The World

of Chess

by Anthony Saidy and Norman Lessing

Special Photography by Norman Snyder | Picture Research by Marion Geisinger

A Ridge Press Book Random House, New York

Editor-in-Chief: Jerry Mason
Editor: Adolph Suehsdorf
Art Director: Albert Squillace
Project Art Director: Harry Brocke
Managing Editor: Moira Duggan
Associate Editor: Mimi Gold
Associate Editor: Barbara Hoffbeck
Art Associate: Nancy Louie
Art Associate: David Namias
Art Production: Doris Mullane

 Published simultaneously in Canada by Random House of Canada Limited, Toronto.

Library of Congress Cataloging in Publication Data
Saidy, Anthony, 1937–
The world of chess.
"A Ridge Press book."
1. Chess. 2. Chess—History. I. Lessing, Norman, joint author. II. Title.
GV1445.S17 794.1'09
74-4375
ISBN 0-394-48777-X
Printed and bound in Italy by Mondadori Editore, Verona.

Contents

Introduction

The Bobby Fischer explosion rocked chess out of its doldrums. It created a storm of interest in the royal game and unloosed an avalanche of chess literature. Not only was there a deluge of new books of every description, but old books were resuscitated as well, decked out in shiny new covers, and freshly distributed at upped prices. All this added to a literature which was already more extensive than that of all other games combined!

Why, then, another chess book? Because the authors felt the need for a very special kind of book, one that would unabashedly transmit their love for the game which has provided them with so many happy hours. The book would combine pictorial elegance with novel insights. It would be of interest to amateurs and professionals alike. Above all, it would be a complete book, covering every facet of the world of chess, presented not as a textbook but as an entertainment.

Through story and lively anecdote, it was hoped to trace the romantic origin and development of chess, following its course from India, Persia, and the Muslim empire to continental Europe, England, the Scandinavian countries, Russia, and the Western Hemisphere.

By highlighting the histories of the great masters and stressing their permanent contributions to the game, the authors wished not merely to express their own strong personal admiration but also to provide a practical course of instruction in chess—instruction without tears—a boon to neophytes and a welcome reminder to more experienced players..

But mainly the authors set out to rectify an all too common failing in most chess books—the neglect of the human element, the passions and frustrations, the idiosyncrasies and humor, not only of the famous players of history but of the millions of anonymous wood-pushers who are the mainstay of chess and the ultimate guarantee of its continued existence.

Chess, the game/art/science which has endured well into its second millennium, is far from being a cold, intellectual exercise. It is a pursuit crammed with tension and emotion, a struggle and a fight whose object is not only to win but also to create beauty and lasting truth. The endless post-mortems in chess, unlike other games where winning or losing is the central fact, are symptomatic of this everlasting search.

Ironically, this computer age, far from causing Caïssa to surrender all her secrets, has only served to confirm the inexhaustible variety of chess. Its moves are as endless as its fascination for people in every walk of life, all over the globe. The future of chess has never seemed brighter.

It may well be that chess, as a worldwide activity which unites competition and cooperation, has a special contribution to make toward peace and, indeed, human survival. The motto of the Fédération internationale des échecs *(F.I.D.E.) is particularly apt:* "Gens una sumus" *("We are one race"). Nowhere is this spirit better exemplified than in the world of chess.*

The authors wish to thank Moshe Czerniak, whose reminiscences forged a link with certain of the greats; Misha Allen, who has kindly provided translations from the Russian press; Edward Lasker, for his informative help; and Bobby Fischer, whose manifold achievements have given chess, particularly American chess, its quantum leap.

—A.S. N.L.

1.

The Wonderful World of Chess

> "Age cannot wither her, nor custom stale her infinite variety." —William Shakespeare

A visiting potentate asked the Caliph Harun al-Rashid, "What is chess?" The Caliph rejoined, "What is life?"

Large questions, indeed! If the Caliph implied that chess, like life, was susceptible of no easy definition, he was right. If he meant that chess paralleled the variety of life, his reply was equally valid. More than any other game, chess has symbolized the wide range of circumstances encountered in daily living. Omar Khayyam wrote:

"We are but chessmen, who to move are fain
Just as the great Chessplayer doth ordain;
He moves us on life's chessboard to and fro,
And then in Death's box shuts us up again."

And in more amatory mood:

"The Queen moved, I became disconsolate,
By harshness fell from knight to pawn's estate.
Then when I tired of king and bishop's game,
Rook to rook I place . . . and so, checkmate."

In Persian *rook* means "cheek" as well as the chess piece.

Chess has exerted a notable hold upon the human imagination for more than a millennium. The game has entranced individuals from the humblest estate to the highest, ordinary men, rulers, the foolish and the brilliant.

The terminology of chess has entered everyday usage. "Stalemate" has come to signify a military or political impasse. The symbolism of the game has been used extensively in literature, from the seventh-century Sanskrit *Vasavadatta* to Boccaccio, Rabelais, Cervantes, and Lewis Carroll. *A Game at Chess*, a political satire by the seventeenth-century dramatist Thomas Middleton, won the author a prison term. But as Machiavelli said, "No tyrant can checkmate the spirit of liberty." In our time, when the president of chess-conscious Argentina thrust his wife into politics, a headline proclaimed, "Perón Advances the Queen." (In Spanish, the chess Queen is called "la dama," or lady.)

Through chess small fortunes have been lost (and rarely won), love affairs have been ruptured (and sometimes cemented), and some creative geniuses have abandoned all else in life. Chess games have been responsible for occasional murders, and even, perhaps, for the discovery of America. The authors have never met a man who succeeded in permanently giving up the game.

The powerful attraction of chess involves elements which elevate it above the category of a mere game. In a world bristling with aggression, chess is the sublimated fight *par excellence*. Chess is also a large body of scientific data and hypotheses which may engage a lifetime of study without exhausting its possibilities. A most felicitous definition of chess—from the *Great Soviet Encyclopedia*—is: "an art appearing in the form of a game." For indeed, the element of beauty is its most captivating quality. We propose an additional characterization: Chess embodies a global community of people united by a common bond that transcends all parochial interests.

Only in contemporary times has psychoanalysis elucidated previously hidden aspects of the mysterious pull of chess. Depth psychologists have related chess to Oedipus and the family romance. The object of the game is, after all, the destruction of the enemy King. The Freudian theory of chess may help to explain why relatively few women have become deeply involved in the game. (Only one per cent of the members of the U.S. Chess Federation are female.) They lack the patricidal motive. This explanation certainly makes more sense than the male-chauvinist remark, "Women don't have the brains for chess."

The rating of the women's world champion, strong chess-player though she is, is exceeded by well over a hundred men. Of course, women have long been discouraged from entering competitive fields. But the grow-

Opening pages: Blitz! Where the hand is quicker than the camera eye. Father William Lombardy (l), Fischer's second at Iceland, and author Saidy play this popular form of speed chess. Clock in background allows only five minutes per man per game.

ing feminist movement may soon produce the first female grandmaster. With traditional ideas about sex roles crumbling apace, more and more women are getting seriously interested in chess. Sisterhood is powerful—and so is checkmating the old man.

Probably the first female chess prodigy was born in West Germany in 1960. Jutta Hempel gave simultaneous exhibitions on television at the age of six. Then she disappeared from view. One can only hope that she was not held back because of her sex. As the *British Chess Magazine* said, "What a joy it would be to get a female Reshevsky!"

Sammy Reshevsky, who checkmated scores of graybeards on tour before the age of ten, was the most famous prodigy of all time, and richly fulfilled his early promise in later life. So did other immortals like Morphy, Capablanca, and Fischer, all of whom played master chess in childhood, while prodigy Arturito Pomar grew up to become Spain's first grandmaster.

Seven-year-old chess "prodigies" continue to make their usually ephemeral appearance. Of interest to brain researchers is that prodigies regularly occur in only three fields, and each has a strong basis in numbers: music, mathematics, and chess. Incidentally, the old misapprehension of chess as an old man's game is rapidly evaporating. The rigors of competitive chess favor youth, and the mid-thirties are the years of peak performance. Most grandmasters decline noticeably after forty-five.

Former World Champion Max Euwe has said that the most instructive approach to chess is to study the historical progress of the game as exemplified by its leading protagonists. It shall, accordingly, be one of the important aims of this book to trace the origin and growth of chess, and to describe the contributions of masters and grandmasters as they served to define the development of chess ideas.

But the world of chess has a more human side. It is not enough to record the master's chess moves without recounting the agonizing pressures as well as some of the lighter moments of tournament play, as described in the chapter "Diary of a Chess Master."

Nor should one make the common mistake of limiting the survey of chess solely to its great players. Even more important are the great majority of woodpushers, addicts, and aficionados whose love and support of the royal game are the lifeblood of chess. "Recollections of a Coffeehouse Player" highlights the homage paid to this doughty breed throughout the book.

The most famous amateur chess-player in American history undoubtedly is Benjamin Franklin. Apart from his well-known panegyric on *The Morals of Chess,* Franklin was a fanatical devotee of the game, often starting to play at six in the evening and not finishing until dawn the following day. In Paris in 1779, he visited the Café de la Régence and watched the great Philidor play, though it is doubtful he ever saw any of Philidor's operas. He preferred instead to play chess. As Franklin himself put it: "I call this my opera, for I rarely go to the operas at Paris."

Many of Franklin's chess opponents were women and, from his own account, very charming women. He apologized to a certain Madame Brillon because his absorption in chess detained her too long in her bath, writing: "Tell me, my dear friend, how you are this morning. Never hereafter shall I consent to begin a game in your bathroom. Can you forgive me this indiscretion?" Dr. Franklin's interests may have tended to pleasures other than chess.

Abraham Lincoln is also reputed to have been a skillful chess-player. Playing a game with Judge Treat of the Illinois Supreme Court, he was interrupted by his favorite son, Tad, who asked a question which Lincoln, absorbed in the game, failed to answer. Irritably, the boy kicked the chessboard, upsetting the pieces. Judge Treat

Opposite: Set made for Thomas Jefferson and presented to him by French government when he was minister to France. Pieces are carved ivory. Below: "Lady Howe Checkmating Benjamin Franklin" depicts the great man at play during his sojourn as envoy to London.

Tab: I.

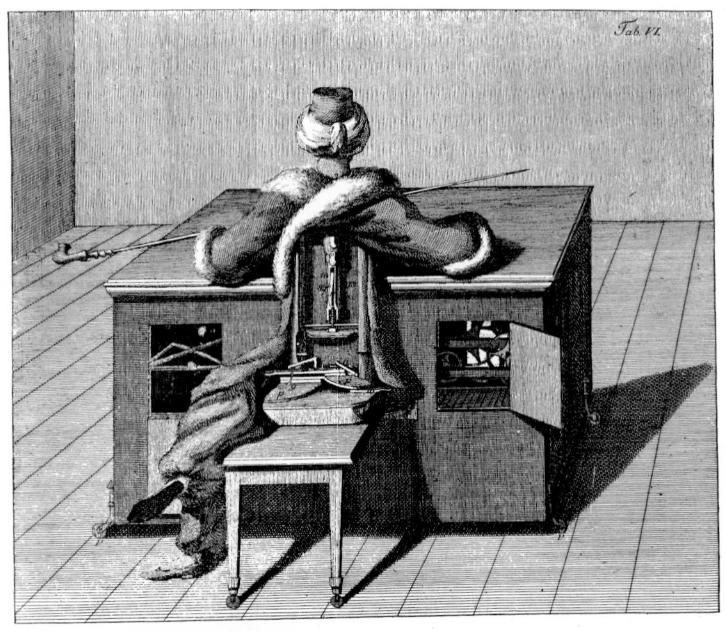

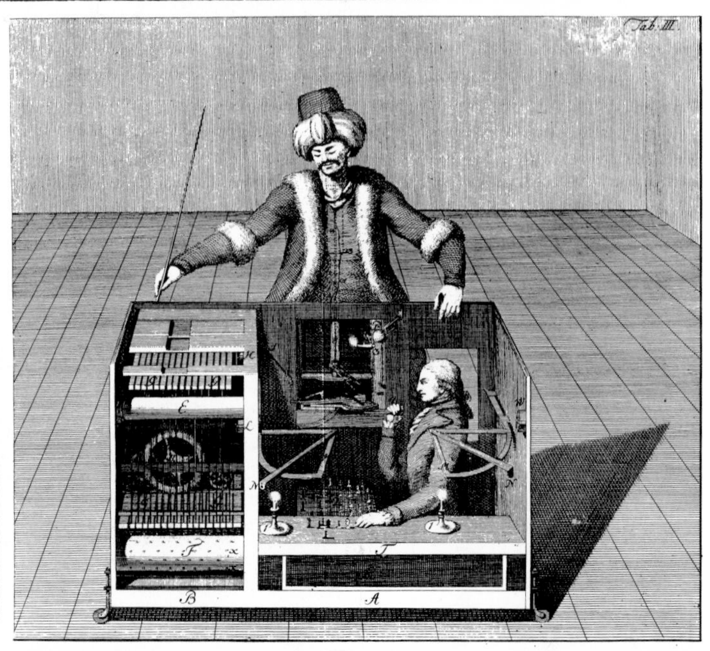

Opposite: 18th-century engravings exposing the operation of von Kempelen's automaton chess-player, "The Turk." Trick was accomplished by small, live player concealed in bottom compartment. Below: An exhibition of simultaneous chess by the 19th-century master, M. Rosenthal.

was furious. "Now we shall never know whose game it was," he snapped. "Well, Judge," Lincoln retorted calmly, "let's call it Tad's game."

Musicians seem to have an affinity for chess: Mischa Elman, the Oistrakhs, Piatigorsky, Richard Strauss, and Prokofiev—to say nothing of Mark Taimanov, a concert pianist, grandmaster, and candidate for the world's championship. Prokofiev called chess "a world of struggle, plans, and passion."

Outstanding among artists is Marcel Duchamp, equally famous among chess-players for his many contributions to the game, including designs for chess pieces, an unsurpassable pocket chess set, occasional writings (as his book on endings with Vitaly Halberstadt) and an unflagging interest and enthusiasm. Before making New York his permanent home, he played for the French Olympic team in Hamburg, 1930, where he drew with American champion Frank Marshall, his ½-point enabling France to tie the match with the United States. Duchamp once said, "All chess-players are artists."

Voltaire, Rousseau, and the eminent British historian Henry Thomas Buckle (one of the strongest players of his time) were devoted aficionados, as were Walter Scott, John Ruskin, Sinclair Lewis, and, today, Nabokov. Of particular interest is the case of Charles Dickens, an avid chess-player, as reported by his playing partner, Victoria Tregear. Whenever she beat him a game, Dickens always insisted on a rematch. They were particularly fond of solving problems—"chess-nuts," as Dickens liked to call them. Once they played a drawn game ending at midnight, which caused Dickens to speculate pensively: "Why not? Man and woman represent an equation, after all. They are, all their mutual traits considered, equals." He went on to say, "The woman who knows the most, thinks the most, feels the most, is the most. Intellectual affection is the only lasting love. Love that has a game of chess in

Opposite: Marcel Duchamp's abstract painting, "Portrait of Chess Players," oil on canvas, 1911. Below: Actual Duchamp, no abstraction, playing with set designed and presented to him by fellow artist, Max Ernst, who also was a dedicated chess-player.

it can checkmate any man and solve the problem of life."

Many rulers have shown a predilection for chess. Tamerlane was reputed to have been a master of the variant game known as Persian Great Chess, a judgment which must be tempered by the observation that had he not been, no one anywhere would have dared to tell him so. More modest and possibly more honest was an earlier great conqueror, Al Ma-Mun (786-833), the son and successor to Harun al-Rashid, who once confessed, "Strange that I who rule the world from the Indus in the East to Andalus in the West cannot manage thirty-two chessmen in a space of two cubits by two."

Napoleon, Frederick the Great, Ferdinand and Isabella, Robespierre, Ivan the Terrible, Charles XII of Sweden, Marx, and Lenin were all chess-players. When Trotsky was amazing the world with his military exploits as commander-in-chief of Russia's Red Army during the Civil War, a chess-player, who knew him by his real name of Bronstein and who had played him at one of the small chess clubs on New York's Lower East Side, snorted contemptuously: "Hmmmff! I could give him a Knight odds." To your true, dyed-in-the-wool chess-player, only a person's ability at chess is important.

Charles XII of Sweden, a military genius, lost most of his chess games, according to Voltaire, because he was fond of moving his King more than any other piece. This tendency was so well known that Frederick the Great, embroiled in his own campaigns, once wrote: "I am like the chess King of Charles XII, always marching."

Blindfold chess has captured the imagination of millions. Actually, the name is a misnomer. The exhibitor is not actually blindfolded but does play without sight of the board, the opponent's moves being called to him. When Philidor engaged three players "blindfold" simultaneously in the eighteenth century, it was hailed as one of the greatest feats ever achieved by the mind of man.

Opposite: Planes of three-dimensional chess. Below: Composer John Cage engaged in electronic chess game at Electric Circus in 1968. Bottom: Four-handed game. Other variations include cylindrical boards and "invisible" pieces.

Living Chess: A ceremonial game dating back to medieval times is replayed at Marostica in northern Italy. Chess has always lent itself to allegory. Rabelais describes a game with living pieces in Pantagruel, *which was published in 1532.*

Morphy played eight strong players blindfold in the Café de la Régence, winning six and drawing two in an exhibition lasting more than ten hours. He was hoisted onto the shoulders of his admirers and carried triumphantly into the streets of Paris. But these feats are now considered relatively routine. Alekhine extended the blindfold-simultaneous record to thirty-two games at Chicago's Century of Progress Exposition in 1933. Days later he could remember and play out each one of these games.

George Koltanowski, a Belgian-American master, beat Alekhine's record by engaging thirty-four players in Edinburgh four years later, and Miguel Najdorf established a new record at São Paolo a decade after that by playing forty-five opponents simultaneously without sight of the board. The feat lasted almost twenty-four hours. He won 39 games, drew 4, and lost 2.

Paradoxically, many leading masters, including some who have excelled at blindfold play, are disposed to belittle it. Morphy wrote of it as "unworthy" and "a mere circus exhibition." Jacques Mieses, a fine blindfold player, published a monograph in 1918 on the psychology of blindfold chess based largely upon his own experience. He described it as "mere show" and "no contribution to the art of chess at all."

Koltanowski, "Kolty" to his many chess friends, could conduct a Knight's tour of the board during a blindfold exhibition, while the audience arbitrarily named a city for each of the sixty-four squares touched en route. The Knight's progress and the names of the cities were duly recorded, and at the end of the exhibition Koltanowski recited in order all sixty-four cities mentioned!

Amazing as such demonstrations are, they are feats of memory rather than chess artistry. Many mnemonic systems use the power of association to produce effects which seem incredible to the uninitiated.

There is one relatively large class of chess-players who must always play "blindfold," as it were—the blind. Chess has always been a great solace to the physically handicapped, but never more so than to those who cannot see. Many blind players have manifested a degree of skill, even against those who play with sight of the board, that is truly amazing. Former U.S. Open Champion Albert Sandrin played master-level chess after he went blind. R. W. Bonham, a leading English blind player, won the Midland Counties Championship on a number of occasions. Blind players also participate in many tournaments among themselves. Blind Chess Olympics were held in Yugoslavia and there is a Blind Chess Club in Sarajevo.

Blind players use a special board with the black squares raised an eighth of an inch above the white squares. The pieces have pegs on the bottom which fit into holes on the board, so that the player can feel them without knocking them over. The black pieces have little points on top to distinguish them from the white pieces.

The great American problem composer, A. F. Mackenzie, was blind. By an extraordinary coincidence, his "two-mover" submitted to the 8th Composing Tourney of the Brighton Society in 1898 was almost identical with the two-mover submitted by an English contemporary, H. W. Lane. Both featured the same sweeping key move: B/KN8–R2. There was an even greater coincidence. H. W. Lane was also blind!

Another taxing form of chess exertion is the simultaneous exhibition. In the "simul," a master plays a number of amateurs at the same time, walking from board to board, usually employing an open, attacking style of play. It affords the amateur a wonderful opportunity to tell his grandchildren, "I once played Bobby Fischer."

Every player remembers the special thrill of his first game with a master. One of the authors (A.S.) was twelve years old when he took part in a "simul" given by Master Eliot Hearst at the Marshall Chess Club. The latter's superiority asserted itself only in the late stages,

MOSTRA·FILA
BANCA POPOLARE

Backstage at Carnegie Hall: Chess has always been a favorite time-killer among musicians awaiting rehearsal cues. The great Philidor learned chess as a choir boy by watching members of the band in idle moments at the court of Louis XV.

when the youngster made a crucial error which cost him the game. The correct move came to him later that night—in a dream!

The simultaneous exhibition places a premium on quick recognition of tactical threats, strong legs, and sheer physical endurance. The exhibitor faces certain hazards. There is usually no limit on the amount of free-wheeling consultation among his opponents. Some customers of the nineteenth-century English star, J. H. Blackburne (nicknamed "the Black Death"), took the added measure of leaving glasses of whiskey en route. Blackburne downed liquor and opponents in record time. When asked the reason for his success, he said, "My opponents left glasses of whiskey *en prise* and I took them *en passant*."

The Swedish grandmaster, Gideon Stahlberg, is credited with the record for the biggest one-man simultaneous—four hundred games—in Buenos Aires in 1940. New opponents were allowed to replace defeated ones. Taking thirty-six hours, Stahlberg won a phenomenal 379 games.

But the biggest chess spectacular took place during the 1966 Havana Olympiad on Capablanca's birthday, November 19, which was proclaimed "World Chess Day." In Revolution Square, 380 masters faced 6,840 amateurs. Unfortunately, most games were washed out by a rainstorm prior to completion, but not before one more diplomatic result: World Champion Petrosian ½—Fidel Castro ½. A foreign spectator was heard to ask, "Who's that fellow playing with Petrosian?"

Between 1883 and 1885, the Bedlam Insane Asylum played a correspondence game with Cambridge University—and won! Because of the length of time it takes to complete a game, some sceptics have observed that you don't have to be crazy to play correspondence chess, but it helps. The tale is told of two chess-players, one living near the North Pole and the other near the South Pole, who were carrying on a game by mail. Every four months for ten years, the North Pole player received a letter containing his opponent's move, pondered his counter-move, and replied. Suddenly, unaccountably, there was a break in the correspondence. No word from the South Pole. A month went by. Two, and still no letter. The game had reached a crucial stage and North, who was playing Black against a Ruy Lopez opening and finding himself attacked on the king-side, was frantic with anxiety. Then, in a swirling Arctic storm, a dog sled arrived with the long-delayed letter. Eagerly, North tore open the envelope. The message said: *J'adoube.*

This story has relevance for everyone familiar with the "touch-move" rule in chess. The rule requires that a player touching a piece must move it. If he merely wishes to rectify the placement of the piece on the square, he says before he touches it, "J'adoube," or "I adjust." So much for North's long wait. Needless to say, the spirit of this chessic courtesy is often violated and has caused many a bitter argument. In a tournament game between Matulovic and Bilek in 1970, the former moved a piece, then saw that it would entail the loss of the game. He quickly said "J'adoube" and calmly proceeded to make another move. The astounded Bilek was too stunned to protest and Matulovic went on to win the game. The chess masters who witnessed the incident thereafter referred to Matulovic as "J'adoubovic."

Postal chess is, of course, a boon to those who live in remote areas where no other kind of competition is available. Such outlanders might subscribe to chess magazines, buy current chess books, engage in a number of correspondence games, and feel themselves well within the mainstream of current chess ideas. But it would be a mistake to suppose that this is the principal function of postal chess.

The majority of correspondence players have no lack of flesh-and-blood opponents nearby. The value of

postal chess lies in the opportunity it gives one for more leisurely contemplation, deeper analysis, and experimentation. A great number of variations in *Modern Chess Openings,* the chess-player's bible, are credited to correspondence games. Conversely, it gives the less-experienced player a chance to brush up on his chess without the bugaboo of touch-and-move.

The United States Chess Federation has a special rating system for postal chess-players and has over seven thousand enrollees in its "Golden Knights" tournaments. A prominent Los Angeles surgeon who acquired a late but intense interest in chess has engaged in as many as twenty-four postal chess games simultaneously. He stoutly maintains that there is no better way for a beginner to receive practical instruction in the game, and he may well be right.

The famous Estonian Grandmaster Paul Keres found little competition as a boy in his home town of Parnu. So, in 1931, he became a correspondence chess-player and soon was conducting as many as one hundred games simultaneously. In his book, *The Early Games of Paul Keres,* the first one listed is a postal game with the following opening moves, Keres playing Black: 1 P-Q4, P-Q4 2 P-QB4, P-K4!? The Albin Counter-Gambit is not seen much in tournament play these days, but postal chess, as noted, gives one the opportunity to experiment. Keres admits he played many risky openings in correspondence chess, seeking complications at any price. But he credits

*Habitués of Chess City, New York.
At far right, Senior Master Edmar Mednis conducts a "simul" exhibition. His opponents are on their good behavior for the camera, concentrating on their own boards and not consulting each other.*

Opposite: World-famous Manhattan Chess Club, with tournament game being played in foreground. Note clocks and score sheets. Below: Quite different in ambience is Chess and Checkers Club, off Times Square. Membership is not required. Passers-by play for small fee.

CHAMPIONSHIP
CHESS
MANHATTAN vs. MARSHALL
0 1
KRAMER MATERA

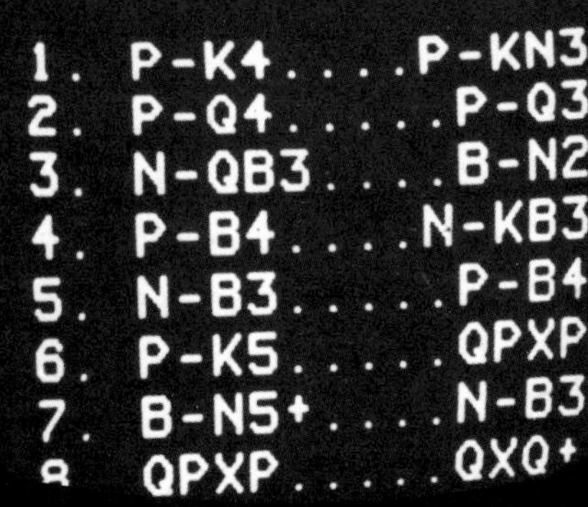

Scenes from televised match in which Sal Matera defeated George Kramer, as shown on New York's Channel 13. Though hardly action-packed, match was enormously popular. Liveliest moments were between-moves commentaries of Shelby Lyman (upper right) and panel of experts.

this course as being instrumental in developing his combinational powers, and with so notable an exemplar, the aspiring player should not hesitate to do likewise.

❧

The latest chess variant, if so it may be called, is also far and away the most popular. It is known as "blitz" or "five-minute" chess and requires, besides the board and pieces, a chess clock. A chess clock is actually two clocks, each with its own operating button or lever. After a player makes a move, he pushes the button on his side, which has the effect of stopping his clock and starting his opponent's. It is, of course, usually used in tournaments where players have an allotted number of moves, duly recorded on their score sheets, to be made before a specified time limit. This limit is usually set at forty moves within two hours, and twenty moves an hour thereafter, although it varies, more time being allowed in international tournaments or matches, and less for lesser tournaments, usually held on weekends, where two and sometimes three games must be completed in a single day.

In blitz chess, however, there are no score sheets and no set number of moves. The clocks are set back to five minutes before the hour, and the only proviso is that the game be completed within this time span of five minutes for each player. It matters not that you have a dead-won position, that you are a Queen and two Rooks ahead, *if* the little flag on your clock falls before your opponent is checkmated. If this happens, you lose—unless the only piece your opponent has left is the King, in which case it is a draw.

David Hafler of Philadelphia has the largest private collection of chess sets and pieces in the United States. The exquisite workmanship of collector's items reflects the art styles of many periods and gives a glimpse of history, as well.

The casual chess club visitor unacquainted with this new pastime might be very much surprised by the wild and unruly action, the loud banging of pieces, especially when the inexorable minute hand approaches zero hour and the flag of the chess clock is poised on its tip, ready to drop. He must ask himself, in the midst of all this insanity, whatever happened to that quiet, analytical game called chess?

The purest form of art for art's sake in Caïssa's realm is the chess problem. It is an unusually rich source of beauty and pleasure and often a valuable means of instruction as well. The greatest problem composer of all time was the American, Sam Loyd (1841-1911). Loyd's credo was: "My theory of a key move is always to make it just the reverse of what a player in 999 cases out of a 1000 would look for."

It is illustrated by the following two-mover, one of his most famous, which he called "The American Indian."

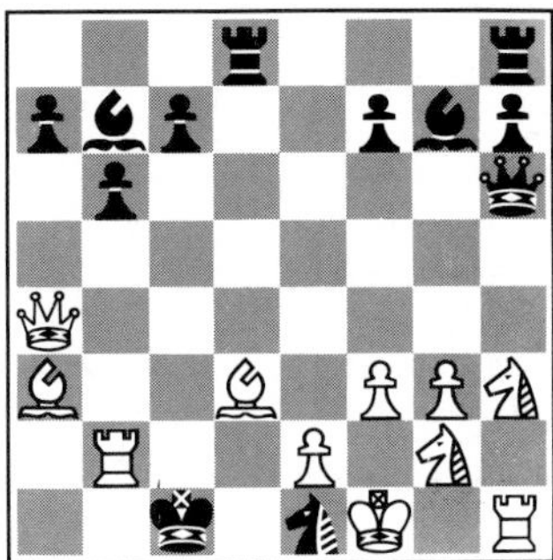

Solution:

1 B-B8!!

Hiding in ambush.

1 . . . BxR

To prevent 2 Q-R1 mate.

2 BxQ mate

Other alternatives also lose but the main line is the prettiest.

Opposite: Pert and amusing, early 19th-century French pieces, made of bone, are typically Gallic in wit and bonhomie. Bottom left: Archeological digs of 1860s inspired these Egyptian and Assyrian forms. Bottom right: 1870s French pieces in Renaissance style.

And now, a three-mover by C. S. Kipping:

White has an overwhelming preponderance of force, but how can he prevent Black from being stalemated? 1Q-B3 achieves this end, but does not mate in three. Therefore, solution:

1	Q-QR1!	PxQ/Q ch	2	BxQ	P-N7
			3	N-B6 mate	

A four-mover by Latzel:

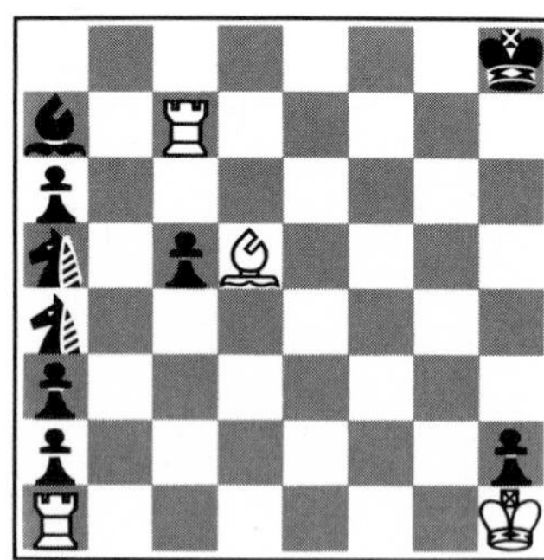

Not a particularly difficult problem, but the concept is ingenious. The white Rook on QR1 will give mate in four moves moving along the QR file, even though this file is currently blocked by no less than *six* enemy pieces. Note that in each case, White will be threatening mate on the opposite KR file, and in each case Black will make the only move to prevent it.

Solution:

1	RxRP	N-N7	3	RxRP	B-N3
2	RxRP	N-N6	4	R-R8 mate	

Finally, we come to a five-mover:

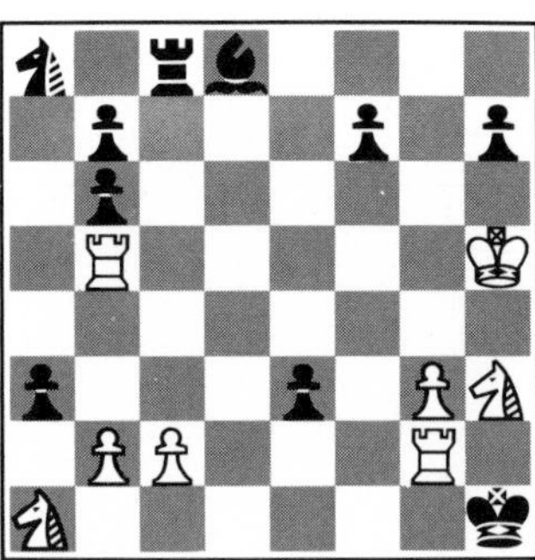

This problem involves a betting proposition. Not only does Sam Loyd stipulate mate in five, but he promises to accomplish this with the least likely piece. The person accepting the wager is asked to select this piece. Logically, it must be the white pawn farthest away from the black King, the pawn at QN2!

Solution:

1 P-QN4

With this move, White threatens mate by R-B5—B1. He cannot move along the rank at once because Black will pin his Rook with 1 . . . R-B4. It is still Black's only defensive move:

1	. . .	R-B4	2	PxR	P-R7

To block 3 R-N1 mate.

3 P-B6 B-B2

The only way to thwart the mate in five via R-Q5 or KB5.

4	PxP	Any	5	PxN=Q or B mate

White might also have promised to mate with a so-far nonexistent Bishop, but this could have given away the theme. There was only one Sam Loyd!

The end-game study differs from the chess problem *per se* in several essential respects. It does not usually stipulate the number of moves to effect checkmate, it has a greater economy of pieces, and, generally speaking, the positions are more realistic. End-game studies afford practical instruction as well as beauty. The Russian

John Harbeson has second largest private U.S. collection of fine chess sets and pieces. Despite Harbeson's studious mien, antique figures are rarely used in actual play. Handling would inevitably lessen their decorative effect.

A. A. Troitzky is honored as the father of the end-game composition. The following unique problem was a clue in S. S. Van Dine's mystery novel, *The Bishop Murder Case.* You think the lone Bishop cannot give mate? Think again!

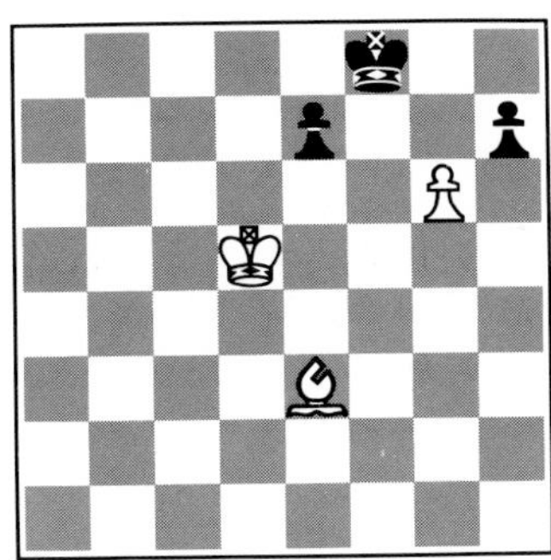

Solution:

1	B-R6 ch	K-N1	**4**	K-K6	K-R1
2	P-N7	K-B2	**5**	K-B7	KP moves
3	P-N8/Q ch!!	KxQ	**6**	B-N7 mate!	

Clearly implicating the live Bishop in the story as a murder suspect. Other variations lose equally.

The wide, wonderful, and wacky world of chess is full of oddballs and oddities. There is hardly any general chess compendium which does not include an account of Baron von Kempelen's fabulous "Turk," the automaton chess-player first exhibited at the court of Maria Theresa of Austria in 1770. After von Kempelen died, the "Turk" was sold to Johann Maelzel, who added music to the attraction and exhibited it in America. Through an ingenious mechanical contraption harboring a concealed player and employing magnetic disks and a device for moving the Turk's arm quite accurately in the deployment of pieces, this elaborate hoax (and its copy "Mephisto") pale by comparison to the actual chess-playing machines of today.

Botvinnik predicted in the sixties that "computers will very soon be able to defeat even grandmasters." A computer chess champion of the world? According to Botvinnik, who held that title a total of thirteen years, the prospect is not only possible but inevitable. An electrical engineer by profession, Botvinnik is noted for his research linking computers to chess. As a champion of the computer's future under the Soviet system, however, he may, consciously or not, have an axe to grind.

The notion of a machine ruling the chess world—dare one include the outside world as well?—has, in the opinion of most experts, a very long way to go before it even comes close to approaching reality. Yet there is no gainsaying the enormous value of chess to computer programming. Chess afforded a valuable insight into the human brain, especially in the study of choice patterns. It was helpful in the solution of exact and inexact problems. Because of the spatial concept in chess, it even helped the robot-computer to "see." These are only some of the things chess did for the computer. The next question was, what could the computer do for chess?

International Master David Levy of Britain has wagered £1,000 that no computer will be able to beat him in a ten-game series before August, 1978. Botvinnik is said to have told him, "I feel sorry for your money." We await the result of this encounter. Whatever the outcome, in the ultimate showdown of machine versus man, given the best of each, we place our money unflinchingly and without hesitation on man. A machine has already been devised to compose music, but no machine will ever be a Mozart. A machine may someday be invented which will write television plays—judging from the current crop, this goal may already have been accomplished—but no machine will equal a Shakespeare or a Nabokov.

If the day ever comes when the monster turns upon its maker, when the Botvinnik computer beats Botvinnik at chess, it may prove to be a sad one for the human race. For the present, we may find consolation in the thought that no computer yet invented can even remotely compare in complexity and creativity with the mind and nervous system, the heart and, if we may revive an ancient word, the soul of man.

2.

The Old Army Game

"Fantastic scenes of mimic war I sing,
Undoubted warriors and a routed King;
How two mock realms, their glory to maintain
Marshalled their squadrons on the checkered
plain."
—Marcus Hieronymus Vida, Bishop of Alba,
16th Century

"War is hell!" —William Tecumseh Sherman

Chess is a game of war. We are the generals. Our chief advantage over actual generals is the clear view of our battlefield and the disposition of our own and the enemy's forces. We are not hampered by the elements as Napoleon was by snow and bitter cold in Russia, by rain and a muddy battlefield at Waterloo.

But our biggest single advantage may have been best expressed by a member of the Cambridge University Chess Club, who wrote in 1858: "To feel the thrilling sense of actual war / Without effusion of the soldier's gore...." To which another chess-player's prayer must be added: "And well 'twould be if Chess alone / Disputes 'twixt nations settle could. / Instead of Pawns of flesh and bone, / The men of ivory or wood."

Someday, perhaps, a moral alternative to war will be found for the settlement of international disputes. In the meantime chess may well serve as a sublimation and healthy outlet for man's aggressive drive, for no more demanding board game has ever been devised.

The exact origin of the game is and must remain a mystery. Fantastic claims have been made that chess is over five thousand years old, but there is little, beyond the wildest theorizing, to support them. One explorer identified a game taken from King Tut-ankh-amen's tomb as an early form of chess, which would date it to 1355 B.C. More knowledgeable experts place the game in the category of *nard,* or backgammon, a Persian game much older than chess.

The first documentary evidence of chess, or of a game approximating chess, goes back to about A.D. 600. But there is supportive evidence that places it perhaps one hundred fifty years prior to that, in North India, about A.D. 455. While some writers have depicted Alexander the Great playing "at chesse" during his invasion of India almost a thousand years earlier, it is probably no more than an imputation, another instance of the rich symbolism of chess in the service of men's imaginations. Certainly there is no hard evidence of Alexandrine chess.

Arab writers endowed the inventor of chess with a name and a family—Sassa, son of Dahir—naturally ascribing the paternity of the founder to an early Muslim invader of North India. This assumption is roughly comparable to the Russian claim to having invented baseball. In any event, the familiar and apocryphal tale has the king offering Sassa any reward he asks, and Sassa, with duplicity worthy of the inventor of the royal game, modestly requests that one kernel of grain be placed on the first square of the chessboard, two on the second, four on the third, and so doubling until all sixty-four squares are taken into account—a sum equal to raising the digit two to the sixty-fourth power minus one, or approximately 18½ quintillion grains, a quantity sufficient to overwhelm the world. Little enough for the inventor of so glorious a game as chess—and for the only time anyone got rich from it until the advent of Bobby Fischer!

It is indeed a measure of the fascination of chess that it has captivated so many, over so long a period of time, without the incentive of appreciable material rewards. Benjamin Franklin wrote: "It is so interesting in itself, as not to need the view of gain to induce engaging in it; and thence it is never played for money." A slight exaggeration, to be sure, but close enough.

There is evidence indicating that, in the very early

Opening pages: Carved ivory set from North China (c. 1790) on elegant Persian board of same era. Squares are inlays of tortoise shell and mother-of-pearl, bordered with ivory. Below left: Possibly the earliest existing chess piece, dating to 6th-century Persia. Right: 10th-century Persian piece of carved jet.

stages of its evolution, the game which was to become chess employed dice. But as it developed, its proponents sought to enhance the elements of skill, leading finally to the abandonment of the dice. From that point on, chess, happily, sacrificed its opportunity to become a gambling game. It was this substitution of skill for chance, the dominant factor in all earlier board games, which raised chess to its unquestioned eminence and earned the loyalty and affection of thinkers and dreamers, of men who, like Franklin, recognized the kinship of chess to the arts and sciences, its symbolic relationship to the precepts of everyday living, its beauty, and its basic morality.

Can one speak of morality in a game of war? We are inclined to think so. It is war without bloodshed. Moreover, it is one in which the good guys—who make the good moves, the moral moves, the right moves—win.

Some psychologists are inclined to belittle the war motif. Ernest Jones has stated that "the unconscious motive activating the players is not the mere love of pugnacity characteristic of all competitive games, but the grimmer one of father murder." Others argue that it is more accurate to describe chess as a substitute for war.

The inevitable paradox of chess persists. It presents a peaceful image, two players quietly hunched over a chessboard. But the game is warlike, and the image of chess-players is not always peaceful. A certain Duke of Burgundy became so enraged during a game that he picked up his solid-gold king and struck and killed his opponent. He was condemned to be hanged. While awaiting execution, he played a game of chess with his jailer and crowned him, as well. This much of the story, considering the weight of the pieces in medieval times, is at least believable. The rest is harder to swallow.

For the rest of his stay, the Duke, quite naturally,

Opposite: Early 14th-century Persian manuscript page from Shah Namah, *the Book of Kings. Written by poet Firdausi, c. 935-1025, it recounts how an envoy from an Indian raja introduced shatranj into court of Khusrau I by challenging Persians to solve the game's riddle.*

had a hard time finding opponents. Finally, a nobleman, equal to the Duke in rank and presumably well versed in the art of self-defense, visited the prison to play against him. They were quite engaged when the hangman and two guards arrived to escort the Duke to the scaffold. The Duke refused to leave until he finished the game. The hangman and guards injudiciously attempted to lay hands on him, whereupon "enraged, he did slay one guard with his bishop, the other guard with his knight, and with his king he slew the hangman." Following which, the worthy Duke quietly sat down to finish his game.

Passions just as violent are aroused in modern chess tournaments, although the contestants, no doubt profiting by the example of the Duke, manage to control themselves a little better. It may also be a fortunate circumstance that modern pieces of the Staunton design, though weighted, are not nearly so heavy and effective as weapons.

For the most part, the game of war remains a peaceful pursuit, except when wives find themselves irked by their husbands' complete absorption in the game—and vice versa. It is well worth noting how many women have taken to chess and how great has been their progress in the game. The time may not be too far off when a woman will emerge to challenge for the world's chess championship, just as Bobby Fischer arose to challenge the Russians. Unlike physical sports, there are no size and weight factors in chess to separate the sexes, only the opportunity for women to prove themselves equal to men in every respect.

Having forecast this vision of the future, let us return to consider the elements of chess in its earliest development.

⋙⋘

The first version of the game of chess was called *chaturanga.* In Sanskrit it was the word for the army. Thus, there is justification in calling chess "the old army game." The word has two parts—*chatur* meaning "four" and *anga* meaning "limb," or literally "having four limbs." Indian armies had four limbs—chariots, elephants, cavalry, and infantry. In the game of war these were four of the six different types of force represented on the board, the other two being the king and his vizier, or minister.

Here we come to a curious contradiction which seemingly invalidates our estimate of the date of origin of chess. Donald M. Liddell, author and chess historian, points out that at the time of the invasion of India by Alexander the Great in 326 B.C., chariots proved a failure and subsequently were discarded by the Indian army. Since the chariot was one of the chaturanga pieces, he deduces that the game itself had a much earlier origin. This is an ingenious theory, but the reasoning is open to question. True, the chariot no longer existed as an element of the Indian army, but it continued to play a great part in Hindu ceremonies and epics. As part of a game, moreover, it made an attractive piece.

That chess is played on a board of sixty-four squares is accidental. It stems from the fact that the early Indian version of backgammon was played on an *ashtapada,* a ruled board of sixty-four squares suitably marked as a race course for the older game. When some Hindu set out to devise a game of war, he simply found the ashtapada handy for his purpose. The board markings were ignored. There was no differentiation in color between the alternate squares; it would be a long time before the adoption of a checkered board such as is used today.

The use of dice was not immediately abandoned, either in two-handed or four-handed versions of the game. The throw of the die determined which piece should be moved. But since each piece had different functions and (with the exception of the foot-soldier, or pawn) could move in any direction, an added element of skill not found in backgammon was brought into play.

Gradually the two-handed game took over. Since

Opposite, clockwise from top: 11th-century Persian piece, possibly a rukh*; 12th-century Arabic Bishop; probably an Egyptian shah, 11th- or 12th-century, with carved words, "the victorious"; ivory raja given to Charlemagne by Haroun al-Raschid. Below: 16th-century Arabic problems and 13th-century ivory pieces from Persia.*

it is human nature for a player to fancy himself more skillful than his opponent—and since the element of luck often beclouded this issue—dice were discarded.

Not completely, however. Indeed, there is evidence that a form of chess with dice existed as late as the thirteenth century, which probably explains why, as a gambling game, it so often incurred the wrath and opposition of the clergy.

In *Huon of Bordeaux,* a romance written about 1200, the boastful, chess-playing hero incurs the displeasure of King Yvorin, who challenges him to a game of chess with his daughter, a master player, on the following conditions: "That if she win, thou shalt lose thy head / and if thou mate her, thou shalt have her one night in thy bed / to do with her at thy pleasure. . . ."

Then Huon asked: "Lady, which game will you play? Will you have it with moves or with dice?"

"Let it be with moves," said the lady in a clear voice.

Which proves the original point. It would be cruel, however, to leave the reader hanging on the outcome of this tale. The lady is winning the game when, luckily for Huon, she falls in love with him and contrives to lose. But Huon is either too chivalrous or too mercenary to insist upon the terms of the wager. Instead, he releases the King in return for one hundred marks, and she is indignant at being cheated of her reward.

The pieces in chaturanga were, as we have seen, six in number, exactly like modern chess. They were arranged on the board as follows: The king and minister occupied the middle squares of the first row (as King and Queen do today). The eight foot-soldiers occupied the second row (as pawns do). The chariots occupied the first and last squares of the first row (in algebraic notation *a1* and *h1*). The horses came next *(b1* and *g1),* and the elephants next *(c1* and *f1).* Considering the functions of these pieces, it can be seen that their position on the

Opposite: Detail of 18th-century Indian traveling set, shown below in full. Pieces are ivory, Moslem in design. Below: Another illustration from the Shah Namah, *possibly depicting the king's minister who did solve the game's riddle and later challenged the Indians with the game of nard.*

Thai set with matching teakwood board, dating from about 1815. Similar sets have been used for past 700 years. Shells or stones are more typical pawns than ivory ones shown here. Opposite: Samlor boys play Siamese chess in front of Trocadero Hotel in Bangkok while waiting for fares.

board corresponds to that of their modern equivalents.

The king *(raja)* moved to any adjacent square not covered by a hostile piece, the same as the King today. The minister *(mantri)* moved to any diagonally adjacent square. The horse *(ashwa)* moved the same as the Knight in modern chess. The chariot *(rat-ha)* moved as does our Rook. The elephant *(gaja, hasti)* differed to some degree, however, from our Bishop. It moved diagonally, but only for two squares, leaping over the adjacent square to the square beyond. The foot-soldier *(padati)* moved to the square immediately in front but captured on the diagonal adjacent square, just like our pawn, except that it did not have the option of moving two squares straight ahead on its first move. When a foot-soldier reached the last rank, it became a minister. The game ended when the king was captured.

While no piece came near to equalling the vast power of the present-day Queen, it is interesting to see the many equivalents to contemporary pieces and how relatively insignificant and few are the differences. We can only pay tribute to the logic and ingenuity of the Hindu inventor of chaturanga. He must have been possessed of great artistic creativity and vast mathematical skill. Chess will forever be his monument.

According to the most eminent of chess historians, H. J. R. Murray, the earliest reference to chess in all literature is in *The Karnamak:*

"When Ardawan saw Artakhshir, he rejoiced and esteemed him highly. He commanded him to accompany his sons and knights to the chase and to the games of ball. Artakhshir did this, and by God's help, he became doughtier and more skillful than them all in ball-playing, in horsemanship, in chatrang [chess], in hunting, and in other accomplishments."

This is a Persian romance written *circa* 600 about events at the beginning of the Sassanian Dynasty, nearly four hundred years earlier. Most noteworthy is that the writer treated chess as a characteristically national game, well suited to the description of a Persian folk hero. It suggests, moreover, that chess may have existed in Persia for a considerable time prior to the writing and that it was held in high esteem. It also would seem to buttress the views of independent scholars that chess was introduced from India to Persia around the middle of the sixth century. The Sanskrit name chaturanga became Persianized into *chatrang*. In the *Chatrang-namak*, a history of chess written some two hundred years later, the Persians conceded the invention of chess to India but salved the national ego by adding that it was soon taken over by great Persian players, who far exceeded the Indians in their appreciation and understanding of the game.

The names of the pieces were changed; two are of particular interest as they relate to the modern lexicon. The rat-ha became *rukh*, from which is derived the English term "Rook." The raja became *shah*. The phrase *shah mat* is used all over the world and has been erroneously translated as, "The king is dead." Its literal meaning is the far more humane, "The king is defeated." Either way, it means checkmate.

Opposite: Large ivory King from Rajasthan, typical of Mogul workmanship. Below: Ivory polychromed Delhi or "John" set, dated 1806, shows mercenaries against Indian troops. Bottom: Ivory Bishop, c. 1800, from traditional Bengalese set (l), and ivory polychromed Indian Knight, also of Delhi type.

Chariot (opposite) and juggernaut carts (below) from late 18th- or early 19th-century Delhi set. The added juggernaut carts make this type of set quite impressive. Chessmen are modeled on famous group of mercenary soldiers known as the John Company.

"What is chess?" the Caliph Omar asked. It was explained to him that it was a game invented to break the news to a Queen-mother whose son had just been killed in battle. Omar replied: "There is nothing wrong in it; it has to do with war."

The conquest of Persia by Islam under the Caliph Omar in 638–651 was the most important development in the history of chess. The spread of Islam led to the spread of chess all over the world. The Persian consonant *ch,* which has no equivalent in Arabic, was replaced by *sh* and the letter g became *j*. Chatrang was transmuted to the Arabic *shatranj.*

The greatest obstacle to chess in Islam was Mohammed's denunciation of images. There was thus a question whether chess was permissible under Muslim religious law. It is related that a certain emir was playing chess when a high-ranking visitor was announced. He immediately threw a napkin over the chess pieces. Having questioned the visitor and ascertained that he knew little of Mohammed's teachings, the emir whisked off the napkin and resumed play. "To the unlearned," he observed, "nothing is forbidden."

To eliminate controversy, chessmen were made to conform to conventional designs bearing little resemblance to images. The literature of shatranj was greatly expanded and, for the first time, chess games between masters were recorded. Great chess-players developed, including many who excelled in blindfold play. Nearly every wealthy household had its chess-player in residence. The fabled Caliph Haroun al-Rashid and his three sons were avid players. The Caliph favored chess masters and granted them liberal pensions.

Opposite: 17th-century Chinese set, not all of which has survived, is one of the earliest existing sets. Large King is 10½ inches high. Below: Ivory-disc Chinese set, c. 1860, has engraved edges and sits on teak board. Bottom: Modern wooden Japanese set has small, 1-inch pieces.

End games played between Jabir al-Kufi and Abdal-ghaffar al-Ansari survive. By 842, the great al-Adli, author of *The Book of Chess,* stood alone in the first class. By 847, the Persian ar-Razi, another chess author, supplanted al-Adli, defeating him in the presence of the Caliph. The most famous Muslim chess player, however, was as-Suli, whose superiority in the following century was acknowledged up to Renaissance times. He challenged the Caliph's boastful resident chess master al-Mawardi to a match and beat him so decisively that at the end, the Caliph said to his former favorite: "Your rosewater has turned to urine!" For many years, people said of someone who showed remarkable skill in chess: "He plays like as-Suli."

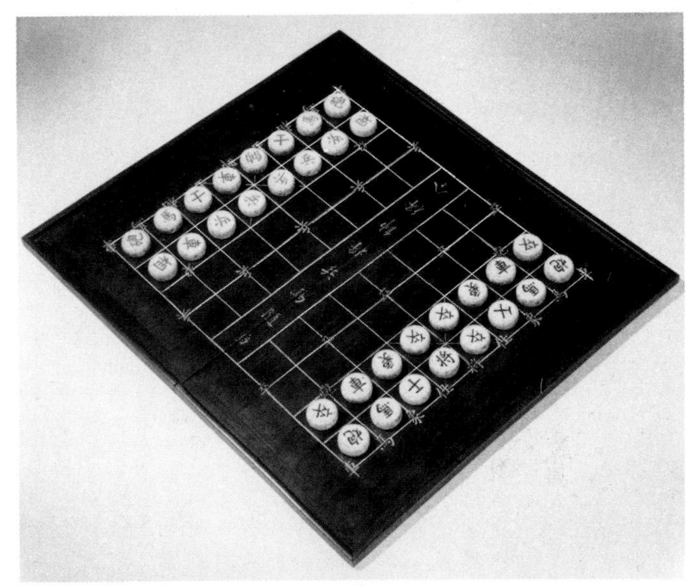

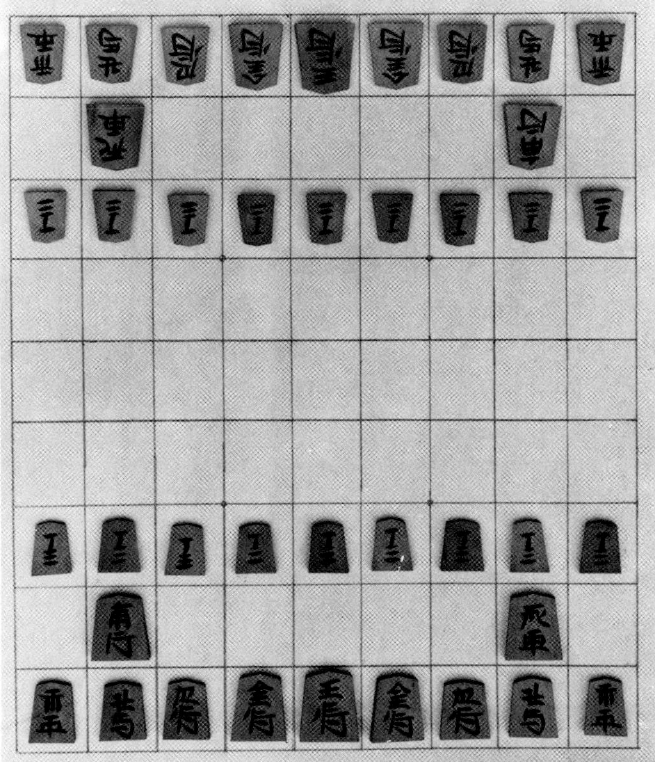

An interesting but little-known facet of chess held sway from its inception in India to Persia and all through the older Muslim period. Nowadays, when we think of chess devotees, we picture people who love to play the game, sometimes at too great length and to the detriment of more practical pursuits. It may come as a surprise to learn that many of the fanatical devotees of the game in ancient times did not play it at all, or, if they did, very rarely. Many did not even know how to go about playing a chess game from start to finish, and most were not interested in learning.

The explanation lies in what modern chess-players would call end-game studies, or mating problems. People were so fascinated by the intricacies of the marvelous new game that the more avid among them used their knowledge of the moves to devise tricky positions, studies, and problems for others to solve. And the response was most gratifying. People were intrigued, much as crossword-puzzle fans today are intrigued by a clever deployment of words.

But there was another and possibly a more pertinent reason for this interest. Remember, this new "game of war" sprang from what was originally a gambling game

These very tall red-and-white ivory pieces belong to a Chinese set from about 1820. The decorative carving, although quite intricate, is considered conventional on sets in this style.

—with dice. The more skilled sought to eliminate the element of chance. In problems the less skilled saw a way to strike back by again resorting to the motive of gain.

One did not have to know *how* to play. One simply bought a composition from the problemist together with the secret of its solution. A victim was sought and a wager made that he could not solve the problem. Among gamblers, this is known as a proposition bet, and the last word of advice on the subject was written by Damon Runyon. Old Man Masterson says to his boy: "Some day, somewhere, a guy is going to show you a nice brand-new deck of cards on which the seal is never broken, and this guy is going to offer to bet you that the jack of spades will jump out of this deck and squirt cider in your ear. But, son, do not bet him, for as sure as you do, you are going to get an earful of cider."

Good advice or not, the lure of such problems must have been hard to resist. After struggling with one for hours or days, the victim might have been ready to pay for the solution, bet or no bet.

Amazingly, a tremendous number of these problems, many of which were preserved for posterity, are remarkable compositions, even by the most exacting modern standards. The one below was selected because the only pieces are Rooks, Knights, pawns, and the two opposing Kings, whose moves have not changed from the inception of chess to this day.

Purists may complain that the problem includes pieces not essential to its solution or thematic idea, but the Muslim composers were interested in making their positions appear the results of real games. This is in contrast to some of the stiffly contrived compositions of today. It is a moot point which approach has the greater aesthetic value.

The problem is labeled "Red plays and wins," Red being the same as White. (Muslim pieces were labeled Red and Black.) It might also be called: "White to play and mate in five."

For those who wish to try it, good luck! The solution is printed below, so cover it with your hand. Should you wish to turn down the "proposition bet" and simply read the solution, you are certain to be charmed by the problem's beauty.

SOLUTION:

1	R-R7 ch	K-N1	3	P-K7 ch	NxP
2	N-B6 ch	K-B1	4	R-B7 ch	NxR
			5	N-K6 checkmate (Shah Mat)	

Every move is forced. White sacrifices his Rook and pawn, but in taking them the opposing Knights block their own monarch's escape, and White (or Red) gives mate with only two Knights. What a delightful conception!

For nearly four hundred years chess was dominated by the Muslim world. Already the game had been divided into the three parts we know today: opening, middle game, and end game. Muslim players were the greatest in the world and they were not about to share their knowledge with heathen Christians. Yet so great was the power of chess and so fascinating its allure for all who chanced upon it, that slowly the game began to trickle into western Europe. The trickle soon became a torrent, far surpassing the flow and development of chess in Eastern countries, until—irony of ironies!—Easterners now have to learn the fine points of chess and the latest innovations from the once-despised Westerners.

Chess triumphed over Shatranj!

3.

Caïssa Begins Her Checkered Career

> "My malediction I utter—May Steini's men fall in heaps! May my fearful incantations bewitch him, so that peril shall beset two or three of his pieces at once! May the Old One [gamla—the Queen] lose her life! May the wee pawns grow fewer and fewer on the squares, and may he be mated both with the low and high mates!"
>
> —Stephan Olafsson

It was not an accident that the Fischer-Spassky match for the World's Chess Championship was held in Reykjavik. The Icelandic chess tradition is one of the oldest in Europe. What a jump from the sun-drenched deserts of Araby to the icy glaciers of the North! Yet so powerful was the thrust of chess that it made the leap without difficulty. Iceland inherited chess from England, which received it from France, which obtained it from Spain, which became the first European country to embrace the royal game, as a result of its conquest by the Moors in the eighth century.

Although virtually isolated from the rest of Europe during the early years of its occupation, Spain after 900 was visited by a great number of European students eager to enroll in its various Moorish centers of learning. Returning home, these travelers brought chess with them—to Sicily and Italy, from Italy through the Brenner Pass to Germany, thence to Switzerland, to Denmark and other Nordic states, and eventually to England and Iceland. The tenth century was the introductory period of chess in Europe. In 1010 the first written reference to it appeared in a will wherein the Count of Urgel solemnly bequested his beloved rock-crystal chessmen to the Convent of St. Giles at Nimes.

As it did in Islam, chess initially incurred the wrath of the clergy, mainly because of its association with dice, although this form of the game was becoming obsolete. In a letter to Pope Alexander II written in 1061, Cardinal Damiani relates how he rebuked the Bishop of Florence for playing chess. The Bishop argued that canon law only forbade dice games and he was playing without dice, but the Cardinal held that the omission of dice was only a subterfuge and imposed a heavy penance.

As with the Muslims, however, the interdiction of chess was soon abandoned, provided that the game was played without dice and not for a stake. The upper classes took up chess, and it was listed as one of the seven knightly accomplishments in the *Disciplina Clericalis*, c. 1110. Pope Gregory XI (1370-8) was an avid chessplayer, as were most of the ruling monarchs in medieval Europe.

Emperor Frederick II of Germany planned to kill a relative while playing chess with him, and two Danish kings, Knut V and Valdemar, were surprised by King Sweyn while playing chess. Knut was killed, but Valdemar escaped by using the chessboard as a shield.

Traveling minstrels and troubadors sang ballads about chess. It was mentioned in poems and historical romances. Many later errors concerning the origin and history of chess may be laid to these writers, who ascribed skill in chess to all their heroes from Alexander the Great to Charlemagne, from Jason to the knights of King Arthur's Round Table. Chess occupied this position of supremacy until the seventeenth century when it was supplanted by cards.

Differences between the Muslim and European versions of chess manifested themselves early. The Muslims never differentiated the color of the squares on their board. Indeed, they rarely used a board, properly speaking. Most commonly their field of play was a mat which could be rolled up for convenience; upon it lines were drawn to form sixty-four squares. Desert Arabs drew lines in the sand and used stones of varying sizes for the pieces.

By 1100, Europeans were using boards with al-

ternating light and dark squares, and Caïssa, the goddess of chess, had begun her checkered career. By 1300 the checkered board was in general use. This had the advantage of creating a certain uniformity, such as the constant placement of the white Queen on a white square and the black Queen on a black.

Rules governing the moves also were differentiated. Most of these are no longer in existence, but one change was important: that which permitted the pawn to move two squares, if so desired, on its initial move. The *en passant* rule came into effect shortly thereafter.

Under Muslim rules, a game could be won by taking off all the enemy's pieces except the King. This rule was revoked by the Europeans to whom mate was all important. Europe also changed the stalemate from a win for the forces hemming in the beleaguered King to a draw.

These rules, along with others no longer in force, were established near the end of the thirteenth century, and although the dates of their adoption by European countries varied, they were in general use by the middle of the fifteenth century. Two major changes still remained to be effected: the revised moves for the Queen and Bishop, the only two pieces whose moves, from their very inception, differed from their function today.

With the impetus of gambling gone, the Muslim emphasis on problems found no parallel in Europe. Play became the thing. It made no difference that the play was not very expert. As Murray correctly points out, this lack fortunately has never hindered anybody's enjoyment of chess.

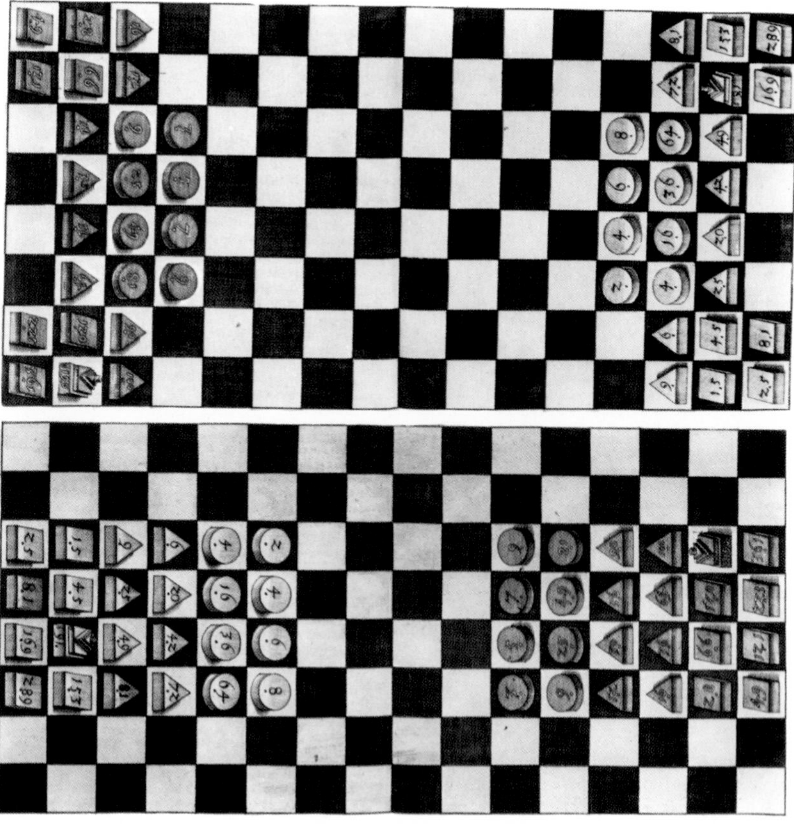

Opening pages: A bevy of Queens symbolize the enhanced role of the Lady in Europeanized chess. Below left: Portrait of Severino, known as Salvio, on frontispiece of his rare book on invention of chess. Right: Diagrams from Das Schach "oder Konig" Spiel *by Selenus, published in 1616.*

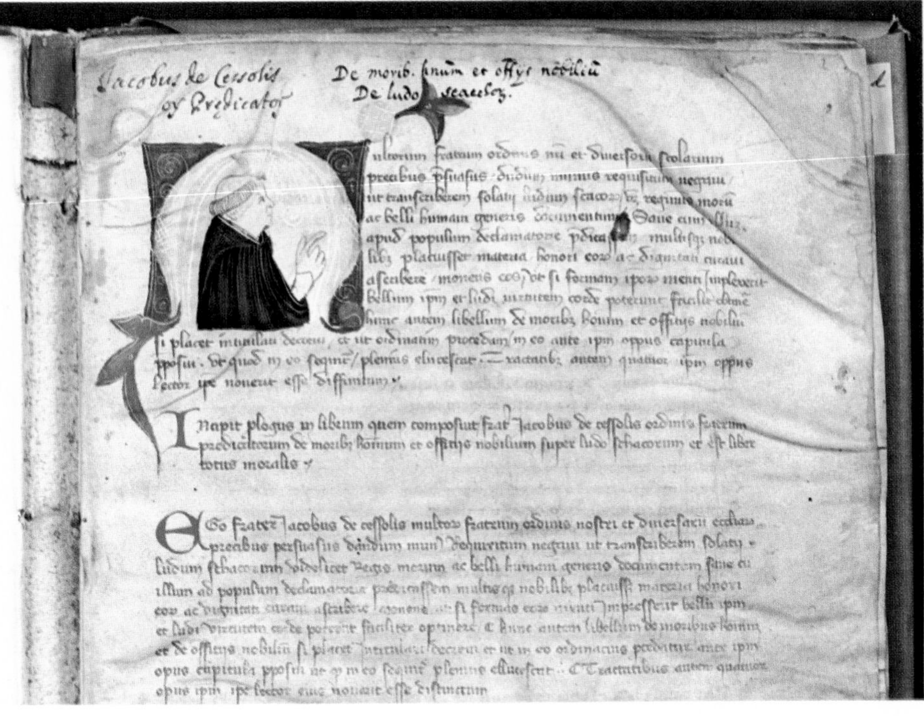
Jacobus de Cessolis Or. Predicator

De morib. hīum et offiys nobiliū De ludo scacoz

Incipit prologus in librum quem composuit frater Jacobus de cessolis ordinis fratrum predicatorum de morib3 hominum et offitiis nobilium super ludo schacorum et est liber totus moralis

Ego frater Jacobus de cessolis ...

119

Essempio 26.°

Altro bel modo di cominciar il Gioco oltre li sopradetti. Come nel n.° 21.° á carte 37.e 38.

Opposite top: Opening of manuscript, Of the Game of Chess, *with possibly the only known attempt at a portrait of Jacobus de Cessolis. Opposite bottom: Illuminated page from Italian manuscript, c. 1730. Left: "Game of Chess," detail from ceiling of Sala de los Reyes, the Alhambra.*

The players of Italy were generally accounted the best, but as late as 1266, the Saracen, Buchecha, engaged three of the best Florentine players simultaneously, playing two of the games blindfold, and was able to win two games and draw the other.

The influence of the Renaissance brought, as it had to so many of the arts and sciences, new breadth and vitality to chess. Henceforth, chess joined the stream of recorded history. It developed a growing body of philosophy and theory. It expanded its horizons, like painting, sculpture, and architecture. It broke the bounds of national provincialism and emerged as the world's most captivating game.

"We have not yet spoken of the woman," says an Arab writer of the twelfth century. "She sitteth at the top of the high places of the city. She is clamorous and willful in her way. She girdeth her loins with strength. Her feet abide not in her house. She moveth in all directions and turneth about her. Her evolutions are wonderful, her ardor untiring. How beautiful are her steps across the plain!"

Even among the Muslims, whose literature mentions women so rarely, the Queen was regarded as a central figure in the folklore of the game. Western writers, fascinated by the parricide motive in chess, are less beguiled by the Queen, noting that in attacking the King-father, the Queen-mother offers the most potent assistance. In fairness, however, it must be noted that it is the *enemy* King the Queen attacks and; moreover, that their countries are at war.

Whatever her psychological or mythological import may be, the Queen for a long time was like the weather. Everybody talked about her, but nobody did anything about her. Despite her popularity in legend, her power on the chessboard was limited to a one-square diagonal move in any direction, the force equivalent of less than two pawns. A pawn which became a Queen on

Clockwise from right: 14th-century German ivory Bishop; 14th-century ivory Scandinavian pieces; mid-13th-century English ivory St. George killing the dragon; 13th-century Danish walrus-bone Queen; 12th-century Rook, probably Danish. Center: Spanish or Sicilian 12th-century ivory Bishop.

reaching the eighth rank less than doubled itself in value.

Invidious references to Lucrezia Borgia aside, the power of women showed a marked upsurge in the latter part of the fifteenth century and continued well into the sixteenth. Catherine de Medici was an excellent chess-player and so was Queen Isabella of Spain, although she is said to have been surpassed by her husband Ferdinand, one of royalty's strongest players.

A remarkable and well-authenticated historical vignette described in Edward Lasker's charming book, *The Adventure of Chess,* would seem to indicate that chess was at least partly responsible for the discovery of America. Lasker came across two letters in the archives of Cordova, written by one Hernando del Pulgar, a name-sake of the famous Spanish author who wrote the *Chronicle of Ferdinand and Isabella.* They are dated February 2 and February 4, 1492, six months before Columbus' first voyage. At that time Columbus was disgusted by Ferdinand's stubborn refusal to accord him the title of Admiral and was on the point of departing from Spain. According to the letters, the news came while Ferdinand was engaged in a game of chess with Fonseca, one of his favorite rivals. Isabella was urged to intercede on Columbus' behalf, but she knew better than to interrupt her husband at chess. She knew also that all depended upon the outcome of the game and its effect on Ferdinand's mood. Unfortunately, Ferdinand's game seemed well lost, and Ferdinand evidently thought so, when Pulgar spied a sudden hope in the position. After considering it, he whispered to the Queen: "If His Highness plays correctly, he wins, and Fonseca cannot outlive four moves." (He was wrong, but only because an extra "spite" interposition delayed the mate one more move.)

Ferdinand was about to make the obvious and losing move when Isabella interrupted with, "Do you not win, my Lord?" Ferdinand lowered his uplifted hand and studied the position again. A smile played on his lips as he saw the winning method.

After such a brilliant victory, it was child's play for Isabella to convince Ferdinand to sanction Columbus' request. A horseman was summoned to overtake Columbus and call him back.

Señor Pulgar, in his letter, recorded the crucial position as follows, with King Ferdinand playing White and Fonseca playing Black.

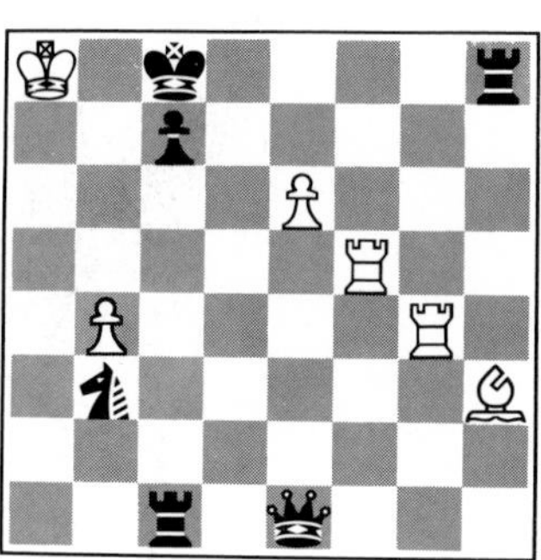

The solution:

1	R-N8 ch	RxR	3	P-K7 dis ch	R-B4 (Spitework!)
2	R-B8 ch	RxR	4	BxR ch	Q-K3
			5	BxQ mate	

Whether or not the increased influence of women contributed to the increased power of the Queen in chess is an interesting though highly debatable question. From the practical standpoint it is much more likely that any game develops in accordance with its own functional needs as a game.

Under the old rules, for instance, there was a long period of immunity in the openings which made this segment of the game rather dull. But toward the end of the fifteenth century, with the all-powerful Queen and increased power of the Bishop (a seemingly necessary corollary), all this was changed. Either side now could be subjected to quick attack in the opening, a wrong move could prove fatal, and making the right moves in the initial stage of the game became all important. This led

"The Chess Players," tempera on wood, by the Paduan, Girolamo de Cremona. The artist's short career (1467-73) suggests that more diversions like the game pictured were needed to lengthen life spans and brighten up a Europe still recovering from the Dark Ages.

to increased emphasis on the development of opening theory, and many books appeared on the subject, one of the earliest and most famous being the Spanish *Repetición de Amores e Arte de Axedres,* written by Lucena about 1497. The Spanish priest Ruy Lopez, famous today for the popular opening which bears his name, wrote his *Libro de la Invención liberal y Arte del Juego del Axedres* in 1561.

The dominating Queen and the more mobile Bishop were soon widely accepted in all the countries of Europe. The pawn also became more powerful; when it reached the eighth rank it could become a Queen, usually leading to a quick decision.

Because of the Queen's greatly enhanced importance, the custom arose of warning the opponent when his Queen was attacked—*Gardez!*—even as we say "Check" when the King is threatened. The admonition to the Queen was gradually abandoned, although some still adhere to it in informal play. In current tournament play it is not even obligatory to say "Check" to the King, although most players do it from force of habit.

The one notable move yet unmentioned is castling. The forerunner of castling was "the King's leap," an ordinary Knight move permitted the King once a game, subject to certain conditions. Dating back to the Muslim game, these conditions varied from time to time and country to country but were reduced basically to those which govern the castling move today: The King must not have moved before, must not be in check, and must not pass over any square controlled by an enemy piece.

Other variations of the King's leap were tried at various stages, some giving the King jumping powers on his first move to the third rank, some extending as far as the eighth rank! None was satisfactory.

In each case, the King's leap was strictly a defensive move. But following the principle of increasing the attacking potential of the pieces—as was done with the

Queen and the Bishop—a move was invented which would insure the King's safety and bring another piece, the Rook, into play. Castling consisted, as it does today, of moving the King two squares toward the Rook, on the unobstructed rank, and transferring the Rook to the square adjacent to the King on the other side.

Castling is, therefore, considered to be a King move. In tournament play, where the rule is that a player touching a piece must move it, the King should be touched first, although we have never seen any player penalized for touching the Rook first if the castling is accomplished in one continuous motion. It is odd how many full-fledged tournament players seem unsure of the correct procedure for castling. It is amusing to see some of them solve this difficulty by using both hands simultaneously, one for the King and one for the Rook, and making the switch so quickly that it can hardly be followed by the eye.

Has chess, as the game exists today, reached the ultimate in its development? It's hard to say. Capablanca, who eventually found the game too simple for his taste, suggested the addition of two major pieces. Just as the Queen embraces the functions of the Rook and the Bishop, the first of Capa's pieces would have combined the Rook and the Knight, the second would have combined the Bishop and the Knight. To accommodate the initial placement and scope of these pieces, the board was to be enlarged to one hundred squares, ten squares a side.

Despite Capablanca's influence and great persuasive powers, the idea never caught on. It does seem a bit much, overbalancing the minor pieces which would virtually be reduced to the status of pawns. When fifty percent of an army's officers are generals, the game of war degenerates from a reasonable facsimile of reality to comic opera.

The development of chess to its present form took many centuries. Many moves were invented and discarded. In other cases, substitutes were found for the newly invented moves, the substitutes discarded, and the new moves reinstated. Castling, as we know it today, was in ordinary use in Rome by 1585. But soon after 1600, "free castling" was adopted which permitted the Rook to be placed on any square up to the King square and permitted the King to move to any square up to the Rook square.

Free castling was soon abandoned, however. Giving pieces greater freedom does not automatically insure a more viable game. Experimentation must be tempered by logic and tested by time. Although most of the moves of today were commonly adopted by the end of the seventeenth century, there were notable exceptions. As late as 1795, French rules confined pawn promotion to a lost piece. If a pawn reached the last rank before a piece was lost, it had to remain a pawn until a piece fell subsequently. It was not until the middle of the nineteenth century that many countries of the world achieved the uniformity enjoyed today.

It will be a long, long time before chess undergoes any new changes or improvements. The harmony and balance in the existing game, brought about by centuries of trial and error, have beauty and depth that are attested to by every new volume of chess theory, every compilation of master games. Indeed, the very extent of chess literature, growing at an unprecedented rate, conspires to make change difficult.

Chess has a quality, like many mathematical formulae, which cannot be expressed in words. The enlarged scope of the Queen was necessary to open up the game, to introduce a force capable of counteracting and enhancing the power of the forces already invented. Similarly, the oblique movement of the Bishops along the diagonals balances the straightforward thrust of the Rooks along the ranks and files. The Knight introduces an element of trickery, the ability of a David to attack the Goliath-Queen without being instantly demolished by

Top: Delicate ivory mirror-back from the 14th century, depicting a game in progress. Below: Title page of German manuscript of 1650, based on Selenus.

the larger piece. The castling move is desirable because it provides the King with an escape and a new fortress, bringing the retarded Rooks into action.

Capablanca's charge that chess had become too routine, too scientific, can be countered by saying that when no more new moves and no more new variations can be found by a Fischer, a Tal, or a Larsen, or, on the theoretical front, by a Pachman, a Suetin, or a Benko, it will be time enough to change the elements of the game.

Chess in its current form retains an abundance of enchantment and mystery, not only for the average player but for the master and grandmaster as well. As in every art form, there are periods of sterility until suddenly a Paul Morphy, an Alexander Alekhine, or a Bobby Fischer bursts upon the scene. The pessimists who claim there is nothing new under the chess sun are sadly mistaken. How else can Fischer's manifest superiority over such giants as Spassky, Petrosian, and Larsen be explained? For that matter, how explain the unprecedented grip upon the public imagination which causes the chess champion of the world to be hailed far and wide by the familiar nickname of Bobby?

The changes in the game of chess did not come about by themselves. They were promulgated by people, some not necessarily famous as chess-players. Jacobus de Cessolis, a Dominican friar, removed the last lingering religious reservations about chess in a sermon written in about 1275. In this most important of chess moralities, which for a brief time almost rivalled the Bible in popularity, Cessolis used the chess pieces as representatives of various classes of men in order to convey religious and practical instruction. It has been widely imitated since and was the precursor of thousands upon thousands of volumes using the rich symbolism of chess. Cessolis' work gave great impetus to the popularity of chess which, in turn, created many players of outstanding skill. To these

This page: Blue and amber Venetian glass set from Murano, c. 1930. Pieces are hollow, but shapes are conventional. Below: "The Chess Players," Venetian painting by unknown artist, c. 1590. Opposite: Marie de Medicis (amber) wages war against Prince de Condé (ivory) on 18th-century marble inlaid Florentine table.

Late 18th-century Spanish set of carved bone. The style is called "pulpit," referring to the leaflike pulpit from which figures arise on most such sets. Modern Spanish pressed-wood sets are modeled after this type, which will probably become "traditional" Spanish.

early masters, we are indebted for the evolution of chess and the birth of chess theory.

By the late sixteenth century, great players had emerged. Some notion of their style has survived to give us an idea of their powers. Between 1560–1590, the two leading Italian players were Giovanni Leonardo and Paolo Boi. Leonardo was slower and more careful, Boi faster and more brilliant. Both excelled at blindfold play. In 1574 they visited Spain to play against Ruy Lopez and Alfonso Ceron, proving their superiority in a number of matches played before King Philip II.

Both Italians led adventurous lives. Leonardo became agent to the Prince of Bisignano and was finally poisoned by a jealous rival in 1587. Boi was a favorite of Pope Pius V, who would have made him rich had he been willing to enter the church. Boi travelled widely, playing before kings and princes. He was once captured by Algerian pirates and is said to have regained his freedom through a wager that he could defeat the best player among the pirates blindfolded. In 1598, returning to Naples, Boi played Dr. Allesandro Salvio. He made a five-move combination to win Salvio's Queen, but Salvio had seen two moves further and won back his Queen and the game. Boi then said, "Youth can do more than age. You are in the prime of life and I am seventy years old." Three days later, he committed suicide by taking poison.

The last of the great Italian players of this period was Gioacchino Greco, called the Calabrese, a brilliant player, if not always sound. He has been credited with inventing the Greco Counter Gambit (1 P-K4, P-K4 2 N-KB3, P-KB4!?), but it seems to have been the work of Leonardo. In any case, Greco's showy style made him a great favorite, especially on his travels abroad. Playing in Paris at the court of the Duke of Lorraine in 1622, he won five thousand crowns, only to be robbed by thieves when he crossed to London. He was always ready to oblige a wealthy patron with a manuscript of annotated games, however, and soon regained his fortune. He died on a trip to the West Indies in 1634. Greco has left many works of historical value showing the wide range of Italian openings between 1560 and 1610.

First Spain and then Italy had dominated the European chess scene. With the coming of the eighteenth century, all this changed. Paris and London became the two great chess capitals of the world, but the superiority of the French and the English did not go unchallenged for long. Chess made great strides in all the countries of Europe and a beginning in the New World, as well. The march of events gave each its place in the sun, in due course, as though Caïssa herself supervised the proceedings and intended to make sure of a proper balance.

But the contributions of Spain and Italy are significant. They took what was still an amorphous game and gave it shape and substance. They invented new moves for the Queen and Bishop, castling, and a new optional first move for the pawn. They changed the old Muslim rule of stalemate and stripping the enemy forces as a means of winning. They clarified and solidified still other rules, introduced the study of modern opening theory, and paved the way for future chess analysis by leaving a recorded history of games and opinions of the masters.

One of the games, a brilliant miniature, is appended below. It has been ascribed erroneously to Jean Jacques Rousseau but actually was played centuries before his time by the Italian, il Busnardo, taking White against an unknown opponent.

	WHITE	BLACK		WHITE	BLACK
1	P-K4	P-K4	6	P-Q4	B-N3
2	N-KB3	N-QB3	7	B-KN5	P-KB3
3	B-B4	B-B4	8	B-R4	P-KN4
4	P-QB3	Q-K2	9	NxNP	PxN
5	0-0	P-Q3	10	Q-R5 ch	K-Q2
			11	BxP	Q-N2

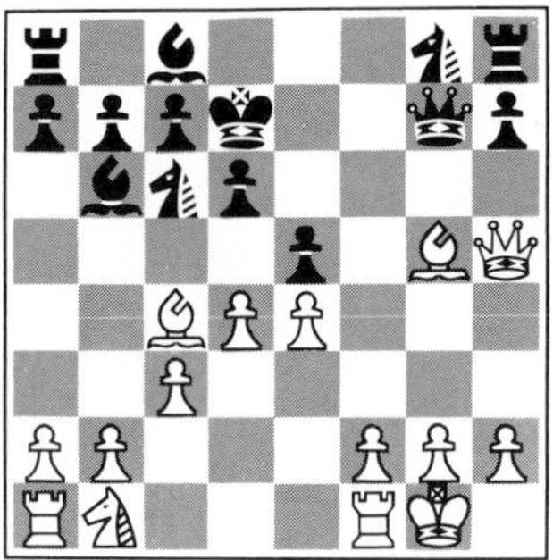

12	B-K6 ch!	KxB	13	Q-K8 ch	KN-K2
			14	P-Q5 mate	

A sparkling game, even by today's standards! Here is another and even briefer game recorded in one of Greco's many manuscripts:

	WHITE	BLACK		WHITE	BLACK
1	P-Q4	P-KB4	3	B-B4	P-KN4
2	B-N5!?	P-KR3	4	B-N3	P-B5

Greco, who seems to have been a master of coffeehouse chess, has deliberately enticed his opponent to advance pawns with a view to entrapping the Bishop. But is the Bishop really trapped?

5 P-K3! P-KR4

The Bishop cannot be taken because of Q-R5 Mate, which the last move prevents.

6	B-Q3	R-R3	7	QxP ch!	RxQ
			8	B-N6 mate	

Amusing!

4.

The Dawn of Understanding

"Pawns are the soul of chess." —Philidor

François-André Danican Philidor was the leading figure of eighteenth-century chess. From 1747, at the age of twenty-one, for forty years thereafter, he held undisputed sway over the chess world. His philosophy as quoted above would indicate that he was far ahead of his time in chess theory, a forerunner of the Steinitzian creed eschewing unprovoked attack in favor of lasting advantages represented by the permanent pawn structure.

Philidor was equally famous as a musician and composer. He commanded the French stage with such operas as *Le Maréchal Ferrant, Le Diable à Quatre, Ernelinde,* and *Tom Jones,* all great popular successes. He travelled widely, often to play chess in London, but also to Italy, Holland, and Prussia, where he was a favorite of Frederick the Great. Among his admirers were chess aficionados Rousseau and Voltaire.

Philidor learned how to play chess while a choir boy in the chapel of Louis XV. He was only eleven when his first composition was played before the king. He was a year younger when he challenged one of the members of the chapel band to play him. Philidor had learned the game from watching the band members play. To everyone's surprise, Philidor won his first game. By the time he left his service as choir boy at the age of fourteen, he was the best player of them all.

His steps led to the Café de la Régence in Paris, where he met the strongest players of the time, among them the redoubtable Phillip Stamma, a Syrian based in London. In 1745, Stamma had brought out a revised edition of his work, *The Noble Game of Chess,* in which he made an attempt to revive the ancient Muslim interest in problems by publishing one hundred end games. They were not particularly noteworthy and neither was his analysis of openings in another section of the book. Philidor must have sensed this because, when he challenged Stamma to a ten-game match, he stipulated that Stamma was to have the advantage of the first move in every game and that all draws were to be counted as victories for him.

The match was held at Slaughter's Coffee House in London in 1747. Philidor won 8 games, lost 1, and drew 1. From that time on, although for lack of need the title had not yet been created, there was no doubt that Philidor was the undisputed world champion of chess.

Unhappily, no record was made of Philidor's games while he was at the peak of his powers. The only games we have are those which took place after the age of sixty-one and these can hardly be considered a measure of the qualities which made him invincible over so long a period. The most widely reprinted game of Philidor's is one with Captain Smith played in 1790, when Philidor was sixty-four. Smith's play was too defensive—he seems to have been overawed by Philidor's reputation—and the game is marred accordingly. Nevertheless, Philidor, playing Black, showed fine positional judgment in exchanging Queens, confident that his attack would still prevail. It led to the following position before Black's 29th move:

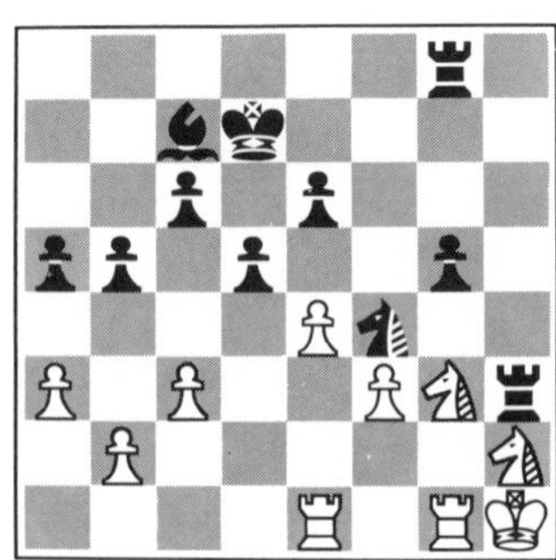

The game continued:

29	. . .	RxN ch!	**31**	N-R5	RxN ch
30	KxR	R-R1 ch	**32**	K-N3	N-R6 ch
			33	K-N4	R-R5 mate

Much of Philidor's reputation was based upon

Opening pages: George Cruikshank's "A Game of Chess" (1814) catches fiercely belligerent mood of contestants. Kibitzer at right enjoys game more than the players. Why not? He has all the fun, none of the responsibility. Below: "The Chess-Players," 1863 engraving of Meissonier painting. Head-in-hand mental struggle has always impressed artists.

what was then considered the astounding feat of playing blindfold with three players at the same time. In the light of contemporary demonstrations like Najdorf's playing forty-five opponents blindfold and Reuben Fine's playing four players simultaneously blindfold and rapid transit—ten seconds a move!—this does not seem too overwhelming an accomplishment.

But the legacy of Philidor remains intact by virtue of his truly distinguished book, *Analyse de Jeu des Échecs.* Philidor's work provided the first organized presentation of chess openings, with the theories behind them and the explanation of each move given in abundant detail, an amount of chess knowledge no master had been willing to impart before. As such, it set the mode for analyzing chess openings by means of listed variations and examples from actual play which exists to this day.

Philidor was only twenty-three years old when the book was written in 1749. It is highly probable that his play at this time matched the sharpness of his written analytical insights. More's the pity that we have no samples of his early games.

Philidor was in London, his second home, at the outbreak of the French Revolution. He wisely decided to remain in England. He had played chess with too many noblemen, both French and English, to make his return a safe one, although he did play chess with Robespierre. Philidor died in 1795 at sixty-nine. His death was a particularly great blow to the patrons of Parsloe's. This chess club, founded for the purpose of keeping Philidor in London, was frequented by the elite of British society.

Here is an analysis from Philidor's book of his own famous defense. Ironically, he was never known to use the Philidor Defense in match play. We give only the gist of Philidor's comments, which are far too exhaustive to reproduce here.

	WHITE	BLACK		WHITE	BLACK
1	P-K4	P-K4	2	N-KB3	P-Q3

These two moves make up the Philidor Defense.

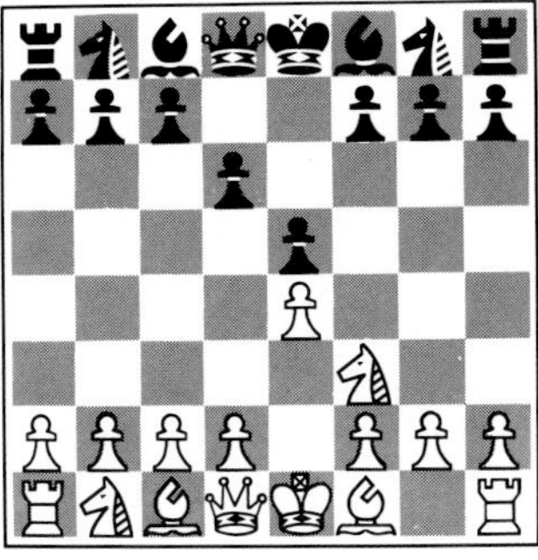

3	P-Q4	P-KB4 (!?)

The punctuation marks are ours. Against White's strong

Philidor playing blindfold at Parsloe's, a London chess club, c. 1794.
Opposite: Hitherto unpublished miniature of Philidor, artist unknown.
Bottom: An array of pawns from Hafler collection. Philidor said pawns are soul of chess.

third move, says Philidor, there are no satisfactory alternatives. He then goes into a number of variations and subvariations to prove that, with any other third move by Black, White emerges with the superior position.

4 PxKP ...

This is certainly the natural move for White although modern analysis has come up with an improvement.

4 ... BPxP
5 N-N5 P-Q4
6 P-KB4 ...

This move is in keeping with the style of the times, but Philidor condemns it as "the losing move" for White.

6 ... B-QB4
7 P-B4 P-B3
8 N-QB3 N-K2
9 P-KR4 ...

To provide a retreat for the Knight without the pawns being doubled by...BxN.—Philidor

9 ... P-KR3
10 N-R3 0-0
11 N-R4 B-N5 ch
12 B-Q2 BxB+
13 QxB P-Q5

Philidor introduced the term "phalanx" in describing two pawns abreast.

14 P-QB5 P-QN4!

The object of White's fourteenth move, says Philidor, was to cut the communication between the black pawns, but Philidor's reply insures their reunion.

15 PxP ep PxP
16 P-QN3 B-K3
17 B-K2 N-B4

This move is decisive, Philidor claims—and rightly—but he continues for another thirteen moves to demonstrate it conclusively.

Today Black's third move of P-KB4 is frowned upon. *Modern Chess Openings* gives, in rebuttal:

4 B-QB4 BPxP
5 NxP!

Leading to a winning advantage, in all variations.

Oddly, in a footnote after White's fourth move of PxKP, Philidor gives this variation, including the bril-

liant fifth move for White, and goes on to demonstrate a crushing attack with the final admission that "the situation is extremely delicate for Black." He then blithely proceeds to ignore the entire line. After all, why should a man belittle his own defense? Or can that be the reason he never played it!

The important thing, however, is not that *M.C.O.* proved Philidor wrong (that's being done every day and to more modern masters), but that Philidor evolved a consistent theory of the game plus the method of thorough and penetrating analysis in universal use today. This, plus his theory about the permanent and lasting pawn structure, is his lasting contribution to chess.

Whether Philidor is right or wrong in the analysis quoted, no chess-player would want to miss the final position visualized by the great French innovator. Where else can one find a better example of the Philidorian pawns, sweeping and majestic, marching as to war?

Left to right: German Queen riding sidesaddle, 1650; an 18th-century French Bishop rides donkey in derisive form of "fou," or fool; a 16th-century French King or Rook (bottom) made of ivory; English King made of silver, 1842. Weight of such pieces made them occasionally dangerous weapons.

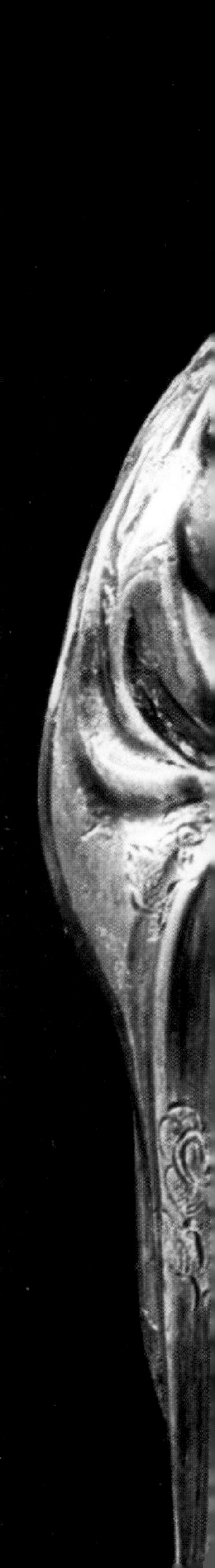

Although England today cannot boast even one grandmaster—"Englishmen never shall be Slavs"—in the mid-nineteenth century, Englishmen dominated the world of chess.

England has always been a most hospitable haven for chess-players. Philidor spent more time playing chess there than in his own country. Chess games were extensively recorded and a large number were published in English periodicals. Still, it is not to be supposed that the English took chess over immediately after the death of Philidor. A Frenchman, Alexandre Deschapelles, reigned for almost twenty years thereafter. His conceit, a trait not unknown among chess masters, though fortunately rare, did little to enhance the game. He insisted upon giving odds of a pawn and two moves to all comers and quit the chess scene when the opposition became more formidable and he faced the possibility of losing in even competition.

Louis de LaBourdonnais, a pupil who hastened his teacher's retirement when Deschapelles found he could no longer give LaBourdonnais a pawn and win, succeeded as the acknowledged chess champion. He was challenged by the Irishman, Alexander McDonnell, and in June, 1834, arrived in London to begin the longest match in chess history: a total of eighty-five games at the Westminster Chess Club.

Actually, the contest was divided into six matches, lasting from June to October. In the first match, McDonnell began by drawing the first three games but subsequently found himself unable to unravel the mysteries of LaBourdonnais' Queen Pawn opening, and he lost by the highly disparate score of 16 to 5 and 4 draws. In the following five matches, however, the scores, though favoring LaBourdonnais, were much closer. The final score was LaBourdonnais 45, McDonnell 27, drawn 13.

LaBourdonnais, more gracious than his predecessor, called McDonnell the finest player he had yet

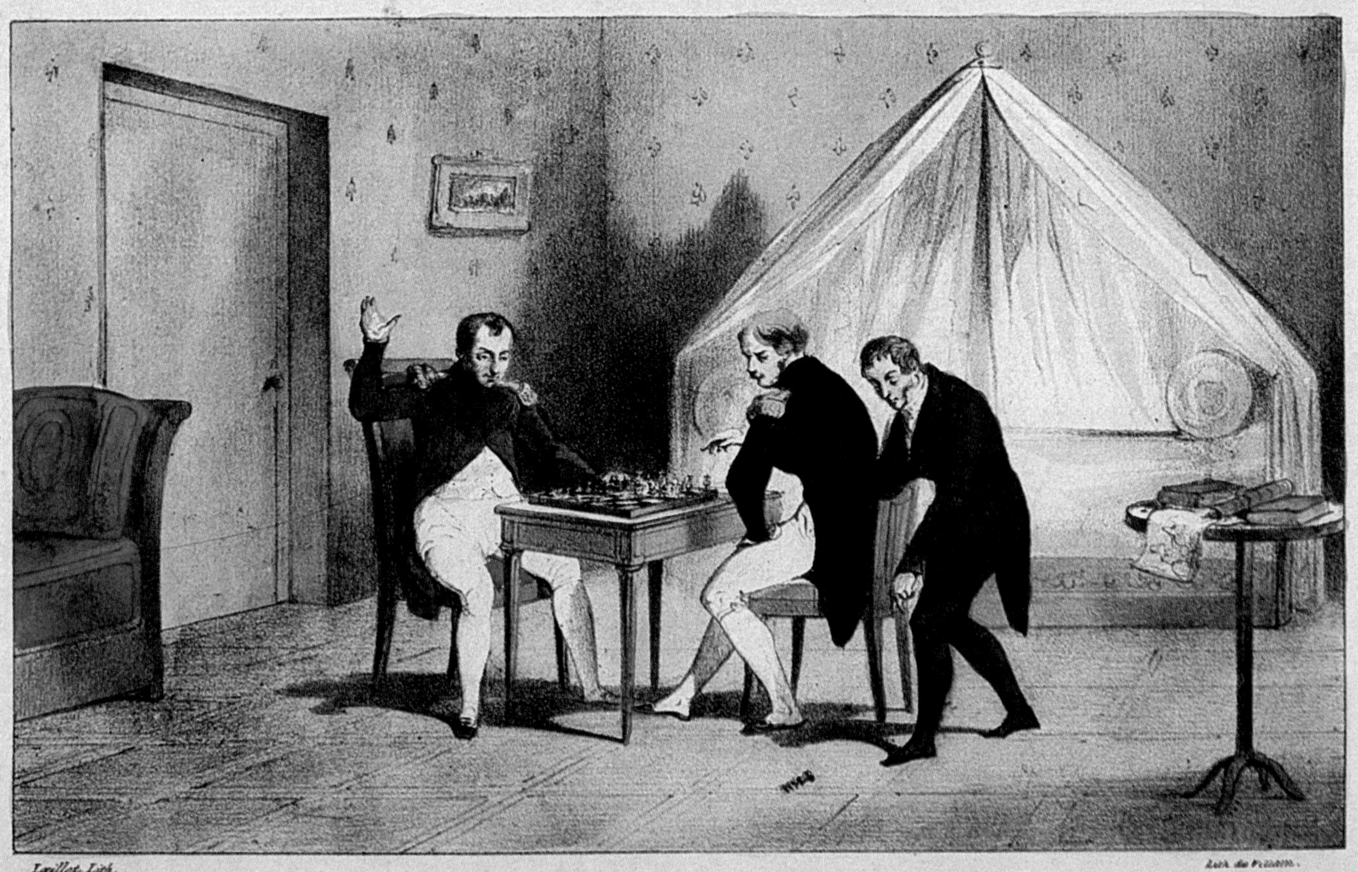

encountered. While McDonnell did not come close to winning, he made an appreciable dent in the score and did much to build up the reputation of British chess.

McDonnell may have contributed to his own downfall by stubbornly persisting in playing openings generally considered inferior, such as the King's Gambit, although it did produce on occasion some brilliant victories. Also, LaBourdonnais, a boisterous, convivial fellow, was a noisy opponent. (His remarks were not addressed to McDonnell, however, since neither spoke the other's language. The only word they had in common was "Check.") In fairness to LaBourdonnais, it must be mentioned that McDonnell was a very slow player and often took from one to two hours to make a single move. There were no chess clocks or time limits in those days, and a very slow player could drive an opponent to distraction.

Be that as it may, the encounter provided wild and woolly chess of a daring rarely seen in match play. George Walker, who recorded every game, pronounced the match the greatest ever played. He commented further that to sacrifice merely one piece was not counted much by either of the contestants.

Here is the famous fiftieth game of the match, wherein McDonnell sacrifices his Queen on the thirteenth move, a sacrifice that only reaches fruition twenty-three moves later!

Opposite: Napoleon playing chess in exile on St. Helena. Of toppled King on floor, the caption has him saying, "My poor King Louis XVIII!" Below: Napoleon figure of early 19th-century French set is polychromed ivory. George III is opposing King, Nelson and Wellington his "Bishops."

LaBOURDONNAIS V. McDONNELL
London, 1834

	WHITE	BLACK
1	P-Q4	P-Q4
2	P-QB4	PxP
3	P-K4	P-K4
4	P-Q5	P-KB4
5	N-QB3	N-KB3
6	BxP	B-B4
7	N-B3	Q-K2
8	B-KN5?	BxP ch
9	K-B1	B-N3
10	Q-K2	P-B5
11	R-Q1	B-N5
12	P-Q6	PxP
13	N-Q5	. . .

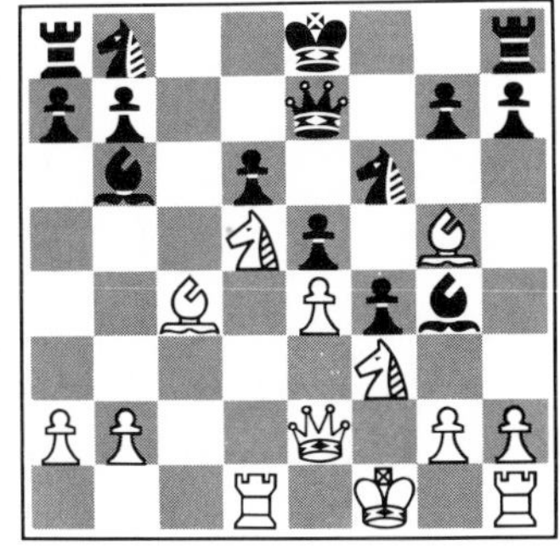

	WHITE	BLACK
13	. . .	NxN!!
14	BxQ	N-K6 ch
15	K-K1	KxB
16	Q-Q3	R-Q1
17	R-Q2	N-B3
18	P-QN3	B-QR4
19	P-QR3	QR-B1
20	R-N1	P-QN4!
21	BxP	BxN!
22	PxB	N-Q5
23	B-B4	NxP ch
24	K-B2	NxQR
25	RxP ch	K-B3
26	R-B7 ch	K-N3
27	R-QN7	N/7xB
28	PxN	RxP
29	Q-N1	B-N3
30	K-B3	R-B6
31	Q-R2	N-B5 dis ch
32	K-N4	R-KN1
33	RxB	PxR
34	K-R4	K-B3
35	Q-K2	R-N3
36	Q-R5	N-K6
37	Resigns	

White is helpless against the threat of . . . N-N7 ch, followed by . . . R-R6 mate.

Beyond inserting a number of exclamation points it is useless to try to annotate this wildly uninhibited game. Howard Staunton, the famous English player, made

Howard Staunton—Shakespearean actor, scholar, and self-proclaimed world chess champion, not without some justice. He was pivotal figure in British chess, wrote a chess column, and organized first great tournament at London in 1851. Below: Staunton (third from right) among cronies.

the attempt some years later, only to give up with the historic remark: "It seems utterly impossible for either player to save the game!"

Howard Staunton clearly earned his right to the imaginary title of World's Chess Champion when he defeated Saint Amant, the leading French player and successor to LaBourdonnais, in Paris in 1843, by a score of 11 wins, 6 losses, and 4 draws.

Saint Amant had defeated Staunton in a previous match. In addition, he had lost the first six games of the second match in short order and actually outscored Staunton in the later stages. Many felt that Saint Amant was the stronger player, and in any case a return match seemed indicated. To this Staunton stubbornly refused to agree. Years later, by persistent evasion, he also avoided a match with Paul Morphy, a factor which is said to have contributed greatly to Morphy's subsequent withdrawal from the game.

Staunton used his central position in chess to intimidate opponents, potential opponents, and chessplayers who had incurred his dislike. His column in the *Illustrated London News* became an instrument for personal vendettas and vilification of the opposition. Evidently unaware of, or not abashed by, the old English proverb which says, "You may knock your opponent down with the chessboard, but that does not prove you are the better player," Staunton vigorously battered his foes more aggressively in print than at the table.

In fairness to Staunton, it is not hard to find the influences which shaped his unpopular and controversial character. The illegitimate son of Frederick Howard, fifth Earl of Carlisle, he was brought up in poverty, with little

Sketch of chess pieces registered at British patent office in 1849 by Nathaniel Cook. In 1852 Staunton authorized his own figure for use as trademark on set boxes, thus leading to common conception that pieces are Staunton's design. Right: Classic 19th-century Staunton set, still without peer for practical play.

education. In spite of these handicaps, he became one of the noted Shakespearean scholars of the age. He can hardly be blamed if the struggles and privations of his youth warped his character so that he became a jealous, suspicious, and vitriolic man.

Staunton may not have been the strongest player of his time, but there can be no doubt that he was the most forceful chess personality. He considered himself chess champion of the world, and such was his persuasiveness that his view was generally shared by his contemporaries. There must have been extraordinarily weak opposition for him to maintain his claim, or perhaps whatever stronger competition existed was hamstrung, so that it was unable to express itself.

Staunton played stodgy games aimed at the acquisition of material. Although his conduct of the English Opening (1 P-QB4) was in advance of his time, not one of his recorded games seems worthy of being reprinted here. Yet the power of self-hypnosis is strong, and Staunton's own high opinion of himself led to his downfall.

In the year 1851, England held a "Great Exhibition of Art and Industry." Staunton seized the occasion to organize a chess tournament, inviting most of the great players of Europe. Many saw fit to decline the invitation, but there was still a fairly strong cross section of players, including Anderssen and Kieseritzky, a duo which gained chess immortality by playing the tournament's most striking game. This classic was fittingly dubbed "The Immortal Partie."

The tournament was an elimination contest. Staunton was naturally favored to win it, but his showing was a great disappointment. He was knocked out by Anderssen in the third round by a score of 4-1.

Whatever may be thought of Staunton as a player and as a person, there can be no denying his great contribution to chess. The tournament he organized in 1851 was the first of its kind and led to the practice of holding

Right: Gentlemen of the French Chess Club of Paris watch Staunton overwhelm their national champion, Saint Amant (making move). Busts of LaBourdonnais (l) and Philidor frown down on French defeat. Below: Portrait of Saint Amant.

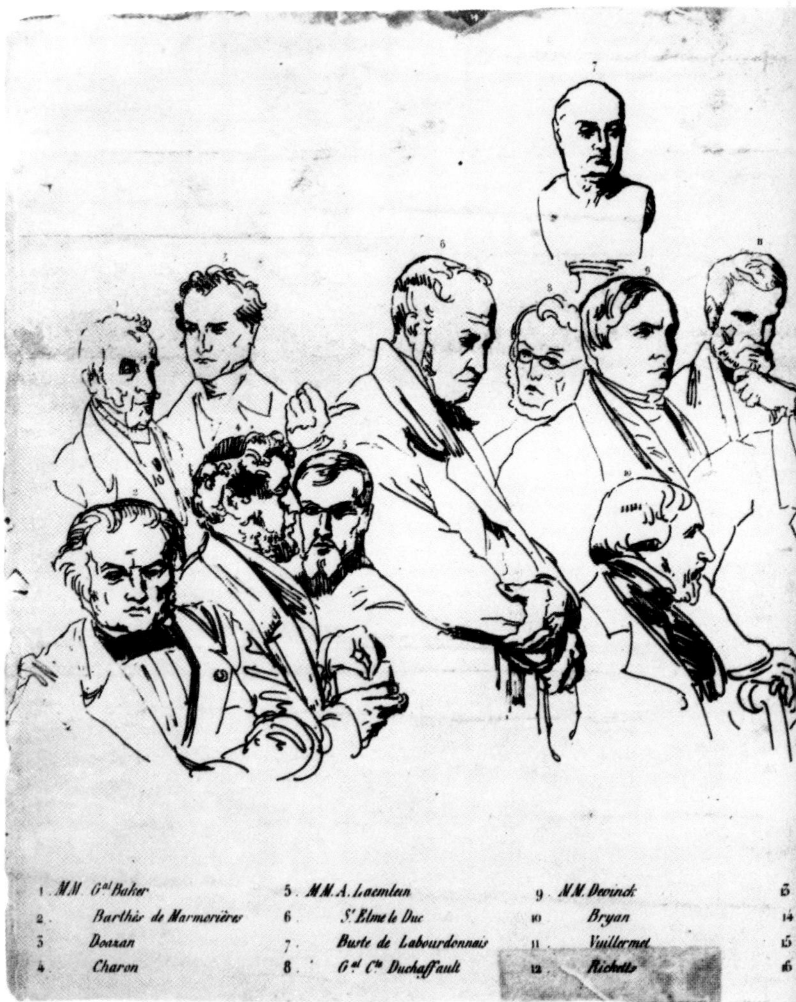

chess tournaments all over the world, although the "knock-out" element was gradually eliminated and no longer exists in modern tournament play. He founded and edited the first chess magazine in England, *The Chess-player's Chronicle*. In 1847, his best-selling *The Chess-players' Handbook* was published, followed in 1849 by *The Chessplayers' Companion*. But his greatest contribution falls into another category.

The Staunton design to keep his mythical chess championship may have been deplorable, but the design for chessmen to which he lent his name is magnificent. There are many original and beautiful examples of chess pieces which are properly classified as art objects. Some are quite ornate and some highly symbolic of the culture which created them. All have undoubted aesthetic appeal. But if a vote was taken among chess-players as to which pieces they most enjoyed playing with, there can be no doubt that the Staunton chessmen would win by an overwhelming margin. They are invariably used in major chess tournaments. No self-respecting chess club would be without them. They afford the most pleasing combination of utility and aesthetic appeal.

Lest this estimate seem too subjective, consider this excerpt from the critique of F. Lanier Graham (*Chess Sets*, New York, 1968): "In the eyes of most chess players, the 'Staunton' design has never been surpassed. . . . The pieces are quite rewarding to the touch and responsive to the move. They are individually well proportioned, and formally interrelated by means of classical balusters, crowning balls and grooves that, in elevation, are either

at the same height or at equally measured intervals. The graduated height of the pieces, although singularly unexpressive of relative power, contributes to the architectonic composition of the whole. The different levels of naturalistic symbolism are distinctly articulated. The Knight and the Castle are obvious. The abstract crowns that cap the King and Queen are clear. The more abstract shape of a Bishop's headdress is also apparent.

"Some neglected details of modern versions of this iconography indicate that functional symbolism may be an integral part of the naturalism. The deep cut into the Bishop may suggest not only a miter but a diagonal move. The points in the Queen's crown, and the crenels in the Castle's parapet, may suggest both the angles and the... directions in which these pieces can move...."

To which it can be added that the tactile pleasure to be derived from handling these well-proportioned pieces, suitably weighted and felted, can only be compared to the soothing effect of a well-balanced billiard cue or to the young child's attachment to his favorite blanket. They have the feel of an old glove and offer the kind of reassurance felt when playing on one's home field.

One carping note: It is more or less accepted that the original designer of the Staunton pieces was not Staunton, but an artist, Nathaniel Cook. What matter! It was Cook who registered the pieces' design at the British Patent Office in 1849, but Staunton influenced their manufacture and introduced them to chess-players of every land. For this his sins are cheerfully forgiven and our undying gratitude acknowledged.

5.

The Flashing Meteor

> "Where are you going, *mon ami?*"
> "Why, to the Café de la Régence to watch Voltaire and Rousseau play at chess."
> "Pooh! Mere scribblers!"
> "True, but today they play with Philidor."
> —*Chess Chronicles*

Café de la Régence! What a surge of emotion every chess-player must feel at the mention of this historic Parisian landmark. It existed from the days of Philidor, with only a brief interruption for the French Revolution. Here were held the greatest chess matches of the eighteenth and nineteenth centuries, featuring such giants as Philidor, Deschappelles, LaBourdonnais, McDonnell, Saint Amant, Staunton, Kieseritzky, Anderssen, Harrwitz, the young Steinitz, and the most glamorous figure of them all, the flashing meteor whose short but brilliant career signalled a new era in chess—Paul Morphy.

These illustrious names do not tell the whole story. Mention must be made of the rapid growth of thousands upon thousands of chess-players during this Golden Age of chess, lesser players whose sole bond with the masters was their great love of the game, those addicts who supported chess and sustained it and became its willing slaves. Perhaps the most accurate description of their fascination with chess may be found in the plaint of the eighteenth-century English clergyman who moaned, "When I have done with it, it hath not done with me."

Quite apart from the pleasure of playing, true aficionados might have been identified by their staying power as spectators. It must be recalled that chess clocks did not exist in those days and no time limit was set on the moves. In match play it was not uncommon for a player to consume more than two hours on a single move. This exasperating state of affairs had its effect upon that eminent British historian Henry Thomas Buckle, who was one of the strongest chess masters of the day. Buckle burst out against a tardy opponent: "Sir, the slowness of genius is hard to bear, but the slowness of mediocrity is insufferable."

A special breed that deserves heartfelt thanks are those lovers of chess who contributed so much to the service of this royal game with no hope of glory or material reward. Such a one was George Walker, previously mentioned as having recorded for posterity all eighty-five games of the LaBourdonnais-McDonnell match. Walker, an effervescent and stimulating writer, offers a delightful account of a visit to the Café de la Régence. Its prelude is a not uncommon mishap:

"Carried away by my zeal, I rushed toward him, but catching my coat-skirts unhappily in a neighboring chess table, down goes the whole concern, the men flying over the floor. This awakens the wrath of a brace of fresh enemies and confusion becomes confounded.

"'Sir,' cries one of them, 'are you mad? Do you ever look before you?' The other screams, 'Sir, you have cost me the game!' 'You had already lost it,' observed his antagonist. 'I had won it, sir—I would have played that game against Verdoni, or Philidor himself.'

"'Well, but gentlemen,' observed poor I, 'do not all talk together. I am ready to pay the stake if the fault were mine.'

"'Pay! Pay! You were not rich enough, were you to coin your brains and bones.' 'For how much, then, were you playing?' 'For honor—for honor, sir. I have come seven hundred miles, post, to accept the challenge of Monsieur here, who fancied himself invulnerable; and but for you, I should have given him a lesson—I should have taken down his pride!'

"'A lesson! What do you mean? You ought to thank the young man for coming to your assistance as he did. I had your Queen won by force in eighteen moves.'

"'Absurd! Ridiculous! I should have mated you in

Opening pages: Lithograph "The Chess Game" by Louis Bouilly, French genre painter (1716-1845). Below: Café de la Régence during telegraphic match between Paris and Vienna. Tchigorin watches move by M. Rosenthal (at table, r). From Le Monde Illustré.

eleven. I had looked through it.'

"'Mated me? Can you dare say so? You it is, sir, I am to thank for this gross insult. Learn, young man, that people don't run in the Café de la Régence.'

"Up jumps another player. 'And learn you yourself, sir, that people don't shout in the Café de la Régence, and that they have no right even to speak here.' The hubbub rises, but one resource remains. I rush forth from the café and take refuge in the Palais Royal."

Walker also tells the story—since much mangled in the retelling—of the man who spent six or seven hours each day for ten years in the Café de la Régence intently watching the play but never playing himself. Finally, a disputed point arose, and the taciturn veteran was called upon to umpire.

The man confessed that not only was he unable to umpire, but he had not the slightest idea how the game was played and didn't even know the names of the pieces.

"What, sir! Then how do you spend all your time here? Why do you not go home?"

"Ah, sir," answered the man, "if you knew my wife, you would never need to ask that question."

In another portion, Walker makes an admirably

To W. J. A. Fuller
as a souvenir
and slight token of friendship
Oct 12th 1859. Paul Morphy

BRADY'S PHOTOGRAPHIC GALLERY 643 BROADWAY NEW-YORK

Paul Morphy in 1859, shortly after his triumphant return from Europe. He was twenty-two and Longfellow, Oliver Wendell Holmes, and James Russell Lowell were among his admirers. Below: Stereopticon view of Morphy and Hungarian master Lowenthal.

exact judgment which has particular relevance today. He writes: "Cigars are forbidden at the Régence. This is as it should be. The same moral rule which permits one individual in a public room to blow second-hand tobacco smoke in your face should be equally lenient to the smokers of opium, valerian, or asafetida. Eat, drink, or suck what you will yourself, but do not force me to go shares against my will."

At length, the players all leave. LaBourdonnais and his noisy, laughing companions have long since left, the waiters yawn as they go about their tidying up, but Walker is still there, gazing at the dingy portrait of Philidor hanging against the wall, haunted by the presence of ghosts, pondering the mystery and beauty of a game to which men, for no material recompense, have devoted their lives. "Even that comes to its end, and the Régence is nearly vacant; the counter is abdicated, the café is cleared; my friend has gone, and the gas seems going. I am alone in the field of battle—the last man of the campaign. Midnight has struck its long, long bell, and I reluctantly prepare to face the cold. Farewell, at least for a season, to the Café de la Régence!"

It is convenient to link schools of chess, as well as the progression of chess ideas, with certain individuals. While this may be a sound pedagogic device, no one man can be held wholly responsible for any school of chess or any specific theory. Steinitz came closest to founding a school which has the right to bear his name, but even Steinitz owed much of his theory of pawn structure to Philidor, and he credited the German-American master, Louis Paulsen, as a pioneer of the new school.

Similarly, Paul Morphy is often hailed as the father of modern chess, the first to grasp modern opening principles. His grasp, on the one hand, fell far short of the formulations of Steinitz. On the other hand, he was

not so far ahead of his time as is generally supposed. Adolf Anderssen (1818-1879), whose chess career both preceded and followed Morphy's, was also cognizant, though possibly not to the same extent, of the principles of rapid opening development, control of the center, and open lines.

If his play lacked something of Morphy's full-blown logic, it is because Anderssen was the chess child of his age, and the emphasis of the age was on combination. Even Steinitz played for "unjustified" combinations in his early playing career which were at sharp variance with his later theories. The truth is that there are styles in chess just as there are styles in writing or anything else, depending upon the times, and no one is immune to their influence. Morphy himself often sacrificed his knowledge of basic chess principles to the quest for a pretty combination.

This emphasis on combination—the search for beauty in chess, to the seeming detriment of chess progress in theory and formal knowledge—is fascinating. Let the pundits make of this what they will. The fact remains that Anderssen could not have perpetrated his magnificent combinations without some recognition—call it instinctive, if you will—of basic chess principles, especially in the opening. While Anderssen represents the peak of romanticism, there are some indications in his play of the positional grasp of open games that emerged full-blown from Morphy's.

What place did Morphy occupy in the development of chess? We have referred to him as the flashing meteor who signalled the advent of a new era. He used his overwhelming clarity and logic like a rapier to penetrate the weaknesses of the old, planless game and to point up the need for a more general knowledge of laws and principles. In this sense he gave birth to a Steinitz.

And if this be so, who, chessically speaking, gave birth to Morphy? There can be no doubt that his was a

Morphy playing eight blindfold games in 1858 at Café de la Régence, against some of the club's strongest players. He won 6, drew 2. Despite wild acclaim, Morphy dismissed blindfold chess as of little importance, signifying nothing.

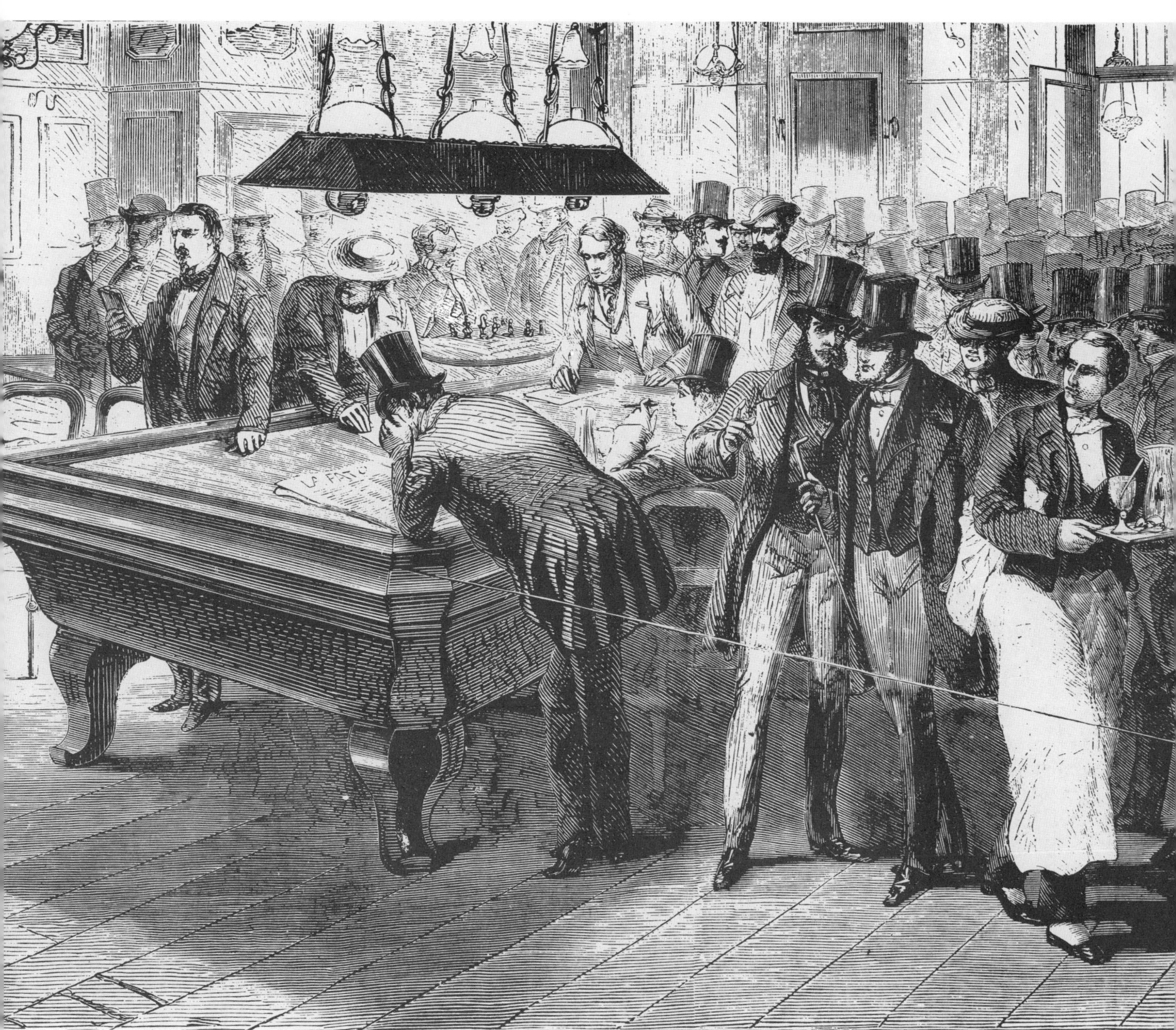

Cast-iron German pieces by Zimmerman foundry in style of famous set presented to Morphy at testimonial dinner in 1859. Actual Morphy pieces were solid gold and silver. Below: Morphy name and portrait advertise a brand of cigars.

hybrid birth, his own chess-oriented family and friends acting as midwives. But of his European progenitors, Anderssen seems to have wielded the most influence. We know that Morphy, though never a "book" player, received and annotated the book of the London, 1851, Grand Tournament, won by Anderssen, and there can be no question that Morphy was familiar with Anderssen's "Immortal" and "Evergreen" games. In his copy, after a listing of Staunton's works, the young Morphy penned in the words, "and some devilish bad games."

It is a paradox that Anderssen, who won these two famous games, has been largely ignored by chess pundits in a consideration of the world's top-rated players. They remember only that Morphy beat him soundly in their match—7 wins, 2 losses, and 2 draws. Seemingly forgotten is that fact that from 1859 to 1866, the period following Morphy's retirement, Anderssen was considered the strongest chess-player extant, a distinction he also held for many years prior to Morphy's appearance.

Morphy's admirers have ever been quick to find excuses for each game their hero lost, but there have been few apologists for Anderssen. Scant mention is made that he was nineteen years older than Morphy at the time of their match, that he had been engrossed in mathematical research and had not played chess for six years, and that he made a tiring mid-winter trip from Breslau to Paris, even though it had been earlier stipulated that the match was to be held in Breslau.

Morphy's illness, psychological or physiological, prompted the change. There can be no doubt that Morphy suffered cruelly from Howard Staunton's refusal to meet him for the world's "championship," but he had no reason to complain of his treatment by Anderssen.

Anderssen was a gentleman in the truest sense of the word. Augustus Mongredien, president of the London Chess Club, described him as "except Morphy, the most splendid and chivalrous player whom I ever en-

Louis Paulsen (below and with Morphy), America's second-best player during Morphy's reign. Their most famous game appears at end of chapter. Paulsen held simultaneous blindfold record at the time—ten opponents. Morphy considered it not worth contesting.

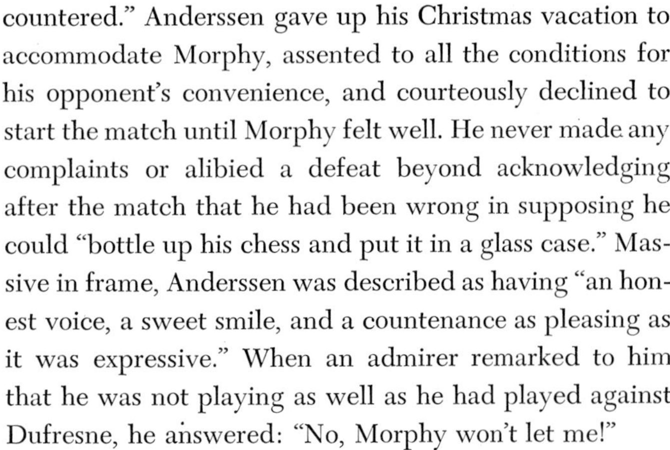

countered." Anderssen gave up his Christmas vacation to accommodate Morphy, assented to all the conditions for his opponent's convenience, and courteously declined to start the match until Morphy felt well. He never made any complaints or alibied a defeat beyond acknowledging after the match that he had been wrong in supposing he could "bottle up his chess and put it in a glass case." Massive in frame, Anderssen was described as having "an honest voice, a sweet smile, and a countenance as pleasing as it was expressive." When an admirer remarked to him that he was not playing as well as he had played against Dufresne, he answered: "No, Morphy won't let me!"

In justice to Morphy, he personally never made any excuses for his rare defeats. It was his followers who claimed he lost the first game of his match to Anderssen on account of illness. But it should be pointed out that all eleven games of the match took place within a period of nine days, and Morphy would have had to make a phenomenal recovery had illness handicapped him in the first game. Study of the game shows that Morphy played with remarkable ingenuity, which would undoubtedly have succeeded against a less formidable opponent. It will also show that Anderssen displayed great coolness under fire and a technical virtuosity in the closing stages equal to Morphy's own. Moreover, he eschewed his propensity for combination and played the black side of an Evans Gambit with all the soundness of a Morphy—or a Steinitz.

No book of this kind would be complete without the inclusion of Anderssen's "Immortal" and "Evergreen" games. Any comment beyond the liberal sprinkling of exclamation points is superfluous. Some modern critics have taken to analyzing these games and questioning their soundness, but this is carping.

The dominant chess motif of the Anderssen era, particularly in the pre-Morphy days, was not positional soundness or scientific accuracy, but *combination.* As examples of the art of combination, the "Immortal" and "Evergreen" games have never been surpassed.

ANDERSSEN V. KIESERITZKY
London, 1851
The Immortal Partie

	WHITE	BLACK		WHITE	BLACK
1	P-K4	P-K4	9	N-B5	P-QB3
2	P-KB4	PxP	10	P-KN4!	N-B3
3	B-B4	Q-R5 ch	11	R-N1!	PxB
4	K-B1	P-QN4	12	P-KR4	Q-N3
5	BxNP	N-KB3	13	P-R5	Q-N4
6	N-KB3	Q-R3	14	Q-B3	N-N1
7	P-Q3	N-R4	15	BxP	Q-B3
8	N-R4	Q-N4	16	N-B3	B-B4
			17	N-Q5	QxP

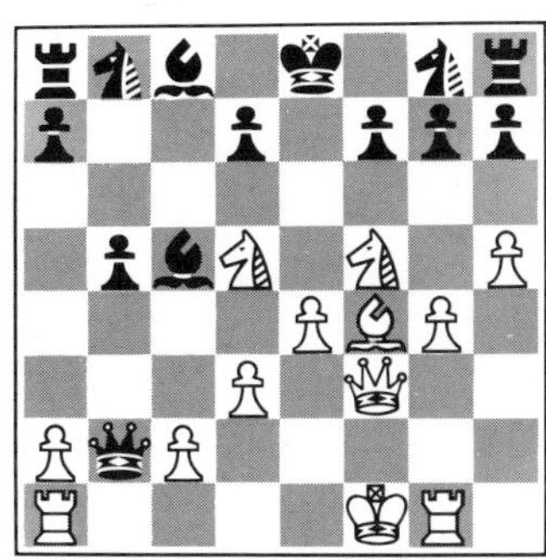

18	B-Q6!	BxR	21	NxP ch	K-Q1
19	P-K5!!	QxR ch	22	Q-B6 ch	NxQ
20	K-K2	N-QR3	23	B-K7 mate	

ANDERSSEN V. DUFRESNE
Berlin, 1852
The Evergreen Game

	WHITE	BLACK		WHITE	BLACK
1	P-K4	P-K4	5	P-B3	B-R4
2	N-KB3	N-QB3	6	P-Q4	PxP
3	B-B4	B-B4	7	0-0	P-Q6
4	P-QN4	BxNP	8	Q-N3	Q-B3
9	P-K5	Q-N3	14	QN-Q2	B-N2
10	R-K1	KN-K2	15	N-K4	Q-B4
11	B-R3	P-N4	16	BxQP	Q-R4
12	QxP	R-QN1	17	N-B6 ch	PxN
13	Q-R4	B-N3	18	PxP	R-N1

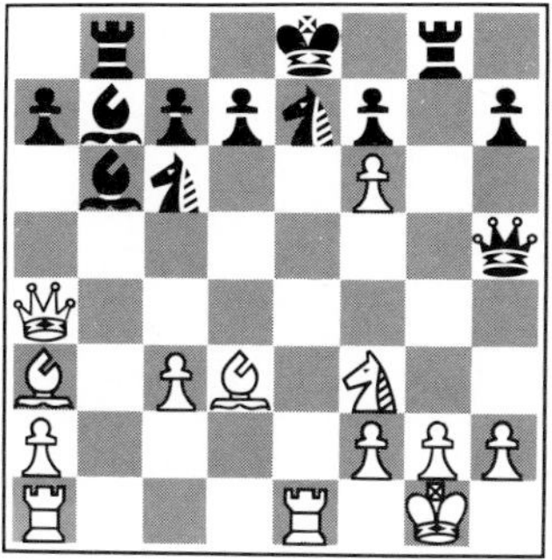

19 QR-Q1!!! . . .

"A move in a billion!"—Napier

Reti attributed the "great charm" of this move to its "inconspicuousness."

19	. . .	QxN	22	B-B5 ch	K-K1
20	RxN ch!	NxR	23	B-Q7 ch	K-B1
21	QxP ch!!	KxQ	24	BxN mate	

It is an ironic coincidence, and of interest to astrologers, that the date of Morphy's birth, June 22, was the same as that of Howard Staunton's death. These two protagonists seemed star-crossed from the beginning.

Paul Charles Morphy was born in New Orleans, a son of Judge Alonzo Morphy of the High Court of Louisiana. His father was of mixed French, Irish, and Spanish ancestry. The French family of his mother, Thelcide Carpentier, came from the West Indies. Paul learned chess at ten years of age from his father and received further instruction in the principles of the game from his uncle, Ernest Morphy, then considered the leading chess-player in New Orleans. At twelve he defeated Eugene Rousseau, a strong player from France; before his thirteenth birthday, he scored a win and a draw in two games played

with the Hungarian master, J. J. Lowenthal. Morphy was so small that it was necessary to place several books on his chair so he could see the chessboard. The master is said to have embraced the boy and declared that he would become the strongest player ever known.

Morphy remained small as he matured, about five feet four inches in height, slight of stature, and with smooth, unlined features. But over the chessboard he was a giant.

Unlike many other masters, Morphy did not neglect his outside life for chess. He studied law and was admitted to the bar before his twentieth birthday in April, 1857. He was fluent in English, French, Spanish, and German, and he inherited his mother's talent for music. It was said that once he heard an air he never forgot it, and that he could recite from memory the whole Civil Code of Louisiana.

Morphy possessed an advantage not shared by the majority of chess masters, that of being independently wealthy. It may have accounted for his stand against commercialism in chess and for his refusal to be considered a professional, a position on which he was adamant to the point of insult.

In the same year that he passed the bar, Morphy participated in a chess tournament for American players in New York and won first prize. The premier American player of the time, Louis Paulsen, took second. By the time he left New York in December, Morphy had lost only five of a hundred games played. His score in the match against Paulsen was 5 wins, 1 loss, and 2 draws. The stage was set for Morphy's triumphant invasion of Europe. It would prove, however, to be a triumph tinged with bitterness.

Prior to Morphy's departure for England the following June, the American Chess Association and the New

Opposite: Mid-18th-century carved and polychromed set from France. Painted figures from this period are very rare. Below left: German boxwood King, mounted on lion, from the 16th century. Right: Pre-1550 French ivory Bishop-Jester backward on donkey.

Orleans Chess Club issued invitations and challenges to Howard Staunton—or any other European player—to come to New Orleans and play a match with the rising young star for stakes of $5,000 a side. This was an extraordinary amount for a chess match in those days. Staunton declined, pleading his heavy schedule of work and the rigors of the journey. Instead, he invited Morphy to participate in a Chess Congress which was to take place in Birmingham at the end of June, where he would meet many champions from England, France, Germany, and Russia "whose names must be as household words to him, ready to test and do honor to his prowess."

The implication was that Staunton himself meant to play Morphy in 1859, at the latest, but this was not and never intended to be. Instead there began a long period of temporizing, exchanges of letters, and finally the breakdown of all communication and Staunton's abuse of Morphy in his chess column, which was in itself an abuse of Staunton's power.

Morphy did, indeed, play Staunton the month following his arrival but, to avoid the sting of man-to-man encounter, they were billed as "consultation games," Morphy and Barnes versus Staunton and Owen. Given the respective stature of Morphy and Staunton over each of their partners, we may safely assume that it was Morphy and Staunton who decided the moves. Morphy won both games played, but it might have been more politic had he managed to lose one. Although Morphy himself did not realize it, from that time on his hope of a match with Staunton was doomed.

Irritated by Staunton's tactics, Morphy ignored the Birmingham Tournament, whose winner was J. J. Lowenthal, the same player Morphy had defeated as a thirteen-year-old in New Orleans. Morphy had the further

Anderssen (l) v. Steinitz. In 1866 Steinitz defeated Anderssen, 8 wins against 6 losses. At forty-eight, Anderssen was the elder by eighteen years. In 1870, however, he got revenge by finishing ahead of Steinitz in Baden-Baden tournament.

satisfaction of having beaten Lowenthal in a London match held immediately before the tournament by a score of 9 won, 3 lost, and 2 drawn.

Morphy proceeded to Paris, the scene of his most brilliant accomplishments. His most important match, held at the Café de la Régence, was with Daniel Harrwitz. Like Fischer in his 1972 match with Spassky, Morphy lost the first two games (some pundits have suggested that Fischer was trying to emulate Morphy when he forfeited his second game), but he went on to win the match by a score of 5 wins, 2 losses, and 1 draw, when Harrwitz pleaded he could not continue because of illness. During one of the interminable postponements caused by Harrwitz, Morphy performed his celebrated feat of playing eight of the café's strongest players simultaneously and blindfold, winning 6 games and drawing 2!

The wildly enthusiastic crowd hoisted Morphy upon its shoulders and carried him into the street. So great was the ovation that he had difficulty extricating himself. Morphy attached no great importance to blindfold play, refusing to compete with Paulsen's record of ten simultaneous blindfold games. This seems like small potatoes compared to Najdorf's 1947 record of forty-five simultaneous blindfold games, but it was considered a great feat in those days, as it was when Philidor played three games blindfold in 1744.

In spite of this adulation and the exhilaration of winning his match against Anderssen, Morphy began at this time to show what can only be described as a hostility to chess. The concept of a love-hate relationship is nothing new, but never has a champion at the height of his powers displayed so much animosity toward the game

which brought him fame.

Being ridiculed by Staunton as an adventurer without financial backing was largely responsible for Morphy's subsequent attitude toward chess and chess-players. Some offer the excuse that Morphy's fine, sensitive nature was sickened by Staunton's ungentlemanly display, but this is letting Morphy off too easily. There must have been some inherent defect of character which led a person of Morphy's great talents to be crushed so easily.

When he returned to the States, he flew into a rage if anyone so much as hinted he was a chess "professional." He considered it more worthy to boast that he had inherited wealth from his father than to lower himself by making money at chess.

Morphy endeavored to return to the practice of law, for which he had shown so much aptitude. It is a sad commentary that his brilliance as a chess-player prevented others from taking him seriously as a lawyer. It was also rumored that a young lady of whom he was enamored turned down his proposal because she would not wed "a mere chess-player." The result was that from 1861 on, only three years after his dazzling successes on the Continent, Morphy retired from chess competition. There were a few instances of blindfold and odds games, but by 1869 even these had ceased. Morphy not only refused to play chess, he refused to discuss it or have any reference made to it. "I am not a chess-player," was his way of terminating any such discussion.

By 1875 Morphy was definitely psychotic, suffering from delusions of persecution. But it cannot be maintained, as some have done, that chess was the cause of his derangement. He had not played chess for many years. He had no nightmares of Knights chasing him across the board or similar fantasies of those whose minds have cracked under the strain of competitive chess. He was actually urged to play chess as a diversion. One contemporary comment, a letter attributed to Morphy's only close friend, Charles Amédée Maurian, which appeared in *La Stratégie* in 1876, puts Morphy's condition into perspective: "As for the causes which have produced in Mr. Morphy this derangement of his faculties, it is the opinion of his doctors that chess is not one of them. They have, I am told, recommended chess as a means of distraction and a change of thoughts. You know, too, that for ten or twelve years Mr. Morphy has completely abandoned chess, and that he never indulged in the game to excess."

On the other hand, his contempt for chess did border on the pathological. It remained forever linked in his mind with Staunton's chicanery. He saw it as a trivial and unproductive pastime divorced from the real business of life.

This is an opportune point to deal with the recurrent question about the effect of chess upon the mental health of its devotees. To put it simply, is chess healthful?

Where chess is a friendly socializing pastime, a stimulating hobby, a respite from the stultifying workaday world, or an invaluable escape from the grim existence of a prisoner or handicapped person, the salutary effect of the game is evident. Chess has been used therapeutically within various institutions. But let's not conceal the fact that the game sometimes has a negative influence.

Some players' compulsion to play the game takes on an addictive quality. For certain periods, they do little but play and think about chess. In consequence other matters, such as work, sleep, or nutrition, may suffer. Fortunately, such chess binges are shorter and far less damaging than other forms of compulsive behavior like drug addiction or gambling.

Then there is the problem of psychosis in certain chess champions. Did chess push them over the brink? If so, why?

Psychoanalysts have uncovered unconscious motivations in chess-playing, including the oedipal theme and the symbolization of the family romance. The classic Freudian paper by Ernest Jones on "The Problem of Paul Morphy" (1931) advanced the thesis that Staunton represented a father-figure to Morphy. Morphy's would-be aggression against the father was frustrated by Staunton's refusal to play him; he overreacted and withdrew from chess and life as a defense against awareness of his own (symbolic) murderous intent.

Dr. Norman Reider has pointed out the role of omnipotence fantasies in the game. Moreover, during a chess game, there is someone plotting against you every minute, laying traps for your destruction. In the context of a society that fosters championships, a tendency to grandiose paranoid thinking may be aggravated to the point of psychosis. Few of us, thankfully, have to bear the potentially unhinging consciousness of a Steinitz or an Alekhine of towering over the entire world, and most of us concede that chess is not the center of the universe.

Morphy died in New Orleans in July, 1884, at the age of forty-seven. He had taken his customary noontime walk along Canal Street and returned home to bathe. He was found dead in the tub.

The legend of Paul Morphy flourished within his lifetime and after his death. To say, as many have, that he was the greatest chess-player of all time is patently nonsense. There is no accurate way to compare the skill of players who lived in different epochs. Any of the scores of today's top masters would easily beat Morphy by virtue of the decades of accumulated chess knowledge. Suffice it to say that by any reckoning Morphy stood a head above his contemporaries. And it is doubtful that he ever reached the limit of his skill. If we are forced to hypothesize, however, and consider Morphy living at the same time as later chess greats, it is difficult to imagine him besting a Lasker, an Alekhine, a Capablanca, a Keres, or a Fischer.

Yet it cannot be denied that Morphy has stimulated and continues to stimulate the imagination of chess-players all over the world. What, exactly, were his achievements, his merits, and his place in the world of chess?

Certainly he was by far the greatest player of his time. He cannot be faulted if most of his contemporaries, with the possible exception of Anderssen, were not strong enough to give him a good fight. By the same token, it is difficult to achieve truly great games without formidable opposition, and there is a paucity of such masterpieces among Morphy's collected games.

Morphy's chief merit was that he understood the principles of development better than his contemporaries and disciplined himself to abide by them. Thus, his attacks always sprang out of positional superiority and he rarely attacked when attack was unwarranted. In this respect he was a forerunner of Steinitz. Emanuel Lasker's sober evaluation was that Morphy was a "rational player" who gradually built up a preponderant development which crushed his opponent, not "a genius who owed his success solely to superior natural gifts and powers of intuition."

The truth is always healthy and cannot detract from true greatness. If Morphy was less than a god, a judgment sure to annoy his legions of devotees, let us make amends by vigorously affirming his brilliant, meteoric impact on the chess scene. By stirring the imagination of millions, he immeasurably advanced the cause of chess, however much he may have abjured it in his later years. His influence on chess theory lay not only in the principles he so forcibly demonstrated—rapid development, control of the center, and open lines—but also in the catalytic role these principles played in stimulating additional precepts and new schools of thought in chess. He raised the level of chess for all who came later.

We cannot forbear adding a wistful note to the saga of this melancholy genius. It is related that in his last years he strode up and down the portico of his New Orleans home, daily repeating the words: *"Il plantera la*

"The Veterans," mid-19th-century oil by Richard Creifelds. Paintings like these fostered illusion that chess was an old man's game. Nothing could be farther from truth. Players usually reach peak in their thirties.

Souvenir lithograph from the First American Chess Congress, New York, 1857. Morphy won this tournament by a wide margin, losing only one game in third round of eight-game finale with Paulsen. Morphy (at right in center picture) won 5, lost 2.

bannière de Castille sur les murs de Madrid au cri de ville gagnée, et le petit Roi s'en ira tout penaud." ("He will plant the flag of Castille on the walls of Madrid to the cry of the city won, and the little king will go away all abashed.")

It is hard to conceive a more fitting epitaph.

PAULSEN V. MORPHY

New York, 1857

Four Knights Game

	WHITE	BLACK		WHITE	BLACK
1	P-K4	P-K4	4	B-N5	B-B4
2	N-KB3	N-QB3	5	0-0	0-0
3	N-B3	N-B3	6	NxP	R-K1

After 6...NxN 7 P-Q4, B-Q3, Black can regain the taken pawn, but Morphy prefers quick development, control of the center, and open lines.

7	NxN	QPxN	10	NxN	RxN
8	B-B4	P-QN4	11	B-B3	R-K3
9	B-K2	NxP	12	P-B3?	Q-Q6!

Of course! Paulsen's slipshod move bears out our comment on the generally poor quality of Morphy's opposition, but we must forgive Paulsen for making possible the beautiful combination on Morphy's seventeenth turn.

13	P-QN4	B-N3	15	QxP	B-Q2
14	P-QR4	PxP	16	R-R2	QR-K1

Threatening QxR ch, followed by R-K8 mate.

17	Q-R6	...

17	...	QxB!!	20	R-Q1	B-N7 ch
18	PxQ	R-N3 ch	21	K-N1	QBxP dis ch
19	K-R1	B-R6	22	K-B1	B-N7 ch

Quicker was R-N7, threatening RxRP and R-R8 mate. Then if 23 Q-Q3, RxBP ch 24 K-N1, R-N7 ch 25 Any, R-N8 mate.

23	K-N1	B-R6 ch	26	RxB	R-K7
24	K-R1	BxP	27	R-R1	R-R3
25	Q-B1	BxQ	28	P-Q4	B-K6
			29	Resigns	

Mate cannot be prevented.

And here is a miniature jewel played in the opera box of the Duke of Braunschweig, in Paris, 1858, between Morphy as White, and two opponents, the Duke and the Count Isouard, as Black.

	WHITE	BLACK		WHITE	BLACK
1	P-K4	P-K4	5	QxB	PxP
2	N-KB3	P-Q3	6	B-QB4	N-KB3
3	P-Q4	B-N5	7	Q-QN3	Q-K2
4	PxP	BxN	8	N-B3	...

Morphy does not wish to allow the exchange of Queens by 8 QxP, Q-N5 ch.

8	...	P-B3	10	NxP!	PxN
9	B-KN5	P-QN4	11	BxP ch	QN-Q2
			12	0-0-0	R-Q1

13	RxN!	RxR	15	BxR ch	NxB
14	R-Q1	Q-K3	16	Q-N8 ch!	NxQ
			17	R-Q8 mate	

6.

The Thinkers

> "Capture of the adverse King is the ultimate but not the first object of the game."
>
> —Wilhelm Steinitz

Wilhelm Steinitz was the first great systematic thinker in chess. He was a true pioneer who put chess on a scientific basis by proclaiming the principles of position play. The first universally recognized world champion, he founded a school which he called "Modern," although we now consider it classical. His influence is comparable to that of Shakespeare on drama, Newton on physics, and Freud on psychology.

Steinitz was born in Prague in 1836, the thirteenth child of a family that intended him for the rabbinate. But as soon as he learned chess from a schoolmate at age twelve, the Talmud took second place.

Sickly throughout his life, he devoted himself to the insecure profession of chess. What sustained him was an indomitable spirit. Once, playing the banker Epstein, he prompted his wealthy opponent to hurry his move. When Epstein asked just who did he think he was, Steinitz replied: "On the Bourse you are Epstein and I am Steinitz; over the board, I am Epstein and you are Steinitz."

One day the aficionados at Vienna's favorite chess café permitted this threadbare student to demonstrate his blindfold skill, and Austria soon had a new champion. It was the heyday of the great Anderssen, and Steinitz began by following the dictate and demand of the time: combination. Thus, at his London debut of 1862, he was acclaimed as the "Austrian Morphy." Morphy had found the correct handling of open games and their winning combinations effortlessly, by unerring instinct. But Steinitz only slowly, through years of profound thought, discovered the very basis of a successful combination—the elements of a superior position. No one before had been able to state a cause for this marvel of combination.

Steinitz' theory began to take shape when he won a match from Anderssen, 8 points to 6, in 1866. He determined that, in order to achieve a decisive combination, indeed, in order to play justly for a win at all, a player must first have a demonstrable advantage in position. He went on to elucidate the various elements that produce a strong or weak position: the strong pawn center; the isolated pawn; the queen-side majority; the bad Bishop; the advantage of two Bishops (over Bishop and Knight); weak squares (which he dubbed "holes") which can't be defended by one's pawns; and the conversion of a transitory advantage (in time) to a permanent one (in force or space).

The romantic ideal had been to win by a bold, sacrificial attack on the King. If it failed, the defender won by his material preponderance. Steinitz deemed such methods crude. He declared to an uncomprehending chess world: "The mere weakness of any square . . . very often will be fatal."

Steinitz introduced the principle of *balance of position.* When a position is balanced the relative strengths and weaknesses of the two sides neutralize each other. With correct play by both sides a draw will be the result. A player should seek to exploit strengths and safeguard weak points. If an opponent is less skillful in doing so, the balance of position will shift against him. The conception is basically mathematical.

Like Philidor, Steinitz affirmed the importance of pawn structure, a static factor. He showed how to accumulate small advantages in position. When these reach a large enough total, dynamic results—a combination—will follow. To the most talented attacking players of his time he said, in effect: "I shall make no weaknesses in my position. Try as you may, you will find no good combination."

After capturing Steinitz' throne, Emanuel Lasker, writing a *Manual of Chess,* became his leading interpreter.

Opening pages: Board overlapping elongated table suggests this picture was set up in photographer's studio. Steinitz (r) plays unidentified opponent while great rival Zukertort (third from l) takes notes. When "world chess champion" was introduced by toastmaster at banquet, both men stood in acknowledgement.

He drew grandiose philosophical inferences for life from Steinitz' ideas on chess, such as the notion that he who has the advantage must attack or suffer the loss of his advantage. He expressed as Steinitz' key principle that the basis of a masterly plan is always a *valuation*.

At the outset of his career Steinitz was a bold gambiteer, influenced by the demands for brilliancy from the people who provided money stakes. He later admitted, "I did not play with the object to win directly, but to sacrifice a piece." As he learned the efficacy of good defensive play, his style changed.

After defeating Anderssen, Steinitz laid a premature claim to the title of world champion. Yet his performance at the Vienna tournament of 1873 gave it some credence. There he finished with a stunning sixteen successive wins to take first prize.

In match play he was unbeatable. Often he started badly, but his superb fighting spirit and faith in his ideas always pulled him through. In 1870 he trounced Blackburne, 7 to 0. The British master, who was fond of the bottle, is said to have become so enraged at one point that he threw Steinitz out of a window. Evidently the results were not serious enough to affect the rest of Steinitz' career or to mellow him.

At London, in 1883, Steinitz finished second to J. H. Zukertort, a Polish physician and writer who was a disciple of Anderssen There arose a dual claim to world supremacy. Steinitz regarded a match victory over Zukertort as necessary to vindicate his doctrine. After acrimonious public arguments, the first acknowledged match for the world championship finally took place in 1886. Zukertort could find no good combinations and, decisively outmaneuvered, could win only five games. Steinitz emerged the victor with 10 wins—a success for his Modern school. According to Lasker, it was the triumph of the greater thinker over the better player, of deep strategy over brilliant talent.

The age of romance was dead, truly, if the most famous attacking player of the day was so convincingly beaten. Even the great Tchigorin, in the matches of 1889 and 1892, could not restore the fallen banner of the romantic tradition. By victories of 10-6 and 10-8, Steinitz confirmed the permanent shift in the center of gravity of chess thought.

In his play, Steinitz was obstinate in clinging too long to discredited moves. He liked to grab a pawn and defend a cramped game for hours, as long as he felt his position to be basically sound. It was unchivalrous! But he declared, "It merely shows primitive taste to prefer brilliancy to soundness."

Steinitz dared his opponents. One of his provocations is the Steinitz Gambit: 1 P-K4, P-K4 2 P-KB4, PxP 3 P-Q4?!, Q-R5 ch 4 K-K2. This he stubbornly played for thirty years, convinced that his strong pawn center outweighed the discomfort of his King. In the Ruy Lopez, he patented a defense, 3...P-Q3, which locks in the King's Bishop in an attempt to maintain the pawn on K4, but he also handicapped himself with irregular moves like 3... KN-K2. Strangely, like the followers of so many revolutionary thinkers in other fields, his pupils later became pillars of orthodoxy.

As a naturalized Englishman, Steinitz devoted many years to imparting his teachings to the world in English newspaper columns, his *International Chess Magazine,* and a book, *The Modern Chess Instructor*. A Viennese player said of him in 1882, "This little man has taught us all to play chess."

But his writings also included a quota of invective, and British hospitality became strained. So, in 1884, he emigrated to the United States, where chess lovers gave him a warm reception. Still, the comfortable life was not to be his. When he returned to the fray at Vienna four years later, an admirer suggested that, having gained enough fame, he could afford to let the younger players

Wilhelm Steinitz (top l) became first world chess champion officially by defeating J. H. Zukertort (bottom l) 10 to 5 in 1886 match. M. I. Tchigorin (bottom r) blundered against Steinitz to miss championship chance. Tarrasch (top r) was too busy to become champion.

have their day. He replied, "I can spare the fame, but not the prize money."

A bright new star was rising. Emanuel Lasker had digested and mastered the modern principles. His fighting spirit equalled that of the champion and he was superior in stamina and tactical skill. When they met in 1894, the aging Steinitz, on crutches from gout, went down by a score of 10 to 5, his first defeat in twenty-eight matches. A return match two years later was even more disastrous. After losing, 10 to 2, Steinitz suffered a nervous breakdown.

Stung by disappointment, Steinitz feared that his practical failures might bring his theory into discredit. With phenomenal resilience, he returned to the tournament circuit, although far beyond peak competitive age, and continued to win prizes almost until the end.

At last he was unhinged by a disjunction between his internal reality ("I am a King of the chess world") and the external realities of poverty and neglect. According to one story, he claimed to be giving God odds of pawn and move. He died a public ward in New York in 1900. A new century had begun which would see manifold developments in chess thought. But all future generations would operate within the Steinitzian framework of position play. Emanuel Lasker wrote, "His theory is and forever remains the classical expression of the idea of chess."

ZUKERTORT V. STEINITZ

St. Louis, 1886

Queen's Gambit

	WHITE	BLACK
1	P-Q4	P-Q4
2	P-QB4	P-K3
3	N-QB3	PxP
4	N-B3	N-KB3

Steinitz already has a plan: to isolate and blockade the QP.

5	P-K3	P-B4
6	BxP	PxP
7	PxP	B-K2
8	0-0	0-0
9	Q-K2	QN-Q2
10	B-N3	N-N3
11	B-KB4	QN-Q4
12	B-N3?!	. . .

A better square for the Bishop was N5 or K5. Zukertort wastes some time in developing against the king-side.

12	. . .	Q-R4
13	QR-B1	B-Q2
14	N-K5	KR-Q1
15	Q-B3	B-K1

Keeping control of Q4 with pieces. But White's seventeenth induces a change of plan.

16	KR-K1	QR-B1
17	B-KR4!	NxN
18	PxN	Q-B2
19	Q-Q3?!	. . .

Better was 19 B-N3, B-Q3; 20 P-B4, producing what Steinitz called "hanging pawns." The coming exchanges only reduce White's attacking chances.

19	. . .	N-Q4
20	BxB	QxB
21	BxN?!	RxB
22	P-QB4	R/4-Q1
23	R-K3?	. . .

True to tradition, White tries an attack on the King without sufficient forces. It was time to go over to defense.

23	. . .	Q-Q3
24	R-Q1	P-B3
25	R-R3!	P-KR3!

Acceptance of the Knight would give White at least a draw.

26	N-N4	Q-B5
27	N-K3	B-R5!

This "tickling" move forces White to weaken the back rank. Steinitz accumulates another little advantage. The counterattack begins.

28	R-B3	Q-Q3
29	R-Q2	B-B3
30	R-N3	. . .

More dangerous was 30 P-Q5, hoping for...PxP? 31 N-B5!. But 30...Q-K4! keeps the upper hand.—Euwe

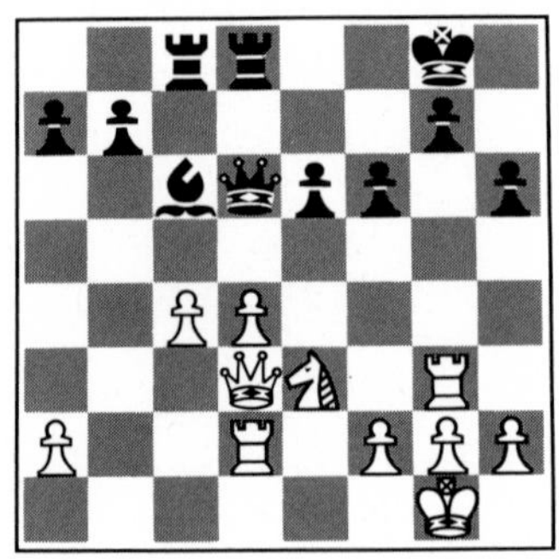

ZUKERTORT & STEINITZ.
MINCHIN
ROSENBAUM. DIRECTOR OF PLAY
MORTIMER
MACKENZIE
MACKENZIE'S PENCIL
ROSENTHAL
MASON
BIRD
WINAWER
AN ONLOCKER
BLACKBURN
RECREATION
THIS IS NO COMMON BETTING MAN. BUT A DISTINGUISKED FOREIGNER TAKING NOTES
THOUGHT
NECESSARY: BUT SUBSERVIENT TO THE GAME OF CHESS.
TAKE A SMALL PAIR OF STEPS WITH YOU - AWFUL EFFECTS OF STANDING TOO LONG.
FOUND ON THE BATTLE FIELD AFTER MIDNIGHT
THE HEAD AND FEET OF A GREAT MASTER
CORBOULD

Dori
52, REGENT ST. W.
& ROYAL AQUARIUM, WESTMINSTER.

Falk
949 BROADWAY, N. Y.

HABANA,
S. A. Cohner
O REILLY 62

London Daily Graphic *cartoon of 1883 tournament won by Zukertort, who finished 3 points ahead of Steinitz and thereupon claimed championship. Blackburne of England was third, Tchigorin fourth. Steinitz settled pretender's claim by beating him decisively in 1886.*

30	...	P-B4!	**31**	R-N6?!	...

The threatened pawn fork shows the error of White's maneuvers of the Rook, but now he'll barely be able to rescue it.

31	...	B-K5	**32**	Q-N3	K-R2

Steinitz said, "The King is a strong piece!"

33	P-B5	RxP	**36**	Q-N2	R-N8
34	RxKP	R-B8 ch	**37**	Q-B3	R-QB1!
35	N-Q1	Q-B5	**38**	RxB	...

The last hope: 38...PxR? 39 QxR, QxR 40 Q-B5 ch and perpetual check.

38	...	QxR/5	**39**	Resigns

For if 39 QxR, Q-K8 mate. Steinitz demonstrated how to punish an unsound attack.

->>><<<-

Tchigorin is the adopted father of the Soviet school of chess and a pioneer of the creative tradition. "Theoretical!" he once exclaimed. "A synonym for unoriginal!" Soviet chess historians have extolled him as a true artist, an enemy of dogmatism, an upholder of creativity against academic conceptions. They are right.

Mikhail Ivanovich Tchigorin was born in 1850 into a Russia very different from today's land of great chess. Although the game had been played there for centuries, there was no tradition of master play and no organized chess life. Through his example and dedicated effort, he left a Russia which had gained a significant place in the world of chess.

Tchigorin was a late learner of the royal game. At age twenty-four he was still receiving odds of a piece. At thirty-one he tied for third place in his first international tournament, at Berlin in 1881. Despite his isolation from the chess centers of Europe, he soon proved himself a peer of the best players of the West.

Meanwhile, he took time from his duties as a government clerk in St. Petersburg to found the first chess club in Russia. In 1876 he started a journal, *Shakhmatny Listok,* filled with instruction and original analyses. Singlehandedly, and at personal sacrifice, he lifted Russian chess to a new level.

Tchigorin lived in the imposing shadow of Steinitz' Modern school, with whose exponents he waged energetic arguments in print and on the board. He himself was unaware of founding any school, but Soviet theorists adopted him decades after his death in 1908. In his time he was honored only for his gallant gambits and attacks and was regarded as a throwback to the romantics. His other facets were not understood. As late as the time of Reti, that deepest of critics, Tchigorin's permanent contribution had not been grasped.

A mischance in the twenty-third game of his second title match with Steinitz at Havana, 1892, caused a long delay in recognition by the chess world. In a winning position, Tchigorin blundered and allowed a mate in two, ending the match. The final score was Steinitz 10, Tchigorin 8, with 5 draws. (Draws still were uncommon in those fighting days before the perfection of Technique!) If not for that stroke of bad luck, Tchigorin might well have gone on to win the match and become the second champion of the world, setting new fashions and inspiring a new generation of young players with his unique ideas.

To appreciate fully the greatness of Tchigorin's thought, one must remember the setting. The Romantic Era was over. Within two decades after defeating Anderssen in 1866, Steinitz had made deep investigations and proclaimed his Modern school, basing the conduct of the chess struggle on scientific principles. These were soon refined by Tarrasch, who became the most lucid teacher of the new orthodoxy.

The message of Steinitz' new Scientific school may be stated as follows: Chess is a finite logical system. Learn the rules of position play, obey them at all times, collect small lasting advantages. Memorize book openings. Generalize. Determine how each position resembles previ-

Opposite: Late 18th-century North Chinese set of carved ivory. All figures on fabulous animals are pawns. Below: Wooden set dating about 1830 illustrates popular theme of Crusaders v. infidels. At bottom are Bishops.

Metropolitan Club, Washington, D.C. Steinitz and Tchigorin, both of whom visited the New World, might have found its atmosphere stiff and formal, impervious to national "chess fever" of the sort that followed Morphy's European victory.

ous areas in the territory of chess knowledge. Gladly accept a defensive position in return for a pawn. Do not seek a combination unless you have accumulated a clear plus. Play chess with fidelity.

To which Tchigorin, the creative counterforce, in effect replied: Chess is a limitless forum for the human imagination. Each position is a fresh challenge. Rules and book openings, to the creative player, are no more than guidelines to be transcended. Individualize. Each position is new—terra incognita that may contain the seed of a beautiful combination. Gladly give up a pawn in return for the attack. Play chess with joy.

These two profound and original thinkers left a large legacy of chessboard battles. Their lifetime score was Steinitz 27, Tchigorin 24. Also fascinating is the Tarrasch-Tchigorin match of 1893, a tie, 9 wins to 9.

Tchigorin espoused the Evans Gambit and the King's Gambit, which Tarrasch called "a decisive mistake." With his sparkling combination play, he endeared himself to a public that was nostalgic for romantic times. But the experts of his day did not understand his strategic side. Today we can assert that his practice stands as a lasting challenge to dogmatism.

To every dogma of the Scientific school, Tchigorin found exceptions. For example, in answer to the rule, "Bishops are generally superior to Knights," he gaily chopped off enemy horses with his orthodox, straight-moving Bishops but went on to work wonders with the tricky, hopping cavalry. Against Tarrasch himself, who proclaimed the evil of a Knight on the side, he played

N-R4, because it accorded with his plan in the specific situation on the board. When *Deutsche Schachzeitung* exclaimed, "Again something new!" he reminded them that "games do not repeat themselves from opening to mate."

Not in the open games but in closed systems do we see Tchigorin's futuristic ideas. He discovered that rapid development is less important in closed games. To Tarrasch's dictum against cramped positions, he replied, "Not every cramped position indicates that the other side has a better game." Tchigorin introduced the King's Indian Defense into tournament play a half-century before its heyday. It flew in the face of the Scientific school, which called for a pawn center and straightforward development of the pieces. Here's an example: 1 P-Q4, N-KB3 2 P-QB4, P-Q3 3 N-KB3, QN-Q2 4 B-B4, P-KN3 5 N-B3, B-N2. Black, seemingly cramped, is ready to fight back in the center with. . . P-K4 or. . . P-B4.

This storing up of the energy of the pieces behind closed lines, as in the still popular Tchigorin Variation of the Ruy Lopez, anticipated the dynamic play of the 1940s and later.

Again, witness the Tchigorin Defense to the Queen's Gambit: 1 P-Q4, P-Q4 2 P-QB4, N-QB3!? 3 N-KB3, B-N5 4 PxP, BxN (off with the Knight!) 5 NPxB, QxP. Black allows White a preponderance of pawns in the center, relying on the power of his pieces to undermine it later. This idea foreshadowed by decades the central thought of the Hypermoderns. Their concept of the individuality of every position was also grasped by Tchigorin long before them.

Nothing confounded the ruling dogma of the day more than Tchigorin's move against the French Defense: 1 P-K4, P-K3 2 Q-K2!? He admitted its origin "half in jest" —but only a Tchigorin would have studied such a move, which retards immediate development in favor of a strategic plan, to deter Black's. . . P-Q4. Tarrasch, when confronted by the move, must have been scandalized.

Thought to be behind the times, Tchigorin was in fact ahead of them. To play over his games today is a fresh adventure in creative chess. And to heed his philosophy is a guarantee against the sterile dead end which is a specter periodically raised by the excessive veneration of Technique.

For the legacy of Tchigorin, Russian chess-lovers are justly grateful. The rest of the chess world is coming to share their feeling. Bobby Fischer, no partisan of the Russians, included Tchigorin in his list of the ten greatest players of all time.

TEICHMANN V. TCHIGORIN

Cambridge Springs, 1904

Queen's Gambit Declined—Tchigorin's Defense

	WHITE	BLACK		WHITE	BLACK
1	P-Q4	P-Q4	3	N-KB3	B-N5
2	P-QB4	N-QB3!?	4	PxP	BxN
			5	PxN	. . .

Preferable is 5 NPxB, relying on the Bishops.

5	. . .	BxBP	6	N-B3	P-K3
			7	B-B4	. . .

Eight years before, Pillsbury had occupied the center with 7 P-K4, but Tchigorin undermined it with 7. . . B-N5 8 P-B3, P-B4!

7	. . .	N-B3	9	Q-N3	N-Q4
8	P-K3	B-N5	10	B-N3	0-0
			11	B-Q3?!	Q-N4!

Intending 12 0-0? BxN 13 PxB, NxKP!, White's Bishop should therefore have gone to K2.

12	Q-B2	P-B4	14	0-0-0	BxN
13	B-K5	R-B2	15	PxB	. . .

By the criteria of the Steinitz school, White has these advantages: Bishop versus Knight, the hole at K5, more central pawns. But these features are static, while Black's plans are dynamic. Watch the play of the agile Knight.

"Chess-Players" by Thomas Eakins, oil on wood, 1876. Edward Lasker once complained that chessboards in paintings rarely had sixty-four squares. This picture should gladden his heart. Count 'em.

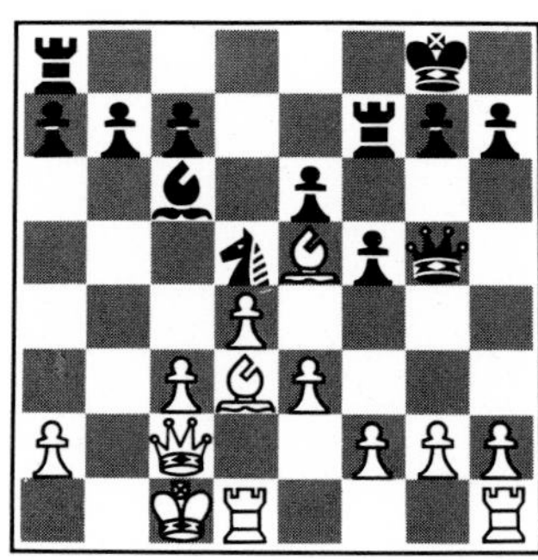

15	...	P-N4!	20	Q-N1	N-B6
16	KR-N1	Q-K2	21	Q-R1	R-Q1
17	QR-B1	Q-R6 ch	22	P-N3?!	N-K5 ch
18	K-Q2	P-N5	23	K-K2	N-B4!
19	P-QB4	B-R5	24	Q-N1	...

Or 24 B-N1, N-N6, winning the Queen.

24	...	NxB	26	K-B3	B-B7
25	QxN	QxP ch	27	Resigns	

In view of 27 Q-Q2, B-K5 ch 28 K-K2, B-B6 ch 29 K-Q3, Q-N6 ch 30 Q-B3, QxQ mate. The Russian giant, nearing the end of his career, showed here how chess would be played in the future.

Dr. Siegbert Tarrasch appreciated beauty enough to say, "Chess, like love, like music, has the power to make men happy." He mastered and refined the scientific system of Steinitz and taught the new dogma to the world.

Tarrasch was born in Breslau, Germany, in 1862, heir to a long patriarchal tradition. As a youth in the city of Adolf Anderssen, he showed scholastic excellence and decided to enter the profession of medicine. The difficulty of pursuing two careers became evident in 1890, when he had to decline an invitation to play Steinitz for the world championship. Thus he lost his last realistic chance at the title, for Emanuel Lasker would soon overshadow him for the rest of his life. But none could surpass Tarrasch's influence as a teacher.

Tarrasch learned chess at age fifteen, but only

Top: Bavarian set of pearwood, c. 1840, against ornate Italian board, c. 1790. Bottom: Late 18th-century French set is carved from ivory and walnut. Note that Knights do not have horse's heads, presaging some of more abstract designs of future.

later did he make the "astonishing discovery" that books were written about the fascinating game. In the cafés of Berlin he met master players but failed in his tournament debut. For two more years he prepared, and in 1883 he gained the title of Master, commencing a competitive career that was to last forty-five years.

His peak years were between ages twenty-seven and thirty-two, when he scored four consecutive first prizes. He again took first honors in the marathon Vienna tournament of 1898, one of the longest ever held, losing only three times in forty games. But in the new century his successes were fewer. In matches he methodically crushed such Neo-romantics as Marshall and Mieses, but he twice succumbed to the superb tactics of Lasker.

Tarrasch's greatest achievement was to take the systematic, scientific approach of Steinitz and change the emphasis, prune it of its eccentricities, and make positional principles available to students throughout the world. Seemingly, he tried to reduce the chess struggle to a series of narrow precepts, such as, "Knights are poorly placed on the side."

Tarrasch's ideas gave rise to two phenomena that he viewed with sentiments ranging from distaste to outrage. They were the prewar generation of colorless technicians who, devoid of fight, carried his doctrine to a sterile extreme, and the postwar Hypermoderns, iconoclasts who scorned it outright.

Tarrasch improved on Steinitz by reasserting function over structure, the mobility of the pieces over the static features of pawn position. Thus, he readily accepted an isolated QP in his patented defense to the Queen's Gambit: 1 P-Q4, P-Q4 2 P-QB4 , P-K3 3 N-QB3, P-QB4 4 BPxP, KPxP. In his famous last book, *The Game of Chess,* he declared, "The future will decide who has erred in estimating this defense—I or the chess world." (Presumably, a dispute of equals. He would have been gratified to see his defense revived by Spassky in the title match of 1969.)

Steinitz' espousal of cramped positions evoked the biggest reaction from Tarrasch. Of the Steinitz Defense (3 . . . P-Q3) to the Ruy Lopez, he wrote: "All lines of play which lead to the imprisonment of a Bishop are on principle to be condemned!"

Tarrasch's emphasis on superior mobility is connected with the factor of space. Advantage in space permits the constricting of enemy piece mobility. (He described his play as "the stalemating style.") With this advantage, winning plans soon present themselves. He had no great flair for combination. The beauty one finds in a Tarrasch game is that of flawless technical execution. It seems to play itself.

In interrelating the three basic factors of force, space, and time, Tarrasch equated the value of a pawn to three moves in piece development. But he approached this enumeration of tempi mechanistically, neglecting the specific situation on the board. He was constantly referring to *a priori* theories instead of empirical data, always generalizing instead of focusing on the individual features of a position.

Tarrasch had the courage to make dogmatic evaluations of opening moves, jumping to conclusions later experts would reject. That fate has befallen his pronouncement about White's still-preferred fourth move in the Two Knight's Defense: 1 P-K4, P-K4 2 N-KB3, N-QB3 3 B-B4, N-B3 4 N-N5—"A typical example of a bungling move." Why did he think so? Because it violates a precept: "Never move the same piece twice in the opening." But experience shows that the threat carried by this move does not permit Black an easy time. Another Tarrasch dictum, "A backward pawn . . . is generally as good as lost," is flouted by today's legions of adherents to the Sicilian Defense.

After World War I, the Hypermodern movement appeared as a revolt against the old values championed

LOLLI
STAMMA

London, 1888. Artistic license has such notables as Salvio, Philidor, Stamma, and Staunton peering from their portraits at Zukertort and Steinitz (second row, 4th and 5th from r). Steinitz' modern concepts outclassed Zukertort, who still seems to be looking for one good combination.

Opposite: Late 19th-century ivory chessmen from Nuremberg carry out an historical theme. Below left: Early 19th-century set of ivory and ironwood. Right: Classic French set of ivory and bone, c. 1820.

by Tarrasch and his school. To the Hypermodern strategy of abdicating the center to the enemy pawns in order to attack them, Tarrasch retorted, "Heresy!" He pointed out that both sides could disdain an early occupation of the center and develop all four Bishops on the flanks. This type of play he called "the horror of all true friends of the noble game." Today it occasions no special horror.

The disciples of Tarrasch were led to believe that all the problems of chess were soluble by adherence to his orthodoxy. Yet chess is a rich game—far too rich to be reduced to any set of sterile maxims. The concrete situation on the board produces endless exceptions, and the imagination transcends the limitations of such formulas, useful though they may be as guidelines for the game.

That he was a great teacher is without doubt. Before his death in 1934, Tarrasch taught more people than ever before how to play chess—but only *his* way to play chess. He promulgated a one-sided science that restricted artistry. He is still instructive today if one approaches him with a healthy skepticism, knowing that there is more to chess than he allowed. In chess, practice is forever outstripping theory, and checkmate awaits those whose minds are not open to innovation.

TARRASCH V. MARCO
Vienna, 1898
Petrov Defense

	WHITE	BLACK		WHITE	BLACK
1	P-K4	P-K4	4	N-KB3	NxP
2	N-KB3	N-KB3	5	P-Q4	B-K2
3	NxP	P-Q3	6	B-Q3	N-KB3

Black could contest more space via . . . P-Q4. He accepts the cramped KB that Tarrasch so despised.

7	0-0	0-0?!	8	P-KR3!	. . .

Tarrasch begins his famous constricting strategy, depriving Black's QB of the N5 square, where it should have gone on move 7.

8	. . .	B-K3!?	13	N-B3!	Q-B1
9	P-B4	P-B3	14	Q-B2	R-N1
10	N-N5	N-R3	15	P-KB5	B-Q2
11	N-QB3	N-B2	16	B-B4	P-QN4
12	P-B4	P-KR3	17	P-QN3	P-B4?!

Offering a pawn for some freedom, but Tarrasch ignores it and seizes more terrain. Black's next move limits his counterplay.

18	P-Q5	P-N5?!	21	P-KR4!	Q-Q1
19	N-K2	P-QR4	22	B-N3	P-R5
20	P-N4	N-R2	23	K-R1	R-R1
			24	QR-K1	N-K1?

Black's pieces seemingly find the worst squares, but there are no good ones. More hope lay in 24 . . . R-K1.

25	N-B4	B-KB3

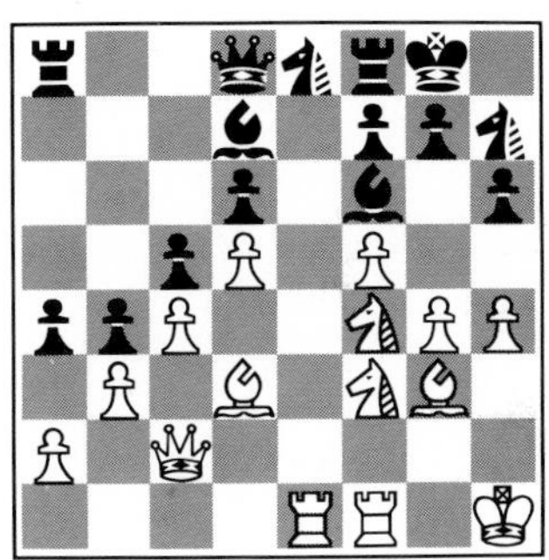

26	N-K6	. . .

Combinations are inevitable in such a dominating position. If 26 . . . PxN; 27 BPxP, there is no answer to the threat of 28 BxN ch. So White first gains the Exchange, then makes the final breakthrough.

26	. . .	PxP	30	PxP	NxP
27	PxP	Q-N3	31	Q-KR2	K-N1
28	NxR	KxN	32	NxN	BxN
29	P-N5!	PxP	33	P-B6	P-N3
			34	BxNP	Resigns

If 34 . . . NxP, then 35 RxN, BxR 36 Q-R7 ch and mate next. The game is a model example of how to exploit an advantage in space.

7.

Chess Enters the Twentieth Century

"Chess is a fight." —Dr. Emanuel Lasker

Dr. Emanuel Lasker, mathematician, philosopher, author, and world chess champion for twenty-seven years, was by all accounts the most equable and gentlemanly grandmaster of all time. His record of success in tournament play extends further than that of any other great player, over a period of forty years.

In 1924, three years after losing the world title to Capablanca, he won the New York International Chess Tournament, finishing ahead of Capablanca and Alekhine. Eleven years later, at the age of sixty-six, he finished half a point behind Botvinnik and Flohr at Moscow, but ahead of Capablanca and a strong contingent of international and Soviet masters, playing nineteen games without a single loss. In a historical study compiled by the Rating Committee of the United States Chess Federation, Lasker had the best twenty-five-year average with 2,690 points, five ahead of Capablanca and thirty ahead of Alekhine. Such figures, however, over so long a time can be misleading. Over the five-year span, Lasker tied with Capablanca and Botvinnik with an average of 2,720, as compared to 2,680 for Alekhine. Again, oddsmakers beware!

Statistics, of course, can never tell the whole story. Yet the incontrovertible facts remain that Emanuel Lasker's exploits are legendary and his position in chess history is unique.

Lasker represents the solid bridge between Steinitz and the modern chess world. Tarrasch may be the great pedagogue, but it was Lasker who, by his example, by his actual play, by his unstinted praise of Steinitz, insured that the theories of that great innovator would endure and receive a full measure of credit.

Emanuel Lasker was a mathematician by training. His companion Edward Lasker—no relation to him—points out that he gave up mathematics for chess because, as a Jew, his chances of obtaining a professorship in a German university were practically nil. Later, fleeing the Nazi holocaust, he had to leave all his possessions in Germany. Neither experience made him bitter. As he explained to Edward Lasker, with a smile, there was another reason for his leaving mathematics: "In mathematics, if I find a new approach to a problem, another mathematician might claim that he has a better, more elegant solution. In chess, if anybody claims he is better than I, I can checkmate him."

Lasker's conception of chess, the source of its attraction for him, was "the fight." Not a fight in the coarser and more brutal context, but a fight of the intellect and the imagination, a fight which combined artistry with scientific principles. Strongly linked with his philosophy of battle was his belief that truth and justice must prevail.

"On the chessboard," he wrote, "lies and hypocrisy do not survive long. The creative combination lays bare the presumption of a lie; the merciless fact, culminating in checkmate, contradicts the hypocrite." Lasker never tried for swindles in chess. If his opponent reached the ending in a level position, he was perfectly content to accept a draw. On the other hand, if there still were opportunities for complications, the fight was not over and ultimate justice had yet to prevail.

It is small wonder that Lasker's popularity was preeminent among chess-players, masters and duffers alike. That keen critic Tarrasch remarked, "Lasker may occasionally lose a game, but never his head." His was a balanced personality. He was interested in the world around him, in people, in philosophy, in mathematics, as well as chess. He was adored by his wife and older brother. In casual conversation Lasker rarely spoke about chess. There were too many other things to engage his attention. As for his views on chess, he let his games and his writing speak for him.

Apart from his works on chess, Lasker wrote three

Opening pages: A 20th-century Swedish set made from ball and roller bearings. One side is gilded, the other silvered. Other oddly attractive sets have been made from nuts and bolts. Chess is always a mirror of the age.

books of philosophy—*Struggle, Understanding of the World,* and *The Philosophy of the Unattainable*—as well as books on contract bridge and other games. He wrote a book on algebra which many mathematicians considered one of the best on the subject. Balance and good humor characterized his attitude, as for example: "Vanity should never tempt a player to engage in combat at the risk of loss of health. It is bad enough to lose without the additional annoyance of paying doctors' bills."

Dr. Lasker's extrachessic activities bear upon his general philosophy which, in turn, typifies his approach to chess. And here arises a curious paradox. It is generally conceded that Lasker, despite his prolific writing and annotations, created no new strategy in chess, no fresh concept dealing with the elements of the game. What then was his contribution?

Before answering, some of the canards circulated about this legendary figure should be put to rest. Fischer, indeed, once called him a "coffeehouse player" and omitted his name from a list of the ten best players of all time. Curiously, this omission may have had something to do with the fact that Lasker's fighting style was so like Fischer's own. They share that same "killer instinct." Like repels like. In fairness, it must be added that Fischer later admitted his befuddlement at how Lasker managed to extricate himself from recurrently inferior positions.

Lasker's style was predicated upon his own philosophy of battle—battle against a human, individual opponent with personal flaws and weaknesses. Knowing for example, Frank Marshall's penchant for brilliant combinations and open lines, Lasker would deliberately play a cramped, stodgy defense and wait for the United States champion to break up as he tried to break it down. But when Marshall began to suspect this plan in a future game and prepared for it, Lasker deliberately turned the tables by out-combining the feared master of combination play. Can one detect in these tactics of Lasker's some resemblance to those employed by Bobby Fischer?

Lasker has left a legacy of games that should be studied by every aspiring chess-player, not for sharp innovative ideas in the opening, but for practical instruction in the art of infighting. With very few exceptions, the average player is incapable of remembering the staggering amount of analysis in the openings now provided by publications like *Chess Informant*. Lacking this kind of memory, it would be more profitable to grasp the general principles behind each opening and—should one fall victim to some slight error—to understand how to salvage the position in practical, over-the-board play. Typically, Dr. Lasker's games in the book of the 1924 New York International Chess Tournament are models of fearless, fighting chess.

The same year he won the New York tournament, Lasker gave a simultaneous exhibition against some fifty opponents at the old Stuyvesant Chess Club in New York City. And half a century ago, one of the authors of this volume was privileged to be among those opponents and the only one, if memory serves, lucky enough to win against the grandest grandmaster of them all. The closing end-game position follows:

It can be seen that Black's two queen-side pawns contain White's three queen-side pawns. The only conceivable way for White to attempt to break the impasse is by P-N3, but then Black responds with . . . P-QN5!, forcing a pawn through to Queen on the Rook file. This

Brilliant assemblage for 1914 St. Petersburg tournament. Front row, from left: Blackburne (2), Em. Lasker (3), Tarrasch (4), Akiba Rubinstein (7), Capablanca (9). Back row, from left: Marshall (2), Alekhine (3), Nimzovich (4). Marshall sent picture to his wife with scribbled plans to play exhibitions, visit Paris and Berlin.

being the case, Black can win by successfully exchanging his KNP for White's KBP, forcing the white King back into a pseudostalemate and compelling the white pawns on the queen-side to commit suicide by advancing and permitting Black to queen. White's first strategy, then, must be to thwart the exchange of pawns, hence:

	WHITE	BLACK		WHITE	BLACK
1	K-R3	K-B3!	2	K-R2!	K-K3
			3	K-N2	K-K4

Now the purpose of Black's triangulation becomes clear. White is on the horns of a dilemma. If he plays 4 K-R2, Black plays . . . K-Q5 and penetrates via K6. If White plays 4 K-B2, Black answers with . . . K-B4 and forces the exchange of pawns at KN5. Therefore:

4	P-B3	. . .

Giving up his last remaining tempo. 4 P-QN4, permitting the immediate entry of the black King, is equally hopeless.

4	. . .	K-B4	6	PxP ch	K-N4
5	K-R3	P-N5 ch!	7	Resigns	

White must relinquish his king-side pawn and the game.

Having gone through the tiring ordeal of engaging fifty opponents, Lasker could certainly have been forgiven some slight sign of pique at having his perfect record spoiled. Instead, he leaned across the table, ruffled the hair of his thirteen-year-old opponent (inadvertently, it must be added, blowing cigar smoke into his face), and said with his warm and gentle smile, "It is a pleasure to lose such a beautiful end game. Congratulations, young man!"

Small wonder that the thirteen-year-old was inspired to spend a lifetime in Caïssa's service, or that he acquired a lifelong passion for cigars.

Lasker's lasting chess contribution, then, was a practical one. His collection of games can serve as a manual for the practical tournament player and show the many ways in which chess games—favorable and unfavorable—can be won against different kinds of players. In these games, Lasker embodied his personal philosophy of "struggle." To him, chess was no mere abstract compendium of opening lines and book knowledge. Chess was head-to-head combat between two individuals. Not merely the game itself, but the style and psychology of the opponent had to be gauged.

Considering Lasker's phenomenal record in tournament and match play, it is surprising that more attention has not been paid to the philosophy behind his success. Instead, modern players seem to rely mainly upon memorizing opening variations and abstract principles of Hypermodern theory, which often leads to the same kind of dogmatism the principles originally meant to counteract.

One of the striking examples of Lasker's applied psychology occurred in the 1914 St. Petersburg Tournament against the usually unflappable Capablanca. Lasker had come from behind with a tremendous finish. Playing two games each against such giants as Capablanca, Alekhine, Tarrasch, and Marshall, he scored 7 out of a possible 8 points—an achievement roughly comparable to Fischer's winning 7½ points out of 9 grandmaster games in a row in the latter half of the 1966 Piatigorsky Cup Tournament in Santa Monica.

Lasker reached the crucial game with Capablanca half a point behind his formidable opponent. All Capa needed to maintain his lead in first place was a draw. The chess world was agog. What bold new plan would the fighting Lasker come up with? Lasker had the white pieces, hence, presumably, the choice of openings. Would it be a gambit or, perhaps, a striking, hitherto unexplored variation of a more conservative opening?

Lasker confounded the experts and, no doubt, surprised Capablanca by choosing the Exchange Variation of the Ruy Lopez, a thoroughly analyzed line which, in the opinion of most of the cognoscenti, would lead to a draw. What was happening? Could the old fighter have lost his nerve and decided to settle for second place? Those who knew Lasker would have laughed at the suggestion.

Undoubtedly, Capa was perturbed. What prepared variation had the old fox conjured up? Or was he trying to lull him into a false sense of security? *En garde!*

The game which follows is a monument of its kind. Here are no striking brilliancies, but a technique aimed at grinding out an infinitesimal advantage and converting it into a full point. This seemed to be the only way to win against a redoubtable adversary like Capablanca, who would be quick to seize any possible opportunity to force a draw. All those who aspire to win at chess should study and restudy this beautiful game.

EM. LASKER V. CAPABLANCA

St. Petersburg, 1914

Ruy Lopez

	WHITE	BLACK		WHITE	BLACK
1	P-K4	P-K4	3	B-N5	P-QR3
2	N-KB3	N-QB3	4	BxN!	. . .

And here it is, the "drawish" Exchange Variation. The exclamation point is appended only because of the circumstances under which Lasker chose this line.

4	. . .	QPxB	5	P-Q4	PxP
			6	QxP!	. . .

What! Permitting the exchange of Queens? The old boy must really be playing for a draw. Again, the exclamation point after this perfectly normal move is occasioned by the fact that this was a game Lasker *had* to win!

6 ... QxQ
7 NxQ B-Q3
8 N-QB3 N-K2
9 0-0! ...

So begins the "psychological" attack. Developing the Bishop, then castling queen-side is more logical, but Lasker wants to give his opponent something to think about. What is Capa to do? Best would be to develop his QB and castle long. Instead, he fears a prepared line and imitates Lasker's move. Score psychological Point One for the old general.

9 ... 0-0
10 P-B4 R-K
11 N-N3 P-B3?

Better was 11 . . . B-K3

12 P-B5! ...

Constricting the enemy pieces, but does it not, according to modern theory, leave a backward pawn at K4? How Lasker turns this minus into a plus will become evident.

12 ... P-QN3
13 B-B4 B-N2
14 BxB ...

Again in apparent defiance of theory. Doubled pawns are held to be a disadvantage, yet here Lasker deliberately undoubles Black's pawns. Why? Because the doubled pawn cannot be attacked, but now Lasker has made a target of the black pawn at Q3. Together with Black's hole at his K3, the winning pattern begins to emerge.

14 ... PxB
15 N-Q4 QR-Q1
16 N-K6 R-Q2
17 QR-Q1 N-B1
18 R-B2 P-QN4
19 R/2-Q2 R/2-K2
20 P-QN4 K-B2
21 P-QR3 B-R1

White's advantage in space is clear. But how can he break through? Capa has been known to set up impeccable defenses before. Lasker calmly builds his position; he is in no hurry.

22 K-B2 R-R2
23 P-N4 P-R3
24 R-Q3 P-QR4
25 P-KR4 PxP
26 PxP R/2-K2
27 K-B3 R-N
28 K-B4 P-N3

Otherwise, P-N5 would be too strong to withstand.

29 R-N3 P-N4 ch
30 K-B3! ...

On 30 PxP, RPxP ch 31 K-B3, R-R1 Black gets some counterplay.

30 ... N-N3
31 PxP ...

If 31 RxP?, then 31. . .N-B5, followed by . . .N-K4 ch gives Black a good game.

31 ... RPxP
32 R-R3 R-Q2
33 K-N3 K-K1
34 R/1-KR1 B-N2

If 34. . .N-B5, then 35 R-R8 wins the black Bishop.

35 P-K5!! ...

And now White finally rids himself of the backward pawn with stunning effect. Black is forced to accept the sacrifice. White has simply cleared the square at K4 for his QN whose entry into the fray quickly decides the issue.

35 ... QPxP
36 N-K4 N-Q4
37 N/6-B5 B-B1

If the Rook moves, then 38 NxB, RxN 39 N-Q6 ch wins the Rook.

38 NxR BxN
39 R-R7 R-B1
40 R-R1 ...

Starting a magnificent square sweep of the board, a fitting way to end the game.

40 ... K-Q1
41 R-R8 ch B-B1
42 N-B5 Resigns

Em. Lasker at table (l) faces H. N. Pillsbury under benign gaze of large Steinitz portrait on wall. Defeated by Lasker in 1896, Pillsbury waited eight years to spring new move on him in very same opening. His patience and secrecy were rewarded with a fine win.

Black cannot prevent the winning check of the white Knight at K6 or N7.

Let those who still harbor the delusion that Lasker's outstanding record of successes was largely a matter of luck or of "blowing cigar smoke at his opponent" closely peruse the above game. The winning conception, from start to finish, bespeaks pure genius. Its originality reflects not merely a philosophy of chess but a philosophy of life. Man utilizes the means at his disposal; there is no such thing as meager resources, asserts Lasker, and he permits the exchange of Queens to prove it.

In describing the event later on, Lasker told what it was like to play before a Russian audience. "The spectators had followed the final moves breathlessly. That Black's position was in ruins was obvious to the veriest tyro. And now Capablanca turned over his King. From the several hundred spectators, there came such an applause as I have never experienced in all my life as a chess player. It was like the wholly spontaneous applause which thunders forth in the theatre, of which the individual is almost unconscious."

Never was an ovation more richly deserved. Lasker had eschewed fancy prepared book variations and beaten his redoubtable opponent in direct over-the-board play. He had utilized his own psychology of battle to demonstrate that there was more than one way to skin a cat—or a Capablanca.

Capablanca was the world champion who brought the Classical Era to its peak. He streamlined all the accumulated technique but did not live up to his own prophetic words: "Let us depart from science. Chess can never reach its height by following in the path of science. . . . Let us, therefore, make a new effort and with the help of our imagination turn the struggle of technique into a battle of ideas."

José Raoul Capablanca y Graupera was born in Havana in 1888. The story of his first chess game is almost as awesome as that of Mozart's first symphony at age four. Capablanca was not even that old when he watched his father play a game and accused him of illegally moving a Knight from one white square to another. His father chided him. Such impertinence from a little boy who had never played a single game! José retorted that not only could he play chess, but he could also beat daddy—which he proceeded to do on the spot. (The story has been vouched for, but, after all, how skilled is an adult player who doesn't know how to move a Knight?)

For five years adult prudence kept the child away from the Havana Chess Club, which had played host to world figures. But within weeks after his admission, little José was considered a first-class player. At age twelve he was matched with Juan Corzo, the national champion. After two initial losses, the youngster pulled himself together and won, 7 points to 5.

Sent to New York for the purpose of entering Columbia University, the young Cuban frequented the Manhattan Chess Club, home of North America's best players in this century. He scored well in local events. But the chess world was in for a major surprise in 1909, when Capablanca played a match with Frank Marshall, United States champion and winner of important prizes in Europe. Losing only one game, Capablanca crushed the astonished Marshall, 15 to 8.

On the basis of that sensational result, Capablanca was invited in 1911 to compete in San Sebastian, Spain. In depth the tournament was considered the strongest aggregation of players ever assembled, lacking only World Champion Lasker. In a concession to Capa, the organizers waived the admission requirement that called for two third prizes or better in major events. The loudest objector was a Russian, Ossip Bernstein. But Bernstein did not reckon with Hispanic pride. In the very first round he was the victim of the most brilliant game Capablanca would ever play. At the end of the tournament, the newcomer, losing only one game of fourteen, took first prize. The chess world had a new superstar.

Capa's partisans have countered the critics of his dry play by citing the number of brilliancy prizes he won during his career. It should be pointed out that he disliked risks and never made speculative sacrifices. His brilliancies were not a way of imposing his will upon the chessboard, but they were always carefully calculated punishments for poor play by the opposition.

Capablanca, having become the most famous of all living Cubans, soon commenced a career in his country's diplomatic service. His chief patriotic function was to win chess games.

Into the late stages of the great St. Petersburg Tournament of 1914, Capablanca held the lead. But, in one of the outstanding comebacks of all time, Lasker overtook him and nosed him out of first place (see above game). A world title match between the two became logical.

Lasker didn't want to play a grueling match with the man he called the "one genius" he had ever seen, and in 1920 he even tried to resign his title. But a record purse of twenty thousand dollars provided in Cuba proved irresistible. (The amount would not be exceeded until 1972.) In 1921 Havana hosted the encounter between its native hero, aged thirty-three, and the champion who had worn the crown for a record twenty-seven years. Lasker was twenty years older and playing in an unfamiliar environment.

After four initial draws, the fifth game developed into an exciting struggle, with Capablanca pressing his initiative. On the forty-fifth move, just when Lasker had a draw almost in hand, he made one of his rare blunders and lost a piece. Four more draws ensued, and then the challenger, refusing to fall into any traps, won two in a row. In the fourteenth game, the champion sustained his fourth loss without a single win. Although ten games remained, he was realistic enough to see that further efforts to breach Capablanca's flawless play would be futile. Lasker therefore resigned the match, and Capablanca became the third chess champion of the world. Never known for his humility, Capa later observed that at no time during the match had he had an inferior position. (The claim would be refuted by Breyer in a published analysis.)

During his reign, a strange myth began to captivate the chess world: the myth of Capablanca as an invincible "chess machine." It fed upon such facts as his losing only one game in an eight-year period (to Reti at New York, 1924). What sort of man was Capablanca, and why was he a fitting subject for a myth?

Capa was a versatile and charming man of the world, a bon vivant, a ladies' man. He was the most detached and effortless chess champion and likely the most talented player ever. He was also, even among chess superstars with their coteries of worshippers, an egoist. Often disdainful of other players, he rarely condescended after a game to explain the sequence of his ideas.

Capablanca's attitude toward chess was paradoxical. Since earliest childhood he had played the game that was virtually a native language to him. He was a professional who made profitable exhibition tours, wrote popular books *(My Chess Career, Chess Fundamentals, A Primer of Chess),* played in tournaments, and ascended to the world throne. Yet he never studied chess, never bothered to learn book openings, hardly ever analyzed. Capablanca to all outward appearances didn't really care about chess!

Later in his career, his play became ever more technical and drawish. He expressed the idea that with the perfection of modern knowledge it would soon be impossible to win a game against a master. Chess would soon reach a "draw death"! He even proposed interchanging the initial positions of the Bishops and Knights to inject new life into the game.

Capa v. Papa: At four and a half, in 1892; at twenty-one, in 1909. Capablanca now has Papa's chair, but chess set and table are the same. Capa had just returned to Cuba from New York, where he catapulted into fame by crushing U.S. Champion Marshall, 15-8.

In retrospect it is easy to see the absurdity of this notion, which vital new schools of thought would soon disprove. Capablanca's despairing idea must have been a rationalization for his own deficiency. He understood chess better than anyone ever had, but he lacked passion for the game and failed to give Caïssa his all. His chess reached rather early a creative plateau and became routine. His earlier quote shows that he correctly diagnosed the problem. But he never summoned the energy to carry out the cure.

New York in the twenties was the scene of two great tournaments. In 1924 Capablanca was second to Lasker, but in 1927 he outclassed the whole field, finishing 2½ points ahead of Alekhine. In that overwhelming victory lay the seed of Capablanca's downfall. It was all he needed to confirm his feelings of omnipotence before the endurance contest with Alekhine later that year.

That title match is decribed in detail later on. But the Cuban's personality—and his genius—are revealed in a little-known anecdote. One game was adjourned in a situation advantageous to the challenger, who had four pawns against a Knight. Alekhine analyzed the position all night with his second, while Capablanca went to a cabaret with a woman companion, returning in the wee hours of the morning. Capa awoke the next afternoon an hour before the scheduled resumption of play and consulted his experts about the position. They said, "It looks bad. Those four pawns are dangerous." Capa replied, "Really? I expect a draw. I'll eat them all up!" As his clock was started, he obtained permission from the arbiter to analyze the position in another room. After a quarter-hour he returned and drew the game.

But it was too late to save the match. In the end Capa's complacency succumbed to Alekhine's passionate will. For the rest of his life, Capablanca, whose lifetime record against Alekhine was a slight plus, never got a chance for revenge.

The dethroned Capablanca continued to garner high prizes, such as a first at Moscow in 1936. But he chafed in frustration that he, born to bask in the adulation of millions, was denied the right to a rematch. His relations with Alekhine, his former friend, degenerated into a public feud. A chess devotee joined one or the other camp, depending upon taste in style, ethnic chauvinism, or which of the two rival titans deigned to say a pleasant word to him one day.

In later years Capablanca developed circulatory troubles. A fatal heart attack came at the Manhattan Chess Club in 1942. He thus followed by only a year the departure of his old rival Lasker into the ranks of mythical heroes. But the Classical Era of which he was the highest personification had ended long before.

Capablanca came upon the scene in the heydey of the Classical school, which chose moves on the basis of general principles, without seeking a total grasp of the needs and potentialities of the position. Capablanca, from whose fingers correct moves flowed as if by instinct, grasped in each position precisely which move would best strengthen his chances. With him it was not a question, as with Alekhine, of complex winning schemes. He perfected the technique of progessively improving his position, leading inexorably to a favorable outcome.

He eschewed dogma. He evolved no system, founded no school, has not one opening variation named after him. Rather, he took classical position play and streamlined it into a model of economy, simplicity, and logic.

Capablanca made a revealing comment about one of his games at his international debut. Against Janowsky, he knew at one point that the move best corresponding to the future needs of the position was P-KN3, followed by the fianchetto of his King's Bishop. But as he had already played P-K3 and could thus develop the Bishop immediately, without a further pawn move, he did so—fearing

Top: Capa in 1914. He was nosed out by Lasker at St. Petersburg that year but had already achieved eminence as a superstar with 1911 victory at San Sebastian. Bottom: One of many simultaneous exhibitions he played.

that the dogmatists, led by Tarrasch, would censure him for losing one tempo! They were still fixated on an abstract principle that dated back to Morphy, while he, who never studied chess books, knew the best move intuitively.

Capablanca never shifted wood, waiting for his opponent to make a mistake. He didn't try to trick or to overwhelm the opponent but went economically, without wasted motion, to the solution. Woe to him who made the smallest weakness in his position. Capablanca would encircle it and often convert it into a full point by perfect end-game technique.

His games have a peerless simplicity, the serene, coordinated action of harmonious forces. He has penetrated the tactical complexities but they are relegated to the notes. Once some colleagues asked why he had not played a brilliant five-move combination that appeared decisive. He blandly answered that he had seen the possibility, but that three moves later, the opponent could have sacrificed his Queen, with a somewhat unclear outcome. Instead, he had chosen the simplest road to victory.

Capablanca's games are an indispensable part of the education of every serious student. His influence is paramount in the play of Fischer (who may be the living answer to the question of how Capa would have played if he had had Alekhine's passion for chess). Whoever studies contemporary chess theory and neglects Capablanca is like the music student who plays only Shostakovich and ignores Mozart. For without appreciating classicism in its highest expression, one cannot rightly master what has come later. And Capablanca is the Mozart of chess.

NIMZOVICH V. CAPABLANCA
New York, 1927

Caro-Kann Defense

	WHITE	BLACK		WHITE	BLACK
1	P-K4	P-QB3	2	P-Q4	P-Q4
			3	P-K5!?	. . .

Lets Black easily develop his QB. For the rest of the game White has but one idea—P-KB5. But Capablanca prevents it, and builds on the queen-side.

3	. . .	B-B4	9	0-0	N-K2
4	B-Q3	BxB	10	N-R4	Q-B3
5	QxB	P-K3	11	NxB	QxN
6	N-QB3	Q-N3	12	B-K3	Q-B2
7	KN-K2	P-QB4	13	P-KB4	N-B4
8	PxP	BxP	14	P-B3!?	. . .

White drifts into passivity. Active was 14 QR-B1, N-B3 15 P-B4.

14	. . .	N-B3	15	QR-Q1	P-KN3
			16	P-KN4?	. . .

This small error is all Capablanca needs. Better was 16 B-B2, P-KR4, but then Black's Knight is easily as good as White's rather hemmed-in Bishop.

16	. . .	NxB	17	QxN	P-KR4!
			18	P-N5	. . .

Virtually ends the chance of P-B5, and weakens the B5 square. But if 18 P-KR3, PxP 19 PxP, Black controls the Rook file.

18	. . .	0-0	21	P-QR3	R-B2
19	N-Q4	Q-N3	22	R-Q3	N-R4
20	R-B2	KR-B1	23	R-K2!	. . .

Hoping to break through with 24 P-B5, KPxP 25 P-K6, but Capa is alert.

23	. . .	R-K1!	24	K-N2	N-B3
			25	R/2-Q2	. . .

Not 25 NxN, QxN, 26 QxP??, P-N3 27 Q-R6, R-R1 winning the Queen.

25	. . .	R/1-QB1	28	Q-R3	K-N2
26	R-K2	N-K2!	29	R-KB2	P-R4
27	R/2-Q2	R-B5	30	R-K2	N-B4!
			31	NxN ch	. . .

Else Black makes headway by taking on Q5. But now Capablanca gets an iron grip on K5 and starts to close in. Black's KRP is immune because of . . . R-KR1-R5.

A Frank Marshall album: Card from Holland, 1906 (top); shipboard picture sent to his beloved Carrie, 1910; pondering one of the famous Marshall brilliancies; and (bottom) at Marshall's Chess Divan, Atlantic City, 1917.

31	. . .	NPxN	37	PxR	Q-B5
32	Q-B3	K-N3	38	K-N2	P-N4
33	R/2-Q2	R-K5!	39	K-N1	P-N5
34	R-Q4	R-B5	40	PxP	PxP
35	Q-B2	Q-N4	41	K-N2	Q-B8
36	K-N3	R/BxR	42	K-N3	. . .

42	. . .	Q-KR8!	44	R-KB3	R-Q8
43	R-Q3	R-K8	45	P-N3	. . .

Also losing is 45 R-N3, Q-K5 46 RxP, R-Q6 ch 47 K-R4, R-KB6. Zugzwang is approaching for White.

45	. . .	R-QB8	46	R-K3	. . .

Or 46 P-R3, R-N8 ch 47 K-R4, R-N5 mate.

46	. . .	R-KB8	47	Resigns

For if 47 Q-KN2, R-KN8, or 47 Q-K2, Q-N8 ch 48 K-R3, R-B7 and wins. A prize-winning example of how to exploit weaknesses.

One can hardly account for when and where a great talent may suddenly appear. A century ago it fell to the small American town of Somerville, Massachusetts, to be the birthplace of a player of world class.

One may imagine that chess was not the great passion of Somerville, for Harry Nelson Pillsbury (1872-1906) learned the game at the relatively late age of sixteen. Two years later, he played three games with Steinitz, who was visiting Boston. The youngster, receiving odds of pawn and move, won two of them. In his all-too-short career he was to have a plus score in a dozen tournament games with the ex-world champion.

Pillsbury mastered Steinitz' positional principles, but his style was utterly different. He was a deep strategist who gradually built up his attacks until the ripe moment for a powerful breakthrough.

Prior to Pillsbury's international debut at Hastings in 1895, his results were modest. The four favorites in that great event were Lasker, Steinitz, Tchigorin, and Tarrasch. The young American was not even considered a dark horse. He lost his first game to Tchigorin. Next he faced Tarrasch and played his patented attacking system in the Queen's Gambit: B-Q3, N-K5, and P-KB4, aiming for mate. The German defended well and got two dangerous passed pawns on the queen-side. Pillsbury's attack on the King, taking fifty moves to reach its climax, at last carried the day. Reti compared the game to the melodrama of an American film.

Pillsbury went on to win the Hastings tournament. It was a sensation. As Morphy did before him and as Capablanca was to do later, the newcomer from America had stunned the chess world in his very first joust with Europe's best.

In multiple encounters with the ten most formidable players of his time, Pillsbury had a minus score only against his countryman, Marshall. He fought such giants as Lasker, Tarrasch, and Tchigorin to standoffs, and piled up a big plus against such a solid player as Schlechter. In two match victories over Jackson Showalter in 1897-98, he joined the line of U.S. champions. Pity that a match for the world championship was never arranged!

Pillsbury was never able to equal his stupendous feat at Hastings, but always finished in the top four until his last tournament at Cambridge Springs, England, in 1904, when he dropped to a tie for eighth place. Still, as a "veteran" of thirty-one, he was able to play one of his finest games against Lasker with a prepared variation in

Dear Friend!
How do you do?

July 4th on Board Dear
1910
we expect to arrive to-
morrow. How do you like
this picture it was taken
on the boat. I am going
to Wildungen as soon
as I can I have not

Marshall's Chess & Checker Divan
Million Dollars Pier
Atlantic City, N.J.

his beloved Queen's Gambit, which he had been saving for eight years! His last serious game was in a club match in 1905 against Hermann Helms, whose indefatigable journalistic efforts in the next six decades were to earn him the title of "Dean of American Chess."

As a blindfold exhibitor, Pillsbury set a world record of twenty-two games simultaneously at Moscow in 1902. The favorite Pillsbury stunt was to play several games of chess and checkers blindfold while conducting a hand of whist and, for the finale, to recite backwards a memorized list of thirty long unrelated words, previously supplied by a spectator.

Truly, his was an exceptional mind. The printed sources are unanimous in ascribing a fatal nervous strain to such repeated blindfold play. But the precise cause of the grand Yankee's tragically premature death at age thirty-three, no writer of that prudish time was bold enough to state. It was general paresis. He renewed the tragic tradition in U.S. chess which would take many years to reverse.

In Pillsbury's centennial year a series of commemorative articles appeared in the chess periodicals of the Soviet Union. American chess-lovers, euphoric over the crowning of their first world champion, neglected to petition the postal service for a Pillsbury stamp. In the country where founding father Benjamin Franklin was the first writer on chess, the idea no longer seems outlandish.

Now, let's have a look at one of Pillsbury's imperishable games:

"Portuguese" playing set of red and white ivory made in Macao in 19th century. Chinese crafted sets of this type for the British market, thus its resemblance to British sets—though ornamentation here is extensive.

PILLSBURY V. EM. LASKER
Nuremberg, 1896
French Defense

	WHITE	BLACK		WHITE	BLACK
1	P-K4	P-K3	5	P-B4	P-QB4
2	P-Q4	P-Q4	6	PxP	N-QB3
3	N-QB3	N-KB3	7	P-QR3	NxBP?!
4	P-K5	KN-Q2	8	P-QN4	N-Q2

Lasker later gave 8 . . . P-Q5 9 QN-K2, P-Q6 10 N-N3 Q-Q5, but 11 P-B3! wins a pawn. Now Pillsbury starts the blockade of Black's game.

9	B-Q3	P-QR4!?	12	B-K3	N/1-Q2
10	P-N5	N/3-N1	13	0-0	P-KN3
11	N-B3	N-B4	14	N-K2	B-K2?!

Better 14 . . . B-N2, defying White to enforce P-B5.

15	Q-K1!	N-N3	17	Q-B2	N/3-R5?
16	N/3-Q4	B-Q2	18	R-N1	P-R4?!

Deters P-N4. Lasker misplaces his defensive trust in a rigid pawn-chain.

19 P-N6! . . .

Further constriction. If 19 . . . NxP, then 20 NxP. Pillsbury sacs two pawns and relentlessly pushes on to destroy the enemy position, as Reti said, "root and branch."

19	. . .	NxB	20	PxN	BxP
			21	P-B5!	. . .

Pillsbury's main theme—the *breakthrough.*

21	. . .	NPxP	22	N-B4	P-R5
			23	R-R1	B-K2

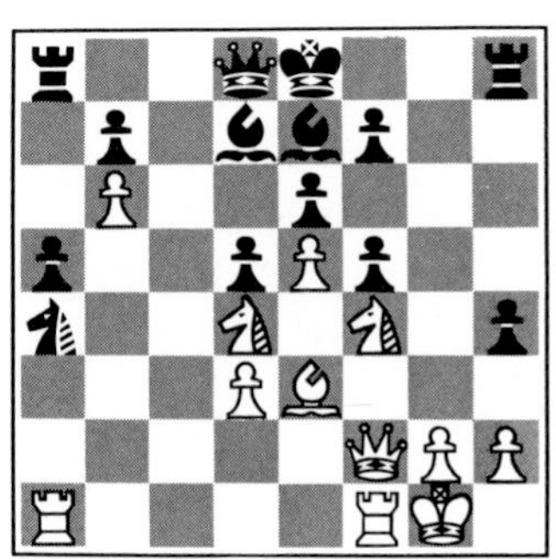

24 RxN!! . . .

The key to the deeply calculated denouement. White sacrifices a full Rook.

24	. . .	BxR	25	N/Q4xKP	PxN
			26	NxKP	B-Q2

Black here holds out longer by immediately giving up the Queen. The depth of Pillsbury's combination is seen in 26 . . . Q-B1 27 QxBP, Q-B3 28 B-N5!, QxP ch 29 P-Q4, Q-N5 30 Q-B7 ch, K-Q2 31 BxB, QxB 32 N-B5 ch, K-Q1 33 NxP ch, K-Q2 34 P-K6 ch, winning the Queen.

27 NxQ

And White won by way of his material advantage, in twenty-three more moves. A magnificent demonstration of Pillsbury's attacking gift.

One of the most artificial aspects of chess, bearing little relation to real warfare, is the draw. While playing, one does not always look for the best move or the best plan. Why not? Because, essentially, there are two programs possible, two logical propositions going on simultaneously in the mind: to play to win, or to play to draw. (It is reasonable to assume that no one consciously plays to lose.)

There are some jaded professionals who seem to ignore the first proposition altogether. When their opponents suggest, "Draw," they just can't say no. They shake hands and go off to sunbathe on the beach. The ranks of the pacific-minded have included no less a figure than World Champion Petrosian.

It is true that playing to win often entails the corollary risk of losing. And some players fear losing so much, or else are so devoid of "killer instinct," that most of their games involve no clash at all. The point is soon split, and they repair to the back room for blitz chess, where prestige and money are not at stake. They are intent not on proving their superiority to their opponents, but on disproving their inferiority.

The prototype of today's drawing masters was

Marshall (l) playing David Janowski in early 1920s. In wing collar, next to Marshall, is journalist Herman Helms, then dean of American chess. Next to Janowski is H. M. Phillips, former president of Manhattan Chess Club.

the Viennese star, Karl Schlechter (1874-1918). He was rightly labeled "the King of Draws." He had mastered Steinitz' principles, but he carried "the balance of position" too far. In a match against Marco in 1893, he achieved a dubious record: ten draws in ten games. In ten matches played with top players of his time, he managed to play eight of them to a tie. His tendency reached a ridiculous extreme at Baden in 1914, where he drew fourteen of his eighteen games—and this in a tournament restricted to gambit openings!

In his match against World Champion Lasker in 1910, Schlechter achieved the level of a tragic anti-hero. After four draws, the champion gained the advantage in the fifth game, only to lose at the end through an uncharacteristic error. Four more draws ensued, and they sat down to play the tenth and last game. Lasker had put through the stipulation that the challenger would need to win by 2 points in order to usurp his crown. So instead of steering the game into his customary peaceful channels, Schlechter willfully, and for the first time, engaged the world's greatest tactician in a tense and complicated seesaw battle that ranged all over the board. On move 39, Schlechter disdained a draw by perpetual check. In the end, Lasker, the precipice-walker, emerged victorious. He thus tied the match and saved his world title.

Because of this twist of destiny, Schlechter's name brings hardly a flicker of recognition from today's young players. But artistry takes many forms, and they would do well to look into his classic games. In Reti's rhapsodic description: "... one loses one's self in Schlechter's games, in which are reflected, side by side with the immensity and simplicity of nature, the airiness of Viennese art and music."

With the privations of war, the gentle chess artist was not aggressive enough even to fight for his daily bread. At the age of forty-four, he died of starvation in a Budapest flat, two days after Christmas, 1918.

"Chess Game," oil on canvas by John Singer Sargent. The artist appears to have realized the Dickensian idyll that "love which has a game of chess in it can checkmate any man and solve the problem of life."

Akiba Rubinstein, born in 1882, was a strategist of consummate technique and the heir apparent to the world title before World War I.

Chess did not come easily to him, but after falling under its spell, he was single-minded in his devotion. A characteristic episode when Rubinstein was a Talmudic student in Lodz, Poland, marked his initiation. He frequented the chess café, where he was one of the most enthusiastic but weakest players. One day he disappeared. Returning after several weeks, he immediately challenged the city's champion, Salwe, to a game. Rubinstein won, and there was a new chess master.

Rubinstein refined the Steinitzian science and converted it into a personal religion. He always followed his chessic convictions and believed that therefore he must succeed. He was a mental wrestler with the vexing problems of the chessboard. Ultimately, when the vexations became too great, he was undone.

Rubinstein set an all-time record for consecutive first prizes: five in 1912. He was thus the logical challenger to the throne of Lasker, whom he had defeated and tied for first in the strong tournament at St. Petersburg, 1909. But in those days before FIDE, Rubinstein was no person to organize a title match, and the chess world was thus deprived of a combative feast.

After the war his big successes became less frequent and he was eclipsed by Capablanca. He had suffered some hard times and was the victim of a sadistic prank, according to former world blindfold champion George Koltanowski. Rubinstein lost a small business that went bankrupt during the war and was being sought by creditors. He was leading a tournament when Alekhine and his sidekick Bogolyubov banged on his door one night, pretending to be process-servers. Next day the frightened Rubinstein left town.

Rubinstein made major contributions to chess theory. There are important Rubinstein variations in four different openings: the Four Knights (4...N-Q5), the Queen's Gambit (6 P-KN3), the Nimzoindian (4 P-K3), and the French (3...PxP). He demonstrated the optimal placement of the pieces in closed positions, so as to maximize their effect when the game opens up. And his skill in endings, especially with Rooks, was legendary. His best games have the mark of the highest strategist—a seeming grand plan from the start to finish. But in his absorption in strategic plans he committed an unusual number of tactical oversights.

Rubinstein was criticized for playing only one opening move: 1 P-Q4. Once he came to the chessboard and touched his Queen's pawn only to find it had been nailed down by a prankster. Later he suffered delusions that his enemies sent flies to distract him, and he became frightened of strangers. His career came to an unfortunate end when he disappeared forever from the chess scene in the early 1930s.

Three decades later, in 1961, Rubinstein's obituary notice came as a strange reminder of a glorious bygone era. It might well have said, "Akiba Rubinstein, Chess Artist. Strongest player never to become world champion. Surviving him: a chess world forever indebted."

RUBINSTEIN V. EM. LASKER
St. Petersburg, 1909
Queen's Gambit Declined

	WHITE	BLACK		WHITE	BLACK
1	P-Q4	P-Q4	3	P-B4	P-K3
2	N-KB3	N-KB3	4	N-B3	B-K2
			5	B-N5	P-B4?!

Versus Rubinstein's beloved Queen's Gambit, Lasker allows an isolated QP, which he soon offers in return for a seemingly dangerous attack.

6	BPxP	KPxP	8	B-N5	PxP?!
7	P-K3	N-B3	9	KNxP	B-Q2
			10	QBxN	...

Rubinstein accepts the sacrifice in fidelity to his conviction that an extra pawn should win. He will soon face the threat of mate on N2.

10	. . .	BxB	**12**	PxB	Q-N4
11	NxP	BxN	**13**	BxN	BxB
			14	N-K3	0-0-0!?

A good alternative was 14. . . BxP 15 R-KN1, Q-R4 ch, but White keeps an end-game initiative after 16 Q-Q2.

15	0-0	KR-K1	**16**	R-B1!	RxN
			17	RxB ch	PxR

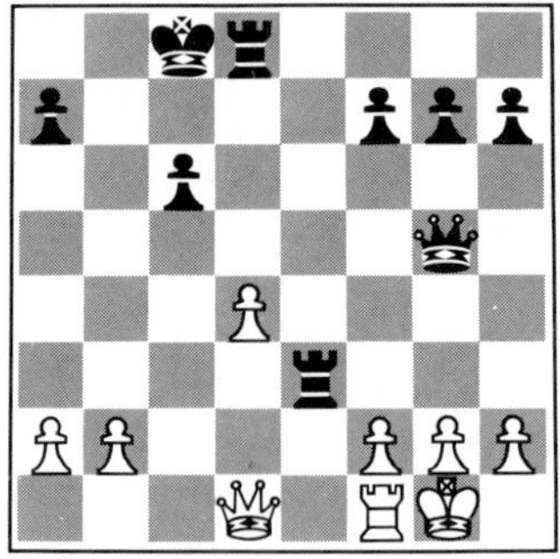

18 Q-B1! . . .

Reti called this move the "miracle" that saves the true believer. The Rook is pinned, and Rubinstein keeps an extra pawn.

18	. . .	RxP	**20**	QxP ch	K-Q1
19	PxR	R-Q2	**21**	R-B4!	P-B4

Not 21. . . R-Q8 ch 22 K-B2, R-Q7 ch 23 K-K1, QxP? 24 R-Q4 ch!, RxR 25 QxQ and wins.

22 Q-B5 Q-K2

Not 22. . . R-Q8 ch? 23 K-B2, R-Q7 ch 24 K-K1, QxP 25 Q-R5 ch and 26 QxR. But now we get a Rook-and-pawn ending, ideal for an example of Rubinstein's famed technique.

23	QxQ ch	KxQ	**28**	R-R6	K-B1
24	RxP	R-Q8 ch	**29**	P-K4	R-QB2
25	K-B2	R-Q7 ch	**30**	P-KR4	K-B2
26	K-B3	RxQNP	**31**	P-N4	K-B1
27	R-QR5	R-N2	**32**	K-B4	K-K2

33 P-R5 P-R3

The hole at N3 will be decisive, but otherwise 33. . . K-B2 34 K-B5, K-K2 35 P-N5, K-B2 36 P-K5, K-K2 37 P-N6, P-R3 38 R-K6 ch, K-Q2 39 R-KB6!! wins.

34	K-B5	K-B2	**37**	R-R6	K-B2
35	P-K5	R-N2	**38**	R-Q6	K-B1
36	R-Q6	K-K2	**39**	R-QB6	K-B2
			40	P-R3!!	Resigns

Zugzwang! The finish might have been 40. . . K-B1 41 K-N6, R-N6 32 R-B8 ch, and White gets two connected passed pawns on the king-side. A fitting refutation of Black's fifth move, in which Rubinstein and justice triumph.

Frank J. Marshall (1877-1944), although he held the United States championship for almost thirty years (1906-1936), would have been the first to tell you this was not his greatest achievement. A genial, popular man who had the look of a Shakespearean actor, smoked strong cigars, and never went a day without playing a game of chess, Marshall was prouder of his pyrotechnical brilliancies over the board than of any title, prize, or mere financial remuneration. It mattered not if it were a match for the world's championship (as in his losing 1907 effort against Emanuel Lasker) or an off-hand game with a comparative duffer, Marshall's main concern lay not so much in winning as it did in creating beautiful combinations. He was, in the truest sense of the word, a real lover of chess.

In this respect he was an incurable romantic, a throwback to the days of Anderssen and Morphy. Moreover, the combinations he enjoyed most were not the aftermath of solidly played games leading to their just reward, but games in which he had much the worst of the position and, by virtue of a spectacular move or sacrificial concept, "swindled" his opponent out of a seemingly sure victory. One of the authors once had the pleasure of being "swindled" by Marshall. So often did "a Marshall swindle" occur that the term became part of the chess lexicon.

Which is to take nothing away from his outstanding record and serious contribution to chess. Apart from holding the U.S. championship an unprecedented number of years, he scored many notable tournament successes: Cambridge Springs, 1904 (ahead of Emanuel Lasker and Schlechter); Scheveningen, 1905; Nuremberg, 1906; and Düsseldorf, 1908. In the strong New York Tournament of 1924, he finished fourth behind Emanuel Lasker, Capablanca, and Alekhine, but ahead of such greats as Reti, Maroczy, Bogolyubov, and Tartakower.

Marshall introduced many sparkling innovations in opening play, notably the Marshall (Counter) Attack in the Ruy Lopez. It runs: 1 P-K4, P-K4 2 N-KB3, N-QB3 3 B-N5, P-QR3 4 B-R4, N-B3 5 0-0, B-K2 6 R-K1, P-QN4 7 B-N3, 0-0 8 P-B3, P-Q4!? This sacrifice of a pawn, so characteristic of Marshall, leads to a lively attacking game in which Black is the aggressor, while White is forced on the defensive. As to its soundness, the jury is still out, but the variation enjoys wide popularity in tournament play. Spassky played it against Fischer in the 1966 Piatigorsky Cup tourney.

Marshall essayed another pawn sacrifice in a different variation of the Ruy Lopez against Emanuel Lasker in the 1924 Tournament. With Marshall playing Black, it went: 1 P-K4, P-K4 2 N-KB3, N-QB3 3 B-N5, P-QR3 4 BxN, QPxB 5 P-Q4, B-KN5!? 6 PxP, QxQ ch 7 KxQ, 0-0-0 ch 8 K-K1, B-QB4 9 P-KR3, B-R4 10 B-B4, P-B4!! Alekhine considered this fine move as leading to a most promising continuation for Black.

Marshall was an indefatigable worker in the cause of chess. He organized the famous Marshall Chess Club in New York City and contributed to the United States successes in the Olympiads of the thirties. He was never too busy to instruct younger players like those who often held their interscholastic team matches at his club. His analysis was a constant source of joy and wonder to the young initiates, who never imagined such moves were possible over a chessboard. When it came to combination play Marshall was second to none.

Frank was fond of good living, took a drop on occasion, and occasionally a drop too much. But his courtesy, ready wit, and conviviality never failed him. With his charming wife Carrie he made the Marshall Chess Club a haven which has never been equalled for warmth and hospitality. To many chess-players it was a home away from home, and possibly something more. Now that Carrie Marshall too has passed on, one can only look back with fond nostalgia to the days when they were King and Queen of their little world on West Tenth Street.

Here is an outstanding Marshall brilliancy, featuring one of the most famous moves ever played, against Levitsky in Breslau, 1912.

Black (Marshall) to play:

1 ... Q-KN6!!!

Into the jaws of death! The black Queen can be taken three ways. Therefore:

2 Resigns

No matter how White takes the proffered Queen, he quickly loses to . . . N-K7 ch, and if he does not take it, he is mated. According to the story, the spectators were so delighted by Marshall's magnificent move, they showered the board with gold pieces!

Juan Gris
3-1917
8.

The Hypermodern Revolution

> "After the first move, 1 P-K4, White's game is in the last throes!" —Gyula Breyer

The Hypermodern Revolution was a chess movement—parallel to the postwar ferment in the other arts—which sought to overturn all the principles of the Classical school. Like their allies in modern art who introduced everything from Cubism to Surrealism, the Hypermoderns were far from being mindless iconoclasts and were able to create new works of lasting value.

Traditional, classical art emphasized form and structure and affirmed the rightness of the existing order. Romanticism permitted the access of feelings but fed upon illusion, like Don Quixote's imagining in a coarse slattern the lineaments of a fair lady. In the same way the Romantic masters took dull, prosaic positions and tried to force into flame the spark of a beautiful combination.

In chess, the chronological order of Romanticism and Classicism was reversed because the uninhibited quest for beauty was an impulse that predated technical understanding of how to build up a strong position. The Hypermoderns neither accepted what was given nor fled, like the Romantics, from harsh reality. Instead, they dared to look upon the chess struggle with fresh eyes.

With the inflammatory statement above, the young Gyula Breyer anticipated the theater of the absurd. It is doubtful that he believed it, any more than the American master Weaver Adams truly believed his own later, symmetrical claim that after 1 P-K4 "White wins by force." But Breyer, a spokesman for the Hypermoderns, meant to shock a chess world that had begun to sanctify the dogmas of the Classical school and transform them into eternal verities. And in time the less extreme ideas of these radicals won lasting acceptance because they were proved in the crucible of practice.

The essence of Hypermodernism lay in distrust of all classical dogma and a revolutionary approach to the center. The importance of the center is easily verified by placing a Knight first in the center and then in a corner of the board and counting the respective numbers of possible moves: eight as opposed to two.

The Classicists counseled White to advance a center pawn on the first move and Black to answer in kind. Thus the defender maintains symmetry and the "balance of position." With correct play he should eventually neutralize the effect of White's first move and equalize the game.

The Hypermoderns dared to challenge these ideas. They eschewed symmetry and went their own way. They answered 1 P-Q4 with 1 . . . N-KB3, thus departing from the seemingly endless series of Queen's Gambits and spawning a whole new family of defenses—the "Indians," a name which seems to have been chosen because it is exotic. In these defenses, Black refrains from an early . . . P-Q4 and instead uses his pieces to prevent White from achieving the goal of P-K4. The enduring popularity of the Indian defenses, whose chief inventor was Nimzovich, testifies to their soundness.

Reti's Opening, now standard, departed further from tradition. With the white pieces he refrained from moving either central pawn and developed both Bishops on the flanks, openly inviting Black to set up a big pawn center, which he regarded as a target for attack.

Alekhine, although he rejected the label of Hypermodern, was even more provocative with his defense, 1 P-K4, N-KB3!? White is invited to set up an apparently formidable pawn center with 2 P-K5, N-Q4 3 P-QB4, N-N3 4 P-Q4, P-Q3 5 P-B4. Classical theory considered the resulting position highly favorable to White. But the Hypermoderns regarded the pawn center as a house of cards, ripe for counterattack. The final word in this argument has yet to be said. Fischer used Alekhine's Defense as a surprise weapon in his 1972 match with Spassky.

Opening pages: "The Chessboard," by Juan Gris, oil on wood, 1917. Although Spanish, Gris lived and worked in Paris most of his life, where he came under the Cubist influence of Picasso and Braque.

Thus the Hypermoderns created whole new contours of position. By no means did they deny the importance of the center. What they did was to put forward a totally new approach to the struggle for the center: control by pieces rather than occupation by pawns.

To all the generalizations of the Classical school, which they regarded as approximations at best, the Hypermoderns raised exceptions. Thus, like old Tchigorin, they reaffirmed the individuality of every position and converted the chessboard to a canvas on which to paint their highly original conceptions. And so they were called Neo-romantics. But Reti pointed out that their "combinations" were positional, not tactical.

The effect of Hypermodernism was a great infusion of fresh ideas into the game that Capablanca had thought was approaching a dead end because of the perfection of technique. "No draw death!" they declared to the world of chess. New continents of thought awaited exploration. Thus they restored creative excitement to the battle of chess ideas.

The Hypermoderns were christened by Saveilly Tartakower (1887-1954), the Russian-born, Viennese-schooled, Polish-French grandmaster, author, poet, gambling addict, and wit. His book, *The Hypermodern Chess Game,* appeared in the early twenties. Tartakower's own style of play was not very typical of the school. He simply loved original moves of any and all sorts. Once, after a visit to a zoo in New York, he introduced into tournament play the opening, 1 P-QN4. He called it the "Orang-Utan"! (As with many opening lines, current Soviet terminology claims the move for its Russian popularizer, Sokolsky.)

He became famous for witty "Tartakowerisms," such as, "It is better to sacrifice your opponent's pieces." After writing a number of books and winning an abundance of prizes in events all over the map, Tartakower joined the Free French Forces during World War II under the name of "Lieutenant Cartier."

Tartakower's dialectical turn of mind is conveyed by his description of his friend Reti, whom he defeated in no less than three matches: "Reti studies mathematics, although he is not a dry mathematician; represents Vienna without being Viennese; was born in old Hungary yet does not know Hungarian; speaks uncommonly rapidly only in order to act all the more maturely and deliberately; and yet will become the best chess player without, however, becoming world champion."

The tragically short-lived Breyer, a Hungarian born in 1894, was one of the most intriguing figures in the history of chess. During his career he carried out deep investigations of existing theory and then, in his games, departed radically from the established norms. Tartakower had Breyer in mind when he described the "state of secession" of the Hypermoderns: ". . . plans which had never disclosed themselves to us before: schemes which gave to the game an unhealthy stamp; moves which scoffed at any endeavor to obtain freer development of the pieces . . . malignant and endless storing up of latent energy. . . .'Not to build up but rather to obstruct a position' is the watchword there given out. The idols of the old school are smashed."

Breyer kept his pieces behind closed lines, avoided the early clash of forces which could lead to simplification, and hatched complex schemes for later attack. In so doing, he foreshadowed the later trend of dynamism which would reveal the hidden power of closed positions.

In various journals that are nearly impossible to find today, Breyer published a wealth of original analyses which challenged classical principles. To him no idea was taboo, so he was able to make pioneering discoveries. The defense named after him shows the typical Hypermodern disdain for moving the center pawns: 1 P-K4, N-QB3!? 2 N-QB3, N-B3!? He also invented an important line in the Ruy Lopez, 9. . . N-N1, and the highly unorthodox move in the King's Gambit, 3 Q-B3!?

Breyer had extraordinary mental powers. In 1921 he set a world blindfold record of twenty-five games simultaneously, scoring 18½ points. He also published a unique, fleeting gazette called *Sport for the Mind,* a collection of difficult puzzles, including chess problems. In one of these, a crazy position was presented in which every piece on both sides was *en prise.* The solution lay in the astounding proof that for the last fifty moves no pawn had been moved and no capture had occurred—therefore, according to the rules of chess, a draw. Of Breyer's tragic death at twenty-seven in 1921, Reti said, "A new Steinitz was all too soon snatched from us."

The paramount figures of Hypermodernism, however, were Aron Nimzovich and Richard Reti. Nimzovich was a strategic innovator, while Reti was a theorist and a philosopher.

Nimzovich was born in 1886 in the Latvian capital of Riga, a city with a strong chess tradition. He is the only chess great whose father was an expert player, and he duly learned the moves at the age of eight. After contact with the masters of Riga, Aron went as a student to Germany, where the beginnings of his playing career were modest. But the young Nimzovich was already laying the theoretical groundwork for the founding of a revolutionary camp of chess thought.

Rejecting the Tarrasch dogmas, he hatched a radical idea of the center. He decided that the rigid insistence on maintaining a pawn on one of the center squares was wrong. He threw down the gauntlet in a series of articles in *Wiener Schachzeitung* in 1913, directly challenging Tarrasch's concept of "surrender of the center," pointing out that the "surrender" by a pawn often means a gain in piece activity. To the question of whether Tarrasch's book, *Die Moderne Schachpartie,* expressed a truly modern understanding of the game, Nimzovich answered a daring "No." He later declared, "I have sounded the call to a revolt."

As well might an obscure priest presume to correct the Pope. To Tarrasch's comment that Nimzovich's "ugly" moves were less forgivable than outright blunders, Nimzovich replied, "The beauty of a chess move lies not in its appearance, but in the thought behind it." The chess world scoffed at the upstart's aggressiveness, but a year later he tied Alekhine for the All-Russian Championship.

His nerves often failed him in crucial battles for first prize. In the key last-round game with Rubinstein at San Sebastian, 1912, each player was so nervous that he overlooked a mate in two. At St. Petersburg in 1914, Nimzovich tasted bitter disappointment when he failed to make the final section.

After the war he emigrated to Denmark. For several years he was absent from the world arena, to the profit of chess in Scandinavia. He returned at Karlsbad in 1923 but could only tie for sixth. Then at Marienbad in 1925 he tied for first with Rubinstein. For the first time the chess world conceded that the bizarre theoretician who had introduced so many strange concepts was in the first rank of the world's players.

But Nimzovich made his deepest mark on the chess world in the mid-twenties with the appearance, first, of his treatise, *The Blockade,* and then of one of the most important chess books ever written, *My System.* There it was, for every player to absorb: a totalistic, mostly original new system of chess strategy. The book won instant popularity which has not dissipated to this day. Later came *The Praxis of My System,* with more of his extraordinarily original games to illustrate the theory.

Nimzovich's postwar record is very impressive. In twenty-eight tournaments, he won or tied for first place thirteen times. His greatest triumph came at Karlsbad in 1929, where he took first ahead of twenty-one other players, including Capablanca, losing only one game. He then declared that the chess world ought to organize a match between the world champion and the tournament

Aron Nimzovich (l) and Richard Reti founded Hypermodern revolt against traditional classicism. To Tarrasch's accusation that moves were ugly, Nimzovich replied: "The beauty of a chess moves lies not in its appearance, but in the thought behind it."

winner. But there were certain conditions, such as a $10,000 purse, that could not be filled. A match between Nimzovich at top form and Alekhine would have been a chessic feast, indeed.

What sort of man was this, who had revolutionized chess play, reviving, in Reinfeld's phrase, "much of the charm and joy of battle"? A very sensitive person, yet one who did not fear to challenge the chess establishment and bring down its scorn. According to Edward Lasker, Nimzovich had a "bizarre streak," repulsing people by his "abnormally nervous behavior." He used sarcasm, yet was free of personal malice. Once, following a doctor's advice to do calisthenics, he stood on his head during a game.

Before a game with the Yugoslav, Vidmar, an inveterate cigar-smoker, Nimzovich got the referee's assurance that his opponent would not smoke. But during the game Vidmar placed a cigar on the table. The agitated Nimzovich rushed to the referee, who pointed out that Vidmar was not in fact smoking. "Yes," Nimzovich replied, "but he is *threatening* to smoke." He was evidently influenced by the old chess adage, "The threat is stronger than the execution."

Nimzovich had to wage a lonely battle against Tarrasch and his disciples for the vindication of his radi-

Jacques Villon's etching, Table d'Échecs *("Chessboard"). On square, practical chessboard, rounded and dreamlike distortion is imposed, with pieces straddling the squares. Underneath, angled boards are stacked like layers of consciousness.*

cal ideas. In this fight he did not even have the help of other Hypermoderns, with whom he was not associated. They did not wish to erect a new orthodoxy in place of the old one they were tearing down. At Liège in 1930 Nimzovich congratulated the Polish master Przepiorka on a fine game. The surprised Przepiorka asked why Nimzovich had not spoken to him for many years. "Oh that!" replied Nimzovich, "I thought you were a member of the Tarrasch school."

After his victory over Tarrasch at San Sebastian in 1912, an excellent illustration of his principle of the pawn-chain, Nimzovich observed, "It is probably not so very difficult to maneuver well if one has a complete system to fall back on." In effect, the System was elevated to a religion. But what if the believer is also the founder of the true religion which brings him persecution and fame? He may then tend toward the messianic.

Thus, to a psychologist it will come as no surprise that Nimzovich later in life thought people were plotting to poison him. At Kissingen he was obsessed with the idea that Alekhine was coming to kill him. If the world champion had actually participated in the tournament, however, Nimzovich undoubtedly would have been more capable of coping with him across the board than in his fantasy life.

Nimzovich died in Copenhagen in 1935 at age forty-eight, a lonely, unhappy man. He had not grasped the extent to which the chess world had already accepted and assimilated his discoveries. He was unaware that his unique ideas would be used by hundreds of thousands of devotees. He could not know that many years later U.S. Champion Robert Byrne would call him "perhaps the most brilliant theoretician and teacher in the history of the game."

In surveying serious chess played today throughout the world, one easily sees the lasting integration of the opening inventions and general strategic concepts of Nimzovich. If he had done nothing more than invent the Nimzoindian Defense (1 P-Q4, N-KB3 2 P-QB4, P-K3 3 N-QB3, B-N5!), he would merit inclusion in a list of the most important contributors to chess theory. Note how effectively the pin nullifies White's threat to usurp the center with P-K4. This flexible, counterattacking, yet safe defense still enjoys a vigorous life a half-century after its introduction.

In Nimzovich's games there often followed an exchange of Bishop for Knight with the consequent doubling of White's pawns. In game after game he targeted these static, hard-to-protect doubled pawns for his maxim, "First restrain, next blockade, lastly destroy!" If White on the third move played instead N-KB3, Nimzovich answered with 3...P-QN3, the Queen's Indian Defense. The fianchettoed Bishop on N2 controls the K5 square, preventing White from advancing in the center. Soon even the Classicists, tiring of 1...P-Q4, were adopting the Indian defenses. Other Indians came later: 3 N-KB3, B-N5 ch (the Bogo-Indian), 2...P-KN3 (the profound King's Indian), and 2...P-KN3 3 N-QB3, P-Q4 (the dynamic defense named after Ernst Grünfeld of Vienna).

The name of Nimzovich is also attached to the defense 1 P-K4, N-QB3!? and the moves 1 N-KB3, P-Q4 2 P-QN3, one of the first "reversed" openings. In these, White undertakes to play a standard defense with a move in hand. The black player, if lured into an overaggressive response, will be punished.

Nimzovich also made numerous contributions in other openings. He liked the move 3 P-K5 in the French Defense, erecting around it his theory of the pawn-chain. Here his chief maxim was, "Attack pawn-chains at their base." He readily gave up the advanced pawns if their squares became available to pieces.

The first game showing his new philosophy of the center was Nimzovich-Salwe at Karlsbad in 1911. It began: 1 P-K4, P-K3 2 P-Q4, P-Q4 3 P-K5, P-QB4! (attack-

Duchamp

"The Chess-Players" by Marcel Duchamp, oil on canvas, 1910. This pleasant, naturalistic painting is a far cry from "Nude Descending a Staircase," which was three years in future. His surrealism may have been offspring of Hypermodern chess ideas.

ing the pawn-chain at its base) 4 P-QB3, N-QB3 5 N-B3, Q-N3! 6 B-Q3!?, B-Q2?! (correct is 6. . . PxP) 7 PxP! (radical! White voluntarily "surrenders" the center), BxP 8 0-0, P-B3!? (attacking the vanguard of the chain) 9 P-QN4! (scholastic conceptions would condemn this move, leaving the QBP backward), B-K2 10 B-KB4, PxP 11 NxP, NxN 12 BxN.

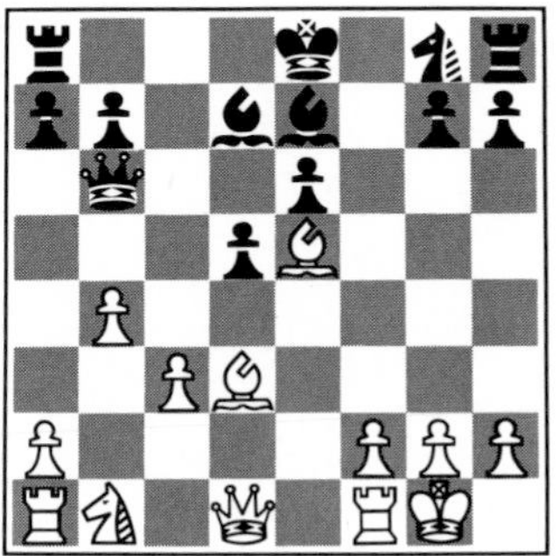

Black has succeeded in destroying the pawns, only to find them replaced by even more dominating pieces. The blockade of the potentially weak, backward KP is in full force, and the key square Q4 beckons White's Knight. As Nimzovich explained, "By counting the heads of the pawns in the center, nothing, literally nothing, is gained."

In *My System*, Nimzovich pays homage to Steinitz and then comments, "Tarrasch took hold of Steinitz' ideas and served them up diluted to the public taste." Rejecting Tarrasch's formalistic conception of the center, he lays down an elaborate, detailed system of play that aspires to comprehend all aspects of the game. He claims it to be the first treatise to go beyond opening theory, the first "to reduce a welter of arbitrary ideas to a definite number of interrelated principles." *My System* is indeed a masterwork of enduring importance, although it is not so original throughout as its author claimed. Today it seems one-sided in emphasis and oversystematized. Who can remember the "five special cases" of the seventh rank? It is sufficient to see every day that a Rook on the seventh is powerful. But *My System* does contain strikingly origi-

Max Ernst with set he designed for important New York chess exhibit in 1944. Dada-surrealist conceptions were order of the day. Yves Tanguy designed a magnificent set from a broom handle! But Ernst's was tops for artistry. Duchamp is shown with this set on page 19.

nal concepts. One is "overprotection" of strategically important points. Nimzovich calls it the *leitmotif* of correct strategy. Here we see one piece after another maneuvered to protect the same point, which is hardly attacked. The idea is part of "prophylaxis" (as is "blockade") against later activity by the enemy forces. The "preventive" play of Petrosian today shows a strong Nimzovichian influence.

Another prophylactic device is the "mysterious" Rook move, placing a Rook where it has no obvious activity, but "giving the opponent a distaste for freeing actions." What with so many efforts to limit their activity, the opponents of Nimzovich sometimes found themselves in virtual Zugzwang. Nimzovich also showed the strength of the "outpost"—the advanced position for a Knight on an open file.

But Nimzovich's treatise is not overly serious. Delightfully, he often personifies the chessmen. There is the passed pawn's "lust to expand": "A passed pawn is a criminal who should be kept under lock and key. Mild measures, such as police surveillance, are not sufficient." The KNP gets "uppish." The pawn, with its "conservative spirit and stability," is the chessman who "works for the least wages." Again: "Master Rook appears in the office, bows to the boss, nods to his fellow employees." It seems that he loved not only chess, but even the chess pieces. Love was not easy for him to find beyond the game.

If Steinitz was the Newton of chess, Nimzovich was its Einstein. He revolutionized the technique of the game and left an indelible mark upon its future. The lonely pioneer who endured so many hardships while sharing his discoveries will forever be studied and remembered.

JOHNER V. NIMZOVICH
Dresden, 1926
Nimzoindian Defense

	WHITE	BLACK		WHITE	BLACK
1	P-Q4	N-KB3	2	P-QB4	P-K3
3	N-QB3	B-N5	6	N-B3	N-B3
4	P-K3	0-0	7	0-0	BxN
5	B-Q3	P-B4	8	PxB	. . .

Here we have the famous static and weak doubled pawns. White should aim for an early P-K4, but instead puts his Knight offside and allows Black a restraining wedge in the center.

8	. . .	P-Q3	10	N-N3?!	P-K4
9	N-Q2	P-QN3	11	P-B4?	P-K5
			12	B-K2	Q-Q2!

One of Nimzovich's "ugly" moves, prophylaxis against White's chief hope for activity, P-N4. The Queen transfers to the King's flank, where the action will be, with a highly original maneuver.

13	P-KR3	N-K2	15	B-Q2	Q-B4
14	Q-K1	P-KR4!	16	K-R2	Q-R2!
			17	P-QR4	N-B4

White is thoroughly blockaded, already faced with the threat of 18...N-N5 ch 19 PxN(?), PxP ch 20 K-N1, P-N6 and mates.

18	P-N3	P-R4!

Restraining White's last hope, P-R5. The "weakness" of the QNP will be insignificant. The same move was used by Fischer against Spassky in 1972, in their fifth game.

19	R-KN1	N-R3	22	P-Q5	K-R1!
20	B-KB1	B-Q2	23	N-Q2	R-KN1
21	B-B1	QR-B1	24	B-KN2	P-KN4!

The beginning of the end. White's pathetically hamstrung pieces can only await doom.

25	N-B1	R-N2	29	KPxP	B-B1!
26	R-R2	N-B4	30	Q-N3	B-R3
27	B-R1	R/1-KN1	31	R-K2	N-R5
28	Q-Q1	PxP	32	R-K3	. . .

Nimzovich planned this pretty finish: 32 N-Q2, B-B1 (alternating strategy versus different weaknesses) 33 NxP, Q-B4 34 N-B2, QxP ch! 35 NxQ, N-N5 mate.

32	. . .	B-B1	33	Q-B2	. . .

Acrylic resin chess set by Richard Filipowski, 1943. Functional shapes are scored on top to show direction of moves. Note eight-directional King, cubic Rooks. Most strikingly, material accommodates twisted body of Knight, an eccentric triumph.

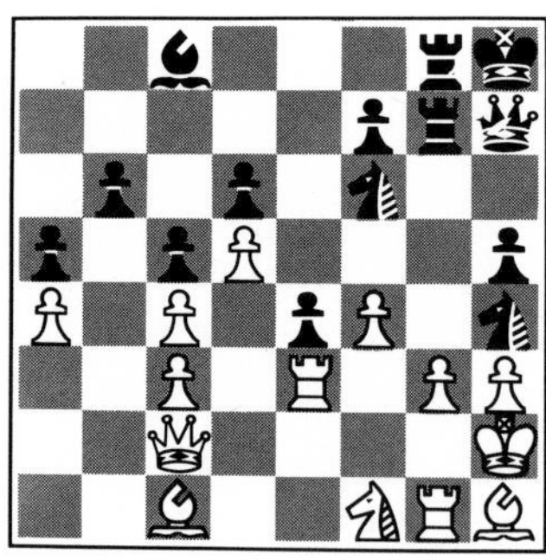

33	. . .	BxP!	**34**	BxP	. . .

Or 34 KxB, Q-B4 ch 35 K-R2, N-N5 ch 36 K-R3, N-B7 dbl ch 37 K-R2, Q-R6 mate. White's game is in ruins and now he loses material, or gets mated.

34	. . .	B-B4	**38**	K-N1	Q-R6
35	BxB	NxB	**39**	N-K3	N-R5
36	R-K2	P-R5	**40**	K-B1	R-K1
37	R/1-N2	PxP ch	**41**	Resigns	

A superb example of the Nimzovich system.

There are men who capture and articulate so well the spirit of their times that they become synonymous with an entire era. For the 1920s in chess, that man was Richard Reti, the foremost theorist of Hypermodernism. "The golden rule," he declared, "is that there is no golden rule."

Born in Central Europe in the town of Pezzinok in 1889, he decided while a university student at Vienna to make chess his profession because it happened to be what he did best.

In Vienna he met Tartakower and other young masters impatient with the dry, drawish technique of the time, and experimented with original strategic ideas which later became part of the substance of Hypermodernism.

In prewar tournaments, Reti's results were good but not overwhelming. Then came his first "moment of truth." In 1914 he teamed with Capablanca in a consultation game at the Vienna Chess Club. In the late opening they reached a position in which there was an obvious developing move that Morphy would have chosen "without considering." Yet Capa insisted on another move, part of his own strategic plan. Reti wrote that "with this game began a revolution in my conviction as to the wisdom of the old principle, according to which in the opening every move should develop another piece." The young man who began to doubt that one principle would later abandon all preconceptions and face the chess struggle armed only with his original ideas.

After the war Reti scored the best results of his his career, with a succession of first prizes. His most impressive victory was at Göteborg in 1920, where he finished ahead of Rubinstein, Bogolyubov, and other stars.

Strategically, he was in a transitional period. Not until 1923 did he introduce the opening that bears his name. The usual first moves are 1 N-KB3, P-Q4 2 P-B4, but various transpositions are possible. The new opening won Reti many successes when opponents following classical ideas hastened to occupy the center, only to find it undermined by White's fianchettoed Bishops. With it he scored a sensational victory in New York against the "invincible" Capablanca in 1924. And against Emanuel Lasker he created the maneuver Q-QR1-KR1 (!), the ultimate example of attacking the center from a distance.

Reti's book, *Modern Ideas in Chess,* published in 1922, became an instant classic. Moreover, his later *Masters of the Chessboard* is a superb work of analysis of the achievements of the great players.

Reti set a world blindfold record of twenty-nine games simultaneously. He was also known for his elegantly composed end-game problems. Britain's Harry Golombek tells a revealing story of one such composition. During a tournament game, Reti suddenly got the idea for a composed study. Without making his move, an obvious one, he jumped up and collared a friend in order to demonstrate his idea on a pocket chess set. The friend insisted that he complete his winning game first. Reti re-

turned to the board somewhat disgruntled, made some hasty moves, and threw away the game. At once he went to his hotel and spent the whole night working out his composition. Fatigued, he lost the next game as well and with it his chance for first prize. His adventure in the realm of chessic poetry was at the cost of his daily bread.

Here is a Reti study, illustrating the beauty of economy of means.

It seems that White's King is too far away to stop the enemy pawn from queening or to assist his own pawn. Here is the solution: 1 K-N7, P-R5 2 K-B6 (threatening to bring the King closer to the White's pawn and thus insure that it also queens), K-N3 3 K-K5 (threatening to catch Black's pawn), P-R6 4 K-Q6, P-R7 5 P-B7 and both pawns promote. The black pawn is like a comet slowed down by the gravitational pull of a distant body.

Reti had a creditable plus-score at New York in 1924 among the world's elite, but he never again scaled the competitive heights. He was preoccupied with evolving and explaining his new ideas. He died in Prague in 1929 at age forty, another unfair blow to the world of chess.

But as a theorist he will always be preeminent. The most beautiful book ever written about chess had its origin in pique at the pretensions of a certain writer, Gutmayer, whose output of chess books far exceeded his degree of comprehension. He was, it seems, the epitome of the vacuous popularizer. Reti employed uncharacteristic sarcasm in saying that Gutmayer "might perhaps in fifty years' time be so advanced as to comprehend Steinitz and has at present achieved this much at least—a partial understanding of Morphy."

Reti was impelled to demolish the man with a series of polemical articles which were later softened and used as the basis of the unique *Modern Ideas in Chess.* It is at once a revelation of the evolution of chess ideas, a reverent study of the great personalities, a manifesto of the Hypermodern movement, and a validation of chess as an art, which places it in the context of all human effort. Its closing words are, "For in the idea of chess and

Interesting confrontation between romantic, swashbuckling Frank Marshall (l) and cool, Hypermodern Richard Reti. Although Marshall was the superior tactician, Reti's ideas prevailed. The flank systems espoused by Reti are now staples of tournament play.

the development of the chess mind we have a picture of the intellectual struggle of mankind."

The chief thesis is profoundly humanistic—that the pioneering works of modern chess, like modern art, no longer conforming to outside nature (the "naturalism of the Steinitz school"), have made paramount the ideas of the individual chess artist. "At least for mankind the human mind is of all things the greatest that nature has provided."

On the Hypermodern style he explains that rules in chess, though useful, are never universally applicable: "It is the aim of the modern school not to treat every position according to one general law, but according to the principle inherent in the position . . . the source of the greatest errors is to be found in those moves that are made merely according to rule and not based on the individual plan or thought of the player."

Whereas Emanuel Lasker used chess as a testing ground for his philosophical notions, Reti through his analysis of chess ideas rose to the level of a philosopher. He pointed out the resemblance between Capablanca's play and the works of modern technology. He showed that the dimensions of chess had advanced beyond a mere game: ". . . he who has felt, for example, the deep sense of devotion that pervades Rubinstein's games knows that we find there a new and ever progressing art."

RETI V. BOGOLYUBOV
New York, 1924
Reti Opening

	WHITE	BLACK		WHITE	BLACK
1	N-KB3	P-Q4	5	P-N3	0-0
2	P-B4	P-K3	6	0-0	R-K1?!
3	P-KN3	N-KB3	7	B-N2	QN-Q2
4	B-N2	B-Q3!?	8	P-Q4	. . .

Since Black has not set up much of a pawn center, White at last does so. Usually Reti's system features P-Q3.

8	. . .	P-B3	9	QN-Q2	N-K5?!

Otherwise White will play Q-B2 and P-K4. But the coming exchanges favor White.

10	NxN	PxN	12	P-B3!	PxP
11	N-K5	P-KB4	13	BxP!	Q-B2?

Leaves White's center too fluid. A better try was 13. . . NxN 14 PxN, B-B4 ch, but Black remains cramped.

14	NxN	BxN	15	P-K4!	. . .

White's belated domination of the center vindicates the whole Reti strategy. According to one Hypermodern slogan P-K4 is stronger on move 15 than on move 1.

15	. . .	P-K4	17	Q-B2	KPxP
16	P-B5	B-KB1	18	PxP	QR-Q1

Or else 18. . . R-K4 19 BxQP, RxKBP 20 B-K4! and the pawn center has been replaced by overwhelming pieces.

19	B-R5!	R-K4	20	BxP	RxKBP

If 20. . . R-Q4, then 21 Q-B4, K-R1 22 P-B6 wins. "Bogo" relies on a combination to maintain material equality, but Reti has seen further.

21	RxR	BxR	22	QxB	RxB
			23	R-KB1!	R-Q1

Otherwise 23. . . Q-K2 24 B-B7 ch, K-R1 25 B-Q5!, Q-B3 26 Q-B8 and wins.

24	B-B7 ch	K-R1

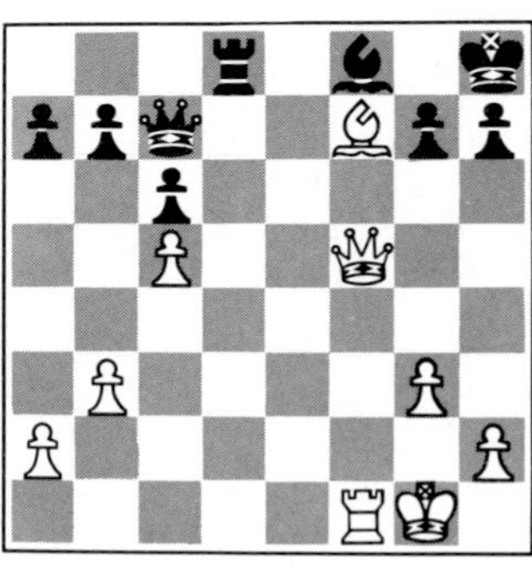

25	B-K8!	Resigns

If 25. . . RxB, 26 QxB ch and mates; if 25. . . B-K2, 26 Q-B8 ch and mates. The interference idea of Reti's final move resembles the beautiful theme of a composed problem.

9.

МАТЧ
НА ПЕРВЕНСТВО
МИРА
ПО ШАХМАТАМ
БРОНШТЕЙН
32
БОТВИННИК

The Age of Dynamism

> "Chess is *not only* knowledge and logic!"
>
> —A. A. Alekhine

Alekhine is the seminal figure of the first half of the twentieth century. He summed up all of chess development to his time and introduced the new and much-needed element—dynamism. His passionate devotion to chess, his mastery of every phase of the game, the soaring feats of his creative imagination were unequaled.

Alexander Alexandrovich Alekhine was born in 1892 to a prominent Muscovite family. Interestingly, he is one of the few chess superstars who learned the game from his mother. Alekhine grew up during the Russian chess renaissance of Tchigorin, played blindfold and postal games, and was a master at age sixteen.

According to Reti, Alekhine's driving nervous energy made him impatient with the static classical technique. Instead he developed a highly original flair for combinations. Even in simple positions he took care to analyze seemingly harmless sequences of moves, with surprising results. He later confessed to a "dangerous delusion . . . that I could always, or nearly always, when in a bad position, conjure up some combination to extricate me from my difficulties."

But combinative genius is not enough to make a world champion. Alekhine's results as a teen-ager in German and Swedish tournaments were mediocre. Reti calls Alekhine's contact with Capablanca, who visited Russia in 1913-14, a turning point: "He learned the latter's new technique, the lively dynamics of which suited Alekhine's disposition, and added a methodical groundwork to his originality." In 1914, the young master surprised the experts by tying Nimzovich for first place in the All-Russian Championship. In the star-studded St. Petersburg tournament he was a very creditable third behind Lasker and Capablanca.

The vagaries of Alekhine's personal life began in the aftermath of the October Revolution. According to a story still told in Russia, two Cheka agents came to arrest him at a coffeehouse in Odessa. He asked to finish the game in progress, and the secret policemen looked on patiently until it was over. (Only in Russia!) According to a Soviet grandmaster, Alekhine's life was spared by Trotsky himself. Always an opportunist, Alekhine worked for the Soviet government, then defected, according to one account, while on a mission to Germany.

Subsequently, he became a French citizen and received a law degree from the Sorbonne, although he never practiced. He married a succession of women much older than he. (One of them was dubbed by Argentine chess fans, "the widow of Philidor.") Alekhine's behavior toward the public was often brusque to the point of rudeness. In the 1930s, his drunken exhibitionism caused frequent scandals. During World War II he lived and played in the German sphere and collaborated on at least one verified occasion. One can hardly imagine a less likely Soviet hero, yet Alekhine's dynamic play was an inspiration to the early Soviet school. The overriding explanation for his acceptance by the USSR is that he was a true chess genius and a Russian.

In the innovative decade of the twenties, Alekhine rejected what he considered the eccentricities of the Hypermoderns but was always alert to the individuality of each position. Reti considered him a practitioner of the "new ideas," one who departed from the classic search for the "best move" in every position and instead sought "the deepest and most far-reaching plan."

Capablanca, the new world champion, had dethroned Lasker with ease in 1921. In subsequent tournaments he rarely lost a game. In 1927 he accepted a challenge by Alekhine and a championship match was arranged for Buenos Aires in mid-September. It was to end when one player reached a total of six outright wins.

Opening pages: Mikhail Botvinnik (l) holds world-championship title against strong challenge of David Bronstein on stage of Tchaikovsky Concert Hall in Moscow, 1951. Below: Alexander Alekhine, greatest creative chess genius of half-century to 1950, but not a likable human being.

Since most of the tightly fought, incredibly accurate games were drawn, the match developed into a ten-week marathon of thirty-four games, the longest world-championship match ever held.

The decision depended not merely on relative chess gifts. Alekhine came to the contest thoroughly prepared and fiercely determined. Capa responded with overconfidence. He had been nourished too long on the myth of his own invincibility. The Cuban's blasé attitude toward the game, which he felt held no further secrets for him, contrasted sharply with that of the Russian, who had given his soul to chess. Alekhine, after losing a game, once aptly expressed his creed with the statement, "Chess will always be the master of us all."

If the chess world had expected a polarized struggle of tactician versus strategist, it was in for a surprise. Alekhine demonstrated the universality of his talent by meeting Capablanca on his own technical ground. The games show a remarkable sameness, each player repeatedly adopting the Orthodox Defense to the Queen's Gambit, and demonstrating that, if Black defended accurately for fifteen, twenty, or thirty moves, equality could be his. (Only in the last stages did Capablanca come up with a new idea for White: the Exchange Variation.)

Alekhine won the first game, but the champion took the lead by winning the third and seventh. In one of his exceptionally fine books of chess annotations, Alekhine called the eleventh game the "crucial point of the match." The initiative seesawed in time pressure, "a true comedy of errors," and the challenger won, equalizing the score. Alekhine seized the lead in the twelfth game and, after eight more successive draws, increased it in the twenty-first. Capablanca's lackadaisical approach to chess was refuted. The experts were confounded. The final blow did not come until the thirty-fourth game. The marathon was over. By a score of 6 wins, 3 losses, and 25 draws, Alekhine became the fourth chess champion of the world.

Alekhine's reign was a glorious one. In tournament play—his exceptional games endure as a permanent record—he scored phenomenal totals. In the strong events at San Remo in 1930, and Bled in 1931, he achieved unparalleled margins of 3½ and 5½ points over the second-prize winner. His lifetime tournament record is unequaled. In seventy events for individuals, he took first prize forty-one times (including nine ties) and won or shared second prize fourteen times. At Chicago in 1932, he played thirty-two simultaneous blindfold games and broke his own world record with 19 wins, 4 losses, and 9 draws.

And yet, for at least a decade, Alekhine dodged a

rematch with Capablanca, the one opponent who posed the greatest threat to his title. He was full of excuses. When the Cuban raised a purse of $10,000, Alekhine cited the instability of the dollar and demanded it in gold. He even sought to bar Capa from tournaments in which he took part and did not play him again until 1936 at Nottingham, a tournament where Capa tied for first while Alekhine did rather poorly. Their individual encounter was a draw.

An incident at the Polish border in 1935 sheds a revealing light on Alekhine's conception of reality. Lacking documents, he informed the policeman, "I am Alekhine, chess champion of the world. This is my cat. Her name is Chess. I need no passport."

That year the chess world was stunned when Alekhine lost his title to Holland's Max Euwe, who, despite his gifts, was not a player of Alekhine's class. The defending champion's play was strangely uneven. His 3-point lead after nine games had disappeared by the fourteenth, and after further vicissitudes, the match ended in a narrow victory for Euwe, 9 wins to 8, with 13 draws. The setback was ascribed to Alekhine's weakness for drink, but Dr. Euwe has assured us in an interview that this factor has been grossly exaggerated.

Next year at Nottingham he finished sixth, his lowest result in twenty-four years. But for the 1937 rematch with Euwe, Alekhine's driving will once more asserted itself. Although the Dutchman held the lead after five games, Alekhine won three in a row and took the match going away, 10 wins to 4, with 11 draws.

In 1941 Alekhine's name was attached to some of the most bizarre essays in the history of chess. They appeared in German newspapers in occupied France and Holland. With a typical Nazi flavor, they attacked the materialistic "defensive thinking" of renowned Jewish players. (The exceptions among Jews were described as sharp, attacking players motivated by money-lust.) Obviously Alekhine knew too much about chess to believe such nonsense. We suggest that he made his statements preposterous so as to show the chess fraternity that the articles were not serious. One example: a description of Steinitz as merely an "adept tactician" who sought to pass himself off as a deep strategist.

After the Nazi defeat, Alekhine denied his authorship of the articles, calling them a "heap of monstrosities." He pleaded coercion, citing fears for the safety of his wife and his desperate need for money. The ongoing debate as to his actual authorship can be laid to rest. After Alekhine's death, copies of the articles, certified to be in his handwriting, were found by a British editor among Alekhine's effects. A veteran master who knew him well told us: "Alekhine's motivation was quite simple—he had no morals. He would do anything for money."

After the war, protests forced the cancellation of an invitation to compete in London. The American contender, Reuben Fine, demanded that the international chess organization, FIDE, strip Alekhine of his world title.

Then came a challenge from the Soviet champion, Botvinnik, backed by a sizable purse from the Moscow Chess Club. Alekhine, just recovering from a heart attack, accepted. The British Chess Federation met and agreed to hold the match. But it was destined not to be. On March 24, 1946, in a Lisbon hotel, Alexander Alekhine, age fifty-three, was found dead in his room, a chess set in his hands.

Alekhine left a rich creative legacy. His penetrating and tireless analysis produced many opening innovations. He introduced the defense which bears his name (1 P-K4, N-KB3), but, oddly enough, never played it again. He is also credited with the Alekhine-Chatard Attack versus the French Defense, and the Kecskemet Variation of the Ruy Lopez.

But far more important than specific moves was Alekhine's whole approach to the opening phase, which before him depended on memorization and was treated merely as a prelude to the real action. Alekhine now proved that it was a forum for dynamic, aggressive planning. Note his conduct of the white pieces in the following opening against the great classicist, Rubinstein, at The Hague in 1921.

	WHITE	BLACK		WHITE	BLACK
1	P-Q4	P-Q4	2	N-KB3	P-K3
			3	P-QB4	P-QR3

Janowski's dubious move, which invites White to grab space on the Queen's side.

4	P-B5!	N-QB3

Threatening the freeing...P-K4. At this early stage, opposing ideas are already in action.

5	B-B4	KN-K2	6	N-B3	N-N3
			7	B-K3!	...

Against principle! White blocks the KP, which in turn blocks the KB. Why? To restrain Black's intended ...P-K4 and ...P-Q5.

7	...	P-N3	8	PxP	PxP
			9	P-KR4!	...

Alekhine strikes out on the other flank, to embarrass the Knight.

9	...	B-Q3?

Better is 9...P-KR4 10 B-N5.

10	P-R5	KN-K2	12	B-N5	0-0
11	P-R6!	P-N3	13	B-B6	...

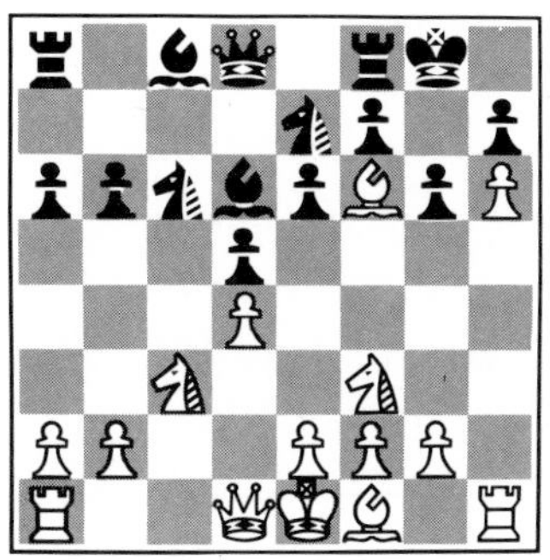

Through highly unconventional play, Alekhine has already achieved a virtually winning position. Black is trussed up and his king-side is full of holes.

Alekhine's was a consummate, integrated talent. His fine appreciation of strategy enabled him to build up positions ripe for combination. Spielmann, the Neo-romantic Viennese master of combination play, once remarked that he could find Alekhine's brilliant moves, but he didn't know how to reach the positions that made them possible.

Alekhine absorbed all the Classical and Hypermodern ideas and introduced the vital new approach of dynamism to the chess struggle. It was to become the mainstream of chess thought. For all players, from amateurs to grandmasters, his games remain an unending source of aesthetic pleasure, an enduring model of the creative impulse in chess. He was the most complete chess artist in the history of the game.

RETI V. ALEKHINE

Baden-Baden, 1925

King's Fianchetto Attack

	WHITE	BLACK		WHITE	BLACK
1	P-KN3	P-K4	2	N-KB3	...

Psychology! Instead of his own opening, Reti plays Alekhine's Defense in reverse. He succeeds in undermining the pawn center and develops a lasting initiative on the queen-side.

2	...	P-K5	10	PxP	N-QN5
3	N-Q4	P-Q4	11	Q-B4	QNxQP
4	P-Q3	PxP	12	N/2-N3	P-B3
5	QxP	N-KB3	13	0-0	R-K1
6	B-N2	B-N5 ch	14	KR-Q1	B-N5
7	B-Q2	BxB ch	15	R-Q2	Q-B1
8	NxB	0-0	16	N-QB5	B-R6!
9	P-QB4!	N-R3	17	B-B3	...

Alekhine foresaw 17 BxB?, QxB 18 NxNP? N-KN5 19 N-B3, QN-K6! 20 PxN, NxKP 21 QxP ch!, K-R1! 22 N-R4,

R-KB1, and if White moves his Queen, he is mated on B1.

17	...	B-N5	21	P-N4	P-R3
18	B-N2	B-R6	22	R-QB1	P-R5
19	B-B3	B-N5	23	P-R4	PxP
20	B-R1!	P-KR4!	24	RPxP	Q-B2
			25	P-N5?!	...

Reti carries too far his avoidance of moving the central pawns. Safe and good was 25 P-K4.

25	...	RPxP	26	PxP	...

26	...	R-K6!!

Typical Alekhine forcing play! The Rook cannot be taken because of ...QxP ch followed by ...NxP and mate. White now neglects his last chance for equality, via 27 B-B3.

27	N-B3?	PxP	28	QxP	N-B6!
			29	QxP	...

On 29 Q-B4, R-R5! 30 Q-N3, NxP ch, the Queen is lost.

29	...	QxQ	30	NxQ	NxP ch
			31	K-R2	N-K5!

"The winning move!"—Alekhine. The advanced Rook is still immune, and a virtually forced twelve-move sequence ensues.

32	R-B4!	NxBP!	37	RxN	N-N5 ch
33	B-N2	B-K3	38	K-R3	N-K6 dis ch
34	R/4-B2	N-N5 ch	39	K-R2	NxR
35	K-R3	N-K4 dis ch	40	BxR	N-Q5!
36	K-R2	RxN!	41	Resigns	

White is only a pawn down, but now a piece goes after 41 R-KB2, NxB ch 42 RxN, B-Q4. As Reti wrote of Alekhine three years before, "It is mostly the final move that takes his opponent's breath away." One of the most beautiful games ever played!

The chief theoretical task of the 1930s was stated well by the American, Reuben Fine: to synthesize the Classical and Hypermodern ideas into a sound modern system of play.

New York at the time was a school of sharp chessic infighting that produced a new generation of U. S. players—including Isaac Kashdan, Samuel Reshevsky, I. A. Horowitz (the father of *Chess Review*), and Reuben Fine—who were to win no less than four Olympiads. With its famous Marshall and Manhattan Chess clubs, the city has continued to be a major source of top American stars, like Larry Evans, Arthur Bisguier, Robert Byrne, his brother Donald Byrne, William Lombardy, and Bobby Fischer.

Kashdan, born in 1905, was the strongest U. S. player in the early thirties, and touted for even higher honors. But he couldn't raise the requisite $5,000 purse, unrealistically high for those Depression days, with which to challenge U. S. Champion Frank Marshall. He later submitted to the economic facts and gave up playing professional chess.

Fine, born in 1914, hit the European circuit in 1935 and soon started garnering first prizes. Very pragmatic, he played positionally but sharply. He rose to the heights in 1938, when he tied for first in the AVRO tournament in Holland which included the eight best players in the world. Oddly enough, Fine never won the U. S. title, explaining that in his encounters with his rival Reshevsky "ambivalence" made him commit errors.

The mind intrigued him, and, instead of pursuing a precarious career in chess, Fine became a psychoanalyst. His monograph, *The Psychology of the Chess Player,*

Vera Menchik, first lady of chess, faces Capablanca, first ladies' man. Menchik was premier woman chess master of modern times and first women's world champion. Her victims were enrolled in "Menchik Club." In encounter shown here, chivalry did not prevail.

stakes out the ultra-Freudian interpretation of chess. His other successful books on all aspects of the game have stamped him as a major theoretician. But from the viewpoint of the American chess-lover, one can only lament his decision "for professional reasons" not to compete for the world championship in 1948.

Reshevsky, born in 1911, was a six-year-old *wunderkind* when he was summoned for a game by the German governor of occupied Poland. Only after beating his powerful opponent did tiny Sammy break the silence. He exclaimed in Yiddish, "You play war. I play chess!"

Sammy was one of the few authentic child geniuses of the game. At age nine he emigrated to the United States, whose championship he was destined to win six times. He was taken on endless exhibition tours. Americans were fascinated by the little boy who could defeat thirty grown men in a couple of hours.

This business exploitation of a child's talent was to have a negative effect upon his future zest for chess. In later years, Reshevsky stood out from his peers of world class by his disinclination to study the game. When he sat down at the board, he took excessive time to find the best opening moves, which his opponents had memorized. The result was that when the crucial phase of the game arrived, Reshevsky had little time left on his clock and had to play "blitz," relying on tactical wizardry and an indomitable fighting spirit. The Soviet press called him an "escape artist." But basically, Reshevsky is a deep strategist of closed positions.

Reshevsky was long unbeatable in match play.

Botvinnik adorned with championship verdure in 1961, after regaining title from Mikhail Tal. "Mr. Soviet Chess" is a methodical scientist, yet a great fighter. He was sixth world champion, held title—with two interruptions—from 1948 to 1963.

After two match victories over Argentina's Najdorf, he laid claim to the title, Champion of the Western World. Then, in 1957, he was stunned to lose his primacy to fourteen-year-old Bobby Fischer. In their 1961 match the score was even after Game 11, when the match blew up in a dispute over scheduling.

Elsewhere a poetic parallel has been drawn between the history of the Jewish people and Reshevsky's chess. While perhaps half of all the greatest players of the past hundred years have been Jews, Reshevsky is the only competitor whose games require special scheduling to avoid conflict with the Jewish Sabbath. Having survived five whole decades of chess struggle, Reshevsky may yet surpass the feats of longevity of the two Laskers.

The Dutchman who upset Alekhine in the 1935 match is virtually an institution. Max Euwe, born in 1901, made his way to chess immortality in unobtrusive fashion. As a teen-ager, his skill was so modest that he played against child-prodigy Reshevsky in one of Sammy's simultaneous exhibitions. But at age twenty he tied a match with Grandmaster Maroczy.

Euwe, a teacher and doctor of mathematics, had only fair tournament results. According to one pundit, his chief achievement before becoming world champion was having lost some matches to Alekhine, Bogolyubov, and Capablanca—narrowly. He was a diligent worker who sought to shape chess by knowledge and method. He catalogued openings and leaned on thorough preparation. When he met Alekhine he was ready to take advantage of the opportunities given him by the unsteady world champion. After losing the title in 1937, Euwe's chess declined. His best results were tying a match with Keres in 1940 and winning second prize at Groningen in 1946.

Euwe's service to the chess world, however, has not slackened. He has written dozens of theoretical works and founded a school of Dutch analysts who issued the periodical, *Chess Archives*. In his lucid book, *The Development of Chess Style,* which outlines the evolution of chess thought, he pays his debt to Steinitz. While Euwe's games lack the clarity of the great classicists, he has played many intriguing games of tactical fireworks. But just there, beyond the reach of all preparation, he was prone to go astray.

In his eighth decade of life, the energetic Euwe became president of FIDE and announced his intention of visiting all seventy-odd member countries in order to boost chess. Caught up in the storm-center of the Fischer-Spassky match, he might have longed nostalgically for those simpler days when he conquered the great Alekhine and became the national hero of Holland.

The first woman in modern times to become a chess master was Vera Menchik, the first women's world champion. She was born of Czech-English parents in Moscow in 1906, and at age nine learned the game from her father. In 1921 the family moved to England, where Vera's career began in earnest. At Hastings she attended lectures by the veteran Hungarian grandmaster, Geza Maroczy. In maturity her quiet positional style was not unlike his. As she started to compete in events with men, the all-male chess world was forced to acknowledge the unprecedented phenomenon: Here was a budding master who was female. As an adult, she did everything that male professionals do. She played widely on the tournament circuit, gave exhibition tours, and published articles on opening theory.

Menchik played a number of serious games with the foremost players of her time. While she defeated many masters, her record against grandmasters was not good. There were two notable exceptions. Reshevsky, with a pawn ahead, overstepped the time limit against her at Yarmouth in 1935. He recalled, years later, the strange feeling he experienced in losing to a woman. And World

Champion Euwe, whom she beat by a score of 2½–1½, told us: "I didn't expect her to see so much."

In 1927 FIDE organized the first women's world championship in London. In a field of twelve women from seven countries, the winner was Vera Menchik, then age twenty-one. She easily retained her title in six subsequent tournaments, amassing a stunning total of 80 points out of eighty-three games. In one event her younger sister Olga finished in fourth place. There was no "sisterly" draw. Vera won.

Vera Menchik died in a London air raid in 1944. She had set a historic example and signaled new possibilities to women. Since the inauguration of the Women's Olympiad in 1957, Soviet women have taken home, every two years, the Vera Menchik Cup.

->>><<<-

The climax of a national championship causes a huge traffic jam as thousands of fans crowd to see a huge demonstration board.

The winner of an international tournament sends a cable brimming with patriotic fervor to the chief of state.

A setback in a chess match is regarded as a blow to an entire culture.

A well-known foreign master giving a simultaneous exhibition to teen-agers emerges with a minus score.

Instead of "hello," people picking up the phone at the largest newspaper answer with the result of a chess match just completed on another continent.

There is only one country in the world where all the above things could have occurred: the Union of Soviet Socialist Republics.

Chess, of course, had roots in Old Russia, where it arrived in the ninth century from Persia. Together with church authorities, Czar Ivan the Terrible in the sixteenth century sought to ban the "diabolic" game, but he did not heed his own ban. Later, Peter the Great fostered "new chess." The great nineteenth-century poet Pushkin wrote, "Chess is indispensable to every well-regulated family."

In the last century Russian theorists began to do serious work. Alexander Petrov (1794-1867) invented the sharp defense that bears his name: 1 P-K4, P-K4 2 N-KB3, N-KB3. He wrote a commentary on Philidor which opposed the great Frenchman's claim that White's first move confers a winning advantage.

But given the backwardness of that vast peasant land, the greatest popularization of chess in history awaited the transformation of the social system after 1917. It may be significant that the founder of the Soviet State, V. I. Lenin, was a sometimes fanatical chess-player in the long exile during which he plotted the socialist revolution. An early comrade, Valentinov, wrote that "the game obsessed him to such an extent that he used to rave about it in his sleep."

The *Great Soviet Encyclopedia* felicitously defines chess as "an art appearing in the form of a game." Chess was seen as a character-builder and a means of raising the cultural and political level of the masses by teaching foresight, patience, circumspection, perseverance, and so forth.

Led by the Bolshevik and chess master, A. I. Ilyin-Zhenevsky, the Third All-Union Chess Congress of 1924 adopted a fateful slogan: "Take chess to the workers!" Only twelve years later the Trade Union Championship drew more than 700,000 entrants. And a half-century later one can verify how well the directive was carried out by engaging almost any Moscow cabdriver in a discussion of the royal game. Regardless of the motives of the totalitarian state, all lovers of chess owe great respect to a movement that has succeeded in registering over three million players and made chess the leading game of the USSR.

In the ubiquitous palaces of young pioneers, Soviet boys and girls learn their first moves and advance to tactics and strategy under the eyes of trainers ever watchful to discover one destined for stardom. Such a one will

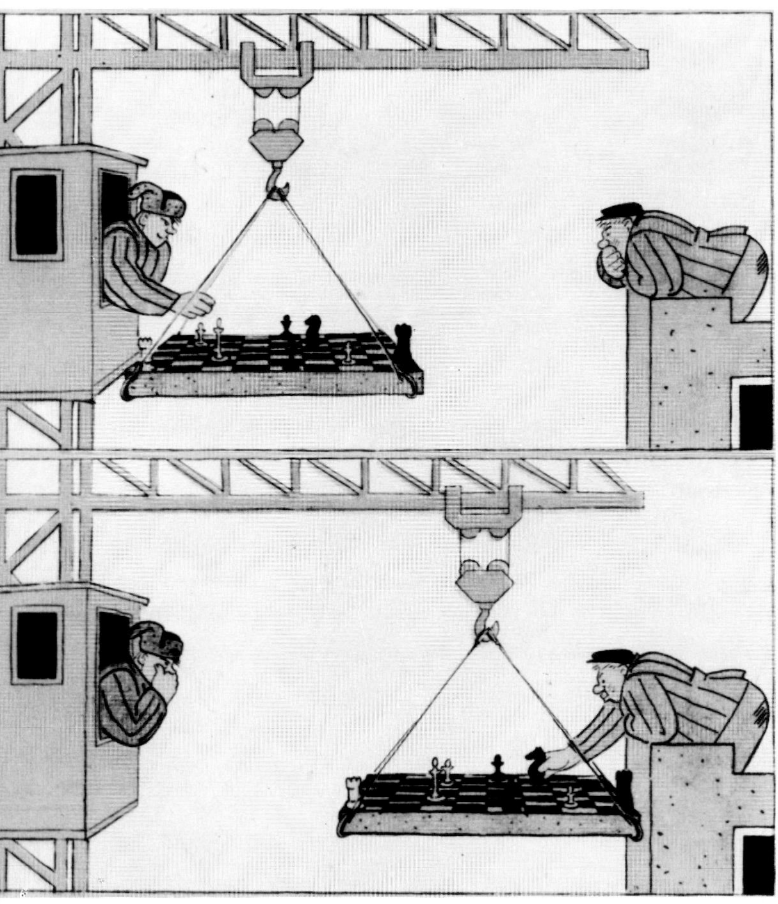

Cartoon from Soviet humor magazine Krokodil *is captioned: "Blitz tournament." Fervent feeling for game recalls Pudovkin's film comedy,* Chess Fever, *which showed Moscow citizenry gripped by mass chess mania during international tournament of 1925. Capa appeared in film.*

receive the personal attention of masters. Moreover, many cities have special chess schools for youth. With a collective spirit, talent is developed for team matches with neighboring cities or republics and for the purpose of qualifying participants for both the Soviet Championship and the international arena.

In the 1930s Soviet masters were already laying the groundwork for postwar dominance. Whether or not directly inspired by Alekhine's games, they were busy analyzing openings for sharp attacking possibilities. Their games reveal an aggressive spirit far from the drawish tendency of some European players. They played dynamic chess, free of a doctrinaire approach.

In 1945, a match by radio was arranged with the United States, which had fielded the strongest team in the thirties. The result: USSR 15½, U.S. only 4½! The chess world was astonished to discover that its capital had moved unobtrusively to Moscow.

Botvinnik, world champion intermittently from 1948 to 1963, is the scientist who led and spoke for the Soviet school of chess.

Born in 1911, Mikhail Moiseyevich Botvinnik grew up in a Leningrad offering rich opportunities for a young chess-player. At age fourteen he beat Capablanca in a simultaneous exhibition. At age twenty he was already Soviet champion.

As an electrical engineer honored for his scientific work, Botvinnik adopted a rigorous, logical approach to chess. He made deep analyses of opening lines, looking for dynamic chances. An example is the Panov-Botvinnik Attack versus the Caro-Kann Defense (1 P-K4, P-QB3 2 P-Q4, P-Q4 3 PxP, PxP 4 P-QB4). He also championed the Winawer Variation of the French (3. . . B-N5) and the Dutch Stonewall, where Black sets up pawns on KB4, K3, Q4, and QB3.

Botvinnik is a technician who considers chess the artistic side of his personality. Basically, his play shows an affinity with the Steinitz-Tarrasch systematizing approach. He heeds Tchigorin's principle of concrete analysis of every position, but the latter's romantic bent is alien to him. A speculative sacrifice by Botvinnik is unheard of.

A good Botvinnik game follows the "grand plan"—a positional strategy resolutely carried out from opening to finish. He can punish the opponent with a vigorous midgame attack but is equally content to exploit a minimal advantage with laborious end-game technique. A perfectionist, he has said that his chief lack is "a weakness of combinational vision." But in his prime he could see as far as anyone. What he really means is that he would have liked to be able to fathom every tactical ramification in every position—in short, to be invincible.

Salo Flohr, born 1908, was the leading new candidate for the world crown in the early 1930s. A classicist, he had a style strongly resembling Capablanca's. He was the hero of Czechoslovakia, where one could buy Flohr

Top: Max Euwe and wife, Moscow, 1948 (l); Reshevsky with Soviet guide (r). Center: Sir Arthur Bliss, composer of ballet Checkmate, *moves for Smyslov, Hastings, 1962 (l); Paul Keres and wife (r). Bottom: Stein plays Black v. Bronstein (l); Viktor Korchnoi (r).*

collars, Flohr eau de cologne, and Flohr cigarettes. Highly impressed by official and popular support for chess in the USSR, he later became a Soviet citizen.

For his match with Flohr in 1933, Botvinnik prepared with what were to become standard Soviet methods: physical training, painstaking study of over a hundred of his opponent's games, and preparation of openings.

The match occasioned great interest. Botvinnik's win in the ninth game was followed by a fifteen-minute ovation punctuated with roars of "Botvinnik!" and "Flohr!" The Soviet public and officialdom were gratified when Botvinnik tied the twelve-game match.

Chosen as a cultural representative of his country to compete at Nottingham in 1936, Botvinnik tied Capablanca for first place. At a time when even chess authors found it necessary to genuflect to the party and its leader, he went so far on the occasion of his big foreign success as to say in a telegram to "beloved teacher and leader" Stalin: "Inspired by your great slogan 'catch up and surpass,' I am glad that I have been able to realize it, if only in that small sector in which our country has entrusted me to fight."

At that time *Pravda* declared, "The USSR is becoming the classical land of chess." The ideological basis was being laid for the postwar proclamation of the "Soviet school of chess." That was the name of a pamphlet by Botvinnik and a book by Kotov and Yudovich which, among other things, rehabilitated Alekhine. In 1944 Botvinnik had written, "Is there a Soviet school of chess? I think there is . . . a characteristic feature of their style is militancy." Kotov and Yudovich admit that a multiplicity of styles can be found among Soviet players, but they cite a common denominator: their resemblance to "Soviet man of the socialist era, an ardent patriot and tireless seeker of the new . . . a struggle against scholastic conceptions of the game." Credit should instead go to the nature of chess itself, in which no ideology, but checkmate alone, is the ultimate arbiter of merit.

In 1948 the vacant world throne, which had once been the exclusive property of the champion, passed into the control of FIDE, which brought together the world's strongest players in a match-tournament for the title. They were Euwe, Reshevsky, the Russians Botvinnik and Vassily Smyslov, and Paul Keres of sovietized Estonia.

Keres, born 1916, became an overnight sensation at the Warsaw Olympiad of 1935 with his daring sacrificial attacks. As co-winner of the powerful AVRO event of 1938, he had long been considered a logical candidate for the world crown. After the war he took the Soviet title three times. In candidates' events, he finished second no less than four times, but always the coveted chance to challenge for the world crown eluded him. Specializing in open games, he has contributed definitive works on opening theory. Although he once confessed, "The older I get, the more I value pawns," he continues to entertain the public with his direct attacking play.

The five-sided world championship event took place in The Hague and Moscow. As expected, the decisive victor was Botvinnik, with 14 out of 20 points. Smyslov was second with 11, Keres and Reshevsky tied for third with 10½, and Euwe trailed with a disastrous 4 points. Thus began a reign which, with two interruptions, was to last fifteen years. With it began the era of Soviet domination of chess.

The record is clearly one of dominance: tenure of the world championship until 1972, at which time the USSR had thirty-three of the world's ninety-six grandmasters and most of the top thirty; victory in every Olympiad in which the USSR participated; and monopoly of all women's championships.

In 1951 Botvinnik had to face his first challenge from another product of Soviet schooling, a brilliant new talent, David Ionovich Bronstein. Bronstein, born in 1924, blazed onto the scene in the Soviet Championship of

1945. He confounded the theorists by successfully adopting a discredited relic from the Romantic era, the King's Gambit. In the Prague-Moscow match that same year his dynamic games with the King's Indian Defense were milestones in chess theory.

Bronstein once claimed, "Chess is imagination." Throughout his career he has remained true to the creative tradition, never ceasing to plow new experimental paths. He is the only big star who plays chess primarily for his own enjoyment and that of the fans, and still brims with original ideas for injecting more interest into the sport. He cares less about victory than he does about vindicating chess as a creative art.

The Botvinnik-Bronstein match was therefore a primordial clash of opposing chessic philosophies. It developed into an intricate and fascinating struggle. As a psychological device, Bronstein adopted Botvinnik's own favorite Dutch Defense. First one player, then the other, took a narrow lead. Exploiting his superior end-game technique, Botvinnik won to even the score in the twenty-third game, drew the next and last, and thus, according to the rules, retained his title.

Years later Bronstein said that his aim in the match was not necessarily to win but to demonstrate that the scientific Botvinnik method was not the only way to play chess. He says that disappointed partisans of the Romantic tradition still approach him in restaurants and ask, "Why did you lose that twenty-third game?"

The other summit battles of the 1950s were waged by a new Soviet star. Vassily Smyslov, born in 1921, had an eminently balanced approach to chess. Without flamboyance he made his way steadily to the top in the rich Soviet milieu. At age nineteen, he was third in the Soviet Championship, a youth who already showed a mature grasp of positional play. At twenty-eight, he tied for the Soviet title with Bronstein. Not brilliant games but sound strategic ideas and good end-game technique were his trademarks. His variation in the Grünfeld Defense constituted a major advance.

At the Zurich Candidates' Tournament of 1953, the Soviet players outnumbered the other participants who, besides Euwe and Reshevsky, included Najdorf, the ebullient romantic from the Argentine, and the solid Gligoric from Yugoslavia. With fine positional and defensive play, Smyslov scored a convincing victory and became the official challenger to Botvinnik.

So began the first of three matches between these two strategists. But unlike Botvinnik, who sought to impose his will upon the chess struggle, the flexible Smyslov was content to probe Caïssa's secrets wherever they led. Their games provide examples of hard-fought, dynamic chess. In the 1954 encounter, Botvinnik grabbed a sudden three-point lead that appeared overwhelming. But Smyslov fought back to an ultimate tie score, 7 wins apiece with 10 draws. Botvinnik had again just barely retained his crown.

After another fine victory in the Amsterdam Candidates' Tournament in 1956, Smyslov was better prepared for the 1957 match. He committed fewer errors and dethroned Botvinnik by a score of 6 wins to 3, with 13 draws. Vassily Smyslov thus became the seventh chess champion of the world.

A year later Botvinnik exercised the deposed champion's right to a return match. At forty-seven, theoretically beyond his peak chess strength, the "iron logician" applied himself to preparing for the rematch with the same single-mindedness that had won him the State Order of the Badge of Honor for his impressive engineering achievements.

For the fourth time running, the world championship match was contested by two Muscovites. At the start, Botvinnik stunned Smyslov with a surprise weapon that he had never used before—the Caro-Kann Defense. Before Smyslov could regain his composure, he had dropped 3 points in three games. The margin proved insuperable, and Botvinnik recaptured his world title with a final score of 7 wins to 5, with 11 draws.

It was an achievement that confirmed Botvinnik's charismatic place in Soviet chess life. He repeated it in 1961 by regaining the crown he had lost the year before to young Mikhail Tal. The Botvinnik era at last came to a close in 1963, with his loss to Petrosian, whom he described as "a computer programmed to play accurate defensive chess." Lamentably, FIDE had abolished the right to a rematch.

Having done battle with every world champion but Steinitz, Botvinnik announced his retirement from chess in 1970. But he left his strong imprint on an entire era and richly merited the appellation, "Mr. Soviet Chess."

BOTVINNIK V. CAPABLANCA
AVRO Tournament, 1938
Nimzoindian Defense

	WHITE	BLACK		WHITE	BLACK
1	P-Q4	N-KB3	5	P-QR3	BxN ch
2	P-QB4	P-K3	6	PxB	P-B4
3	N-QB3	B-N5	7	BPxP	KPxP
4	P-K3	P-Q4	8	B-Q3	0-0
			9	N-K2	P-QN3

White plans to expand with P-B3 and P-K4, while Black seeks to exploit weaknesses on the queen-side.

10	0-0	B-R3	12	B-N2!?	Q-Q2!
11	BxB	NxB	13	P-QR4	KR-K1?!

Good is 13...PxP; 15 BPxP, KR-B1. But instead Capa forestalls P-K4 and plans to win the QRP via a long Knight maneuver.

14	Q-Q3	P-B5?!	15	Q-B2	N-N1
			16	QR-K1!	...

A classicist would not lightly leave his QRP in the lurch. Botvinnik decides to stake it on the dynamic chances he has on the other side. A decision well made.

16	...	N-B3	21	Q-B2	P-N3
17	N-N3	N-QR4	22	P-B4	P-B4
18	P-B3	N-N6	23	PxP ep	NxBP
19	P-K4	QxP	24	P-B5	RxR
20	P-K5	N-Q2	25	RxR	R-K1
			26	R-K6!	RxR

Black would lose shortly after 29...K-B2 30 RxN ch! KxR 31 PxP ch, KxP 32 Q-B5 ch, etc.

27	PxR	K-N2	28	Q-B4!	Q-K1
			29	Q-K5	Q-K2

30	B-R3!!	...

The start of a twelve-move combination! Black must accept the Bishop, for if 30...Q-K1, then 31 Q-B7 ch, K-N1 32 B-K7, N-N5 33 Q-Q7 wins.

30	...	QxB	31	N-R5 ch!	PxN

Or 31...K-R3 32 NxN, Q-B8 ch 33 K-B2, Q-Q7 ch 34 K-N3, QxBP ch 35 K-R4, QxP ch 36 N-N4 ch! and wins.

32	Q-N5 ch	K-B1	36	K-N3	Q-Q6 ch
33	QxN ch	K-N1	37	K-R4	Q-K5 ch
34	P-K7!	Q-B8 ch	38	KxP	Q-K7 ch
35	K-B2	Q-B7 ch	39	K-R4	Q-K5 ch
			40	P-N4	...

Not 40 K-R3?? P-KR4 and draws!

40	...	Q-K8 ch	41	K-R5	Resigns

As Botvinnik foresaw on move 30, mate follows. He called this deep brilliancy "the game of my life." Because it signifies the eclipse of static classical concepts by the new dynamic ideas, we call it "The Dynamic Evergreen."

10.

Recollections of a Coffeehouse Player

"You castle your way and I'll castle my way..."
—George Treysman

In chess, "coffeehouse" is a generic term having many facets. As a description of playing sites, it includes not only coffeehouses, equally popular with chess and coffee addicts, but also park benches, public beach tables, city-sponsored recreation rooms, chess emporiums where players are charged by the hour, card parlors where chess is also played, the smaller chess clubs, and even the larger and more prominent clubs on those frequent occasions when serious tournament chess yields to "pots" and blitz chess, usually for a minor financial consideration.

As a description of the players themselves, coffeehouse refers to those trappy, psychologically oriented players, generally but not always a shade below master rank, who seek quick wins, time being equated with money when giving odds to patzers foolish enough or rich enough to wager on the game. Fischer once slightingly called Emanuel Lasker a coffeehouse player, being irked by Lasker's propensity for getting the worst of a position, then squirming out of it. Bobby has since seen fit to modify his position.

Lastly, as a description of chess play, coffeehouse usually means favoring highly combinative lines, often unsound, over more solid positional considerations. Tal's play, on occasion, has been described as coffeehouse, but Tal's ideas are so brilliantly imaginative that in this instance the word takes on the connotation of admiration.

The experiences of a master engaged in an important tournament (Chapter 12) have their coffeehouse counterpart in the recollections of the co-author (N. L.) as a player in that most coffeehouse of all atmospheres, the Stuyvesant Chess Club of New York.

There has never been another place like the Stuyvesant Chess Club, nor is there likely to be. It was a world in itself, peopled by strange creatures who would rather play chess than do anything else, and play chess they did, from early in the morning until closing time, which was usually between 3 and 4 A.M. Did these people have homes? Some of them evidently did, because they were quick to show snapshots of the wife and kiddies, a form of conscience appeasement, perhaps. A few others were permitted to sleep on tables after the place locked up, a practice tolerated by the pudgy, easy-going proprietor, Jacob Bernstein, more familiarly known as Yonkel.

Located on New York's lower East Side, on Fourteenth Street just west of Second Avenue, the Stuyvesant Chess Club was actually a front for a gambling emporium. It consisted of a long loft in an old brownstone, half a story above street level, with a number of chess tables in front and card tables toward the rear. Back of that, a kitchen catered to the customers' needs—everything from coffee and Danish to a full-course dinner. Since chess-players were not charged for playing and paid no dues, it was expected that they would patronize the restaurant portion of the establishment, some of them doing so when they were solvent. The majority settled for a cup of coffee, more often than not neglecting to pay for it.

The noise and smoke were thick enough to cut in chunks. Bare light bulbs with green mandarin-hat shades hung over the tables, forming illuminated triangles of smoke. One would expect noise from the card players, arguments being common, but truth to tell, most of the noise came from the chess group. Epithets like "patzer!", "pfuscher!", "dummkopf!", "nebbish!", "schlemiel!" rent the air, or what was left of it. Certain established short-cuts were taken in the constant barrage of insults. For instance, Player A would make a move and Player B would immediately volunteer, "You're an idiot yourself!" The stranger looking on might be puzzled, but the meaning was quite clear. "If A makes this move," reasons B, "he must think I'm an idiot." He therefore eliminates the

Opening pages: Café de la Régence in 19th-century Paris, historically the most famous abode of coffeehouse chess. Below: Charles Jaffe, dubbed "Crown Prince of East Side Chess," playing author Lessing (with more hair than today), c. 1931.

middle phrase by responding, "You're an idiot yourself!"

It must not be supposed that the cultural level was low. Indeed, there were those who could discourse quite eloquently on literature, music, and art, and their ranks were occasionally swelled by visiting artists, musicians, and the like from uptown. The big question remains, how did the habitués of the Stuyvesant Chess Club make a living? The mathematically improbable answer is—from each other. No game was played without a cash stake, which ranged from a dime to a dollar, usually something between the two. Of course, the ranks were swelled by local storekeepers and neighborhood job-holders, who contributed to the general fund, but the basic question remains a mystery. One thing was certain—nobody got rich.

Some of the denizens sported proper names, but most were immediately labeled with some more colorful appellation. One who chanced to bear the surname of the Krupp munitions family as well as a huge nose was dubbed "Krupp mit der cannon." "City College," a thin, bitter little man, earned his title by constantly springing such snappish questions as, "You think you're so smart? How do you spell avoirdupois?" (He pronounced it "avoyer-dupoyz.")

"*Fahrfahlen*" was the nickname attached to a rubicund, elderly gentleman simply because of his aversion to the word. It is the Germanic-Yiddish equivalent of "all is lost" and, in another sense, "fallen" or "caved in." He was playing a gadfly of a man named Miller one night, when Miller, urging him to resign, said, "You have a lost position. *Fahrfahlen!*"

"Don't say that word!" screamed the old man.

The gadfly's face lit up with joy. "You mean I shouldn't say '*Fahrfahlen,*' Fahrfahlen?"

With each repetition the old man yelped in pain. That's all it took. On successive nights similes abounded. "Fahrfahlen! Fahrfahlen like string and spaghetti! Fahrfahlen like a duck's behind!" Once the old man was peacefully carrying a glass of tea on a saucer from the kitchen when Miller entered. "Fahrfahlen!" he shrieked in greeting.

The old man's hands shot up in the air, the tea splattering and scalding a table of irate card players. Miller, of course, was in ecstasy.

Dr. Slowly, a retired dentist, garnered the adverb from his habit of admonishing, "Slowly, slowly . . ." whenever his opponent made what appeared to be a forceful move. Doc Slowly had a weird fixation about "the bones of Christ," and spoke often of financing an expedition to recover them, which would, in some mysterious way, bring fame and fortune to all participants. His harangues sometimes got on the listeners' nerves. "Hey, Slowly," a chess-player some tables away would yell out, "do you believe in the hereafter?"

"So?"

"So hereafter keep your mouth shut!"

Another chortled, "Finance an expedition! That guy wouldn't pay a nickel to see the Statue of Liberty do a split." But more of Slowly later.

The Stuyvesant Chess Club had an amazingly high complement of strong players, often fielding a team in the city interclub competition which defeated the highly vaunted Manhattan and Marshall clubs. Jacob Bernstein himself was a strong chess master, his love of chess accounting for his many kindnesses toward chess-players. His living quarters were on the third floor of the building, and he was married to a plump, ebullient Irishwoman who obviously adored him. Mrs. Bernstein had a large number of brothers and cousins on the police force, and it was something, on a Friday night, with Mrs. Bernstein preparing her husband's favorite Jewish dishes, to see Yonkel holding court before an admiring audience of police in uniform, right above his illegal gambling domain.

Yonkel was a patient, unflappable man, as indeed he had to be to arbitrate the inevitable disputes among card- and chess-players. Once, long ago, at a Wilson-for-President rally, he raised his hand to ask a question. "Mr. Wilson, is it true that if you're elected, every man will have work?"

Wilson answered that such was the case.

"But, Mr. Wilson," Yonkel protested, "I don't want to work. I'm a gambler."

Charles Jaffe, a slight, gypsy-like man, whom Alfred Kreymborg, the poet, dubbed "the Crown Prince of East Side Chess," held court most often at the Stuyvesant. He came by his title because of his many devoted subject kibitzers for whom Jaffe could do no wrong. He was especially good at giving huge odds to grossly inferior players and pulled off many a sparkling combination in the process. Jaffe was famous for his poverty, a circumstance which prompted many a wag to remark: "Charlie Jaffe? I knew him when he was poor!" Nevertheless, he scraped his pennies together in order to send a cable to Alekhine, then engaged in his world-championship match with Capablanca at Buenos Aires. The cable contained an analysis of a variation of the Queen's Gambit with a new move suggested by Jaffe, which Alekhine is thought to have adopted.

Not many nice things are said about Alekhine as a person, so it is pleasant to record that upon his return to New York he returned the favor by agreeing to play a two-game match with Jaffe, without financial remuneration, at the Hotel Astor. The match proved nothing, of course, and Jaffe was soundly trounced, but it was a generous gesture on the part of Alekhine.

Jaffe was a spirited player who always took a dare over the chessboard. His style was inimitably coffeehouse which, win or lose, made it a delight for the spectators. He beat me in many brilliant games, and on occasion I managed to do the same. That I have the score of one of these offhand games, which I happened to win, is due to a friend who jotted it down, a well-known violinist, who at that time used to like to watch me play until the wee hours of the morning. The crucial position is appended because it is a prime example of coffeehouse chess.

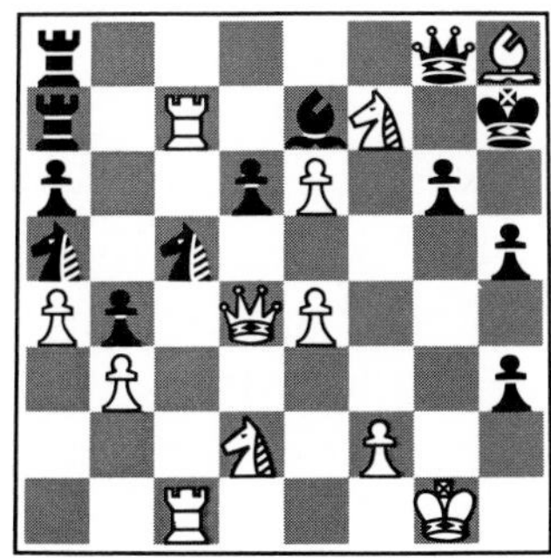

Jaffe, playing the black side of a Ruy Lopez, had defended ingeniously against mounting pressure. Now, after his last move of 36. . ./Q2-B4, he threatens NxP/K3 as well as the exchange of Rooks. He seems out of the woods, but:

37	RxB!	RxR
38	RxN!	PxR
39	N-B3!!	. . .

The point of the last two sacrifices. The third offer, of a Queen, cannot be accepted because of 40 N/3-N5 mate. White now gains an all-important tempo. The rest of the moves are more or less forced.

39	. . .	RxN
40	N-N5 ch	K-R3
41	NxR ch	K-R2
42	QxBP	NxP
43	Q-K3	Q-KB1
44	QxN	Q-B4
45	Q-N2	R-KN1
46	B-Q4	Q-K2
47	B-B6	Q-B4
48	N-N5 ch	K-R3
49	Q-Q2	Q-KB1
50	P-K5	R-R1
51	P-K7	Resigns

It was close to 3 A.M. when the game was finished. My violinist friend promised to send me a copy of his score sheet. "Why do you waste so much time here?" I playfully chided him. "Why don't you stay home and practice?"

"I can practice any time," he answered, "but where else can I see such beautiful chess?"

One of the most interesting members of the old Stuyvesant Club and probably the strongest natural player I have ever known was George Treysman. Treysman never cracked a chess book or, I suspect, many books of whatever description. Nevertheless, he was possessed of a keen intelligence and a biting, mordant wit. Playing in his only major event—the first modern United States championship in 1936—Treysman, a virtual unknown, as-

George Treysman, coffeehouse player par excellence. *Though Treysman played only for cash stakes, he astounded the chess world by emerging from relative obscurity to tie with Reuben Fine for third place in the U.S. championship tournament of 1936.*

Opposite: Chess House, New York City. Note backgammon game in foreground—only fitting, since an early precursor of chess, played with dice, had its roots in backgammon, a game the ancient Persians called nard. *Chess has come a long way since.*

tounded the cognoscenti by leading much of the way and tying for third with Grandmaster Reuben Fine.

Jaffe was too soft and easygoing to take undue advantage of the suckers he played, but Treysman was the chess hustler *par excellence,* combining psychology and insult in a way that made his chess victims eager to play him, even against their better judgment. I was quite young and inexperienced when we first met, and he gave me many a sound drubbing. As my game developed and I became accustomed to his style, I was able to hold my own. One day when I challenged him to a game, Treysman, who never played except to make money, said, "Look, kid, why should we play each other? It's like the horses betting on the horses." I swelled with pride. It was as though I had just received my diploma. From that moment on we became fast friends.

George, like another player nicknamed "Caruso," was fond of singing little songs as he played, especially with a win in sight—such tender old favorites as "Who Hit Nelly in the Belly with a Flounder?" and one whose constant refrain went, "They call me Shirley, because my hair is curly." He was so fond of the latter that after a while we really did call him Shirley.

Since I was less dependent on chess for a living than he was, I often steered customers his way. Spotting a well-dressed prospect, I'd call out, "Hey, Shirley, here comes a live one."

George would approach his prey courteously enough. "Would you care for a game of chess, sir?"

This usually produced a wary response. "Chess? No, I don't think so."

"Pinochle, maybe? Clabriash?"

"Not interested."

"Casino, dominoes? Maybe you'd like to shoot a game of pool? They got a nice pool hall across the street." The customer would try to wave him off but George was a hard man to shake. "Ping-Pong, tiddlywinks? What's your best game? I'll play you anything you want and give you odds, that's how much I think of you."

By this time the man was angry. "Okay, I'll play you chess. What odds will you give me?"

George would pretend to be deeply offended. "Odds? A man comes in wearing a double-breasted English suit with patch pockets and he asks for odds!"

"You said you'd give me odds."

"Okay, stuck is stuck. I'll give you pawn and move."

Like as not, as the odds and stakes increased with each game, George would end up giving the man a Queen. The fish was firmly hooked.

A famous Treysman story concerns the time he was giving Queen odds to a player a little too strong for that tremendous handicap. To iron out the difference Treysman devised a new way of castling on the king-side. Instead of placing the Rook on the King Bishop square, he moved it at once to the King square, thereby gaining a full move. Finally, the pfuscher caught on.

"How come," he asked, "when I castle, my Rook ends up on the Bishop square and when you castle, your Rook ends up on the King square?"

Then Treysman uttered his immortal remark.

"Look," he said reasonably, "you castle your way and I'll castle my way, okay?"

"Okay," agreed the fish.

Besides the United States championship, George played in only one other tournament, to my knowledge, and that was for the Stuyvesant Chess Club Championship, which I was fortunate enough to win by a score of 11½ to ½. My last-round draw occurred with George, who finished second. But in all fairness, I must acknowledge that Treysman played under a serious disadvantage. He lacked the incentive of immediate financial gain. True, Yonkel Bernstein generously donated a purse for the winner, but this constituted a long-term arrangement of no

Opposite: The Olive Tree, another New York coffeehouse featuring chess. From time immemorial, atmosphere of coffeehouse chess has been the same, spiced with wit and occasional invective, outspoken kibbitzing, and—contrary to a commonly held view—noise.

practical use to a man who had to pay for his dinner that same night. George Treysman had only one weakness as a chess-player. He liked to be paid after every game.

»»««

The year was 1933 and I still remember the excitement when I entered the club. "He's here . . . Alekhine's here!" And, sure enough, there he was in the Stuyvesant Chess Club, large as life, playing not chess, but bridge. Alekhine was obviously drunk, chain-smoking like a fiend, slapping down his cards, and finding fault with his partner. Finally, he accused his partner of being in league with the opposition, angrily threw down his cards, and stalked off toward the chess section. "Who's the strongest player here? I'll give good odds," he challenged.

There was a deep silence. City College sidled up to me, sneering. "*Nu,* big shot, how come you're so quiet?"

I asked, "What kind of odds, Mr. Alekhine?"

Alekhine sized me up shrewdly. From the smiles and expectant attitudes of the others, he sensed that I was a strong player. "Draw odds?" he offered.

I shook my head. "Not enough."

"Pawn and move."

"For how much?"

"Whatever is your pleasure."

"Ten dollars," I said.

There was a buzz. Ten dollars at the height of the Depression was a lot of money to chess-players. One of the chess tables was dragged out from the wall to the center of the room. A fresh linoleum board was provided and the genial Bernstein brought a brand new chess set out of his private closet. The set, like most in use then, was a genuine Staunton made of wood, and very beautiful.

We were immediately encircled by a ten-deep ring of spectators. Those on the outer fringes stood on chairs and tables to see better. Even the card-players deserted their tables. Some of them didn't even know how to play chess. Most amazing of all, it became very quiet, probably for the only time in the history of the club.

Although the smoke was thick as usual, it was even thicker around Alekhine. He kept puffing away and seemed very nervous. By contrast, I appeared calm. Odds of pawn and move meant that I had the move with the white pieces; Alekhine removed his King Bishop pawn. I played the usual move against those odds of 1 P-K4. It meant that Black could not play P-K4 in response, nor the Sicilian P-QB4. In both cases, 2 Q-R5 ch would win at least another pawn. The usual answer for Black is P-K3. To my surprise, Alekhine played 1 . . . P-Q4! In retrospect, my best reply would have been 2 PxP, but I saw a quick chance to grab another pawn. The truth is I was overconfident! (Overconfident against the World Champion? Well, I was young. I aged rapidly during the game, however.) Thus, I played: 2 Q-R5 ch, P-N3 3 QxQP, QxQ!

And now, Alekhine, with two pawns down, was actually exchanging Queens! Who could ask for anything more? Play continued: 4 PxQ, N-KB3. After this ordinary and expected move, I experienced my first slight chill. I saw I could not hold the pawn with the natural 5 N-QB3. Black could bring his Queen's Knight to QN3, castle queen-side, and win a pawn back with better development. Where was the initiative I was supposed to get with pawn and move? As compensation for this lack, I determined to hold the pawn at all costs. So:

5 P-QB4 P-B3!

Alekhine didn't give a hoot about the pawn. Like Morphy, all he wanted was quick development.

6 PxP NxP **7** N-KB3 P-K4
8 P-Q3 . . .

I had to stop 8 . . . P-K5.

8 . . . B-KB4!

What to do? 9 N-R4, N-Q5 10 NxB, PxN 11 K-Q1, 0-0-0 allows a dangerous offensive thrust for Black. I was no longer so confident. Now Alekhine appeared calm and I was nervous. It looked as though my backward pawn

at Q3 had to fall. I would still be one pawn ahead, but Alekhine would have a superior position, enough to win back the pawn, perhaps. And then, with an even game. . . .

If Alekhine were alive today, he might possibly remember the exact order of the ensuing moves, as he did in so many of his unimportant games. Frankly, I cannot—except for the general impression that it all came out exactly as I had sensed. The Queen pawn did fall, and Alekhine kept applying pressure until I was only too happy to give up my original pawn-plus for an opportunity to bring about a flurry of exchanges. With scant material left, the position was a dead draw, which Alekhine conceded after a few ineffectual maneuvers.

Alekhine was no longer drunk. He seemed much less irritable now, quickly setting up the black pieces, minus the King Bishop pawn, for another game. It was at this point that I made my wisest move of the night.

"*Encore une partie?*" he invited.

"*Merci, non,*" I politely declined.

By fair means or foul, the coffeehouse player has only one object—to win. At the Stuyvesant almost any method was tolerated. Only violence was frowned upon.

Once, in a heated argument over a wager, a chessplayer pulled a gun on his opponent. A shocked silence fell. Attracted by the lack of noise, Bernstein quickly made his way to the scene. He cast a Jovian look of reproach and scorn upon the would-be gunman. We fully expected the offender to be struck dead by a bolt of lightning. As Yonkel opened his mouth to speak we waited for the rumble of thunder. "Feh," he said quietly, "that's not nice." The man put the gun back in his pocket.

There is a familiar story about the ancient who hid his Rook at the corner of the board with his long beard. At the propitious moment he surprised his opponent by lifting his beard and sweeping down the board with his hidden Rook to capture a piece. The story may very well be true. The technique, however, is useless to those without the necessary hirsute equipment.

The more generally approved method is, while moving another piece, to brush your Rook with your elbow so that it is half-off the square. Another move may be all that is required to brush it off the square entirely. Your partner either overlooks it or, noticing it, hopes that you have overlooked it and are playing with a Rook down. At the crucial time, when the Rook can come into play with devastating force, you pretend astonishment and say, "Where's my Rook? Didn't I have a Rook here?" Your opponent, of course, is helpless to deny it. You smoothly snip off his Queen.

Participating in the National Open at Las Vegas some years back, I had occasion to try a coffeehouse trick. Playing blackjack till 4 A.M. is not conducive to a morning tournament round of chess starting at 9 A.M., even against a lower-rated player. My opponent had the white pieces and the game went: 1 P-K4, P-K4 2 N-KB3, N-QB3 3 B-B4. I was about to answer with 3 . . . B-B4, when I had the uncanny premonition (later confirmed by my adversary) that he intended to play the Evans Gambit. The game would then have continued: 3 . . . B-B4 4 P-QN4, BxP 5 P-B3, B-R4 6 P-Q4. This was okay with me. I knew the line well, and the pawn sacrifice usually leads to a favorable game for Black.

The only trouble was that in making my third move, instead of stopping with the Bishop at B4, I placed it at once at its ultimate destination, QN5. This was a horrible blunder. White now had all the advantages of the P-B3 move without sacrificing anything.

Though immediately realizing my error, I put on a cool and smiling act. My opponent, suspecting some deep trap, thought a full fifteen minutes. Then, just as he was about to make the right move, I inquired casually, as though surprised by the long delay, "What's the matter? Haven't you ever seen the Kravetz Defense?" His hand hung suspended in midair. My remark cost him another fifteen minutes of his precious playing time. I would like to be able to report that he lost the game on this account. Candor compels me to admit, however, that my position was too compromised and I lost. But it was a good try.

In most cases the moves are all that matters. In coffeehouse chess it's how you make the moves. The object is always to disconcert, intimidate, or infuriate the opposition. Listed below are some common techniques for the aspiring student:

"The Hammer"—The piece is lifted high in the air and brought down on the square with great force. It is designed to terrify your opponent.

"The Sledgehammer"—This should only be used in a dead-lost position. The piece is brought down with such power that all the other pieces are sent flying. Efforts to reconstruct the position fail. You start another game.

"La Delicatesse"—This is the most potent reply to the "Hammer." Pinky in the air, the piece is not lifted at all but delicately shoved into position. The more violently the "Hammer" responds, the more delicately you make each ensuing move. Guaranteed to drive the "Hammer" berserk.

"La Delicatessen"—This is done by chewing a sandwich, preferably hot pastrami, while leaning across the board. The fumes should engulf your opponent.

"La Patisserie"—Much favored by Donald Byrne. Substitute cream puffs for pastrami.

"The Rapier"—Thrust swiftly *through* your opponent's pieces to skewer the piece you intend to capture.

Other pieces you knock off can be replaced to your advantage.

"The Straddler"—Put a piece down where it straddles two squares. As the position develops, take your choice.

"The Screw"—Screw the piece firmly into the square. This gives the impression of great scientific solidity. Practiced by World Champion Smyslov.

"The Palsy"—Don't put the piece down at once but let it hang suspended while your hand shakes violently. Your opponent will feel so sorry for you, he'll throw the game.

"The Feint"—This is designed for the pro to keep a new sucker on the hook. He acts as if he is about to put the Knight down on a square which would permit an immediate mate by the patzer's Rook. Then, as if changing his mind on a whim at the last moment, he makes a move forking the King and Rook. The sucker, convinced the pro has won by sheer luck, can't wait to pay up and start the next game.

"The Trill"—Preceded by a certain amount of normal singing. Then, as if struck by an extraordinary combination, let your voice rise higher and higher in a crescendo which can only be terminated by checkmate.

"The Trill Is Gone"—Looking intently at the board, choke off the trill in mid-note, as though struck by a combination even more magnificent than the original inspiration. Your opponent will find the sudden silence even more unnerving.

There are many more we could list: "The Sweeper," "The Swinger," "The Grovel," "The Hovering Hand," "The Punchboard," "The Swimmer," "The Nibbler," "The Mouse," "The Snake," etc., but the student should have enough here for openers. One of the most successful practitioners of these devices, particularly "La Delicatesse," was the previously mentioned Dr. Slowly. His steady opponent was a man called "Mutik with the Scar," who was a "Hammer." As noted before, "Delicatesse" invariably beats "Hammer," and such proved to be the case.

Mutik was a dour, apoplectic individual with a certain ready wit, unfortunately too scatological to be quoted here. Dr. Slowly almost literally drove him up the wall. As each game progressed Mutik's rage mounted, the scar on his chin glowed whiter and whiter, and a steady stream of invective poured from his lips. But Slowly was impervious to insult. As Mutik banged each piece down with increasing force, Slowly raised his hand in mock alarm, cautioning, "Slowly, slowly..." then made each move more delicately than the last, little finger poised aloft, slowly sliding each piece into place like a pianist caressing a Chopin nocturne.

Their constant stake was fifty cents a game and Mutik always had a plentiful supply of half-dollars handy, since he always lost. The method of payment never varied. Mutik took out a half-dollar, spat on it, and tossed it contemptuously on the board. Slowly picked up the coin delicately between thumb and forefinger, wiped it carefully on his vest front, and inserted it into his vest pocket. Calmly, he proceeded to set up his side for the next game. Mutik glared at him for a long moment, then followed suit. The ritual was repeated time after time, day after day, rain or shine, for at least ten years that I remember.

Then one day the good doctor met with an accident. A truck had, apparently, not heeded his admonition of "Slowly, slowly...." With Slowly's death, Mutik's whole attitude changed. He still came to the club, but he sat quietly next to the table where they used to play, rarely speaking, never raising his voice. Once in a great while he would try to play a game of chess, even make an attempt at the old rhetoric of insult, but it was done without spirit. Eventually he stopped playing altogether, and finally he stopped coming to the club. A short time later we learned that he too had passed away. Some whispered that he had died of a broken heart.

11.

Champions of the Sixties

> "There are two kind of sacrifices—correct ones, and mine!" —Mikhail Tal

While sojourning on the Baltic Sea early in his reign as world champion, Botvinnik was approached by a slight youngster who boldly challenged him to a chess game. Within a dozen years, the boy was to play him in a championship match. The boy was Mikhail Tal.

Mikhail Nekhemovich Tal is the most brilliant player of our time. He's never sacrificed two Rooks and a Queen like Anderssen, but in this day of advanced defensive technique, Tal's speculative offers of a Knight are even more impressive. His exciting play electrifies every stage on which he performs.

The frail youth with the striking black eyes, born in Latvia in 1936, rocketed to the top at age twenty, winning the Soviet championship. The new star had a style unique for this or any era. He always attacked. He plunged into the most hair-raising complications with carefree abandon, seemingly able to turn any position into wild channels despite the contrary will of the most experienced opponent. Gaily sacrificing pawns and pieces, he saw further than anyone else and emerged victorious.

Tal made sacrifices that could not stand the cold, objective test of post-mortem analysis, yet he could beat the very best. Soon he became known as a wizard, a magician, a mesmerizer. One grandmaster opponent even wore dark glasses to his game with Tal to avert the "evil eye."

Tal defied the whole orderly, methodical approach to the game by which others lived and breathed. His heritage goes back to Lasker, who preyed on the psyche of the opponent, and Alekhine, who could shake brilliant surprises out of placid positions. Correctness or the high risk of losing did not matter to "Mischa"—only the joy of battle.

His secret: an incomparable sense of humor. To spend an hour with Mischa is to hear sixty quips, puns, and witticisms. Urged to wear an overcoat because he is a national resource, Tal responds, "Yes, like caviar." Informed of a new government campaign against alcoholism, "State vs. Vodka," Tal says, "I'll play for the Vodka team!" Asked if sixteen-year-old Bobby Fischer, one of the eight qualified candidates for the world championship in 1959, had any chance, Tal replied, "Yes—for the junior title."

The winner of that candidates' event was Tal himself, and in 1960 he faced Botvinnik for the world crown. Tal jumped into the lead in the very first game. After four draws, he chose Game 6 to unleash one of his typical, incalculable piece sacrifices, disturbing Botvinnik's methodical conduct of the position. In the maze of complications, first one, then the other, played dubious continuations. Then a single path presented itself by which the champion could secure a clear advantage. Alas, he missed his way, and Tal went on to regain his piece and win. It was almost as if the twenty-three-year-old Tal had trifled with "Mr. Soviet Chess." At last, by a score of 6 wins, 2 losses, and 13 draws, Mikhail Tal became the eighth chess champion of the world, the youngest ever.

For the 1961 rematch, Botvinnik did his homework. He was determined to get Tal into closed positions with restricted piece activity. There Tal's flaming imagination would be confined. It worked. Finding himself trailing at midway, Tal abandoned all caution and compromised his positions with futile attempts to gain activity. At match's end, Botvinnik had for the second time recaptured the world crown, with 10 wins, 5 losses, and only 6 draws. Tal had lost his magic.

Soon a new factor made itself felt in Tal's career: ill health. His play became quieter and his results declined. With the onset of the 1970s, Tal underwent kidney surgery, and his fortunes turned upwards. Prior to the Leningrad Interzonal of 1973, he was first in five consecutive events, playing eighty-three games without a

Opening pages: Early Soviet set pits Workers v. Capitalists. Worker King has peasant-pawns holding sickles, Queen holding wheat. Capitalist King has death's head and pawns in chains. Russian Czar fell in Revolution, but chess King survived.

single loss. The global press was abuzz with predictions that Tal was heading again for the summit. Soviet officialdom, eager to recoup the world title, hovered expectantly.

The Interzonal began with a shock. Tal lost to two outsiders! The magician who had once faced down all the greats in the game of "chicken" confessed, "It was my nerves." Then he got food poisoning. Soon all hope for another challengers' berth was dead. People had demanded too much. The conjurer was, after all, only human.

But no matter. Mischa was soon joking again, playing rapid games for the sheer fun of it. The immortal Tal had already given more joy to the world of chess than all the dry technicians who ever existed.

TAL V. KELLER
Zurich, 1959
Queen's Gambit Declined

	WHITE	BLACK		WHITE	BLACK
1	N-KB3	K-KB3	4	P-Q4	P-B3
2	P-B4	P-K3	5	B-N5	PxP
3	N-B3	P-Q4	6	P-K4	P-N4
			7	P-QR4!?	. . .

Usual in this sharp line of Botvinnik's is 7 P-K5, P-KR3 8 B-R4, P-N4 9 KNxP. Now Black should play 7. . . B-N5.

7	. . .	Q-N3?!	10	0-0	B-QN2
8	BxN	PxB	11	P-Q5!	BPxP
9	B-K2	P-QR3	12	KPxP	P-N5
			13	P-R5	Q-B2

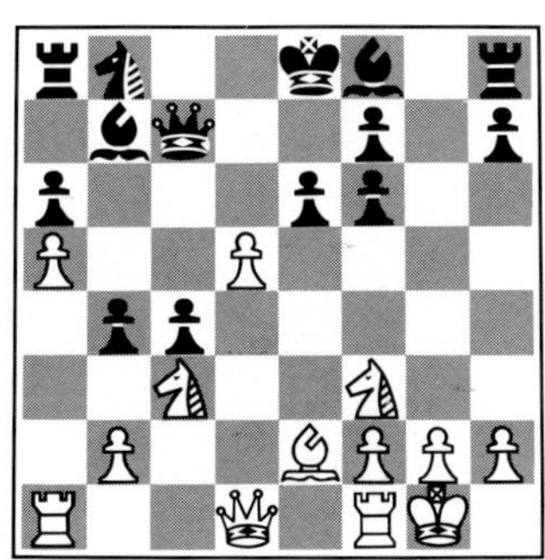

14 PxP!!? . . .

Tal's element! He offers a Knight, attacks the exposed King, and brings on incalculable complications.

14	. . .	PxN	15	N-Q4!	. . .

Planning something like 15. . . PxNP 16 Q-R4 ch! N-B3 17 PxP ch, QxP 18 NxN! PxR/Q 19 RxQ and "the naked King cannot survive."—Clarke

15	. . .	R-N1	17	P-KN3	B-Q4
16	Q-R4 ch	K-Q1	18	KR-Q1	K-B1
			19	NPxP?	. . .

Even Tal may go astray in his own labyrinths—19 Q-K8 ch, K-N2 20 NPxP probably wins.

19	. . .	B-B4	20	P-K7!	N-B3?

The Swiss master falters. Necessary was 20. . . BxP and holds on.

21	B-N4 ch!	K-N2	22	N-N5?!	. . .

A new Knight offer which can hardly be accepted. But 22 NxN! wins, e.g. 22. . . QxN 23 RxB! QxR 24 B-B3! QxB 25 Q-Q7 ch, K-N1 26 R-N1 ch and mates.

22	. . .	Q-K4!	24	QR-N1!	RxB
23	R-K1	B-K5!?	25	RxB!	QxR

Or 25. . . RxR 26 N-Q4 ch, N-N5! 27 Q-Q7 ch with a likelihood of perpetual check.

26	N-Q6 ch	K-B2	27	NxQ	RxN
			28	Q-Q1	R-K4??

A typical blunder due to time pressure and Tal's "sorcery." It was time to end the pawn's charmed life. After 28. . . RxP, Black would have more than enough compensation for the Queen. Now comes the last and most crushing of Tal's blows.

29	R-N7 ch!	KxR	32	QxR ch	K-N2
30	Q-Q7 ch	K-N1	33	Q-Q7 ch	K-N1
31	P-K8/Q ch	RxQ	34	QxN	Resigns

In 1950 the women's world championship was revived. Invariably, the title has gone to Soviet representatives. These champions include Ludmilla Rudenko,

Young Tal (l) beats Botvinnik in opening game of 1960 title match at Moscow's 1,000-seat Pushkin Theater. Harry Golombek officiates. Opposite: Overflow crowd watches progress of fourth game on demonstration board in street. Brilliant Tal is a crowd pleaser.

who held the title until 1953, Elizaveta Bykova (1953-56 and 1958-62), and Olga Rubtsova (1956-58). All were born before the Revolution. In 1962, Bykova lost her title match by a score of 9-2 to a newcomer. And therein lies another story.

Honored chess trainer of the Georgian Soviet Socialist Republic, Karseladze, who had a sharp eye for talent, was visiting a provincial town in 1953. There he spied a twelve-year-old girl who looked promising. Her name: Nona Gaprindashvili.

He persuaded her parents to send her to live with an aunt in Tbilisi, the capital. There she could get lessons and develop her skill at the Palace of Young Pioneers, whose most famous alumnus was Petrosian. The trainer's hunch was right. At twenty-one, Nona was women's champion of the world. To American ears, Flohr's description of Nona's return home sounds incredible: "Young and old, great and small mobbed to see her, shake her hand, embrace her, and kiss her. Day after day she was feted in banquets.... Wherever she went crowds gathered.... It was like Gagarin [the astronaut] over again."

This native daughter of the Georgians, a warm and hospitable people proud of their ancient heritage, was a better chess-player than any woman from Great Russia.

ВИННИК
ТАЛЬ

Mass interest produced Soviet champions. Red Army Club chess room in Moscow (top). Lessons for twelve- and thirteen-year-olds at Leningrad Palace of Pioneers—a scene repeated throughout USSR (bottom l). Russian sailors playing on hatch cover at sea.

She was, in fact, the best in the world. Georgia had a new national heroine overnight, and suddenly every girl in the republic wanted to play chess. Soon one, then another Georgian girl became a champion. In the meantime Nona retained her title in three matches with Moscow's Alla Kushnir. (When Kushnir won the first game of one match, Petrosian called it "a palace revolution in the amazon kingdom.") Dr. Euwe rates Nona as equal to Menchik.

Gaprindashvili's talent is well-rounded. Her ability is evident in every aspect of the game, as several international masters have had to learn on the few occasions when she has taken part in men's events. Here is an example of her skill and daring in attack.

GAPRINDASHVILI V. RINDER
England, 1967
Sicilian Defense

	WHITE	BLACK		WHITE	BLACK
1	P-K4	P-QB4	3	N-B3	P-Q3
2	N-KB3	P-K3	4	P-KN3	. . .

A closed system which here serves, after passive deployment by Black, as a prelude to aggression.

4	. . .	N-Q2	7	P-Q3	P-QR3
5	B-N2	KN-B3	8	P-QR4	R-QN1
6	0-0	B-K2	9	N-Q2	. . .

Preparing a pawn-storm. Black needs counterplay with . . .P-QN4.

9	. . .	0-0	11	P-KN4!	B-N2
10	P-B4	P-QN3?!	12	P-N5	N-K1
			13	N-B3	P-Q4?

Giving White a target. Black should contest the king-side buildup with 13. . .P-N3 and . . .N-N2.

14	PxP	PxP	17	B-Q2	N-B1
15	N-R4	N-B2	18	Q-R5	B-B1
16	N-B5	R-K1	19	N-N3?!	. . .

White could get excellent chances with the piece sac, 19 NxNP! KxN 20 P-B5 followed by P-N6.

19	. . .	N/1-K3	21	Q-R4	N-Q5
20	QR-K1	P-N3	22	R-K5!	N-B3

If 22. . . B-K3, then White has a very promising Exchange sacrifice: 23 P-B5!, PxP 24 NxBP! NxN 25 R/5xN. But now Nona plays in brilliant style.

23	RxP!	NxR	24	BxN	N-N5?!

Better 24. . .N-Q5, but 25 BxP ch! KxB 26 QxP ch, K-K3 27 P-B5 ch PxP 28 NxP should still win, despite the investment of a Rook.

25	BxP ch!	KxB	26	QxP ch	K-B1

Or 26. . .K-K3 27 P-B5 ch, and with B-B4 ch in the offing, White wins easily.

27	P-B5	Q-Q5 ch	29	NxP	B-N2 ch
28	K-N2	PxP	30	K-N3	Resigns

For mate is inevitable.

A visit to Tbilisi in 1973 revealed a totally female-oriented chess community. In the city of chess amazons, even the top male players devote less time to their own careers than to coaching budding female talents. One of them confessed, referring to his favorite girl, "I spent the whole night with her—analyzing her adjourned game." It could only happen in the USSR.

Tigran Vartanovich Petrosian, born in 1929, caused no big splashes. He played quiet, refined chess. In his Soviet championship debut at age twenty there was no promise of anything world-shaking in his result: sixteenth place. It would take him eight tries before becoming Soviet Champion.

Petrosian hardly ever attacked. His play was characterized by many draws. Wins, often in long end games, were fewer. His mastery of strategy owed much to Capablanca and Nimzovich. He was very hard to beat. Strong players tried to attack him but could rarely corner him. He always seemed to slip out.

After a while, experts began to notice something unique in his unspectacular play. He was conducting his

campaign according to a negative principle—that of preventing every active chance of the enemy pieces. Aloof from the fans' complaints, he played not so much to win as to avoid loss.

Petrosian calls his unique chessic philosophy "Prevention." While it offers little to those fans who clamor for brilliancies, connoisseurs have come to appreciate his uncanny ability to foresee and abort every enemy threat. Once done, he can exploit the most minimal weakness and win in as many as a hundred moves.

Petrosian had won very few first prizes before Curaçao in 1962, where, thanks to a last-minute upset suffered by Keres, he nosed out both Keres and Geller by a mere ½-point and found himself in a role he did not wholly want—the official challenger to World Champion Botvinnik.

After the first game of their 1963 match, Petrosian admitted that he'd played like a "small child" who felt himself up against a "national institution." The fifth game took a characteristic course: 1 P-QB4, P-KN3 2 P-Q4, N-KB3 3 N-QB3, P-Q4 4 N-B3, B-N2 5 P-K3 (a modest move against the Grünfeld Defense) 0-0 6 B-K2, PxP 7 BxP, P-B4 8 P-Q5, P-K3 9 PxP, QxQ ch 10 KxQ, BxP 11 BxB, PxB.

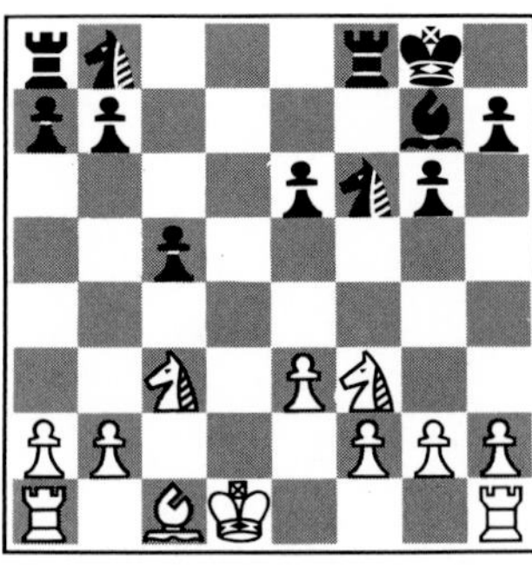

White's minimal advantage consists of a strong point on K4 for a Knight, in front of Black's isolated KP. Petrosian had anticipated this very position before the match and told his second that he would win it. In a display of fine technique, he did in fact win in another thirty-seven moves, evening the match score.

Frustrated by Petrosian's subtle preventive play, Botvinnik could win only one more game in the match. He tired in the late stretch and fell behind. At last, by a score of 5 wins, only 2 losses, and 15 draws—the largest number of draws ever for a title match of this length—Petrosian became the ninth chess champion of the world.

The reigning spirit of the 1960s became the doctrine of Prevention. But it, too, would pass.

Bent Larsen is today's leading standard-bearer for the creative tradition in the art of chess. Born in Denmark in 1935, he grew up in the era of Botvinnik, the Scientist, in which young players all over the world were learning chess technique from tomes of accumulated knowledge. Unlike the Soviet aspirants, Larsen developed his talent without a vast machine of trainers, seconds, and economic security, and he took a different approach. He is the Neo-romantic who said: "Chess is a beautiful mistress to whom we keep coming back, no matter how many times she rejects us."

A true lover of Caïssa, he refuses to accept limitations. He tries out new ideas in every game and approaches each as a fresh, creative challenge. He is not only an artist but a great fighter too. He plays always to win, disdains the draw, and is immune to the pang of defeat, from which he rebounds to greater victories.

Larsen plays ultra-Hypermodern ideas as well as openings that had their heyday in the Romantic era; he plays intricate strategical maneuvers and also sparkling sacrificial attacks. He delights in the infinite variety of Caïssa's beauty.

But in his style of play, Larsen more resembles the Hypermoderns. His openings are indeed the most original since the 1920s. Not only has he resurrected the Bishop's Opening (1 P-K4, P-K4 2 B-B4) and Bird's Open-

Nona Gaprindashvili, women's world champion, in simultaneous exhibition against twenty-eight men at English atomic-energy installation in 1965. Soviet heroine from Georgia undoubtedly would refute youthful Fischer's offer of Knight odds to any woman.

ing (1 P-KB4), but in this age, when theorists burn midnight oil to find innovations on move 15, he has introduced an increasingly popular novelty on the first move: 1 P-QN3. Recalling that Nimzovich was a Danish citizen, he has humorously referred to "the Danish School of Chess."

Larsen's early results were mixed, his games sought out chiefly by connoisseurs who valued original ideas. Then, in 1964 at the Amsterdam Interzonal, he tied for first with Tal, Spassky, and Smyslov, and joined the world's elite. The new superstar subsequently reached the candidates' semifinals three times, only to have his ambitious predictions thwarted by more realistic rivals.

Nonetheless, Larsen is one of the few authentic heroes of chess history. Not only his sparkling games but his bright, multilingual personality have won him a large following throughout the world. And the lifetime ambition of most other players would have been satisfied by the following game—a ticket to immortality.

LARSEN V. PETROSIAN
Piatigorsky Cup, 1966
Sicilian Defense

	WHITE	BLACK		WHITE	BLACK
1	P-K4	P-QB4	5	B-K3	B-N2
2	N-KB3	N-QB3	6	P-QB4	N-B3
3	P-Q4	PxP	7	N-QB3	N-KN5
4	NxP	P-KN3	8	QxN	NxN
			9	Q-Q1	N-K3

All "book." White's Maroczy Bind gives him an edge.

10	Q-Q2	P-Q3	13	QR-Q1	B-QB3
11	B-K2	B-Q2	14	N-Q5	R-K1
12	0-0	0-0	15	P-B4	N-B2
			16	P-KB5	N-R3?!

Petrosian takes liberties because he thinks Larsen can no longer enforce P-K5. Better was 16. . . NxN.

17	B-N4!	N-B4!	18	PxP	RPxP
			19	Q-KB2	R-KB1

Below: Bent Larsen rekindled romantic flame.
Bottom: Polugaevsky winning the XXXVII USSR Chess Championship in 1969, which he tied with Petrosian.
Opposite: Tigran Vartanovich Petrosian being crowned world champion at Moscow in 1963. Armenian victory chant was irresistible.

Petrosian, fresh from his first and successful world title defense, is ready to usurp control in the center. If 20 BxN, PxB 21 N-B6 ch, Black gets adequate compensation for the Queen. Larsen finds an extraordinary way to keep his attack going, with a deflecting sacrifice of a pawn.

20	P-K5!!	BxP	**22**	RxB	N-K3
21	Q-R4!	BxN	**23**	R-B3!	B-B3
			24	Q-R6	B-N2

The attack seems spent. But now comes one of the most beautiful moves in the history of chess.

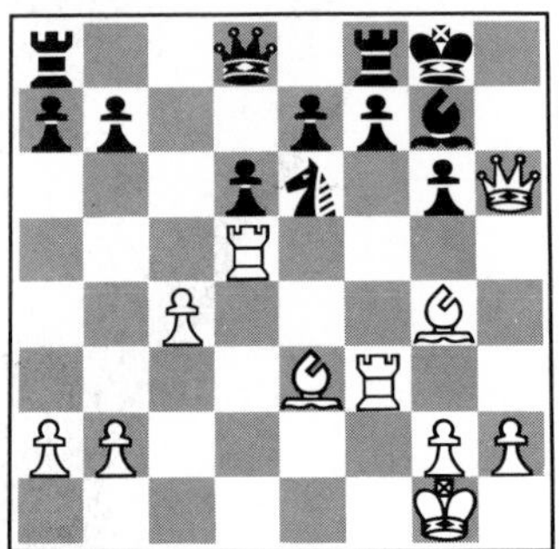

25 QxP!! N-B5

Accepting the Queen immediately makes no real difference.

26	RxN	PxQ	**27**	B-K6 ch	R-B2

Or else 27...K-R2 28 R-R4 ch, B-R3 29 BxB, R-B4 30 RxR, PxR 31 B-B7!! P-K4 32 R-R3, Q-N3 ch 33 K-R1 and mate follows with B-B8—a lovely line, which Larsen had to foresee on move 25.

28	RxR	K-R1	**29**	R-KN5!	P-N4

Or 29...B-K4 30 RxNP, Q-R4 31 R-R6 ch, K-N1 32 R/7-B6 ch, K-N2 33 R/B-N6 ch, K-B1 34 R-N8 mate.

30 R-N3 Resigns

Mate can be averted only by surrendering the Queen. A new Evergreen game, which circled the globe with a renewed affirmation of the beauty of chess.

Of the many strong players of our time produced by the Soviet school of chess, Boris Spassky, born in 1937,

атч на первенство мир
1969
Вечера

Opposite: Sell-out crowd at variety theater in Moscow, site of 1969 title match.
Below: Bronstein comments on Petrosian-Spassky match in 1966. (Petrosian kept title.)
Bottom: Boris Spassky with world championship medal and laurel wreath after 1969 win.

is the most Russian of all. For despite his troubles with bureaucrats, he remains a loyal son and represents what is best in that nation which has contributed so much achievement and suffering to the heritage of artistry. And in his bold, expansive play one can perceive the chessic equivalent of the legendary, passionate Russian soul.

Schooled at the Leningrad House of Pioneers, Boris scored a sensation at age sixteen, when he beat Smyslov at Bucharest. It was an open game typical of the classic attacking style, sparkling with original strokes, which would become his trademark.

SPASSKY V. SMYSLOV
Bucharest, 1953
Nimzoindian Defense

	WHITE	BLACK		WHITE	BLACK
1	P-Q4	N-KB3	3	N-QB3	B-N5
2	P-QB4	P-K3	4	B-N5!?	. . .

Spassky's favorite.

4	. . .	P-KR3	5	B-R4	P-B4
			6	P-Q5	P-Q3

A tame reply that does not challenge White's central preponderance. At Tallinn, twenty years later, Tal would rebuff Spassky with the pawn sac, 6. . . P-QN4!

7	P-K3	PxP	12	B-N3	N-R4
8	PxP	QN-Q2	13	B-Q3	NxB
9	B-QN5	0-0	14	NxN	N-K4
10	KN-K2	N-K4	15	B-K2	BxN
11	0-0	N-N3	16	PxB	Q-R5
			17	P-KB4!	. . .

The teen-ager fearlessly attacks the world champion-to-be.

17	. . .	N-N5	18	BxN	BxB
			19	Q-R4!	. . .

Embarrassing the Bishop by the threat of P-B5 and R-B4.

19	. . .	B-B1	22	R-B2	P-QN4!?
20	P-K4	Q-N5	23	P-K5	P-R5
21	Q-B2	P-KR4!?	24	N-B1	B-B4

25	Q-Q2	PxP?

Smyslov is playing overconfidently, and gives Spassky a strong passed pawn. Better was 25. . . QR-Q1.

26	PxP	B-N3	28	P-Q6	B-K5
27	R-K1	P-R6	29	N-K3	Q-K3

The recommended 29. . . Q-N4 should also fail after 30 N-B5! QxQ 31 N-K7 ch, K-R2 32 RxQ, BxP 33 P-Q7, when Black is trussed up.

30	R-B4	BxP

If 30. . . QxKP, then 31 N-N4, Q-Q4 32 N-B6 ch! wins. If 30. . . P-B4 31 RxB! PxR 32 Q-Q5 and the passed pawns are decisive.

31	N-B5	KR-K1	32	R-K3!	QR-Q1

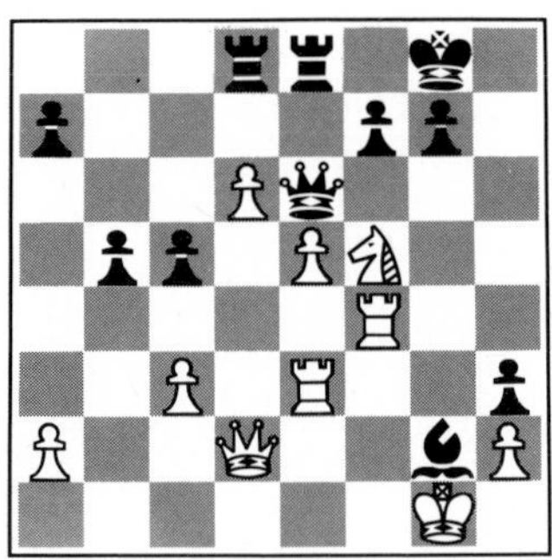

33	NxP!	RxP

Or 33. . . KxN 34 R-N3 ch, K-B1 35 RxP ch! and mate in two.

34	NxQ	Resigns

In view of 34. . . RxQ 35 R-N3 ch, K-R2 36 R-R4 mate. The annunciation of a great new talent.

At nineteen, Boris already qualified for the World Candidates' Tournament at Amsterdam, where he tied for third place. He was the "crown prince of chess," and the very highest honor seemed imminent.

Spassky may resemble a blond matinee idol, and he has charmed many female fans. Yet his story unfolds not in Hollywood, but in Russia, and to our hero has been ascribed a Dostoyevskian melancholy. In the next two world cycles he tasted bitter frustration, failing to qualify.

After Tal eliminated him with a lucky win in the XXV Soviet Championship, he wept in the street.

Spassky, who has not contributed a single book, has called himself "lazy." Yet his struggle for the world crown, which resumed in the mid-sixties, can only be called herculean. In its five-year course he fought no less than eight matches with some of the world's toughest players—and won seven of them! No one in history had remotely approached such a feat.

He had disposed of countrymen Keres, Geller, and Tal before his 1966 match with World Champion Petrosian. His strategic psychology for that encounter was ambitious enough. Faced with the craftiest defensive player of all time, Spassky felt that overt aggression would be too crude. So, as if to show his universality, he joined the Armenian in games of closed maneuver. After six draws, Petrosian uncorked one of his patented preventive Exchange sacrifices, squelched all of the challenger's chances, and won nicely. The champion was later tied but never headed. With a strong finish Petrosian kept his crown with a score of 4 wins, 3 losses, and a new record 17 draws. Spassky's strategy—"The secret of chess is: You must know the rules, and you must know when to break them"—had proved faulty.

Spassky's superior strength in tournament play was manifest later that year in the Second Piatigorsky Cup at Santa Monica, California. There he beat off a strong finish by Fischer to take first prize (a record $5,000) undefeated, while Petrosian finished in the middle of the strong pack. The unfailingly courteous and good-humored Spassky made an excellent impression on American fans, who gathered in greater numbers than ever before.

In the next candidates' matches of 1968, Spassky proved that his grand attacking play had only been in abeyance. He unleashed some of his finest creative chess to defeat Geller, Larsen, and Korchnoi in elegant style. Thus 1969 brought his second chance against Petrosian for the world title. He took a new approach, no longer attempting to beat the Great Preventer at his own game. Spassky attacked!

Spassky lost the first game via a late error but was undaunted. In Game 4 he sprang a surprise weapon, the Tarrasch Defense, which would prove sturdy throughout the match. Accepting an isolated Queen's pawn in return for active piece play, he piled on the pressure until the champion buckled, evening the score. With a slashing attack in Game 5, he inflicted the unheard-of: Petrosian's second consecutive defeat. The crucial battle was Game 19. Spassky went into the game with a minimal 1-point lead. He rose to the occasion with a pretty mating attack against the Sicilian Defense and won in only twenty-four moves, virtually clinching the match. By a final score of 6 wins, 4 losses, and 13 draws, Boris Spassky became the tenth chess champion of the world.

With the onset of the seventies, big new talents made their bid for a place in the chess sun. Outstanding were Canada's Duncan Suttles, the most original strategist since Nimzovich; the temperamental classicist, Henrique Mecking, hero of Brazil; Yugoslavia's wildly imaginative Lubomir Ljubojevic; the dynamic Walter Shawn Browne, multiple U.S. Open Champion; and the extraordinarily cool and solid young Russian, Anatoli Karpov. Karpov, the strongest player in at least a generation, was proclaimed the great Soviet hope. These same players await the chance to change the course of history set down by Bobby Fischer when he challenged the man who had beaten the Great Preventer.

Spassky, meanwhile, had proved that Prevention could not withstand the onslaught of creative ideas and thus vindicated the ever-fertile richness of chess. And he did it by fidelity to his true nature as a chess artist. Thus, having shouldered the most heroic labors ever demanded of an aspirant, Boris Spassky entered on the fateful road that led to Iceland.

12.

האיגוד הישראלי לשחמט
ISRAEL CHESS FEDERATION
Tournament NATANYA '73
Round 8
Date 6-4-73
Y. KRAIDMAN
A.F. SAIDY
WHITE
BLACK
c4 Nf6
Nc3 g6
g3 Bg7
Bg2 0-0
d6
Nc6
Bg4
Nb5 Rxc1
Rxc1 a6
Nd4 Nc7
Be3 Nba8
Ne6 Nxe6
dxe6 Qb8
Qd5 b5
Qc6 Bb2
Rc2 Bf6
Qxa6 d5

ara, who is destined for last place. I improvise in the sharp Grünfeld Defense, and on move 21 he tries a dubious combination. I ponder for forty-five minutes and counterpunch into a slightly better ending. Why so long? The endless quest for perfection, the desire to plumb the position to its depths. But it is foolishness. Now I have only twenty minutes for eighteen moves. With seconds left on move 38, I see that my only chance to win is by grabbing the "poisoned" RP with my Bishop, à la Fischer. Intuition, the sense that comes from playing and inspecting thousands of master games, tells me I can get it out of the trap. Unlike Fischer in his first match game with Spassky, I prove right. I soon adjourn in a winning position.

May 30. We resume play in the morning. The time limit is now sixteen moves per hour. With one minute left I have to decide whether to take a second pawn, leading to an ending I have never seen in the book. If I do, can he get a freak draw? I disdain it, wrongly. Close to move 72, under time pressure for the third time in one game, I stumble into a draw! After seven hours of hard effort, I bemoan my terrible luck. But I recall Alekhine's dictum that the excuse of time pressure is as invalid as a criminal's plea that he was drunk at the time of the crime.

The same afternoon, against Porath, I am hurting for a win. I go for a double-edged line against the Nimzo-indian that I have studied ever since Padevsky crushed me in a famous game in 1959. A timely Exchange Sacrifice blunts his counterattack, and when he gives away a pawn I adjourn in a promising end game.

May 31. Porath's first move in the morning is a mistake that tells me he lacked the stomach to analyze the position during the night. In no time I push a pawn to the seventh, and he resigns just before it queens. At last I am in the plus column.

The fifth round pits me against Yanofsky, Canada's first grandmaster, who made a sensational debut at age fourteen at the 1939 Olympiad. Now he is one of the best part-time players in the world. Again I play the dynamic Grünfeld Defense, and he responds with Spassky's favorite Exchange Variation. On move 14 he surprises me with Q-R4, after long thought. Does he know the Gligoric-Portisch game of a few months before? Next move, I know the answer is no, because he chooses a feeble continuation that hands me the initiative on a gold platter. Soon I have accumulated enough advantages to delight old Steinitz. On move 27, running behind on the clock, Yanofsky makes an error that loses a pawn. I trade Queens to reach a winning ending. With some more sharp play, I gain two Bishops for a Rook. We adjourn, but he can safely resign.

June 1. After only one move this morning, Yanofsky turns over his King, thus becoming the fourteenth grandmaster I have beaten in my career. (Many more have beaten me.)

After eight playing sessions in five days, I suddenly appreciate the value of the Sabbath. Friday is a night off and a chance to meet people, one of whom is a young woman named Shula, who is very friendly.

June 2. I am White against Romm, an unknown in international circles, who so far has amassed five goose eggs. (Later he will make a fine recovery.) There was no way to prepare for him. Against others one spends time studying their published games, trying to find weak spots, planning an opening. Romm plays the Benoni Defense in unapproved fashion, ceding space and the two Bishops. But I play too quietly, too much like Petrosian, and by move 33 my advantage is microscopic. I am beginning to worry. I need to win this game. Then he does it. Too boldly he advances a Knight to K5. All I have to do is exchange it off, and then he'll have an isolated pawn right in the center of the board, juicy, completely undefendable. Too good to be true. I double-check my calculation, and then I feel good. It is hardly a noble way to win, but isn't it about time that a break went *for* me? I grab the booty. On move 41 I seal my move in the envelope.

June 3. Two hours of play in the morning suffice to bring in the point. It is my third in a row, and this modest winning streak gives me a score of 4½-1½. My campaign is in good order.

I repair to the swimming pool. (Swimming is my only physical tonic, before or during a tournament. Not for me the mountain retreats of the Rumanian national team, or Botvinnik's walks of exactly two hours. Fischer prizes physical training, but Lasker was sedentary. Who knows?)

The pool is the daily meeting place of the foreign players for banter, gossip, and political argument. I run into Kavalek, my opponent for this afternoon.

"Lubosh," I say, "after lunch I have an important date with a young woman . . . a very lovely person . . ."

"So?"

"Well, I am just wondering whether I'll be needing a lot of energy for our game. I mean, are you out for blood?"

To my surprise he takes my question seriously. Kavalek is a top grandmaster, he has the white pieces, and he is gunning for first prize ($1,000—the circuit has not yet caught up with Fischer economics). He has prestige at stake and a previous score of 2½ out of 3 against me. Never in my life have I prearranged a draw. I have turned down such offers from grandmasters three times. As Fischer has pointed out, such arrangements give an unfair advantage to the players who thereby receive a rest day, and in any case they are against the spirit of the game.

Kavalek answers, "When I played in Eastern Europe I was sometimes pressured before games. Some bureaucrats felt it was unpatriotic to beat a countryman. Now I just play normal chess."

I show up for the game relaxed after a most pleasant interlude. Maybe too relaxed. He opens with the move hardest to meet: 1 P-K4. How to answer? With the modest Caro-Kann, designed for a draw at best? Impulsively, I play the sharpest, most popular, and riskiest defense—the Sicilian. I might lose, but also it gives me a chance to win, and if I win I'll be in first place and in easy reach of the grandmaster norm.

On move 9 we reach a known position from the book by Gligoric and Sokolov, *Sicilijanska Obrana,* which I always carry with me on the circuit. For years, despite my limited knowledge of Serbo-Croatian, it has been my bible. With my marginal notes alone I could write a new edition. But what is the book move? My mind goes blank. I can't remember. Why hadn't I prepared for this game more seriously? I give up a pawn, but the expected counterplay doesn't materialize. If I exchange Queens at move 20, my end-game prospects will be bleak. Suddenly he penetrates deep into my position. The specter of disaster looms, and fatalistically I blunder. With an elementary combination he wins a Rook. In only twenty-four moves, I am beaten—and badly. Why has Caïssa chosen such a crucial time to remind me of my ability to play like a patzer? I leave the room shattered.

June 4. My opponent, or, as the Russians say, "partner," is Kraidman, perhaps Israel's most talented natural player but, like the others, weak in the opening. On the eighth turn he plays a move condemned by every book on the King's Indian Defense. It hands me the two Bishops and a semi-open file which, added to my edge in space, are the germs of a win. Steadily, I increase the pressure, while his pieces squirm ineffectually. He even retreats a Knight to the corner. On move 24, my King's Bishop springs to life on the long diagonal and he loses first one, then another pawn. On move 37, faced with the loss of a third foot-soldier, he turns over his monarch.

My spirits swell again. A colleague congratulates me on a "beautiful game." It has been a model of the exploitation of a positional advantage. And Shula was watching.

June 5. Sabbath again, and I certainly need the

Kavalek (r) attacks Saidy at Las Palmas International Tournament, 1973. Spain's Canary Islands have become a major new chess center. Mass simultaneous exhibition with 3,000 school children playing visiting stars closed festival. Kavalek tied for U.S. championship later in year.

rest. Shula takes me home for dinner with her family, which has come from Morocco. The hospitality reminds me of my grandmother's.

June 6. Black against the very bookish Tatai, the leading player of his adopted Italy. Why has that nation with such a rich cultural and chessic heritage failed to produce a grandmaster in modern times? Again, I play the Grünfeld, and he is so well prepared that he takes only one minute for his first fourteen moves! To avoid "home-cooking," I vary from the way I played against Yanofsky and expand on the queen-side to offset his dominance in the center. It takes me a long time to equalize, and by move 30 both of us are short of time. Then Tatai makes a mistake in judgment. Anxious to avenge previous defeats, he concedes the Q-file and stakes all on a king-side attack. My weaknesses there are small. My Queen swoops from KB1 to QR6; he has to drop a pawn. His few feints at my King are harmless. I adjourn with an overwhelming pawn-roller on the other flank.

An hour later my phone rings. It is Tatai.

"Hello, Saidy? I resign."

"Thank you for saving us from getting up in the morning. It was a tough game."

I now have 6½ points out of 9, and 5 of my last 6. I am tied for second place with Reshevsky, only a ½-point behind Kavalek. For the grandmaster norm I need but 4 out of my remaining 6, and my strongest opposition is already behind me. Am I at the crossroads of my career?

June 7. My opponent, Domnitz, who looks like Leonard Bernstein, plays instead like Leonid Stein, my friend and thrice Soviet champion, a virtuoso of the King s Indian. (A month later the chess world suffers a blow when Stein, at the age of thirty-eight, drops dead in Moscow.) Should I play the ultra-complex Saemisch Attack, which requires the profundity of a Botvinnik? I do, and by move 23 I am regretting the decision. I give up a pawn on speculation, and four moves later I see that he can sac the Exchange with fine chances. I have a good score to conserve and I lack the Larsen spirit (optimism at all times). I offer a draw. Right after he accepts, I am most chagrined to learn that he planned an inferior move! What a pity to see more deeply than the opponent and not be rewarded. During this game I make my third request to the referee for crowd silence. Will organizers ever learn? Don't they know that *my* norm is at stake?

June 8. For religious reasons, the eleventh round is scheduled for the ungodly hour of 10 A.M. Despite my written appeal, I am informed in classic bureaucratese that no exceptions can be made. Yet all sorts of exceptions have always been made for Reshevsky, one of whose opponents, Tatai, refuses to cooperate with some weird scheduling, convinced that Sammy is trying to give him a hard time. (Some chess masters venerate Morpheus more than Jehovah.)

My friendly antagonist, Czerniak, had played for the Palestine team in the Olympiad of 1935 in his native Poland. He is a rotund old fighter of massive *Sitzfleisch* who has played the longest game on record—a twenty-hour, 191-move draw with Pilnik at Mar del Plata in 1943. The leading promoter of chess in Israel, he is still tough at sixty-three, but I certainly expect to beat him as I have once before. What's more, I must.

Knowing he has faced the Sicilian a thousand times, I choose the modernistic defense known by the Yugoslavs as the Pirc, by the Russians as the Ufimtsev, and by Western Europeans as the Robatsch. On move 11, I think for a half-hour and plunge into tactical complications for strategic purposes—to destroy his pawn center. Shortly, I have two alternatives, and in my morning haze I choose the wrong one! Soon I find myself in an ending a pawn down, theoretically lost. But do I have to compound matters by losing a Knight with my worst blunder of the year? I give up the ghost.

A disastrous setback! I vow never again to consent to begin a game in the morning. If I am to reach my goal, I must have 3½ points out of my last four games.

At lunch someone asks, "Is it true you were born in Syria?" I am not in the mood. I answer, "I do play the Aleppo Gambit—Queen's Gambit to you. Did you know that algebraic notation was invented by a Syrian, Phillip Stamma?" My interlocutor volunteers his racial and military theories.

June 9. Round Twelve. I play the English against Kaldor. The early phase is a Hypermodernist's delight. He sets up a pawn-center and I destroy it with rapier thrusts from the side. Soon I force the win of the Exchange, but, in view of some weaknesses around my King, I have to exercise extreme care. At adjournment I know there will still be a lot of work.

June 10. On move 59 I find a sharp pawn-push to force a trade of Queens and the rest is easy. At the end of seventy-five moves and nine hours of play, Kaldor resigns. Later he criticizes my deliberate "technique." Some players have a reverse psychology and praise only those who lose.

After a good lunch of what seems to be the favorite local meat—turkey—I have to sit right down again and face Damjanovic. He opens with Larsen's 1 P-QN3. I am out to win, so on move 9 I make a crucial decision to unbalance the game, gaining a queen-side majority of pawns in return for his menacing central mass. It leads to the most exciting sort of chess struggle, one in which the conflicting plans of the antagonists dictate a long series of strategically and tactically forced moves. Blow is traded for blow. I have cast the die, but now I am carried along by the momentum of the battle, not knowing who will emerge on top. What's more, I don't care so much. I am playing for big stakes. I am playing fighting chess the way chess should be played. Let the better man win!

The crisis comes in the center, where a major tactical skirmish chops most of the wood from the board. When the smoke clears, I find myself in an inferior end game, with two Rooks and four pawns versus his Rook, Bishop, Knight, and three pawns. Just before adjournment, both sides blunder as I give him, and he overlooks, a quick way to finish me off. (After my further complaints about crowd noise, the assistant referee tells me I have been around Fischer too much.) I have one advantage overnight: I will be studying the position while, I am sure, Mato will be playing cards.

June 11. Soon after resumption my hope is confirmed. Damjanovic makes a weakness in his pawn structure which produces virtual equality. The way opens for wiping out his last pawn, thus assuring a draw. He crumples visibly as his win slips away. Then I get an insane idea. I have his King confined to the back rank by one of my Rooks. If I can slip the other Rook past his defenses, can I even checkmate him? I have the draw in hand, but my own King is also under attack. Suddenly I look at the clock. I have only seconds left for two moves! I reach out. My hand hovers a moment in the air—and I make a fatal move! In undue fear of his Bishop and Knight, I grab them in return for a Rook, only to find myself in a dead-lost book ending. Soon I extend my hand. In broken German I say, "I had an easy draw." He replies, "I know. *Natürlich.*"

My hopes are crushed. In effect, the tournament is over for me. I stand up slowly, drained of all energy, like a runner at the end of a marathon. I think of Spassky's thirteenth game against Fischer, in which he fought so long and so valiantly, only to blunder it away at the end. Sometimes I have played like a grandmaster, sometimes like a patzer. I shall never be a Spassky. I shall not be a grandmaster this year, but someday I shall have another chance. Will the fruit ever dangle so tantalizingly again?

At lunch I see Lubosh, who has rescued a losing ending from Camara. Since Reshevsky had made a strange blunder of a Rook to Czerniak, Kavalek's lead looks secure.

"Looks as if you have got it wrapped up now, Lubosh. As for me, I can't get the breaks. After throwing away this morning's game, I have no more interest."

"Why, Tony? You're still in the running for second."

In Round Fourteen, the sixth straight game without a rest day, I completely outplay Friedman, the twenty-year-old "baby" of the event, with the Maroczy Bind. (Later I advise him on getting into European tournaments—difficult without an international title.) On move 19, I play a *petite combinaison* and win a clear pawn. Moreover, it is protected, passed, and on the sixth rank. Obviously, the game is easily won. I am carefree, more interested in the evening's date with Shula. I play rapidly in a double-Rook ending, thinking the win automatic. Then on move 38 I make a horrible oversight! When he takes my prized pawn in return for a worthless one, it is all I can do to keep my poker face. At adjournment, I know he can draw with correct play.

An adjourned position, especially a bad one, is an albatross that saps both free time and sleep. But I don't look at this one all night. I am angry at myself and at my fate. If Caïssa insists on acting like a bitch-goddess, there are other women less fickle, made of flesh and blood.

June 12. We resume in the morning, my eighth adjourned game of the tournament. I am tired and don't feel like looking at the chessboard. But as a pro I have to try to extract a victory as long as any winning chances remain. My inexperienced opponent refuses to go wrong.

On move 79 I extend my hand in peace.

It is an off day, but Reshevsky and Tatai are playing their postponed game. The two inveterate time-pressure artists, who each have to make about fifteen moves in two minutes, lose track of the written score. When Tatai's clock-flag falls, Reshevsky seeks a forfeit. Fortunately for the Italian, the reconstruction shows that more than forty moves have been completed. Then he plays a move that forces a simple draw, yet Sammy stares at the position for an hour before agreeing. After this unpleasantness Tatai cannot be expected to go all-out in the last round to beat Kavalek, just to give Reshevsky a chance to tie for first.

June 13. The last round. After a few minutes of play, I see Kavalek and Tatai agree to a draw, thus guaranteeing first prize to Lubosh. Strangely, the moves are identical with a previous game of Tatai's, played in the last Olympiad. The game does not appear kosher.

Reshevsky sees that his last hope for a share of first prize is dead. He disgustedly offers Friedman a draw on move 7—the shortest game in his long career. The young Israeli accepts, unaware of an old New York adage, "When Reshevsky offers a draw, see if you have a forced mate."

Meanwhile, I am playing the Slav Defense against Pachman, who essays the unusual 4 Q-N3. Not having memorized my opponent's tomes on the openings (*Geschlossene Spiele*, etc.), I do not follow the stem game Pytlakowski-Smyslov, Helsinki, 1952. If Pachman can win, he will tie Reshevsky for second. I equalize with an early exchange of Queens, and the point is halved on move 20.

The tournament is over. The final standings of the leaders: Kavalek 11-4, Reshevsky 10-5, Damjanovic and Pachman, each 9½-5½ to share third and fourth places, Kraidman and Saidy, each 9-6 to share fifth and sixth places, and Yanofsky 8-7.

June 14. The closing banquet and prize ceremony take place in the usual atmosphere of conviviality. But there is always a melancholy feeling at the end of a tournament when the members of the fraternity break up.

This time there is another reason for sadness. I shall soon have to bid farewell to Shula, who has been a gracious friend and my consolation after the sorrows of battle. One is fortunate to find friendship in any circumstances and the more so in the temporary setting of a chess tournament. Yet the day of leave-taking arrives and the itinerant chess master sets out for another land of strangers.

June 15. At the airport the security men note my surname and my recent visit to Tunisia, the chief chess center on the African continent. They start to interrogate me in earnest. How did I arrive in Israel? By air, but I have misplaced the ticket. I must look like a suspicious character! (When for a while I sported a beard, Pal Benko in *Chess Life* described me as resembling a "Bulgarian anarchist.") I begin to feel nervous. My plane leaves in a half-hour. I may lose two days or worse . . .

I say, "Look, I can explain. I have many Israeli friends who can vouch for me."

"Who?"

"Chess-players. I've just been playing in a big tournament with them."

"What are their names?"

"Czerniak, Domnitz, Friedman . . ."

"What about Kagan?"

"Not him. He's preparing for an event in Brazil next month."

My interrogator smiles for the first time. "That's right, Mr. Saidy. He's a friend of mine. He was telling me that the other day. You can go right through. And a pleasant flight to you. *Shalom.*"

Gens una sumus. Chess has given me deep satisfactions, stimulating adventures, friends in every corner of the globe. And now chess has gotten me off the hook. Caïssa, why did I ever doubt you?

Less than four months later, there is war again in the Middle East.

13.

"Bobby"

"All I want to do, ever, is play chess."

—Robert J. Fischer

Phone calls . . .

Four in the morning. The phone rang in the home of Larry Evans. The day before he had been analyzing a puzzling opening variation with Bobby Fischer. The stunned grandmaster woke up and groped for the phone.

"'Lo?"

A boyish, rapid-fire voice at the other end. No preliminaries, not even to identify the variation.

"I found the right move. It's. . . .

Not a few friends and chess colleagues of Bobby Fischer, and their relatives, have been awakened by the telephone at unusual hours. It wouldn't occur to Bobby that a call from him at 2 or 3 A.M. might be an inconvenience. It happens that *he* sleeps late and does some of his sharpest thinking during the wee hours. The day, after all, has a million curious eyes; the night is a time for undisturbed analysis. Some of the moves that helped Bobby win the world title came to him while the city slept.

Bobby can't be bothered by the social niceties. He has no time for unnecessary words—or moves. Like many other geniuses, he is self-centered. His powerful ego has been a valuable asset, channeling the brimming energy which has elevated him to the pinnacle of chessdom.

1972. The day before the scheduled start of the world championship match in Iceland. That island country of two hundred thousand chess-loving Vikings was as tense as if one of their volcanoes had been about to erupt. One of the two principals, Bobby Fischer, the unpredictable American, was not there. And no one knew whether he would show up.

While his aides tried to negotiate an acceptable agreement with the Icelanders, Bobby was at the Long Island residence of the family of one of the authors. There he had sought refuge from a bumptious band of newspeople and photographers who, for the first time in history, were treating a chess-player like a superstar. Uninvited, they swarmed around the house. One daring cameraman even took up a perch in a tree across the street, hoping to get a shot of his prey through upper windows.

The phone rang. A woman's voice said, "Mr. Henry Kissinger is calling from the White House. He would like to speak to Bobby Fischer, please."

Bobby came to the phone. The Fischer-Kissinger conversation was, presumably, not recorded, and will likely never be revealed. It is not improbable that the presidential adviser, an alleged master of the global chessboard, urged Bobby to go through with the match in the interests of United States prestige and of scoring an American counter-coup against Soviet propaganda. Bobby did go, but not because of Washington pressure. Patriotic as he is, Bobby is his own man. The clincher was that British financier James Slater had just doubled the purse.

And so history was not denied.

⁂

More words have been written about Fischer than any other chess champion, possibly because he is the most difficult one to comprehend. His rival, Tal, called the unpolished youth from Brooklyn "the greatest genius to have descended from the chess heavens."

For years, the shadow of tragedy loomed over his career. More than once, associates wrote off his future as hopeless. Those who cared about Bobby and about American chess went through cycles of exultation and depression, false starts, soaring hope and agonizing despair. But in 1972, miraculously, the American dream came true.

Born in Chicago on March 9, 1943, Robert James Fischer was raised by his mother, who was divorced from the father he never knew. He learned the moves of chess at age six from his older sister. Fortunately, Bobby was living then in Brooklyn, New York, near the biggest con-

Opening pages: Bobby Fischer Day in New York, 1972. Wearing city's gold medal and accompanied by Mayor John Lindsay, Bobby shakes hands with some of 3,000 fans attending. Such displays are rare for Bobby.

centration of chess talent in the hemisphere. Within a few years, word got around the clubs regarding a twelve-year-old boy who could play like a master.

In 1956, Bobby was invited to play in the prestigious Rosenwald Tournament, where his 4½ points in eleven games constituted a fine debut for a thirteen-year-old. He played a brilliant game against Donald Byrne that the wires carried around the globe, and the world of chess learned of the arrival of a new star.

DONALD BYRNE V. FISCHER
New York 1956
Grünfeld Defense

	WHITE	BLACK		WHITE	BLACK
1	N-KB3	N-KB3	5	B-B4	P-Q4
2	P-B4	P-KN3	6	Q-N3!?	PxP
3	N-B3	B-N2	7	QxBP	P-B3
4	P-Q4	0-0	8	P-K4	QN-Q2

The boy shows understanding of this Hypermodern system. If now 9 P-K5, N-Q4! 10 NxN, PxN 11 QxP? NxP! favors Black.

9	R-Q1	N-N3	10	Q-B5!?	B-N5
			11	B-KN5?	. . .

Allowing a fine combination; 11 B-K2 preserves equality.

11 . . . N-R5!!

Fearless youth! Bobby's idea is 12 NxN, NxP 13 Q-N4, NxB 14 NxN, BxR 15 KxB, BxP, when White has an insecure King and a slight material deficit. But Donald thinks he can outplay Bobby in complications.

12	Q-R3!?	NxN	13	PxN	NxP!
			14	BxP	Q-N3!

A bold Exchange sac. If 15 BxR, BxB 16 Q-N3, NxP(6)! Black stands well, for if 17 QxN? then. . . B-N5.

15 B-B4!? NxP(6)!!

Bobby's third combination in five moves! If now 16 QxN, KR-K1 or 16 BxR, BxB 17 QxN? B-N5 and wins. But Byrne's next appears to win material, so Bobby had to foresee all the ramifications of the next two notes.

16	B-B5	KR-K1 ch	17	K-B1	. . .

Now if 17. . . N-N4, 18 BxP ch! K-R1 19 Q-Q3 wins the Exchange, or if 18. . . KxB, 19 Q-N3 ch, B-K3 20 N-N5 ch wins outright. The stage is set for the move that went around the world.

17 . . . B-K3!!

The point! If now 18 QxN, QxB! or 18 B-Q3, N-N4 Black keeps a pawn with an easy win, while 18 BxB leads to "Philidor's legacy": 18. . . Q-N4 ch 19 K-N1, N-K7 ch 20 K-B1, N-N6 dbl ch 21 K-N1, Q B8 ch 22 RxQ, N-K7 mate! So Byrne accepts the Queen offer, allowing multiple discovered checks.

18	BxQ	BxB ch	20	K-B1	NxP ch
19	K-N1	N-K7 ch	21	K-N1	. . .

Or else 21 R-Q3, PxB 22 Q-B3, NxN 23 QxB, R-K8 mate.

21	. . .	N-K7 ch	23	K-N1	PxB
22	K-B1	N-B6 ch	24	Q-N4	R-R5!
			25	QxP	NxR

Below: Bobby at fourteen, when he won U.S. Closed Championship for first of eight times.
Opposite: Bobby at Marshall Chess Club. Here, and at his own club, the Manhattan, he honed his talent in blitz tournaments. In later years, he demanded distance between himself and spectators.

And with overwhelming material for the Queen, Fischer won easily, giving checkmate on move 41. Kmoch called it grandiloquently the "Game of the Century."

Fischer's career was a crescendo of achievements. At fourteen he won the United States championship undefeated, a point ahead of Reshevsky, who would remain forever eclipsed. He thus became the youngest player ever to win a major event. He played extraordinarily well. He had voluminous knowledge of a few openings, conducted direct and vigorous middle games with a sure tactical grasp, and displayed the end-game finesse of a veteran.

At fifteen he was already qualified for the Interzonal Tournament for the world championship. At Portoroz he played steadily, with flashes of brilliance against Gligoric and Larsen, and ended in a tie for fifth—making him the youngest grandmaster ever and a candidate for the world crown.

In those years of pinched chess budgets, there was doubt whether enough funds could be raised to send Bobby to the candidates' event in Yugoslavia. An incident related by his biographer, Frank Brady, sheds light on the individualistic, independent Fischer character that would become world famous. A wealthy New York manufacturer called Bobby in and offered to underwrite his trip. There was only one string attached—Bobby was asked, if he emerged the victor, to plug his benefactor. He promptly refused, saying, "I win the tournament myself, with my own talent." Fischer would do it all alone.

In the event, which was won by Tal, the teen-ager finished tied for fifth with such an experienced grandmaster as Gligoric. On the home front, he continued to win the national championship each time it was held.

Bobby became known as a nonconformist who had special ideas about the need for optimal conditions for playing top-flight chess. His first public crisis occurred in 1961, during a match with Reshevsky. When organizers attempted to force him to start one of his games in the morning, he adamantly refused and was handed a peremptory forfeit. The match, with the score tied, broke up in acrimony, leading to lawsuits.

The year 1962 was pivotal for his career. It opened with the appearance of a damaging, distorted interview in *Harper's* magazine, which poisoned Bobby's attitude toward journalists for a long time to come. At the Stockholm Interzonal, he swept all before him, finishing 2½ points ahead of Geller and Petrosian. This time, he fully expected to win the eight-man Candidates' Tournament at Curaçao and became, at nineteen, the challenger for the world title. The opinion of Gligoric was more realistic: "Five Soviet grandmasters cannot be weaker than one Fischer."

Maturing grandmaster. In late teens, Bobby began to wear impeccable suits and ties as befitted a high-class chess-player. When he won 1962 Interzonal, a Soviet spokesman —usually grudging in praise of non-Russians—said: "Fischer is going to be world champion!"

In a typical round of the long event on that tropical isle, Bobby Fischer found himself locked in strenuous combat, while the Soviet players agreed to perfunctory, energy-conserving draws and stood around whispering about his game. His well-rested opponents were quick to seize upon his errors. Although he won many games, he could finish no better than fourth, 3½ points behind winner Petrosian.

Justice had been denied. Never one to look within himself for the roots of any setback, Fischer was convinced that the competition was rigged. He subsequently published his accusation, "The Russians Have Fixed World Chess." He has said, "I had the best score of anyone who didn't cheat." He vowed never again to compete for the crown again unless the system was radically changed, and later efforts to arrange a match with Botvinnik were unavailing.

The intensity of Fischer's vendetta against "the Russians" is not to be minimized. But in 1973, he was to send the following telegram on the occasion of the premature death of a Soviet colleague (quoted in the Russian monthly *Shakhmaty v SSSR*): "I am shaken by untimely end of Leonid Stein—outstanding international grandmaster and good friend. I express sympathy to family and brotherhood of chess-players."

Thus began Bobby Fischer's self-exile. He continued to win the national championship with annual regularity, setting a record of eight consecutive first prizes. In the 1963-64 event, his superiority to all other Americans became embarrassing. He outplayed theoretician Larry Evans after surprising him with that romantic relic, the King's Bishop's Gambit. Against Robert Byrne he played one of his greatest combinations, so deep that a grandmaster commentator, just before Byrne's resignation, was still predicting Fischer's defeat. And against Benko, he produced a move which is unsurpassed for beauty and originality.

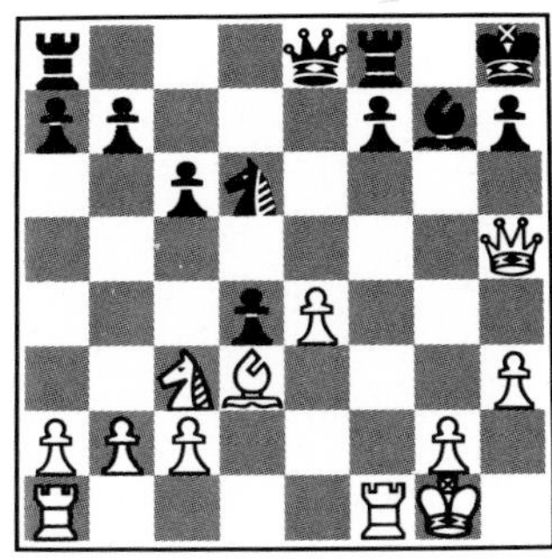

If White threatens mate on R7 by 19 P-K5. . .P-KB4! is a perfect defense. Fischer played: 19 R-B6!! If Black takes the obstructing Rook, then 20 P-K5 forces mate. The Hungarian-American grandmaster, faced with a choice between mate and loss of material, soon had to resign.

Bobby won his first ten games. One of the authors was the eleventh and last opponent. He played resolutely for the draw, in order to break Fischer's streak, and adjourned in an end game that offered a forced drawing sequence. After forty-five minutes of thought, Saidy, distrusting his analysis, chose the wrong sealed move. Next day, when the secret move was removed from the envelope, a smile flickered over Fischer's face. He went on to win the eleventh game in a row for another record likely never to be broken.

Fischer was invited to the Havana International Tournament in 1965, but the U. S. State Department denied him permission to go to Cuba. He decided to take part by teletype from New York and managed despite the handicap of playing twenty-one sessions of eight hours or more to tie for second—but not before exchanging sharp tactical moves by cable with Fidel Castro on the world political chessboard. They met the next year at the Havana Olympiad, where the leader of the Cuban Revolution was a frequent spectator and the U. S. team was a distant second to the Soviet gold-medalists.

In the first half of the powerful Piatigorsky Cup of 1966, Fischer was in bad form. His standing at the bottom caused alarm. But in the latter half he scored 7½ points out of 9, rising to second place. It was the greatest comeback in chess history, but not Bobby's last.

Very few organizers could meet his specifications, ranging from money to fluorescent lighting. To play in only one event per year was a sad waste of talent and deprived the chess world of a wealth of stirring games. There seemed to be an irrevocable breach with FIDE, even though the international body had converted the candidates' tournament into a series of matches, as a safeguard for non-Soviet participants.

After a lapse of five years, Fischer entered the 1967 Interzonal at Sousse. The inexperienced Tunisians were ill-equipped to deal with his demands for better lighting and scheduling (his church prohibits work on the Sabbath). Bobby surged into the lead, only to withdraw from the tournament.

In 1970 Fischer emerged from an idleness of over a year and a half to man a board in the historic match, USSR v. Rest of World. He obligingly acceded to Larsen's proud demand to play top board. Against the super-solid Petrosian, Bobby scored two wins and two draws, while Larsen split three games with Spassky and won one from Stein. But the Soviet team, dominating the lower boards, won narrowly, 20½-19½. Fischer's very presence excited Yugoslav fans and spawned speculation that he might someday again try for the summit.

For years many had considered him the best player in the world. But if he was to be persuaded to prosecute a quest for the world title, many off-the-board problems would have to be ironed out. So Ed Edmondson of the U. S. Chess Federation agreed to become his personal manager starting with the 1970 Interzonal at Palma de Mallorca. At last, things went smoothly. Gaining momentum as he went, Fischer won the tournament with a 3½-point margin. For the first time since the introduction of candidates' matches at his prodding, Bobby was in them.

Buenos Aires crowd numbered more than 10,000. Opposite: USSR v. World match at Belgrade in 1970. Najdorf stands at left, behind Fischer, who faces Petrosian. Bobby almost fell asleep during game—one of his best! Bottom: Fischer pondering at Buenos Aires, 1971.

Hopes were rising in the chess circles of the United States. Early in 1971 Fischer met Soviet Grandmaster Mark Taimanov at Vancouver and demolished him in six straight games. Russian commentators were stunned, implying that Taimanov had collapsed under a mysterious force. Others called it "Fischer-fear." Then, in Denver, Fischer faced Larsen. Together they had shifted the center of chess gravity away from Moscow. After Bobby won the complex first game, the word "draw" seemed to have escaped from Larsen's vocabulary. With increasingly desperate attempts to win a game, the Dane suffered defeat after defeat. The match ended in another 6-0 victory for Fischer! *Sovietsky Sport* declared, "A miracle has occurred."

At last, the "kid from Brooklyn" was only a step away from a world title match. In the fall of 1971, the eyes of the chess world were riveted on Buenos Aires, where Bobby met ex-champion Petrosian in the final candidates' joust.

In the first game the well-armed Petrosian, out of character, sprang a sharp innovation in the Sicilian Defense and put Fischer under heavy pressure. But a late error cost the Armenian the point—Fischer's twentieth consecutive win in elite company. Bobby insisted on playing the second game on schedule despite a head cold (he believes that his Soviet opponents take time-outs for dubious "illnesses") and Petrosian played a fine attack to even the score. In the next three drawn games, Tigran kept

Fischer confronts Petrosian in final candidates' match at Buenos Aires, 1971. Emblem of Argentine Federation has FIDE motto: Gens una sumus. *Tigran later complained: When Bobby says, 'Drink coffee,' you have to drink coffee." But he could not explain worst defeat of his career.*

the upper hand.

At Moscow's Central Chess Club they were breathing easier—at long last the terrible American had been stalled. But in Game 6 Petrosian reverted to his passive way, and Bobby seized the initiative as early as the third move with the black pieces: 1 N-KB3, P-QB4 2 P-QN3, P-Q4 3 B-N2!? P-B3! Carrying the advantage into the ending, Fischer coaxed the position until a crucial inaccuracy gave him the game and the lead. Then Petrosian went the way of Fischer's other opponents—he collapsed. Fischer won the next three games with unexpected ease. By a score of 6½ to 2½, to the noisy acclaim of the Argentine throng, Bobby Fischer was hailed as the official challenger for the world chess championship.

Fischer always plays to win. He excoriates "grandmaster draws," in which a peace agreement is concluded in a few desultory moves, labeling the perpetrators "chicken." Despising quiet maneuvering, he once made the pithy comment, "The players have gotten soft on the Botvinnik-Barcza-Benko diet." He sees the chess struggle as an end in itself, and in it he pursues and comes close to his rigorous standard of perfect play.

People from Toronto to Moscow have asked how Fischer keeps in form during his prolonged absences from the arena, how he keeps abreast of new developments in theory, and how he can bear to be away from the game he loves. The fact is that chess is never far from Bobby's consciousness. Even on a foray to a restaurant, he is apt to bring along the latest chess periodicals. He has said that his subconscious mind is always working on chess: "Things are coming to me all the time."

One of the authors (A. S.) has seen more than one uncanny demonstration of Fischer's chess powers. I once showed Bobby a game from the U. S. Championship in which I felt my opponent's innovation dubious, although I hadn't been able to discover a win either during the game or in the post-mortem analysis with my grandmaster antagonist. After five minutes, Bobby's restless attention went on to something else, and he never looked at the position again. A few days later Bobby remarked, "Oh, by the way, you missed a winning move—Q-B3." He had just "thought it up."

The "secret" of Fischer's chess is accuracy. His method is to apply steady pressure until the opponent, whoever he is, breaks. The beauty of a Fischer game springs from no romantic impulse but is, rather, the by-product of winning execution.

His styles resembles one facet of his personality—it is very direct, even over-sharp. Although subtlety, stealth, and a capacity for passive defense have helped others to win many games, they are not notable Fischer qualities. Spassky has called him "straightforward in chess, like a child."

The Great Match was a tale of two titans. It was the best of matches, it was the worst of matches; it was a chess-lover's dream, yet it hovered on the brink of nightmare; it was a feast of exciting chess, but it disappointed the connoisseur. It was match in which the King's pawn player *par excellence* emerged as a Queen's Gambiteer and won. It was a historic necessity that almost neglected to happen. It was jeopardized by one man's demands for money, yet in the preliminary draft of an apology statement he renounced the entire purse and offered to play for the love of chess alone. It was the heyday of Fischer, the man of paradox.

It was a revolution, in which the Soviet chess colossus had to release its grip on Caïssa's most coveted crown to a brash outsider who violated the established order. And in revolutions regimes crumble, values are transformed, the young do outrageous things and the old make adjustments all too painful.

These few words serve to characterize the historic match between Bobby Fischer and Boris Spassky

GENS
F.I.D.E
FISCHER
DERACION ARGENTINA DE AJEDREZ
JUGADA
43

Fischer and Larsen scored personal triumphs in USSR-World encounter, although Soviets pulled out of the match. But the pillars of the Soviet chess colossus were shaken, and Fischer and Larsen henceforward posed a substantial threat to the Soviet-held world championship.

toric match between Bobby Fischer and Boris Spassky that unfolded in Iceland in the summer of 1972. It signaled a radical shift not only of power but in the attitude of the Western public toward the royal game. The chess world would never again be the same.

The basic question about the match was whether Fischer would play it at all. In a world which rewarded prize-fighters with millions for a single bout and had permitted more than one chess champion to starve, he now demanded rewards commensurate with the stature of chess. He decided to play only because of the "deus ex machina" intervention of British patron James Slater, who at the last minute doubled the purse to an astounding $250,000, over twelve times the size of the largest previous chess purse.

After acrimonious disputes and Fischer's contrite apology for "my disrespectful behavior," the match started nine days late, on July 11, 1972. In the first game, Bobby committed what looked like a beginner's blunder and lost. Then, irate at the distracting presence of television cameras, he refused to appear for the second game and was handed a forfeit. When his appeal was denied, he booked a flight home.

Thickest gloom reigned in the chess clubs of New York, whose habitués as well as millions of chess neophytes followed Shelby Lyman's replay of the moves of each game on public television. Telegrams of support began to pour into Fischer headquarters in Iceland. Spassky later said that he had every right to return to Moscow at this point, and some circles there wanted it. But the superb Russian sportsman did not wish such a hollow victory—which would likely have meant the end of Fischer's career.

A phone rang in Los Angeles. A friend of Bobby's answered. It was Iceland calling.

"Things look terrible here. Bobby is going to quit the match."

"Can't the lawyers work out some compromise?"

"We don't see how. The committee's decision can only be overruled by the FIDE Congress—too late."

"How is Bobby taking it?"

"I saw him once last night. He looked bad. This may be the end of Bobby Fischer. He'll never play again. He'll be destroyed."

"Don't worry too much about that. He still knows he's the best. But his life won't be easy. What a tragedy!"

"Got any ideas?"

"Tell Bobby we all want him to continue the match. The country's behind him. This is his last chance. We all know he can win it anyway. Tell him to do it for all the kids just starting in chess."

Rescue was found through a compromise—to have the third game played offstage in a room. Even then, the start of the game was marred by a dispute. But it was resolved and Bobby settled down to play chess, essaying the ultra-sharp Modern Benoni Defense. On move 11, he surprised Boris by moving his Knight to the rim, allowing doubled Rook pawns if it were captured by a Bishop. The move was against principle—the ghost of Tchigorin smiled. Spassky pondered for more than a half-hour before taking it but missed the best follow-up and drifted into complete passivity. Before adjournment the champion lost a vital pawn.

A player will generally retire while his second probes the intricacies of an adjourned position for most or all of the night. Then, next day, the second shows the results of his analysis and the player checks it and resumes the game well rested. At Reykjavik, this function was Grandmaster Lombardy's. Fischer at times got advice from Grandmaster Kavalek as well. The practice is overwhelmingly sanctioned by tradition, if not by law. But Fischer, never one to trust others' ideas, would stay up long after the midnight sunset and study every possible ramification of each adjourned position for himself. His reliance on physical training before and during the match (he demanded exclusive nocturnal access to the hotel pool) made it possible for him to play sharply despite a sleep deficit.

As usual, Fischer arrived a few minutes late for the resumption of play of the third game, but Spassky had already left. Referee Schmid explained that the champion, directly upon seeing Bobby's sealed move, had resigned. For the first time in his life, Fischer had beaten Spassky. He left the arena feeling that his oppressive burden had lightened. Meanwhile, the relieved chess world again looked forward to a monumental struggle.

But the manifold disturbances had taken a serious psychological toll on Spassky. In Game 4 he dissipated a good position into a draw, and in Game 5, in an uncomfortable situation, he committed one of the worst blunders of his career, losing instantly. The score was then even, and in the next game Fischer further crushed the champion's morale by fashioning the finest artistic achievement of the whole match.

FISCHER V. SPASSKY
Game 6
World Championship, 1972
Queen's Gambit Declined

	WHITE	BLACK		WHITE	BLACK
1	P-QB4 (!)	. . .			

Surprise! Fischer had played this move only twice before.

1	. . .	P-K3	4	N-B3	B-K2
2	N-KB3	P-Q4	5	B-N5	0-0
3	P-Q4	N-KB3	6	P-K3	P-KR3
			7	B-R4	P-QN3

Tartakower's Defense, a Spassky favorite.

8	PxP	NxP	11	R-B1	B-K3
9	BxB	QxB	12	Q-R4	P-QB4
10	NxN	PxN	13	Q-R3	R-B1
			14	B-N5	. . .

Fischer had never before played the Queen's Gambit, but

Reykjavik, 1972: Poster of long-awaited match; Fischer arriving at Exhibition Hall for first game; Spassky-Fischer opening game in progress. Furors, disputes, ultimatums enlivened match, resulted in—among other things—minimal photographic coverage.

he knew this move of Soviet G. M. Furman.

14 ... P-QR3
15 PxP PxP
16 0-0 R-R2?!

Rather than disconnect the Rooks, 16... Q-R2 is a convenient way to safeguard the "hanging pawns" in the center.

17 B-K2 N-Q2!?

Allows White's next. But 17... P-B5 accepts an inferior end game.

18 N-Q4! Q-B1?!

A lesser evil was 18... N-B3 19 N-N3, P-B5. Now Fischer gains Bishop for Knight and keeps hitting at the pawn center.

19 NxB PxN
20 P-K4! P-Q5?!

Gives a strong square to the Bishop. More counterplay lay in 20... P-B5.

21 P-B4 Q-K2
22 P-K5! ...

Before Spassky can consolidate with...P-K4, Fischer applies constriction.

22 ... R-N1
23 B-B4 K-R1
24 Q-R3 N-B1
25 P-QN3 P-QR4
26 P-B5 ...

The open KB file now becomes decisive. The beginning of the end.

26 ... PxP
27 RxP N-R2
28 R/1-B1 ...

Not 28 R-B7? N-N4.

28 ... Q-Q1
29 Q-N3 R-K2

Fischer's turn to wear the laurel. Dr. Max Euwe, head of FIDE and himself world champion from 1935 to 1937, presents Bobby with championship medal. As Euwe has played every other champion since Steinitz, this picture symbolizes all summit encounters of the twentieth century.

30 P-KR4

Further cramping the Knight. The next move only seems to allow . . . N-B3—then RxN would be lethal.

30	. . .	R/1-N2	**32**	Q-K5	Q-K1
31	P-K6	R/1-B2	**33**	P-R4	. . .

A "nothing" move, showing that Spassky is reduced to marking time helplessly.

33	. . .	Q-Q1	**35**	R/2-B3	Q-Q1
34	R/1-B2	Q-K1	**36**	B-Q3	Q-K1
			37	Q-K4!	. . .

Threatening 38 R-B8 ch, NxR 39 RxN ch, QxR 40 Q-R7 mate.

37 . . . N-B3

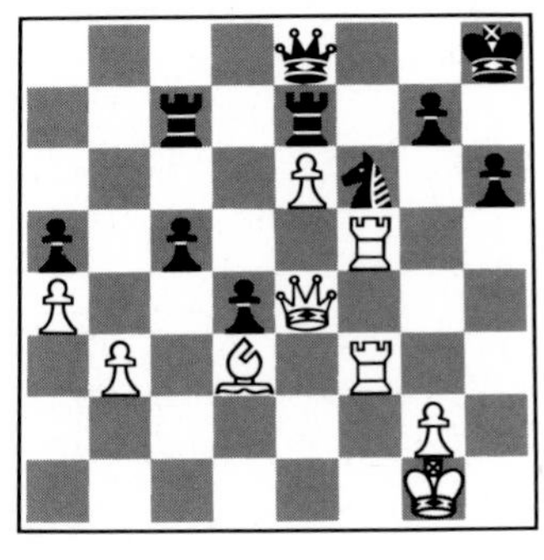

38	RxN!	PxR	**39**	RxP	K-N1
			40	B-B4	. . .

The exposure of the black King has no remedy. White now threatens 41 R-B7.

40	. . .	K-R1	**41**	Q-B4	Resigns

White wins as he pleases, for example, 41. . . K-N1 42 QxRP, R-KR2 43 R-B8 ch, QxR 44 P-K7 ch, R-B2 45 PxQ (R) mate.

Even Fischer was touched when Spassky, great sportsman that he is, joined in the applause for such a Capablanca-like game of elegant simplicity.

Through Game 10 Spassky's form was mostly unrecognizable. Fischer surged ahead to a lead of 6½-3½. The champion appeared to be destroyed, but the fans counting on the return of the old Spassky were not to be completely disappointed. In Game 11 Fischer captured the notorious "poisoned pawn" in the Sicilian Defense, as he had often done before with impunity. This time it proved truly venomous, and hardly out of the opening stage, Fischer had to lose his Queen and the game. The game proved chiefly that chess retains the power to humble even its greatest exponent. The challenger's lead was now shaved to 2 points.

If Game 3 put Fischer back in the match, then Game 13, the most interesting battle of all, put Spassky out of it. Spassky, surprised again, this time by Alekhine's Defense, lost a pawn early but developed dangerous king-side chances that he misplayed, pressed for time. (Fischer, with amazingly quick "sight of the board," has almost never been short of time.) At adjournment, the challenger seemed to have a winning end game, but on resumption the champion found a perfect defense against ingenious threats. Just before the third time-control in the ninth hour of play, Spassky erred and threw the draw away. After such protracted effort, it was the bitterest defeat.

Fischer once again enjoyed a 3-point lead. In the next seven games, the challenger known for deadly play and 6-0 shutouts coasted with draw after draw, moving ever closer to his goal. In the fourteenth, Fischer again entered the unfamiliar waters of the Queen's Gambit, losing a pawn. But six moves later Spassky blundered it back, turning his face to the wall in disgust.

At this stage the Soviet delegation made public a most bizarre allegation that the Americans might be influencing the world champion's behavior by "chemical substances or electronic means." The only evidence uncovered by a solemn scientific investigation, including the dismantling of Spassky's chair, was two dead flies in a light fixture. It was Boris who had earlier said that Bobby suffered from a "persecution complex." The press corps agreed that this episode was the best comic relief since a

Spassky in simultaneous exhibition at Chess City, New York, early in 1974. Forty-one opponents each paid $25 for privilege of facing ex-champ. One, age six, said: "He's a very nice man." He is. Event could not have taken place without changes wrought in chess by Fischer and Spassky.

first-week story from Moscow that Fischer was to be helped during the games by a New York computer.

In Game 21 Fischer adopted for the first time the Paulsen Variation of the Sicilian, and on move 7 sprang another innovation. It was a simple idea, based on the classical principle of occupying the center with pawns, but nobody had thought of it before. Spassky, with real hope long since gone, misplayed the ending. After pondering the adjourned position overnight, he discovered he had sealed a weak move, and decided to resign.

On September 1, 1972 Bobby Fischer learned by phone that with a score of 7 wins, 2 losses, 1 forfeit and 11 draws, he had become the eleventh chess champion of the world. The news merely made official a destiny he had sensed as a boy in Brooklyn many years before. Without it, Bobby's world, in which the art of chess occupied the paramount place, could not be said to be in order.

Boris Spassky told the press, "Fischer is a man of art, but he is a rare human being in the everyday life of this century. I like Fischer and I think that I understand him." It was the generous tribute of one great artist to another. Thus ended ten weeks that shook the chess world.

If much had been written about Fischer prior to his great victory, the floodgates were now opened to a veritable torrent of newspaper stories, magazine articles, and books. Fischer made the front covers of the leading magazines in America and abroad. Radio and television broadcast his exploits. On many programs the King himself deigned to appear and comported himself amazingly well.

In spite of Fischer's overwhelming achievement, not all the comment was favorable. Nowhere was Fischer more misunderstood than in his own country. As his sister Joan once observed: "Bobby is a boy who requires an extra amount of understanding."

The most common accusation was that Fischer was greedy, mercenary, more interested in the almighty dollar than in promoting the interests of chess. It should be made clear that Fischer made demands not only for himself, but for Spassky as well. But, in the larger sense, the demands were not for himself or for Spassky, but for chess.

Fischer understood the psychology of the American public only too well. He knew that in our society, the symbol of a man's achievement is money. Fischer's motive was a selfish one, admittedly, but not in the way most people thought. He wanted respect for the game in which he excelled and, through it, a deeper respect and recogni-

tion for himself. He has turned down a number of very lucrative commercial offers.

The next most frequent accusation leveled against Fischer is that his tantrums are all part of a game of psychological warfare against his opponents, especially against Spassky. Let's not kid ourselves, friends. Fischer simply doesn't need it.

Certainly Spassky ought to be the person best qualified to know. We refer the reader to Spassky's statement about Fischer at the end of the match. This accolade is not that of a man who feels he has been subjected to unfair or underhanded tactics. The truth of the matter is that Spassky likes and respects Fischer, and vice versa.

If Fischer seems to make an undue fuss about playing conditions, noise in the hall, movie cameras, equipment, etc., it is only because he feels that respect for the game of chess makes optimal conditions imperative. The casual spectator can have no idea of the dynamos pounding inside each contestant in an important chess match. In this furious battle of wills, all else being equal, it may take very little outside diversion to distract one player and present the victory to the other.

Again, it must be stressed that Fischer's demands were not unilateral. They were as much for his opponent—

and for chess—as they were for himself.

One more footnote must be added. When a person is described as modest, the sad corollary, all too often, is that he has plenty to be modest about. No such hang-up applies to Fischer. How can anyone who presumes to know anything of Fischer's character believe that he would settle for beating his opponent any way except through his superior playing ability? Fischer plays the board, not the man. As he himself put it, "I don't believe in psychology. I believe in good moves."

In the Spassky match, Fischer departed from his invariable P-K4 opening move on several occasions and from his usual Sicilian with Black to play as unpredictable an opening as Alekhine's Defense. Again the cry was raised of "psychological warfare"—though perfectly permissible this time. Psychology, our collective foot! Fischer knew that Spassky had been engaged in exhaustive preparation to meet his usual openings, so he simply switched to lines that Spassky was less likely to have studied. This is not psychology, just plain common sense.

Accusation number three may be broadly categorized as the "monsterizing" of Fischer. He is depicted, all too literally, as an ogre over the chessboard. The distinguished *New York Times* critic Harold Schonberg has accused him of "psychic murder." The implication is both gratuitous and misleading.

Let's face it. Chess, like all competitive sports, is an outlet for aggression. Frankly, we look forward to the day when athletes will discard the phony-modest "we were lucky" in favor of "we won because we're the better team."

Accusation four is usually put in the form of an inquiry: Why shouldn't Bobby be good? He spent his whole lifetime on nothing but chess! Answer: Thousands upon thousands of chess-players have done precisely the same with little to show for it, except an occasional divorce. Chess is a most absorbing game, but no amount of study will take the place of championship talent. On the other hand, many talents in chess and other fields have withered through lack of application. We should be thankful for Bobby's monomania. It has made him champion of the world and given chess-players everywhere a heritage of beautiful games and creative innovations.

Accusation five: Fischer has bad manners. Granted, but let's consider a few instances:

1. *He comes late to important chess games.*
   So what? It's Fischer's clock that's running.
2. *He is anti-social and likes to be alone.*
   So did Thoreau. Don't bother him and he won't bother you.
3. *He glares at the spectators.*
   Stop eating popcorn. Also, you can avoid the glare by studying his latest move on the wall-board.
4. *Many of his complaints are unreasonable.*
   Many aren't. Have you tried playing chess with a camera watching your every move, off the board and on?
5. *He is grouchy and uncooperative.*
   He has also been known to be cheerful and obliging. Take his good-humored participation, after the Larsen match, in the big New York Rapid Transit Tournament in August of 1971.
6. *He is hostile, lacks poise and self-composure.*
   Did you catch him on the Dick Cavett, Bob Hope, and Dinah Shore shows? He was a doll.
7. *As a public figure, he should give more interviews.*
   He was burnt once—badly. A great chess-player doesn't repeat the same mistake.
8. *He is aloof and unapproachable.*
   Ask for his autograph and see where that gets you. (Actually, Bobby made a surprise appearance at the final round of the 1972 American Open in Santa Monica and was liberal with his autographs.)
9. *He has a low opinion of women.*

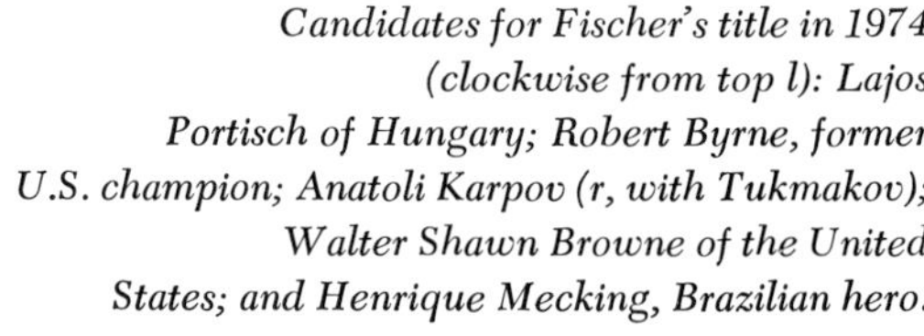

Candidates for Fischer's title in 1974 (clockwise from top l): Lajos Portisch of Hungary; Robert Byrne, former U.S. champion; Anatoli Karpov (r, with Tukmakov); Walter Shawn Browne of the United States; and Henrique Mecking, Brazilian hero.

Picture Credits

AS —*Albert Squillace*
BH —*Burt Hochberg Collection*
DH —*David Hafler Collection*
DL —*David Lawson Collection*
JFH —*John F. Harbeson Collection*
MET —*Metropolitan Museum of Art, New York City*
NS —*Norman Snyder*
NYPL—*New York Public Library*
TL —*Time-Life Picture Agency*

Chapter 1
10-11: NS. 14: Eric Schurl/TL. 15: Manson Collection, Yale University Art Gallery. 16: NYPL, Rare Book Division. 17: Cleveland Public Library, John G. White Department. 18: Philadelphia Museum of Art, Louise and Walter Arensberg Collection. 19: Mark Kauffman/TL. 20: Yale Joel. 21: (top) Alfred Statler/TL; (bottom) UPI. 23: IRI Foto. 25: Alfred Eisenstaedt/TL. 26-27: Baruch Katz. 28-29: NS. 30: Jack Nowack. 31: Harold Messing. 32: AS. 34-35: NS, courtesy DH (l and bottom r) and JFH (top and bottom l). 36: NS.
Chapter 2
38-39: NS, courtesy JFH. 40-44: MET. 45: (bottom) MET. 46: AS, courtesy DH. 47: (l) NS, courtesy DH; (r) NYPL, Manuscript Division. 48: NS, courtesy DH. 49: Kessel/TL. 50: NS, courtesy DH. 51: (top) AS, courtesy DH; (bottom) NS, courtesy DH. 52-54: NS, courtesy DH. 55: Philadelphia Museum of Art. 56: AS, courtesy DH.
Chapter 3
58-59: AS, courtesy DH. 60-61: Library of Congress, Rosenwald Collection. 62-63: (top and bottom l) Cleveland Public Library, John G. White Department; (r) Photo Service. 65: (r) Bayrische Nationalmuseum; (bottom) Philadelphia Museum of Art; (center and top l) Nationalmuseet, Copenhagen; (center) MET. 66-67: MET. 69: (top) Photo Service; (bottom) Cleveland Public Library, John G. White Department. 70: (top) NS, courtesy DH; (bottom) Berlin-Dahlem Staatliche Museen. 71: NS, courtesy JFH. 72: AS, courtesy DH.
Chapter 4
74-75: NYPL, Print Division. 77: Photo Service. 78: Culver Pictures. 79: (top) Cleveland Public Library, John G. White Department; (bottom) AS, courtesy DH. 80-81: NS, courtesy DH. 82: David Namias, courtesy JFH. 83: AS, courtesy JFH. 84: courtesy DL. 85: NYPL. 86: Jaques & Son, Ltd. 87: NS, courtesy Mrs. J. Russell Twiss Collection. 88: courtesy James Gates. 88-89: courtesy DL.
Chapter 5
90-91: courtesy JFH. 93: NYPL. 94-95: courtesy DL. 96-97: NYPL. 98: AS, courtesy DH. 99: Library of Congress. 100: (l) Cleveland Public Library, John G. White Department; (r) courtesy DL. 102: AS, courtesy DH. 103: NS, courtesy DH. 104: courtesy DL. 107: Brooklyn Museum Collection. 108: Photo Service.
Chapter 6
110-111: courtesy DL. 115: (top) Cleveland Public Library; (bottom) courtesy DL. 116: NYPL. 118: NS, courtesy DH. 120: NYPL. 122-123: MET. 124: NS, courtesy JFH. 126-127: Photo Service, courtesy National Portrait Gallery. 128: (top) AS, courtesy DH; (bottom l) NS, courtesy DH; (bottom r) NS, courtesy JFH.
Chapter 7
130: NS, courtesy DH. 134: courtesy BH. 137: courtesy DL. 141: courtesy Mrs. Capablanca Clark. 142, 145: courtesy BH. 146: NS. 148-149: courtesy DL. 150: courtesy Harvard Club of New York City.
Chapter 8
154-155: Museum of Modern Art Collection, New York City. 159: courtesy Manhattan Chess Club. 160: Museum of Modern Art, New York. 162-163: courtesy Philadelphia Museum of Art, Arensberg Collection. 164: Bob Towers/TL. 167: NS, courtesy Philadelphia Museum of Art, gift of JFH. 168: courtesy BH.
Chapter 9
170-171: Sovfoto. 173: courtesy DL. 177: courtesy BH. 178: Sovfoto. 181: Krokodil/TL. 183: (top l and r, center r) courtesy BH; (center l) Pictorial Parade; (bottom l) courtesy BH; (bottom r) UPI.
Chapter 10
186-187: NYPL. 189, 191: Author's collection. 193, 195: Nigel Eddis.
Chapter 11
198-199: NS, courtesy Mrs. J. Russell Twiss Collection. 202: Pictorial Parade. 203: Sovfoto. 205: (top) Thomas McAvoy/TL; (bottom l) Howard Sochurek/TL; (bottom r) UPI. 207: Pictorial Parade. 208: (top) Author's collection; (bottom) Sovfoto. 209-211: Sovfoto.
Chapter 12
214-215: NS. 220: Author's collection.
Chapter 13
224-225: UPI. 227: NYPL. 229: courtesy Manhattan Chess Club. 230, 232: courtesy BH. 233: (top) courtesy BH; (bottom) NYPL. 234: courtesy BH. 235: Rapho Guillumette. 236, 238: courtesy BH. 239: (top) UPI; (bottom) Chester Fox. 240: Chester Fox. 242-243: Baruch Katz. 245: (top l and r, center l) courtesy BH; (bottom l) Nigel Eddis (bottom r) Author's collection.

Candidates for Fischer's title in 1974 (clockwise from top l): Lajos Portisch of Hungary; Robert Byrne, former U.S. champion; Anatoli Karpov (r, with Tukmakov); Walter Shawn Browne of the United States; and Henrique Mecking, Brazilian hero.

Only as chess-players. Wait till he meets the right girl.

10. *He is egomaniacal, has tantrums when he doesn't have his own way, is devoted to only one thing to the exclusion of everything else, thinks the whole world should kowtow to him, is suspicious of everybody, and considers his genius an excuse for everything.*
Are you talking about Beethoven? Don't be too hard on him, he's dead. Anyway, the only thing the world remembers now is his music.

The only thing Fischer wants the world to remember him for is his chess. He has earned this right. It is carping and petty to attempt to judge him by ordinary standards. They no longer apply.

When, as a youth, he boasted that he would one day become world champion, the effect was distasteful and presumptuous. A Yiddish word describes it best—*chutzpa*. It spawned an anti-Fischer prejudice which became magnified over the years. This onus must now be lifted—once and forever. Fischer was right. He has proven himself an accurate prophet.

In that disastrous interview of long ago, Fischer was asked if he considered himself greater than Capablanca, Steinitz, and Morphy. His much-quoted reply: "Well, I don't like to put things like that in print, it sounds so egotistical. But to answer your question, yes." You can drop the apologetic tone, Bobby. You have made your point.

Bobby Fischer's unprecedented Elo rating of 2,780 points stamps him as the strongest chess-player who ever lived. The burden of proof rests on those who would seek to dispute the validity of this statistical measure.

Fischer is that rare instance of a modern man who has always been true to his principles. Virtually assured of first prize in the Interzonal Tournament at Sousse in 1967, Bobby threatened to withdraw if certain conditions relevant to scheduling (in conformity with his religious requirements) were not met. The tournament committee failed to accede. Bobby withdrew, even though it meant giving up, for the time being, his lifelong dream of a chance to play for the world title.

When he played his 1961 match with Sammy Reshevsky in Los Angeles, the sponsor, Mrs. Piatigorsky, wife of the famous cellist, tried to change the twelfth-round playing schedule to an earlier hour so she could attend a concert that evening given by her husband in tandem with Jascha Heifetz. Bobby indignantly refused and forfeited the match. "I should get up early in the morning just because she wants to listen to some fiddler!" In Bobby's mind, chess plays second fiddle to no one, not even Heifetz.

Using strangely involuted logic, some of the same detractors who took Bobby to task for complaining when he was so far ahead also accused him of having used poor playing conditions as an alibi for his infrequent defeats. This is simply not true. Bobby has made demands and accusations on various occasions, but rarely has he offered excuses for any specific losses. In the 1966 Piatigorsky Cup Tournament, Fischer scored only 3½ points out of the nine rounds which constituted the first half of the tournament. No whimper of alibi or protest crossed his lips. As Bobby once expressed it, "I play honestly and I play to win. When I lose, I take my medicine."

And take his medicine he did, with highly salubrious effect! In the last nine rounds, he scored a magnificent 6 wins and 3 draws to take second place, only ½-point behind Spassky. The mark of a true champion is his ability to come back as Fischer once again stunningly demonstrated in the big match.

On the ideological level he represents the triumph of the individual over bureaucracy, specifically, the rigid bureaucracy of the Soviet Union. It was the Soviets who introduced the symbol of chess as a badge of their superiority over the bourgeois world. So ingrained was this belief that when Spassky was defeated, it was seen not as the result of an encounter between individuals, but as a direct slap to the Soviet social system. Marx and Lenin (and possibly Tchigorin too) had presumably been betrayed. The Soviet grandmasters, and especially Spassky, were depicted as fat cats, lazy and indolent, neglecting their duties to the State.

Henceforth, it was decreed, the grandmasters would be put to work. No longer would they be permitted to shirk their responsibilities, to pick and choose whatever tourneys they personally desired to enter. All of the strongest active players in the Soviet Union were obliged to participate in that country's forty-first annual championship tournament.

Alas, for dialectical materialism! Pity the poor Soviet State Committee on Physical Culture and Sport! The splendid victor turned out to be the most bitterly berated Soviet grandmaster of all, the same Boris Spassky whose "moral qualities and determination" they had attacked after his resounding loss to the bourgeois upstart from Brooklyn, U.S.A.

But the reign of Bobby the First produced more than merely political repercussions. It set off a chess explosion which was heard around the world. Never before had chess achieved such an all-time high of interest and popularity. Membership in the United States Chess Federation more than doubled. There came forth a flood of magazine and newspaper articles, chess books, and chess paraphernalia—fancy chess sets, pocket sets, variations upon the game, collector's items, postal chess equipment, pins, emblems, souvenirs, and trophies.

Ironically, those who castigated Bobby most severely made more money than ever before through their chess books and articles. The public's thirst for chess literature was insatiable. New books were published and old ones re-issued. The paperback market for chess books, at upped prices, enjoyed a prosperity it had never experienced before.

More and more tournaments were held. Many of the weekend variety were open to all, while others were organized for the more elite chess-players. In many cases, the prize money was dramatically increased, often more than doubled. There is no such thing as pure amateurism in chess. There are occasional small tournaments for book or subscription prizes, but in over ninety percent of the events, the trophies in every section are accompanied by cash.

Youngsters were encouraged to learn chess by their parents, not merely as a hobby but as a possible valid and worthy occupation. A goodly amount of new talent was uncovered and is continuing to be developed. Someday, perhaps, this phenomenon may bring forth new contenders to challenge Bobby or his possible successors.

Those engaged in the field of chess—players, writers, publicists, manufacturers—all felt the new prosperity. The millennium has not been reached, but there are hopeful signs that future chess greats may be spared the financial anxiety that plagued Steinitz, Lasker, Rubinstein, Alekhine, and so many others.

One man and one man alone was responsible for this incredible upsurge, a man variously described as cantankerous, egomaniacal, boorish, and paranoid. A man with a monomania for chess to the exclusion of all else. A man given to unreasonable and outrageous demands—he actually insisted upon being paid and paid well for something he enjoyed doing the most! Who ever heard of such effrontery?

Would that someone had had the temerity and bargaining power to make such demands before! Chess might have been rescued from its doldrums a long time ago. Every true lover of chess in every part of the world must feel a bond of gratitude to Bobby Fischer.

No more worthy aspirant ever graced the chess throne. We wish him an active and fruitful reign.

Long live the champ!

Picture Credits

AS —Albert Squillace
BH —Burt Hochberg Collection
DH —David Hafler Collection
DL —David Lawson Collection
JFH —John F. Harbeson Collection
MET —Metropolitan Museum of Art, New York City
NS —Norman Snyder
NYPL—New York Public Library
TL —Time-Life Picture Agency

Chapter 1
10-11: NS. 14: Eric Schurl/TL. 15: Manson Collection, Yale University Art Gallery. 16: NYPL, Rare Book Division. 17: Cleveland Public Library, John G. White Department. 18: Philadelphia Museum of Art, Louise and Walter Arensberg Collection. 19: Mark Kauffman/TL. 20: Yale Joel. 21: (top) Alfred Statler/TL; (bottom) UPI. 23: IRI Foto. 25: Alfred Eisenstaedt/TL. 26-27: Baruch Katz. 28-29: NS. 30: Jack Nowack. 31: Harold Messing. 32: AS. 34-35: NS, courtesy DH (l and bottom r) and JFH (top and bottom l). 36: NS.
Chapter 2
38-39: NS, courtesy JFH. 40-44: MET. 45: (bottom) MET. 46: AS, courtesy DH. 47: (l) NS, courtesy DH; (r) NYPL, Manuscript Division. 48: NS, courtesy DH. 49: Kessel/TL. 50: NS, courtesy DH. 51: (top) AS, courtesy DH; (bottom) NS, courtesy DH. 52-54: NS, courtesy DH. 55: Philadelphia Museum of Art. 56: AS, courtesy DH.
Chapter 3
58-59: AS, courtesy DH. 60-61: Library of Congress, Rosenwald Collection. 62-63: (top and bottom l) Cleveland Public Library, John G. White Department; (r) Photo Service. 65: (r) Bayrische Nationalmuseum; (bottom) Philadelphia Museum of Art; (center and top l) Nationalmuseet, Copenhagen; (center) MET. 66-67: MET. 69: (top) Photo Service; (bottom) Cleveland Public Library, John G. White Department. 70: (top) NS, courtesy DH; (bottom) Berlin-Dahlem Staatliche Museen. 71: NS, courtesy JFH. 72: AS, courtesy DH.
Chapter 4
74-75: NYPL, Print Division. 77: Photo Service. 78: Culver Pictures. 79: (top) Cleveland Public Library, John G. White Department; (bottom) AS, courtesy DH. 80-81: NS, courtesy DH. 82: David Namias, courtesy JFH. 83: AS, courtesy JFH. 84: courtesy DL. 85: NYPL. 86: Jaques & Son, Ltd. 87: NS, courtesy Mrs. J. Russell Twiss Collection. 88: courtesy James Gates. 88-89: courtesy DL.
Chapter 5
90-91: courtesy JFH. 93: NYPL. 94-95: courtesy DL. 96-97: NYPL. 98: AS, courtesy DH. 99: Library of Congress. 100: (l) Cleveland Public Library, John G. White Department; (r) courtesy DL. 102: AS, courtesy DH. 103: NS, courtesy DH. 104: courtesy DL. 107: Brooklyn Museum Collection. 108: Photo Service.
Chapter 6
110-111: courtesy DL. 115: (top) Cleveland Public Library; (bottom) courtesy DL. 116: NYPL. 118: NS, courtesy DH. 120: NYPL. 122-123: MET. 124: NS, courtesy JFH. 126-127: Photo Service, courtesy National Portrait Gallery. 128: (top) AS, courtesy DH; (bottom l) NS, courtesy DH; (bottom r) NS, courtesy JFH.
Chapter 7
130: NS, courtesy DH. 134: courtesy BH. 137: courtesy DL. 141: courtesy Mrs. Capablanca Clark. 142, 145: courtesy BH. 146: NS. 148-149: courtesy DL. 150: courtesy Harvard Club of New York City.
Chapter 8
154-155: Museum of Modern Art Collection, New York City. 159: courtesy Manhattan Chess Club. 160: Museum of Modern Art, New York. 162-163: courtesy Philadelphia Museum of Art, Arensberg Collection. 164: Bob Towers/TL. 167: NS, courtesy Philadelphia Museum of Art, gift of JFH. 168: courtesy BH.
Chapter 9
170-171: Sovfoto. 173: courtesy DL. 177: courtesy BH. 178: Sovfoto. 181: Krokodil/TL. 183: (top l and r, center r) courtesy BH; (center l) Pictorial Parade; (bottom l) courtesy BH; (bottom r) UPI.
Chapter 10
186-187: NYPL. 189, 191: Author's collection. 193, 195: Nigel Eddis.
Chapter 11
198-199: NS, courtesy Mrs. J. Russell Twiss Collection. 202: Pictorial Parade. 203: Sovfoto. 205: (top) Thomas McAvoy/TL; (bottom l) Howard Sochurek/TL; (bottom r) UPI. 207: Pictorial Parade. 208: (top) Author's collection; (bottom) Sovfoto. 209-211: Sovfoto.
Chapter 12
214-215: NS. 220: Author's collection.
Chapter 13
224-225: UPI. 227: NYPL. 229: courtesy Manhattan Chess Club. 230, 232: courtesy BH. 233: (top) courtesy BH; (bottom) NYPL. 234: courtesy BH. 235: Rapho Guillumette. 236, 238: courtesy BH. 239: (top) UPI; (bottom) Chester Fox. 240: Chester Fox. 242-243: Baruch Katz. 245: (top l and r, center l) courtesy BH; (bottom l) Nigel Eddis (bottom r) Author's collection.

Index

Page numbers in italics indicate reference to illustrations.

Beatrix Potter's Art

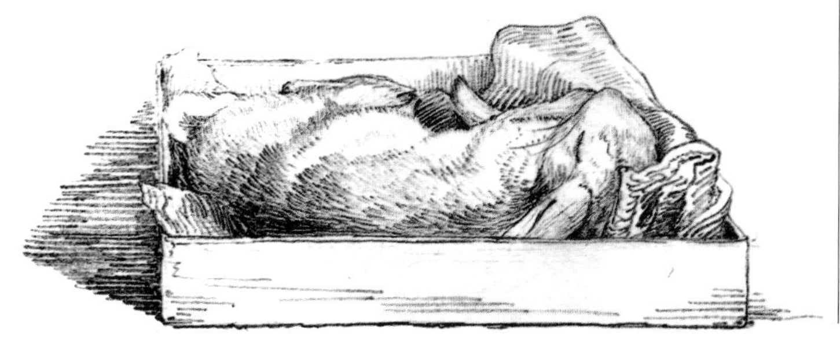

Beatrix Potter's Art

Paintings and Drawings
Selected and Introduced by

ANNE STEVENSON HOBBS

FREDERICK WARNE

FREDERICK WARNE

Published by the Penguin Group
27 Wrights Lane, London W8 5TZ, England
Viking Penguin Inc., 40 West 23rd Street, New York, New York 10010, USA
Penguin Books Australia Ltd, Ringwood, Victoria, Australia
Penguin Books Canada Ltd, 2801 John Street, Markham, Ontario, Canada L3R 1B4
Penguin Books (NZ) Ltd, 182-190 Wairau Road, Auckland 10, New Zealand

Penguin Books Ltd, Registered Offices: Harmondsworth, Middlesex, England

First published 1989
10 9 8 7 6 5 4 3 2 1

ISBN 0 7232 3598 8

Designed by Yvonne Dedman

Set in Linotron Aldus by
Rowland Phototypesetting (London) Ltd.
Colour Origination by Anglia Graphics Ltd., Bedford.
Printed in Italy by L.E.G.O. Vicenza

British Library Cataloguing in Publication Data available

Title page:
Esthwaite Low Grounds, February 1911.
A quick sketch which summarizes an effect of light.
Pencil and watercolour; 140 x 228; FLP

Preface

Beatrix Potter's Art could equally well have been given the title 'Beatrix Potter's Other Art'. As a selection of her less familiar drawings, some never before published, it is meant to surprise as well as delight. It is not intended as a critique of Beatrix Potter as illustrator for children, and so contains tantalizingly few of the 'book pictures'. Those that do appear are seen in the context of her work as a whole, as compositions in their own right. More comprehensively represented are her illustrations to others, and especially to 'Anon.'.

Not all her best drawings could be included. The longer narrative sequences, with their lively line drawings, had to be omitted, and with them some of her humour. Examples mentioned but not illustrated can be investigated in her 'Tales', or in recent publications.

Beatrix Potter may have been in a higher class as a book artist than as a landscape watercolourist, but she holds her own as an illustrator of natural history. This selection may help to remove the 'taint of smiling toleration', deprecated by Sickert in relation to another artist, which still clings in some quarters to the work of Beatrix Potter.

She neither wanted nor expected fame or popularity through her art. Her privacy has been posthumously invaded – but there is surely compensation in the delight she has given to all ages, and the indirect influence her work has had in encouraging both a love of the countryside and its inhabitants and a determination to save its beauty for the future.

Acknowledgements

The Armitt Trust, the Book Trust, several Sections of the British Museum (Natural History), the Frederick Warne Archive, the Rare Book Department, Free Library of Philadelphia, the Trustees of the Linder Collection, the National Art Library, Victoria and Albert Museum, the National Trust, the Board of Trustees of the Victoria and Albert Museum.

Brian Alderson, Elizabeth Battrick, Dr Hugh Chapman, Dr Sydney Chapman (AT), Joan Duke, Gail Engert, Doris Frohnsdorff, John Gavin (AT), Dr Pamela Gerrish Nunn, Michael Glover, Avril Hart (V&A), Wendy Hoare, Mary Hobbs, Maureen Lambourne, Margaret Lane, the Countess of Huntingdon, Karen Lightner (FLP), Dr Mary Noble, Brian Riddle, Charlotte Robinson, Judy Taylor, Dr Michael A. Taylor, Jan van der Wateren (National Art Library, V&A), John and Kate Veale, Miss Laura Wakely, Dr Roy Watling, Irene Whalley.

Joan Broderick and Derrick Witty (photographers, Philadelphia and London), Richard Davis (photographer, V&A), and especially Yvonne Dedman (designer), Diana Syrat (editor) and her colleagues at Frederick Warne and Co.

Introduction

Background and Influences

The numbers which appear in the Introduction refer to the illustrations.

Repetition and variety, the keynotes of nature, are also the keynotes of Beatrix Potter's art. Repetition, because she continually returns to favourite themes, redrawing and re-copying, endlessly attempting to capture the world about her; variety, because within her own limits that range of subjects and styles was as wide as her experience allowed.

Associated in the public imagination with one style, she experimented with medium, technique and scale. The 'miniaturist' painted spiders and fungi ten times larger than her vignettes. The practitioner of naturalism and precise detail played with broad washes and a palette of bright primaries. The investigative scientist used her knowledge with wit. The discipline of the camera and the microscope guided her vision, but she had, in her own words, the 'seeing eye': a memory both for places and for the sentiments they evoked. From ordinary, everyday objects she created a microcosm of the world.

For some people her 'little books' have overshadowed her other achievements. The reference books almost ignore her. Many of her most original pieces, independently invented and untouched by publishers, were neither exhibited nor printed in her lifetime. She painted and drew to please herself, believing 'the more spontaneous the pleasure, the more happy the result'. Her essentially private and unshowy art demands, and deserves, close attention.

Beatrix Potter was born into a prosperous family whose fortune came from the Lancashire cotton trade. Her father, Rupert Potter, a qualified barrister, was rich enough to lead a life of almost perpetual leisure. Beatrix's cloistered existence at No. 2 Bolton Gardens, Kensington was relieved by visits to Camfield Place in Hertfordshire, much loved home of her paternal grandparents, by spring holidays at the sea, and by the annual three-month exodus, when the entire household moved from London to a rented country estate, at first in Scotland and later often in the Lake District.

74.

The Potter family belonged to the contemporary art world, as connoisseurs and patrons, and as practitioners. Edmund Potter, Beatrix's manufacturing grandfather, had been President of the Manchester School of Art; her uncle Edmund Crompton Potter was a notable collector. Rupert, her father, something of a collector himself, was a man of taste. He was a member of the Photographic Society of London; his work includes posed portrait groups and over one thousand experimental views of London.

Opposite:
View across Esthwaite Water, November 1909 (detail).
Watercolour; 180 x 255; V&A

5.

Spending at least half the year out of London, he recorded landscape too and specialized in 'artistic' compositions. He supplied photographs of models and landscape backgrounds for John Everett Millais, a close friend: 'Mr Millais says the professionals aren't fit to hold a candle to papa,' Beatrix wrote.

Beatrix's mother, a fine embroideress, had in youth been an accomplished watercolourist in the fashionable manner, but Mr Potter was above all a draughtsman. 'Note the direct work and touch,' Beatrix commented on his painstaking studies of dogs and birds. An 1853 sketchbook contains caricatures in the spirit of *Punch* or even Lear; he later painted nursery plates and table mats with birds for Beatrix and her younger brother Bertram, who actually became an artist.

Rupert Potter had no understanding of the difficulties of painting, however. 'Seeing Mr Millais paint so often and so easily, would make a man hard on other painters. It prevents me showing much of my attempts to him, and I lose much by it.' Millais understood the problems only too well, advised Beatrix on mixing paints, and was reassuring about the value of working alone. 'I shall always have a most affectionate remembrance of Sir John Millais, though unmercifully afraid of him as a child . . . He gave me the kindest encouragement with my drawings . . . but he really paid me a compliment for he said that "plenty of people can *draw*, but you and my son John have observation".'

Like the Brontës, Beatrix wrote and drew at an early age, benefiting from a rich diet of reading. Expression and imagination matured sooner in her words than in her pictures. In a secret journal she kept from 1881 to 1897, she recorded impressions of places, people and animals, scraps of gossip, social comment and observations on art. Written in code, the journal provided both outlet and task. 'Her journal is an enormous sketchbook in which she tried to teach herself how to see and write' (Maurice Sendak, 1966). Her descriptive writing always conjures up vivid images.

Drawing was indulged and not always supervised: 'Thank goodness, my education was neglected and the originality was not rubbed off.' She copied from life or from popular natural history books: dead game and garden birds, humming birds and budgerigars, and a profusion of flowers in watercolour. She knew the work of Bewick and Harrison Weir; she must have seen copies after Gould, Wolf and Lear, and Grandville's *La Fontaine*. On her tenth birthday she was given, to her joy, *Birds Drawn from Nature* by Jemima Blackburn, from whose bird fantasy *The Pipits* she copied that same year.

Real animals surrounded her too: a menagerie of pets, from snails to mice. Her brother Bertram shared her enthusiasm and augmented the animal population with pets of his own, bats, a kestrel and a jay included. Alert and curious about the world, brother and sister found a stimulus to creativity in their holiday escapes from London. They studied and drew

26.

animals with scientific precision. At home they contrived to reconstitute the skeletons of dead creatures and even to stuff them. Rabbits were an important addition to Beatrix's nursery and her repertoire; the most memorable were Benjamin Bouncer and his successor, Peter Piper, whom she drew from life in every attitude and later immortalized as Benjamin Bunny and Peter Rabbit. Her earliest known fantasy drawings, from 1876, show rabbits skating in a high wind; they are remarkable for their characterization, composition and sense of movement. Even more remarkable were her application and single-mindedness: 'It is all the same, drawing, painting, modelling, the irresistible desire to copy any beautiful object which strikes the eye. Why cannot one be content to look at it? I cannot rest, I must draw, however poor the result. . .'

4.

From the ages of twelve to seventeen she studied with a Miss Cameron, and took in July 1881 her only formal qualification, the Art Student's Certificate, 2nd Grade, of the Science and Art Department. Summing up her time with Miss Cameron, she wrote, 'I have learnt from her freehand, model, geometry, perspective and a little water-colour flower painting. Painting is an awkward thing to teach except the details of the medium. If you and your master are determined to look at nature and art in two different directions you are sure to stick.'

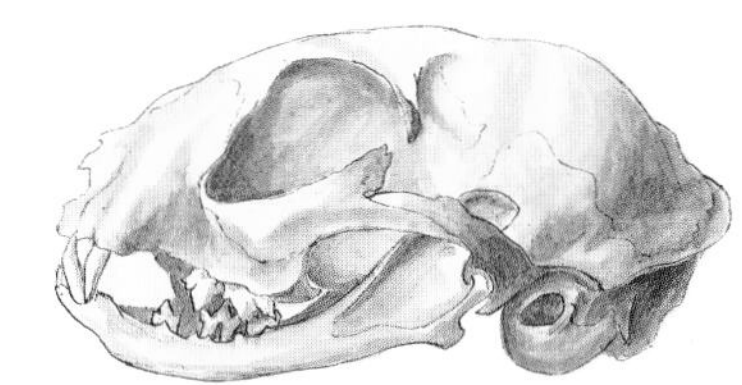

36.

Conventional still lifes, with or without flowers, date from this period. In late 1883 she was producing strong but static fruit-pieces and interiors in a heavy bodycolour imitating oils (9). This technique she owed to a brief and unsuccessful flirtation with oil and figure painting: twelve expensive lessons twice a week with a still unidentified 'Mrs A' (possibly Sophie Anderson), recommended to her parents by Lady Eastlake. 'I may probably owe a good deal to Mrs A . . . I did to Miss Cameron, but I am convinced it lies chiefly with oneself. . . It is a risky thing to copy, shall I catch it? I think and hope my self-will. . . will guard me here.' The experience was not entirely regrettable, however: 'This time last year I hadn't tried oils, don't think I've done badly considering all things.' She intended to resist Mrs A's insidious influence. The oils were spoiling her for watercolours, and she instinctively disliked underpainting, though many painters used it.

By the end of 1884 the painting question had thankfully been dropped. Technique was not enough. 'I don't want lessons, I want practice. I hope it is not pride that makes me so stiff against teaching, but a bad or indifferent teacher is worse than none.' Only two of her finished oils survive. 'Have lost completely several paintings. Should be amused if I ever met them in after life, not that they are worth stealing.'

7.

The Potters regularly visited galleries, and not just the fashionable Royal Academy whose Summer Exhibition opened the Season; in spite of her tastes and talents Beatrix had hardly been included in these expeditions before the age of seventeen. Perhaps because she was exposed so late to real pictures, when she was herself already grappling with problems of

43.

expression and technique, she was at first quite overwhelmed. She soon made up for lost time, visiting or revisiting at least fifteen exhibitions each year from 1883. Opinions on viewers and viewed were forcibly expressed at home. Beatrix said little but wrote much – increasingly from an artist's standpoint and never passively accepting the general view. Her journal catalogues and criticizes each exhibit, with the iconoclasm of the child in 'The Emperor's New Clothes'. Rereading her entries at the great age of twenty, she was much embarrassed: 'it is rather appalling to find one was such a goose only three years since.'

Her reviews could be devastating – but she also recognized that different artists have different ways of looking at things. Technical problems did not escape her: fading, the flatness which results from over-restoration. She is perceptive about the peculiarity of Pre-Raphaelite painting – an almost total absence of shadow, and everything in focus at once.

She is rude about Rossetti, and 'Dislike is a mild word for my feeling towards Burne Jones', but she shares Lear's admiration for Holman Hunt: real honest work and no pot-boilers. She is contradictory about Millais, and comes to prefer his early, Pre-Raphaelite style, epitomized in *Ophelia*.

One remark looks forward to her adult concern with preserving her country's heritage: 'There will be few great collections left in England soon. All the best works of Old Masters leave the Island. The Government is too stingy to buy them, and in the market they are bought cheap for foreign museums, . . . or for rich Americans.'

All her life she was to criticize bad draughtsmanship. Style without sentiment and effects without power, all were beyond the pale. 'I had rather a picture I can't understand than one with nothing to be understood.' Turner had been the first painter to impress her as a young child: he was 'the greatest landscape painter that has ever lived'.

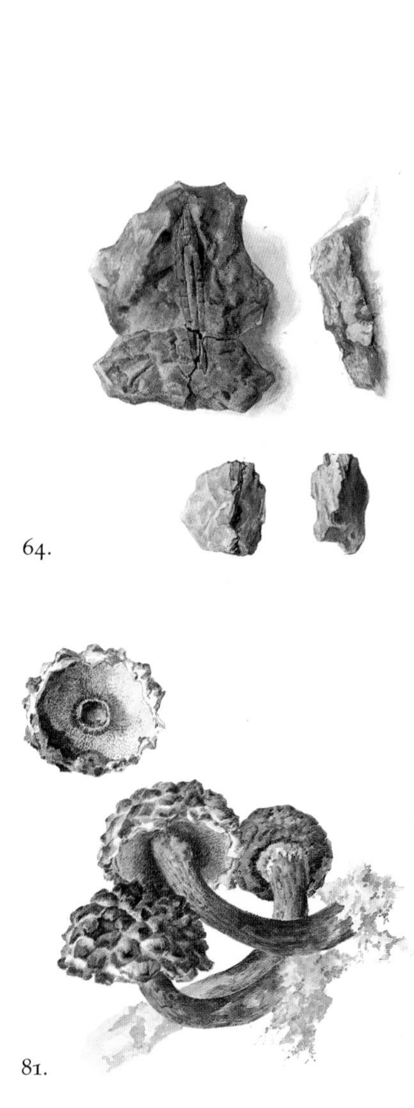
64.

81.

Her first experience of the Old Masters, in January 1883, had occasioned her much surprise. 'I never thought there *could* be such pictures.' It was 'rather a painful pleasure', and at first she was disheartened – but resolved 'I *will* do something sooner or later.' At the National Gallery the sight of swarms of young ladies 'painting frightfully for the most part', and in a 'sickly chocolate', spurred her on; perhaps her colours were not so bad. 'O dear, if I was a boy and had courage!' She was cheered by the achievement of women artists whose work she saw at exhibitions: Angelica Kauffmann, Lady Waterford, Rosa Bonheur.

Becoming more blasé, she began to enjoy looking at people as much as pictures, and no longer listed every exhibit ('you can read the newspapers for them'). By 1895 her art reviews tailed off. New interests were absorbing her, and giving a fresh impetus to her work – the study of fossils and insects and, above all, fungi.

She began to record fungi from about 1887, but was collecting and painting them most intensively from 1893 to 1898, mainly during her holidays in Scotland or the Lake District. Amateurish and imprecise at first, her drawings benefited from the instruction and encouragement of Charles McIntosh, the 'Perthshire naturalist'. Beatrix first met 'that learned but extremely shy man' on family holidays at Dunkeld, where he was the local postman. He showed her how to improve her botanical drawings by making 'separate sketches of sections showing the attachment of the gills; the stem if it be hollow or otherwise, or any other detail that would show the characteristics of the plant more clearly'. She incorporated his recommendations into later drawings. He 'spoke with quite poetical feeling about their exquisite colours', and sent her specimens to draw during the winter months.

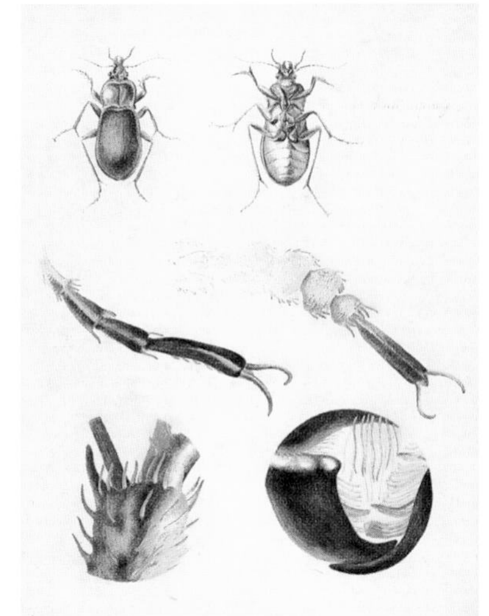

28.

Virtually self-trained, by 1895 she had the skill of a fully-fledged scientific illustrator. A project 'for a Miss Martineau' (33) would have brought together the fruits of her entomological work in a set of twelve lithographed plates (apparently only three were ever completed).

Meanwhile she tried her hand too at illustrating favourite books for her own pleasure. The illustration and design of books always concerned her. She was early exposed to work by graphic artists of the 'Sixties', such as Birket Foster. She saw Cruikshank's illustrations to *The Brownies*, by Mrs Ewing. She admired Doré and Phiz, and considered Flaxman and Fuseli underrated. Not surprisingly, with her receptive eye and memory, she could hardly avoid unconsciously absorbing some of these influences. Yet she never aped another artist's manner, but selected, digested and modified. The statement 'I can't invent, I only copy' meant only that like the Pre-Raphaelites she painted what she saw, aiming (as did Constable and Cézanne) to *'realize'*.

Copying as a necessary discipline was another matter. It trained observation and co-ordination, and improved both her drawing and her science. Picturesque fairy tale designs by Ludwig Richter and Otto Speckter supplied congenial models for practice in architectural and figure drawing. She studied too the great masters, as recommended by Reynolds. Among the academic copies which have survived are a 'study subject figure' in line and wash from a Bartolozzi engraving after Holbein, a stately dead stag in chalks after Landseer (43), and a convincingly muddy early Constable of Sty Head Tarn, Borrowdale at noon.

171.

An irrepressible lava of wit and fantasy continually bubbles through, apparent from the earliest sketchbooks. No child could have been more receptive to Tenniel and Lear. Though declaring that 'Dickens, and Alice-in-Wonderland, have been illustrated once for all,' she herself attempted some *Alice* designs. In a juvenile sketchbook is a copy from *The Baby's Opera* by Walter Crane. Few contemporary fashions passed her by. The Grosvenor Gallery, as well as Walter Crane, had introduced her to 'japonisme', and occasionally she was to echo the glaucous colouring and tendril ornament of Art Nouveau (171).

25.

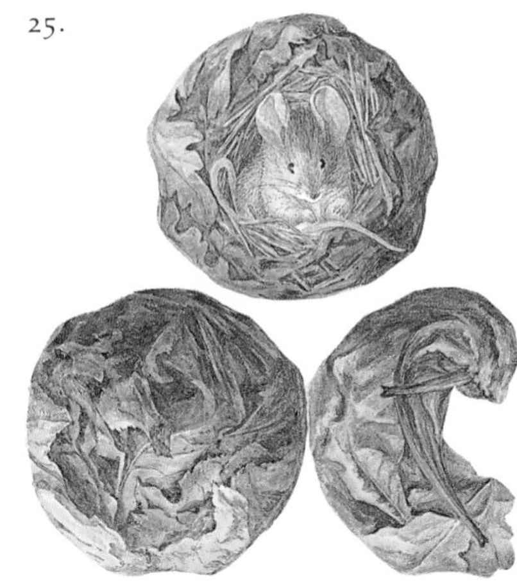

51.

52.

Caldecott, her most obvious mentor, died when she was nineteen. 'We bought his picture books eagerly, as they came out,' and her father managed to secure about thirty of his paintings. Artists from Van Gogh to Maurice Sendak have respected Caldecott as one of the foremost illustrators of all time. Beatrix admitted that she had tried 'in vain' to copy Caldecott and wrote: 'I have the greatest admiration for his work – a jealous appreciation; for I think that others, whose names are commonly bracketted with his, are not on the same plane at all as artist-illustrators.' His followers were 'lifeless and wooden': Kate Greenaway for one designed well but 'could not draw'.

Beatrix exercised her maturing talents with elegant trivia of everyday life, painting butterflies on menu cards for her aunt's bazaar and constructing, on the lines of the popular 'movable' books, ingenious toy pictures for favoured children. 'Pique', and the need for £6 towards a printing machine, soon encouraged her to put to serious use the skills she had practised in fun. Guinea pig models were turned to profit as greetings cards – as was Benjamin Bunny, who proved a veritable gold mine.

Her first paid work had not been entirely to her taste. Only at this period, and in response to public demand, does she descend to 'tweeness'. Six designs using Benjamin as model were accepted in May 1890 by Hildesheimer and Faulkner, who 'showed a mysterious desire for more'. Jubilant passages in the journal celebrate her triumph, and record her opinion of Mr Faulkner. 'He did not strike me as being a person with much taste, in fact he rather gave me to understand . . . that it was the humour that signified, not the likeness.'

The greetings cards which she was later to deplore give no idea of the quality of her original drawings; they are much better executed than most contemporary work of the kind, but their refinement was particularly difficult to reproduce. The cards were instantly repackaged, in a booklet by Frederick Weatherly entitled *The Happy Pair*. Other commissioned designs are still being discovered in little gift books published by Hildesheimer and Faulkner or Ernest Nister.

For Ernest Nister she produced the Caldecott-inspired nine-picture sequence 'A Frog he would a-fishing go'. The influence of Caldecott can be seen in her uncrowded designs and her economical but eloquent line (172, 177). She too knew that the art of leaving out is a science: 'the fewer the lines, the less error committed'. Her flair for story-telling, in the tradition also of Hogarth, Cruikshank and Lear, is evident here in the almost strip-cartoon approach. Among her other narrative sequences the most fetching are 'The Rabbits' Christmas Party' and 'Three Little Mice' sextets, the 'Appley Dapply' trio, and paired designs such as the White Cat and White Rabbit duos. Less known are the narratives in her picture letters.

Like Carroll, Caldecott and Lear, Beatrix sent illustrated letters to children. From 1892 onwards letters with 'pen-and-ink scribbles', dramatic and action-packed, beguiled her child friends, in particular the Moores, the large family of her former governess. A few of the more worked-out picture sequences were made up into little booklets, so that the picture letter becomes a picture story proper; the most famous example is, of course, 'The Tale of Peter Rabbit', first written for Noel Moore in 1893. Only Lear and Caldecott matched the sometimes ribald humour; only Beatrix Potter took the picture letter to its logical – and lucrative – conclusion. Its success with children and adults alike gave her the confidence to go ahead with her own text.

118.

Beatrix Potter always had the instincts of an illustrator, and responded to words. Her accomplished but idiosyncratic designs for *Alice* and *Uncle Remus* were pursued no further, and never published; but she took *The Tale of Peter Rabbit*, her own story, into print with entrepreneurial determination. Once established as author-illustrator, she resisted the suggestion that she might illustrate other people's books and it is as her own interpreter that she is most in sympathy with the text.

The fruitful years between 1901 and 1913 produced nineteen 'little books' for children. Success brought financial independence and practical changes to her life. In 1905 she bought her first property, a Lake District farm called Hill Top in the village of Sawrey. In 1913 she married local solicitor William Heelis and went to live at Castle Cottage, also in Sawrey. She kept on Hill Top both as a quiet and private place where she could write and draw, and as a working farm. Her best books behind her, she was making the transition from writer and illustrator to hill farmer. As Mrs Heelis, the complete countrywoman, she became first woman president of the Herdwick Sheepbreeders' Association and was active in annexing over four thousand acres of Lake District land and saving them for the National Trust.

203.

She still sketched and drew but painted less. It was 'a refreshment' to sketch out of doors at Sawrey, however uncomfortable the conditions. She sketched in all weathers: 'I spent a very wet hour *inside* the pig sty drawing the pig. It tries to nibble my boots which is interrupting!' As an incomer she had joined the growing number of artists settled in the Lake District by the 1900s – but farming left little time for painting, except in winter. Not surprisingly, many of her later Sawrey landscapes are snow scenes. Out of doors or indoors, she continued to 'copy what she saw' according to her creed. The 'highest and lowest in nature' were 'both equally perfect', from the swill bucket to the 'peculiar blue' of snow in a white frost, and the Lakeland hills whose watery atmosphere had captivated so many artists before her, from Farington to Turner. Whatever the subject, she tackled it with professional detachment: 'I see no reason why common-sense should not foster a healthier appreciation of beauty than morbid sentimentality.'

187.

She was equally unsentimental about her own art. Always honest about her weaknesses, she had welcomed her brother's help and her publisher's

199.

advice. When she knew her work was good she said so without false modesty. In the case of her fungus studies, which were based on solid research, she had battled with her shyness and, armed with the drawings, bearded the scientific establishment at Kew. Knowing that they represented her best work, she kept them and other drawings with special care in portfolios home-made from fabric samples. She was adamant about the future of her book pictures. Any reproduction should be as close to the original as possible; the originals should not be sold but, like her Caldecotts, be given to some public collection.

Her critical faculties remained into old age, voiced in letters to publishers or to friends from the worlds of books and art. She saw art journals and enjoyed American illustrators, but railed against the vulgarity of London booksellers with their 'gaudy, ugly, toy book style'. 'It is impossible to explain balance and style to people if they don't see it themselves.' Her later, more adventurous colour work, in a style few would associate with 'Beatrix Potter', reflects an awareness of contemporary trends (198, 199). By her sixties she was working mainly in black-and-white, and in yet another idiom (206–209).

She was disparaging about an article in *The Listener* in January 1943, less than a year before her death, which described her as a watercolour artist of the English school, comparing her with Samuel Palmer, Bewick and Constable. 'Absolute bosh. I revere the names of the Immortals, and I have this much in common with them, that, like them I have tried to do my best, and taken satisfaction in so doing . . . but to compare the manner of my work with theirs is silliness – especially the great, and *broad-painting* – Constable.' All the same, she shared his passion for painting and for nature, and achieves something of his 'dewy light and freshness'.

Her rational, level-headed approach is itself just one manifestation of her Englishness, like the naturalism and nostalgia, the pastorals and the sense of place, the preference for watercolour, the interest in detail and narrative – and not least, the insularity which like Constable she makes a virtue. Unusually for a nineteenth-century artist, her social concerns hardly affected her art – except perhaps indirectly, in the selectivity of her subject: an unspoilt rural landscape.

208.

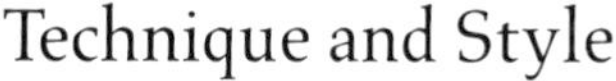

Technique and Style

All her life observation inspired experimentation. Back in the schoolroom Beatrix and her brother had tried everything from transfer printing to etching. Beatrix took readily to modelling; it helped her figure drawing. (Later she made a 'rather good clay Peter'.) She was a skilled photographer and by 1895 had her own camera, with 'a lovely mahogany complexion'. That same year she took 'two excessively expensive lessons' in learning Platinotype printing at the Polytechnic – difficult but satisfactory. Soon after, she studied lithography with its chalky effects. Chalk was another medium she enjoyed. Rough-textured brown paper flatters her large-scale chalk heads of sheep and ducks; she used this medium for some impressive architectural studies 'in singularly good perspective' at or near Bush Hall, Hertfordshire, in 1884.

Beatrix liked to work on several subjects simultaneously; equally she could look at similar subjects in different ways and tackle them in varying styles and techniques. Meticulous drawings of a rare fungus (81) were made only the day before she sent Noel Moore the Peter Rabbit picture letter. Coexisting with the Caldecott-like manner in which she was still feeling her way was her stipple method.

This technique, seen by Sickert as anticipating the Impressionists, was pioneered by William Henry Hunt. Minute touches of pure colour mixed with opaque white (bodycolour) are applied with a fine dry brush held almost upright, the colours coming together in the eye of the beholder. Hunt also invented a lacquer-like ground of Chinese white (apparently tried out but disliked by Beatrix), which made possible a virtuosic rendering of bloom and texture. The method was taken up by the Pre-Raphaelites and then by Birket Foster and Frederick Walker. This pointillism produced the effect which so delighted Beatrix in Fred Walker's 'gems of concentrated colour and light'.

58.

Beatrix admitted that the Pre-Raphaelites, with their 'somewhat niggling but absolutely genuine admiration for copying natural detail', had influenced her; she worked with the same heightened, even disquieting intensity, but her pictures are more carefully composed.

Later she was to prefer her unstippled paintings in imitation of Caldecott. Artists' comments on their own work can be revealing but must sometimes be taken with a pinch of salt. Beatrix could be contradictory in her self-criticism, since some of her best work was done in a stipple technique, often combined with wash. She could convey subtle and surprising differences of tone in hair or plumage, and the infinite gradations from light to dark. Like some other watercolourists towards the end of the century she preferred transparent colour to bodycolour. Minute subjects demanded minute strokes: with Bewick, William Hunt and Birket Foster, she is a descendant of the pictures 'in little' approach of the Elizabethans.

65.

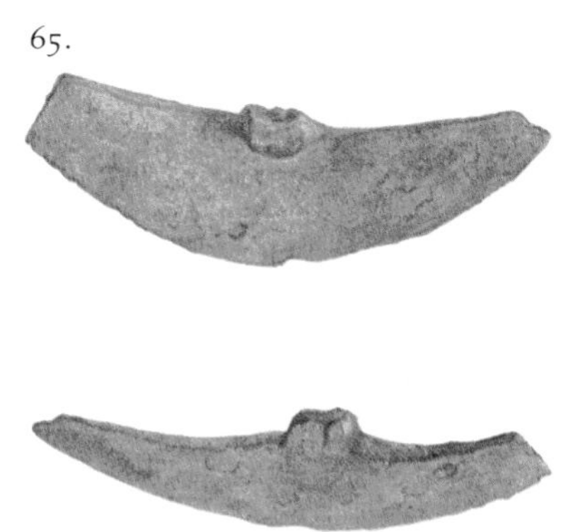

She makes one see, smell and touch what she paints, and has a sensuous awareness of the essential shape and feel of each object: crumbling leather and flaking rust, mould-encrusted branches, the crunchy dryness of seed-pods and papery rustle of onion skins – and the stiffness of a small dead fish with its accusing gelatinous eye (60). Her tactile sense is as insistent in the 'book pictures': a polished crab-apple; flowers embroidered in silk; the cold hard gleam of a dresser, redolent of beeswax; the highlighted lusciousness of a strawberry.

177.

93.

44.

Except for her book pictures, she abandoned this miniaturist technique around 1900, adopting a bolder, more fluid line in pliable quill pen or brush. Line as well as colour inspired her to experiment. She often used pencil like a brush, to achieve nuances of tone, but occasionally the drawing is at first sight indistinguishable from pen-and-ink. For pen work she preferred free-flowing Indian ink to 'stodgy process black', or sometimes the fashionable and even freer flowing 'sepia'. Where the line illustrations of her books are in brown ('The Sly Old Cat' and many of the late Tales), the watercolours too have 'sepia' outlines. This brown ink may have been used in emulation of Caldecott, or to counteract excessive blackness in printing.

Considering herself primarily a draughtsman, she was also a colourist. Her colour not only enhances the line, it models (175). In her limpid, quasi-Oriental waterlilies and her posy of flowers (112) the line is unobtrusive: she had learnt to compose in colour.

The muted palette of her commercial work, toned down from the opaque richness of her early set-pieces, was dictated by the demands of chromolithography. Intensity returns with the sumptuous greens and flaming reds of parrot and toadstool (44, 73), and denser, darker hues for the dead blackbird and furry spider, or for the fossils and the jackdaw, at the blacker end of the grisaille spectrum.

'Grisaille', a technique of minute greyish-white brushstrokes, produces a striking sculptural effect (61). A natural progression from her exploration of the versatility of pencil, it had more three-dimensional possibilities. Sometimes the brushstroke lengthens and thickens into a near monochrome; in a few small landscapes she adds a misty blue-grey.

A range of jewelled, rather gaudy hues, purples and greens in particular, seems to have been a passing and part-time phase, between the stipple and 'sepia and wash' styles. A clear watery blue-green gives an impression of coolness; fir green gives depth to the snow scenes, occasionally warmed by touches of orange (187), a colour she uses to great effect. 'Mr. Pricklepin' is painted in multi-hued brushstrokes, an experiment extended further for the sheep's head in a looser pointillism and an even brighter palette (204). A dash of colour may act as focal point, sometimes doubling as light source (a candle, an open doorway, a glowing fire), sometimes in drawings which otherwise depend on line (101).

Like Rackham, she could exploit the new three-colour process, which favoured a painterly rather than a linear style and was better adapted to watercolours than chromolithography – but she complained about the 'horrid clay-faced paper' on which it had to be printed, and which muddied the colour and line. Drawing paper could cause problems too: the thinner sort cockled and so had to be mounted on boards, but the thicker paper turned yellow. Small sheets suited her mouse pictures particularly, and made for accuracy of reproduction. By 1905 she was beginning to feel cramped, and so a more generous format was chosen for *The Pie and The*

Patty-Pan, to do justice to the colour and detail. This book, and *The Tale of Samuel Whiskers,* have some of her finest book paintings – strong and unexpectedly large.

Colour work later became an effort. 'The country is looking beautiful enough to give me inspiration; but I seem as if I can't screw it out, and my eyes are always tired.' She blamed the deterioration in her eyesight on the microscopic work and fungus drawing, but her housekeeper blamed it on working late by candlelight at Hill Top. Many of her last paintings – *Peter Rabbit* re-copied to make money for the preservation of Windermere, the *Fairy Caravan* colour plates, the 1930 *Pie and Patty-Pan* cover – are sadly pallid, or garish. No longer able to see clean colours, she could 'still draw'. What her paintings lost in detail they made up for in dynamism, as is shown by the mature versions of some *Appley Dapply* designs (1917), redrawn from her stippled 1890s originals.

169.

Composition and Design

Beatrix Potter had definite ideas about the visual relationship of picture to text, liking to dictate the layout of her books. She studied pages designed by others – Crane, Caldecott, the medieval illuminators – and made up her own dummies, cleverly using italics or white space for dramatic effect. Her occasional choice of framed illustrations as opposed to vignettes was intentional. Illustrations with edges needed borders: 'the black frame pulls them together & sends back the distance.' Endpapers should rest the eye, 'like a plain mount for a framed drawing'.

Even the merest scraps of informal sketches show her flair for pictorial composition, where objects of the same type are compared, or their particular idiosyncrasies analysed: insects or parts of insects, the convexities and concavities of potsherds, the elegant assemblages of artefacts in which not a single element is swamped.

175.

Her modish round or oval vignettes set off the forms they enclose – a hollow forest glade, the flattened arch of a cart. 'The Toads' Tea Party' is all roundedness, from the bun-shaped toadstools and plump toads to the curved format, which elsewhere invites us in to cosy interiors.

181.

A rising or receding zigzag, another compositional device, both breaks up the picture and increases the sense of recession and depth (140, 180). One's eye is coaxed not inwards but up and outwards, 'over the hills and far away'.

The viewpoint, never chosen at random, can be a curious one. Parts of the picture may be only half-present, or dash off the page; centrifugal movement is accelerated when a peaceful clustering of mice turns into scampering mayhem (52). Imagining an animal's perspective, she portrays the creatures large in relation to their backgrounds. Samuel Whiskers on the landing is seen from cat height; the Puddle-ducks of Sawrey, higher than the viewer, gain in self-importance (181, 178).

189.

She sometimes exploits conventional compositional devices which draw attention to middle distance or background, as when interpreting an airy spring landscape or the dappled shade of a Sawrey lane (189, 200). Moonlight reflected on swirling water, the play of light on polished surfaces – all are instances of her fascination with the effects of light and shade.

Through a subtle combination of composition, light and colour, more senses than sight are stimulated – the feel of smooth slate or dry leaves, the taste and smell of fog and frost, the unheard airs which accompany her dancing line.

Subjects

144.

Reopening her portfolios in 1920, and surprised by the quality of what she saw, she wrote, 'It seems a pity . . . that some of my miscellaneous drawings cannot be published.' Those 'miscellaneous drawings' remained largely unknown until 1955, when Leslie Linder published over three hundred in *The Art of Beatrix Potter*. They reveal the catholicity of an ardent observer. A brief survey of her pet themes gives an idea of their relative importance: over five hundred botanical studies, for example, but only a handful of figures.

Flowers and fruit had been an obvious and conventional choice; she drew them as conscientious student, as enquiring botanist, or for sheer enjoyment. Roses and lilies, clematis and carnations reappear in her Tales, with more robust foxgloves and the geraniums featuring as cottage decor (or occasionally as missiles). Next came gardens, their paraphernalia, and the food that grows in them, from the precise formality of a tree-lined path by the Tay to the box edging at Gwaynynog and the studies of Fawe Park used as backgrounds for *Benjamin Bunny*. Her Sawrey gardens, celebrated in *The Pie and The Patty-Pan* and *Tom Kitten*, have a Gertrude Jekyll lushness.

73.

Trees, the subject of letters, articles and fairy tales, intrigued her both scientifically and imaginatively. So many professional woodland landscape painters had never considered how the branches grow from a tree trunk, she wrote to Delmar Banner. *'In the right place'* (here speaks the conservationist) trees are 'as beautiful as rocks, and they have a nobility of growth which is usually intirely over looked. I did so many careful botanical studies in my youth, it became easy for me to draw twigs. And little details like that add to the reality of a picture.'

She understood too the close association between certain trees and fungi (76). Her fungi are mostly shown in their natural settings, nestling among pine-needles and dry leaves, squatting in lichen and moss, or profiled among stiff grasses, in the tradition of Dürer's *The Great Piece of Turf*. Sometimes the setting is barely indicated, and nothing allowed to detract from the 'brittle', ethereal grace of the central subject.

The 'funguses' generated more than three hundred watercolours. It took two generations for Beatrix Potter's botanical illustrations to be valued as they deserved, and her pioneering discoveries were not acknowledged for sixty years. She was the first in Britain to succeed in sprouting the spores of agarics, and one of the first to realize the symbiotic nature of lichens. Dr W.P.K. Findlay encountered her drawings at the Centenary Exhibition in Kendal, and afterwards published fifty-nine of them in *Wayside and Woodland Fungi* (Warne, 1976). Today leading mycologists have at last begun to appraise both discoveries and drawings.

Quality is not dependent on quantity: the handful of fossil studies ranks with her best work. Fossils, like the fungi and the pine-cone, were painstakingly recorded as specimens in true Ruskin spirit.

Beatrix's interest in geology, and also in archaeology, was encouraged by Canon Hardwicke Rawnsley, a friend of Rupert Potter and unlike him an admirer of Ruskin. By happy chance another friend, Tom Squire, lent her some Roman artefacts from the Bucklersbury excavations just when she was at her peak as a scientific illustrator. Determined to find out how things work, she takes each item apart visually, just as she dissects the fungi, bats and beetles. These studies of objects identifiable today in books on the archaeology of London are redeemed from being mere inventories by the exquisite drawing and composition: a spiky pattern of nails, or a delicate tracery of needles and toilet utensils laid out like regimented spillikins (66, 70).

The round of gallery visiting took in archaeological museums and, a few months after these drawings were made, two visits to the Silchester exhibits at Burlington House. Antiquity in itself failed to impress: 'I was more than ever struck by the bad taste of the Roman art.' She was more complimentary about the pottery, and collected the modern variety (Staffordshire and Wedgwood included), drawing it in her domestic scenes: 'Mr. Pricklepin', Ribby's kitchen and the Tailor's dresser.

Good design, and 'that appreciation of the fitness of things which is the soul of artistic taste', were important to Beatrix in all the arts – in architecture, textiles and, rather unexpectedly, in dress. 'I suppose not since the Empire whose gigot sleeves they emulate, have the dresses been so graceful as now,' she wrote in her journal in 1890. She revelled in the elaborate costumes from the Victoria and Albert Museum, redrawn for *The Tailor of Gloucester*.

Even at eighteen she longed to possess old furniture: 'If ever I had a house I would have old furniture, oak in the dining room, and Chippendale in the drawing room.' She drew, in every medium, cane and bentwood chairs as well as Chippendale, and long-case clocks for fairy tales and rhymes, and for the Tales. More than a hobby, furniture collecting became a mission. She wrote informed notes on carved oak and corresponded on the subject with specialist friends in America. She secured good pieces for her

68.

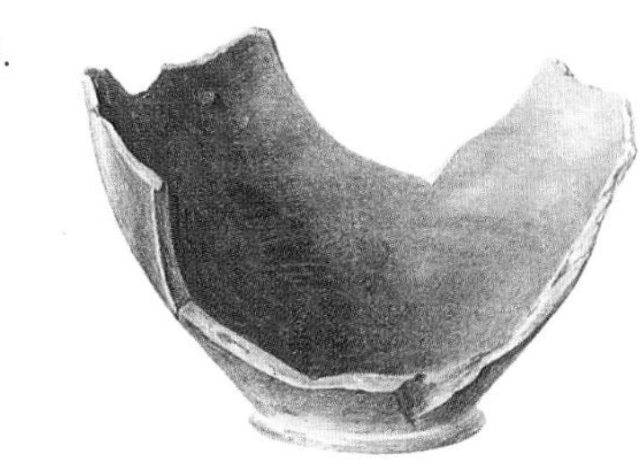

153.

135.

152.

Lake District farms, and marked her Hill Top belongings with their provenance and intended positions.

A particular piece of furniture inhabits a particular space. Beatrix recorded rooms wherever she stayed, and especially the bedrooms where she slept, at Camfield, Bedwell Lodge, and at Winchelsea during a wintry week in January. She drew the schoolroom at Bolton Gardens and the library at Wray Castle, a grand staircase at Lingholm and staircases in little at Lakefield Cottages and Hill Top. The drawings were more than run-of-the-mill mementos. Staircases, passageways and empty attics provided useful exercises in perspective; a doorway sometimes served as a frame. She painted fireplaces of every date and degree, grand and curvaceous, empty and chilly or warm and inviting.

Following the nostalgia of her time for roots and rusticity, she became drawn to North Country vernacular. In these cottage kitchens, conviviality seems always in preparation if not in progress. The same snug cosiness pervades her more authentic settings. Safe burrows are hinted at behind hedgehog and vole or actually pictured from inside. It is a temporary safety only, contradicted by the alert ears and the little wild eyes. Outside is a cruel and uncosy world of murderous gardeners, foxes and wolves.

'What she instinctively felt about spaces – that they should be comforting, responsive and protective – was part of a general realisation about spaces common to artists,' writes Alison Smithson in *Architectural Design*. 'Beatrix Potter succeeded in portraying forms entirely suitable for their purpose.' Equally suited to its purpose, and inseparable from its landscape, is the indigenous architecture of the Lake District, which became part of the fabric of her books.

Architecture interested her from a young age. She drew the Duchess of Atholl's dairy at ten and other buildings soon after. Her fairy stories have medieval backdrops; familiar houses, also drawn in their own right, supply backgrounds for her Tales. In *The Tailor of Gloucester*, the only book in the series with a period setting, all her treasures come together: architecture and furniture, china and clothes.

121.

Landscapes too appear in the early sketchbooks, dating from 1875-76. By 1884 she was painting the Hertfordshire panorama as seen from Camfield Place. The composition improved with her photographic skills, and in the 1890s she joined a small Drawing Society. The criticisms on the back of her circulated pictures (some partly torn off!) reflect as much on her fellow-members as on the paintings. 'I notice that those with a bit of landscape are the favourites,' she wrote to her publisher. Their titles, so typical of a period when literature and art in England were closely linked, are often tags of poetry (mainly Goldsmith and Gray): 'At evening's close', 'A sheltered cot', and a coast scene, 'Like some tall cliff' (121, 128).

Maritime subjects and harbours were part of the English artist's repertoire. Beatrix painted the sea but never crossed it. She drew Holyhead in black ink, Lyme Regis and the Cobb in black or brown and Teignmouth in luminous watercolour wash. *The Tale of Little Pig Robinson* was an amalgam of Lyme Regis and its local thatch, Ilfracombe, Teignmouth shipping and the net sheds of Hastings. 'So the illustrations are a comprehensive sample of our much battered coasts.'

Where necessary, she resorts to artistic licence to 'improve' the composition, bending both the rules of naturalism and the arrangements of geology. Apart from such occasional leanings to the Picturesque (149), her places are actual rather than ideal. Lingholm near Keswick and the Scottish Borders near Lennel inspired between them nearly one hundred sepia drawings. As she began to spend more time in the Lake District, she sketched by Windermere and her favourite Esthwaite Water, which she drew for the sketching society and thereafter at every season and in every mood, most happily in its wintry aspect.

105.

Like Helen Allingham, Beatrix Potter has been called a 'fairweather painter'. The smiling landscapes of the Tales, mainly unrelieved by rain, may give this impression – but as children's stories they were after all meant to be enjoyed. There is plenty of weather in her watercolour sketches: 'Spring' at Harescombe Grange is balanced by 'Rain' at Lingholm, in which she is already using wetted paper to convey damp slates and sodden sky (122, 105). 'A November Day' (154) is reminiscent of Whistler, but closer perhaps to an Atkinson Grimshaw twilight. The landscapes have little movement, and scarcely a rushing stream – though there are exceptions among the rough wash sketches, the sepia views and in her skies. Some atmospheric effects, not unlike Ruskin's cloud formations, are a reminder too of her lifelong respect for Turner.

194.

A group of snow scenes dates from March 1909, and some little-known summer sketches survive from this period, done at speed in blobs of melting colour. These daringly impressionistic, almost abstract wash landscapes recall late Wilson Steer – Steer had himself earlier experimented with pointillism. Quick sketches tend to look avant-garde in comparison with finished work. Even so, these studies seem startlingly modern. Most British artists of her day remained suspicious of Impressionism; Steer was an isolated figure.

Amateurs, usually behind the times, make little progress through their careers – but Beatrix Potter was more than an amateur. As she wrote to Delmar Banner, artists move on, leaving behind the 'topographically-exact-in-detail' stage. Her diversity of styles was caused not just by deteriorating eyesight, but by a changing inner vision.

92.

The name Beatrix Potter brings to mind not landscapes but figures in a landscape. The figures are usually animal ones, but play their part like humans. Landscape backgrounds, conveniently ready in her portfolios, are redrawn with figures skilfully placed (140, 200). The scenery is much more than a backdrop, and even in the best compositions the figures need

85.

29.

23.

their landscapes more than the landscape needs figures – though occasionally the figures add to the sense of distance. Since the figures were put in last they are sometimes visible in unfinished designs as faint outlines (152).

Human intrusion was avoided, and she found human anatomy 'a terrible bother'. Adult models made her shy, though photographs were a help. Perhaps the mystique attached to life-drawing made her self-conscious, or perhaps she tried too hard, since her dashed-off figure sketches and the picture-letter stick people have plenty of life.

Human beings reminded her of animals, and 'a few of the animals were harmless skits or caricatures'; it is tempting to speculate on the targets. The creatures themselves are treated with affection and respect: they behave in character while satirizing human foibles and mannerisms: the confidence trickster wolf, his paws crossed in apparent relaxation, Tom Kitten's dumb insolence, Jemima's sheer silliness. The body language is half-human, the bodies are not.

Even in the nursery she had observed the behaviour of her pet animals as well as their anatomy – their resting and running positions, their hibernating and breathing patterns. Criticizing Landseer and his 'sleek pretty creatures', she had remarked that 'the legs are primarily wooden pegs to support [the] body, the balanced springs superadded to give ease in motion.' Having analysed both skeletal structure and musculature she was well equipped to draw animals in all their grace and power, and did so with a detached but loving realism.

Her microscopic work in particular is both appealing and accurate. Beetles, butterflies and moth wings, water creatures, claws and feet were compared at different angles and magnifications, and often provided with scale diagrams. Her scientific studies metamorphosed into imagined characters. The invertebrates provide supporting cast and local colour: a snail on the wall, a fly on the doll's house roof, a whole corps de ballet of butterflies, beetles and bees in *The Tale of Mrs. Tittlemouse*. The amphibians and reptiles creep or hop into fantasy and book pictures; Sir Isaac Newton's waistcoat imitates the colours of a crested newt.

Rabbits inspired an exceptional number of drawings, but mice populate the early rhyme pictures. They are painted in wash, stippled in miniature, or sketched with a more supple brushstroke suited to their quicksilver movements. She pictured them as busy and active, spinning or even stealing. Squirrels, less domestic, could be difficult models. Rats carouse or sleep, cheerful pigs perch on straight-backed chairs, peel potatoes or are ensconced in tubs. Sheet after sheet is filled with studies, of several animals, of one animal, or of one particularly arresting feature: the translucent ears of mice and bats; the heads of rabbits and pigs. In a delightful self-parody she deals in the same way with a Teddy-bear.

Parody – sometimes tongue-in-cheek, sometimes concealed – was irresistible. Peter Rabbit at the door is a sly reflection of Anna Lea Merritt's

Love Locked Out (1889) – one of the first paintings by a woman to be acknowledged by the British art establishment. Duchess on the sofa mimics Briton Rivière's *Cupboard Love* (168). She pays her respects to Tenniel's sheep in Mrs. Flock of *Little Pig Robinson*, the *Tailor of Gloucester* frontispiece is a rather bland adaptation from Hogarth's *Times of the Day*, and Jemima Puddle-duck, in her frontispiece, with updated bonnet and shawl, has waddled straight out of a folk-tale illustration by Otto Speckter, *Hanne Nüte un de lütte Pudel*. Beatrix Potter seems to challenge her audience to find her out – to court discovery.

125.

Away from the books and the fantasy pictures such subterfuge is redundant. The artist is herself challenged by her subject. The strongest subjects demand portrait treatment. In convenient repose they seem even more arresting: minute spiders, spreadeagled over her largest sheets, deceptively enlarged by the microscope; the bat, the weasel and the parrot, momentarily frozen yet wary-eyed; the skulls, eyeless but equally emphatic; and, glazed and sightless, the ram's mask, the crisply profiled orange fish, and the tragic stag, sprawled in the abandon of death. Long since stuffed, newly deceased or just resting, her animals have as glossy a presence as her fungi, which celebrate a decay teeming with new life.

Death and sleep are recurring themes in Victorian art, sleep and dream in Beatrix Potter's art. Rabbits lie on hearthrugs or in boxes, or like the mice are tucked up in brass bedsteads. Less comfortably, shadowy mood-paintings, moon- or candle-lit, can suggest oppression and even nightmare: a long panelled corridor, a wood from fairy tale (90, 85). In the nocturnes of her late books one senses unease, loneliness and fear. The haunted solitude of a moonlit wood can be strange and other-worldly.

A sense of mystery never left her, nor did an underlying melancholy. Anxiety, vulnerability and pathos are implicit in the attitudes of her animals, belied by the outward serenity of her sunlit paintings. Always understated, never obvious, her pictures like her texts have hidden resonances; they are suffused with emotion and atmosphere.

'Black shadows flung across the silver road'. One of Beatrix Potter's favourite pictures for *The Fairy Caravan*, 1929. Pen-and-ink; 50 x 118; WA

NOTES AND SOURCES

All sizes given refer to the image size of the illustration unless otherwise stated. Sizes are given in millimetres (height x width).

Currently accepted names for fungi are used. Since these now sometimes differ from the names used by Beatrix Potter, earlier names are also given.

Key to abbreviations of sources:

AT	The Armitt Trust
FLP	The Free Library of Philadelphia
LT	The Trustees of the Linder Collection, Book Trust
NT	The National Trust
TG	The Tate Gallery
V&A	The Victoria and Albert Musuem (Linder Bequest, National Art Library)
WA	Frederick Warne Archive

The Plates

The difference between a
bad artist and a good one is:
the bad artist seems to
copy a great deal.
The good one really does
copy a great deal.

WILLIAM BLAKE

1. Caterpillars from the 'Dalguise 1875' sketchbook. These were drawn when Beatrix Potter was nine years old. On the next page of the sketchbook she added observations on their habits.
Pencil and watercolour; 170 x 152 (page size); V&A

2. Trees, June 1879.
Drawn before Beatrix was thirteen,
this was probably a copy.
Black chalk; 335 x 225; V&A

Opposite:
3. The Three Witches from *Macbeth*, 1878.
Several of Beatrix's pictures have Shakespearian titles, but this seems to be the only true illustration. The asymmetric composition, focusing on the fire, is as effective as the sense of mist and mystery.
Pencil and watercolour; 350 x 254; private collection

4. Harebells and marguerites, July 1880.
Painted not long before her fourteenth birthday. Flower painting was *de rigueur* for the accomplished Victorian girl.
Pencil and watercolour; 168 x 150; V&A

5. Early painting of a rabbit at rest. By 1880 Beatrix Potter was already making serious studies of rabbits, with feathery brushstrokes, and transparent colour which allows the paper to provide the highlights.
Pencil and watercolour;
102 x 174; V&A

6. 'Silver Urn, modern copy of old pattern, about 20 inch', *c.*1880.
The liquid sheen and delicacy express her feeling for craftsmanship and form, whether man-made or in nature.
Pencil and watercolour; 162 x 110; FLP

7. Pomegranates and vase, November 1881.
A painting that shows an awareness of form and mass.
Pencil, watercolour and bodycolour heightened with white;
227 x 258; LT

8, 9. Grapes and peaches, 1882 and 1883.
Still lifes painted by Beatrix at the ages of sixteen and seventeen. The later painting (*right*) is in a luscious but heavy style of bodycolour against which she soon reacted. Such fruit-pieces, made fashionable by William Henry Hunt, became especially popular with women artists.
Watercolour heightened with white; 231 x 267; LT (above); Pencil, watercolour and bodycolour heightened with white; 231 x 294; V&A (right)

10. Pineapple with cherries
and 'the little lizard Judy', 1883.
A bold variation on the still-life theme.
Watercolour and bodycolour heightened
with white; 231 x 294; LT

11. The lizard Judy, 1884.
A study of Beatrix's pet against an unfinished background of bell-heather and grasses. 'I have had a great deal of pleasure from that little Creature.'
Pencil, pen-and-ink and watercolour; 100 x 161; V&A

12. From the drawing-room window at Camfield Place, Hertfordshire, 1884. 'In summer the distant landscapes are intensely blue,' Beatrix wrote in a memoir on her grandparents' house. Pencil and watercolour heightened with white; 187 x 265; V&A

13. Hyacinth in a pot. An early drawing. Pencil; 111 x 56; V&A

14. From the terrace at Camfield Place, December 1884.
The low horizon increases the importance of the sky.
Pencil and watercolour; 128 x 232; V&A

15. Common long-eared bat (*Plecotus auritus*), 1885.
One of several studies of bats crouching, hanging upside-down, or stripped to their skeletons.
Pencil and watercolour heightened with white;
70 x 73; V&A

16. Common long-eared bat (*Plecotus auritus*), 1887.
Pencil, pen-and-ink and watercolour heightened with white; detail from a sheet of bat studies
268 x 366 (sheet size); V&A

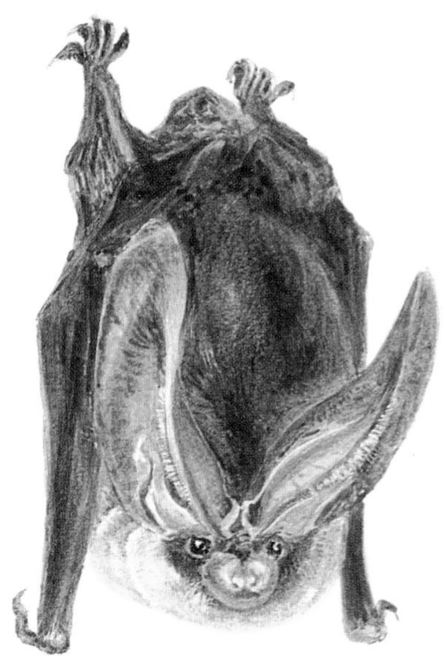

17. Weasel, drawn at Camfield Place in 1888.
A treatment ideally suited to suggesting the sinuous shape under the glossy coat.
Pencil, pen-and-ink and watercolour heightened with white; 69 x 217; LT

18. 'The little Lizard, Bill', 1893.
One of half a dozen designs made for *Alice in Wonderland*. Unlike Tenniel the caricaturist, she avoids human subjects. Only early works are signed 'HBP', as here, and only the earliest with her full name.
Pencil, pen-and-ink and watercolour; 150 x 203; LT

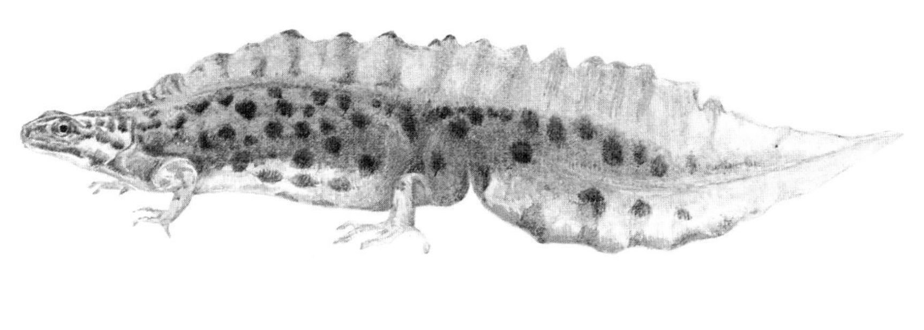

Opposite:
19. Common lizard (*Lacerta viviphera*), 1885.
Beatrix became particularly attached to her pet lizards. She painted several varieties, from different angles, showing how their skin differs in texture from that of a newt.
Pencil and watercolour; 130 x 160 (detail); LT

Above:
20. Common newt (*Triturus vulgaris*), 1886.
The top example shows a male in the breeding season. The translucency and sheen of the skin is well expressed in watercolour.
Pencil and watercolour;
17 x 98, 23 x 90, 29 x 108; LT

21. Bank vole (*Clethrionomys glareolus*).
Beatrix studied all varieties of voles, mice and dormice. Here a soft-textured brushstroke perfectly conveys the softness of fur.
Pencil and watercolour heightened with white;
170 x 120; FLP

22. Timmy Willie and strawberry,
for *The Tale of Johnny Town-Mouse*, 1918.
Pen-and-ink and watercolour; 85 x 93; NT

23. Wood mouse (*Apodemus sylvaticus*), 1886.
Beatrix came to prefer mice as subjects; she grew 'a little tired of rabbits'. This mouse was painted for a Christmas present.
Pen-and-ink and watercolour; 52 x 72; LT

24. The mouse-trap lesson, from *The Tale of Two Bad Mice*, 1904.
'I think some of the new mouse drawings are rather good,' she wrote in 1904.
Pen-and-ink and watercolour; 86 x 102; NT

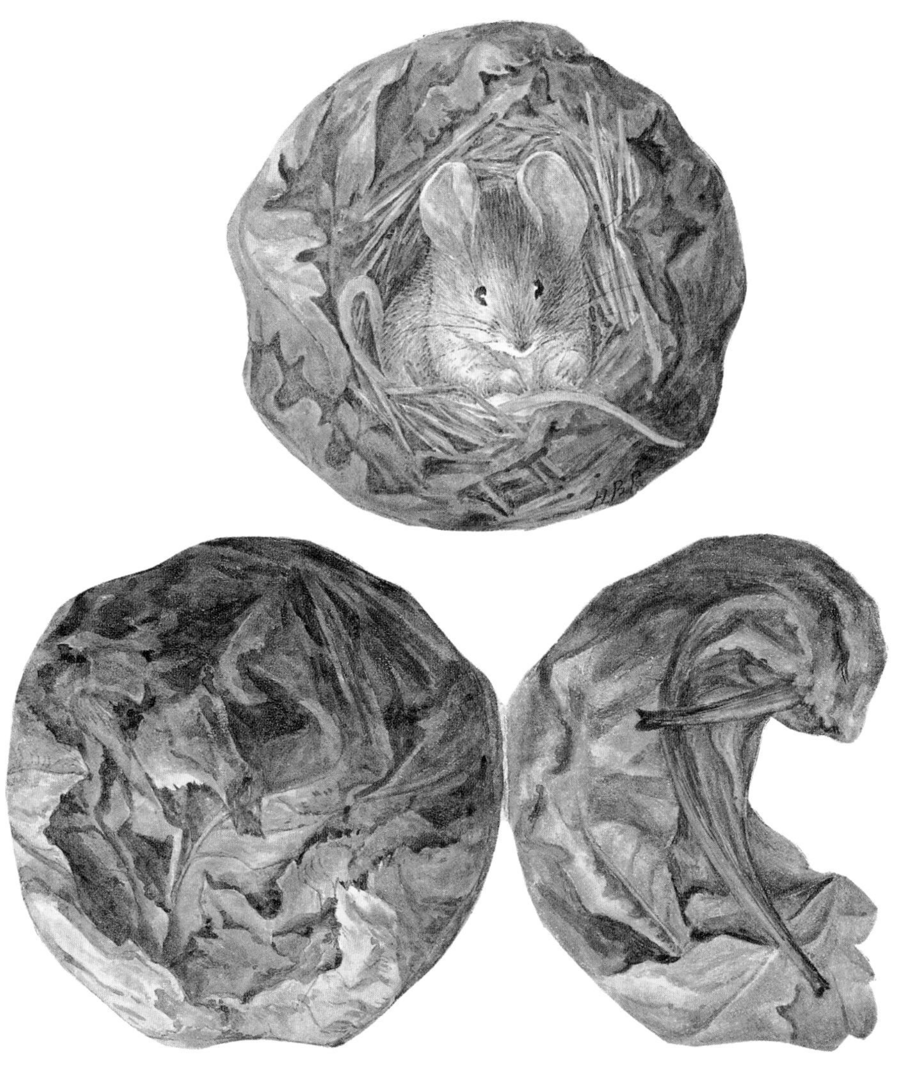

25. Mouse in its nest, *c.*1891.
A greetings card design for Hildesheimer and Faulkner, showing both the inside and the outside of the nest. Complementary designs include mice in a coconut and guinea pigs in a lidded basket.
Pen-and-ink and watercolour; 66 x 66 (mouse), 68 x 115 (open nest); V&A

26. Studies of a Hazel dormouse (*Muscardinus avellanarius*), 1887. 'When I was a child I had a favourite dormouse – a sleepy little animal . . .' This was Xarifa, a much-loved pet, named from a ballad by J. G. Lockhart. Pencil and sepia ink; 169 x 108; V&A

27. Jumping spider (*?Sitticus pubescens*, male) magnified, 1886.
Like her other spider paintings, full of character and designed on a lavish scale.
Watercolour and bodycolour heightened with white; 360 x 268; FLP

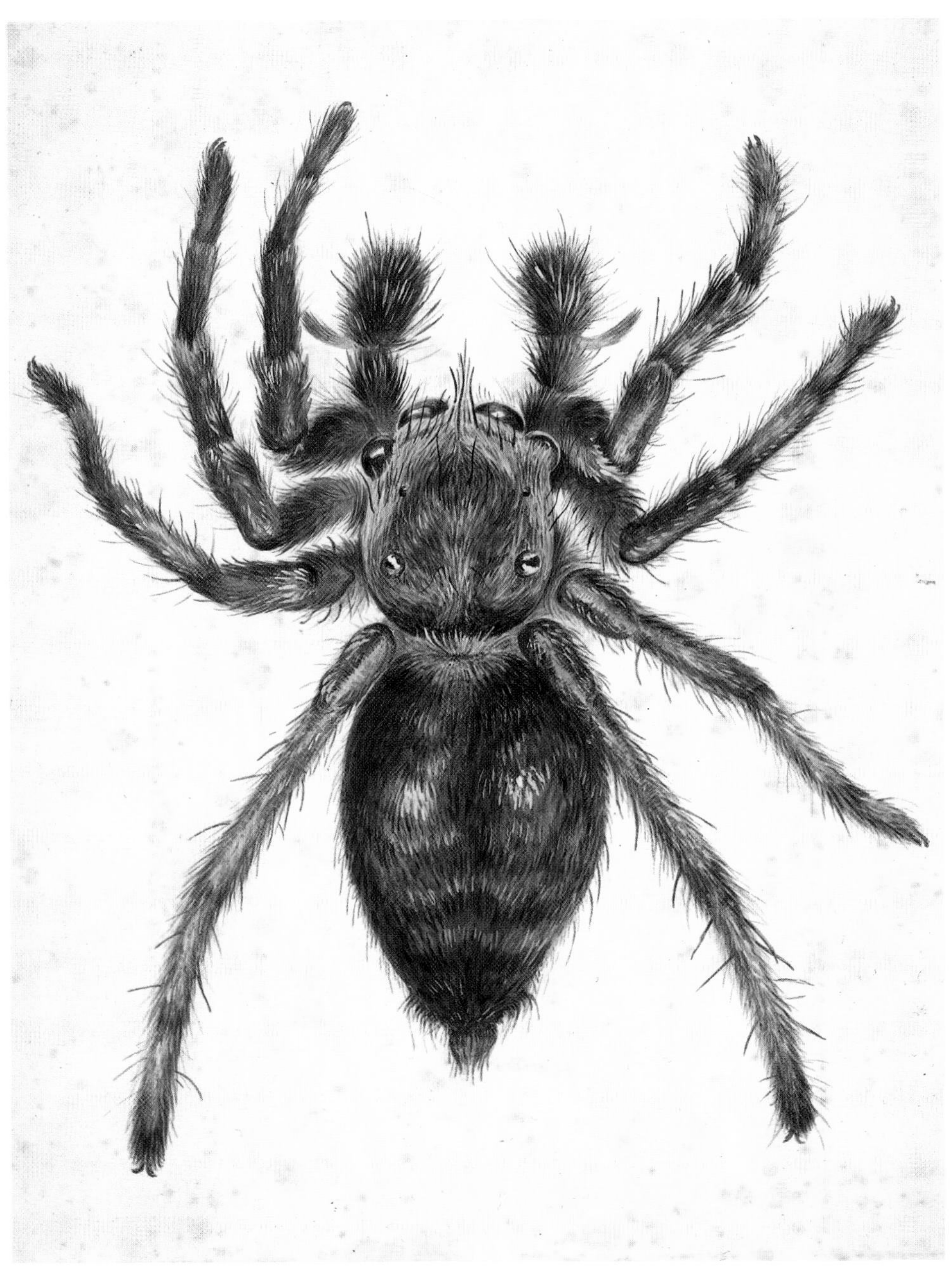

Opposite:
28. Ground beetle (*Carabus nemoralis*), *c.*1887.
Examined microscopically at different magnifications, from above and below. The same species of beetle reappears in *The Tale of Mrs. Tittlemouse*, published in 1910.
Pencil, pen-and-ink and watercolour; 363 x 268 (sheet size); V&A

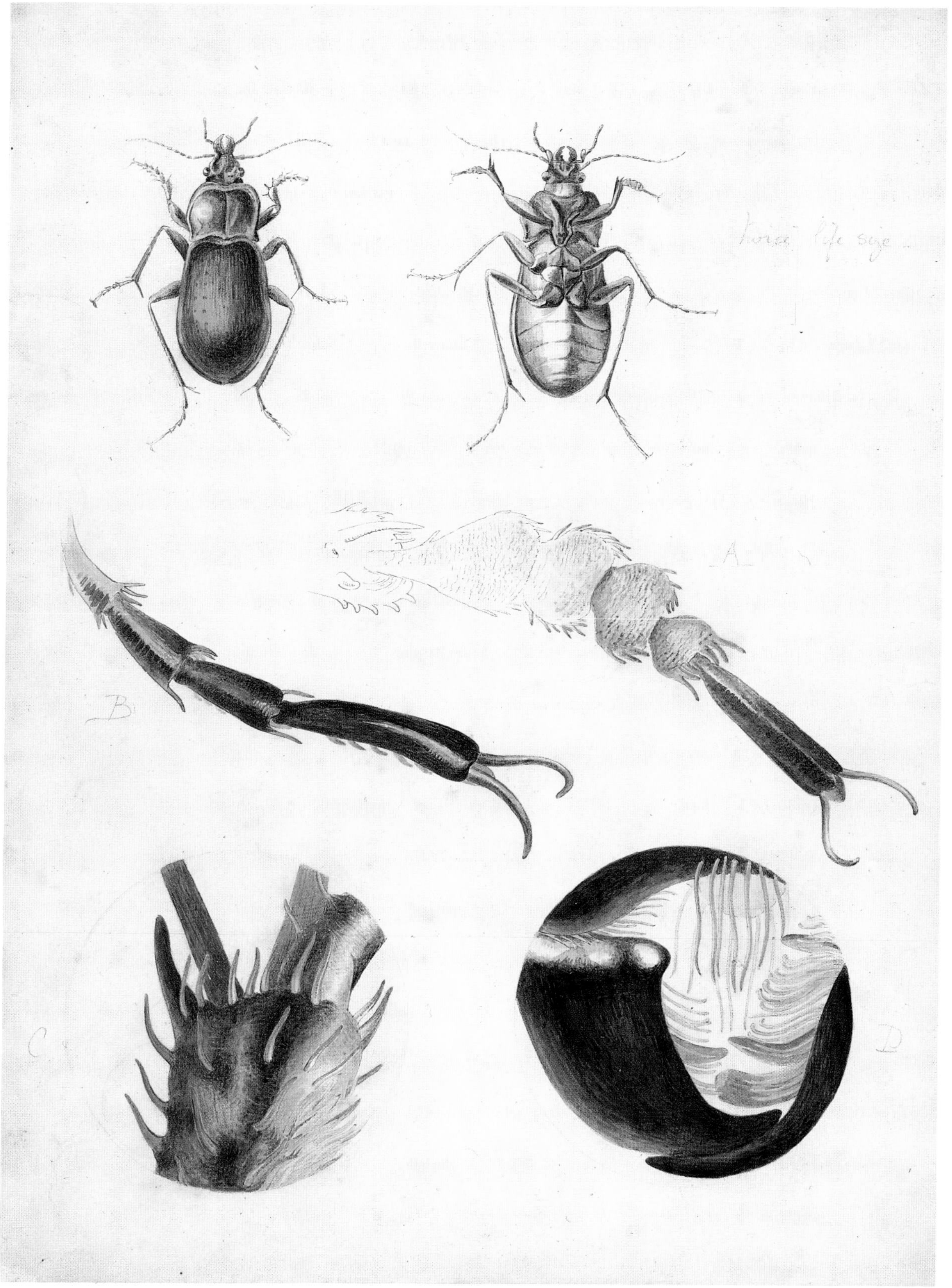
twice life size
A
B
C
D

29. Red Admiral butterfly from *The Tale of Mrs. Tittlemouse* (1910).
Insects often play a part as secondary characters in the 'Tales'.
Sepia ink and watercolour; 85 x 78; NT

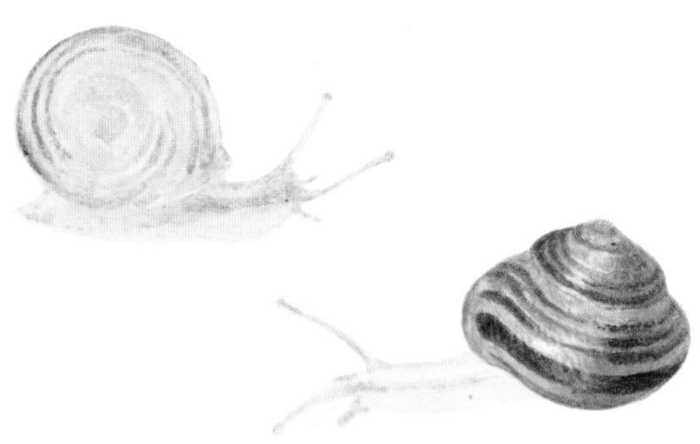

30. Two snails, *c.*1887.
One reappears on the wall of Jeremy Fisher's house.
Pencil and watercolour heightened with white;
60 x 35 (here repositioned); V&A

Opposite:
31. Painted Lady and Small Tortoiseshell butterflies (*Vanessa cardui* and *Aglais urticae*), 1887.
These microscopic studies show magnified scales from lower and upper sides of wing.
Pen-and-ink and watercolour; 355 x 265 (sheet size); V&A

Painted Lady Butterfly.
Vanessa Cardui.
Scales on lower side of wing highly magnified.

Small Tortoise-shell Butterfly.
Vanessa Urticae.
Scales on upper side of wing highly magnified.

Opposite:
32. Small and Large White butterflies (*Pieris rapae* and *Pieris brassicae*, females), ?1887. The scales 'rub off like dust on the fingers when one touches a moth or butterfly', she wrote on the reverse of this study.
Pen-and-ink and watercolour;
364 x 268 (sheet size); FLP

Below:
33. Microscopic studies of Sheet Web spider (*Linyphia triangularis*).
One of three known lithographed plates for a planned set of twelve, *c.*1895. Beatrix modestly doubted whether they were of any educational value 'because they were not drawn with design'.
Lithograph and pencil; 239 x 350; V&A

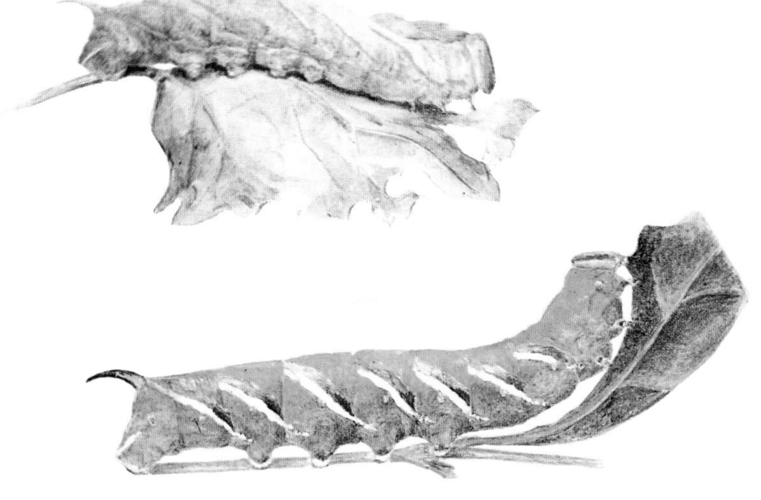

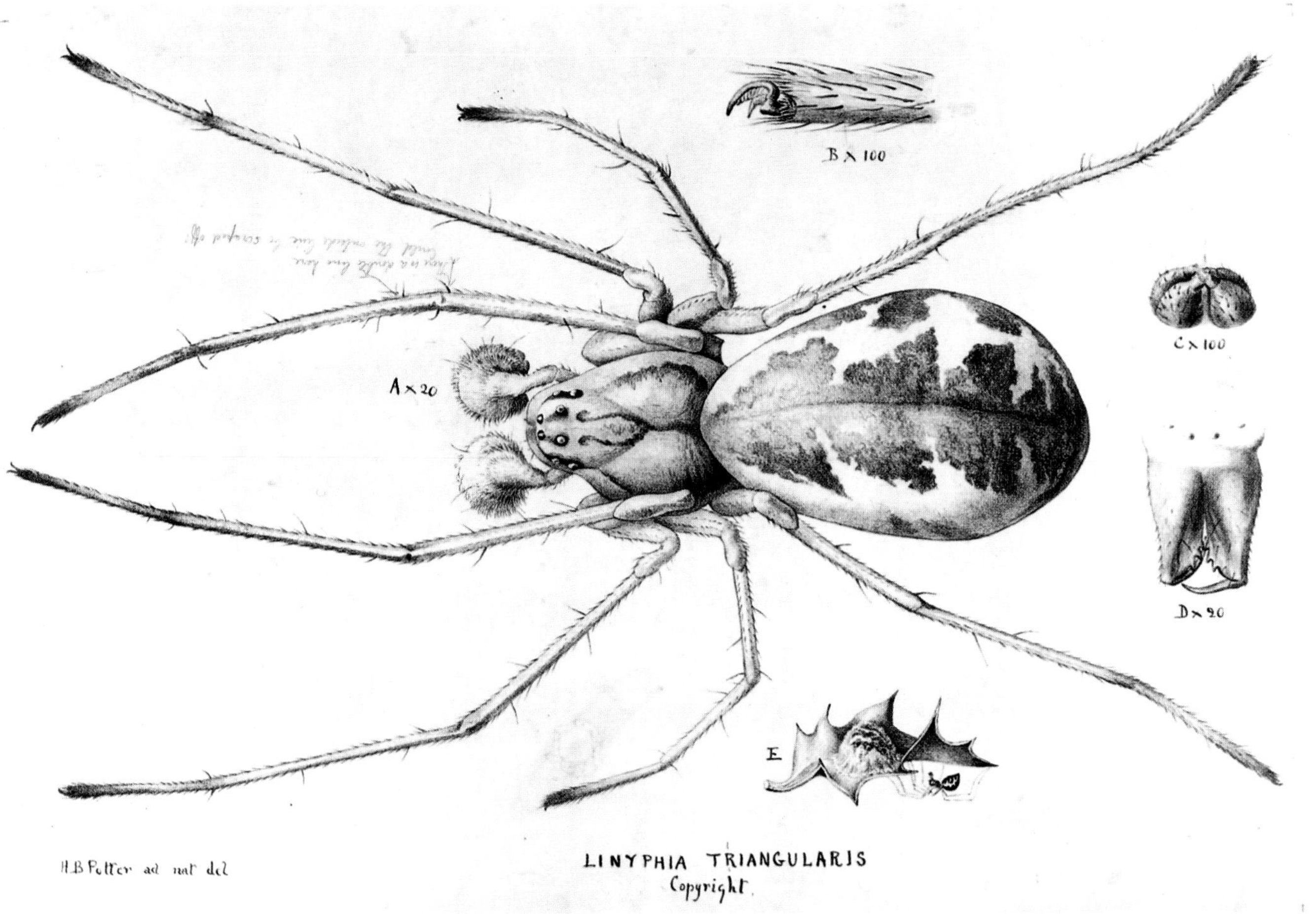

34. Caterpillars of Poplar Hawk-moth (*Laothoe populi*) and Privet Hawk-moth (*Sphinx ligustri*), *c.*1887.
Beatrix drew caterpillars singly or as one of several developmental stages.
Pencil and watercolour; 39 x 82, 40 x 100; V&A

B x 100
C x 100
A x 20
D x 20
E

H.B. Potter ad nat del

LINYPHIA TRIANGULARIS
Copyright

35. Five beetles, *c.*1885.
Top row: Longhorn beetle (*Prionus coriarius*), Dung beetle (*Geotrupes* sp.), Burying beetle (*Nicrophorus* sp.); bottom row: Ground beetle (*Pterostichus* sp.), Oil beetle (*Meloe* sp.).
Drawn on a sheet of writing paper headed 'Gorse Hall, Staley Bridge'.
Pencil, watercolour and bodycolour;
83 x 106 (here repositioned); V&A

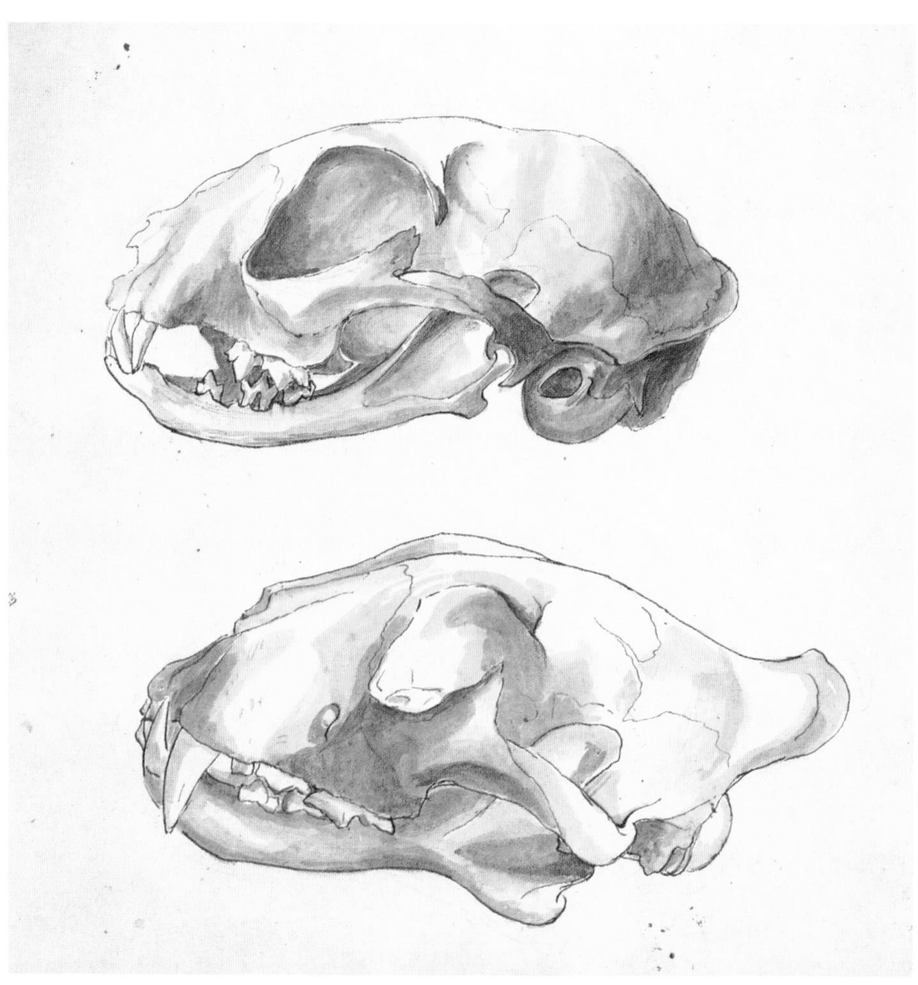

36. Skulls of the cat family in line and wash, ?1887.
Mass is emphasized rather than detail. The smaller cat (*Felis* sp., above) may have been drawn larger than life to make a clearer comparison with the tiger skull (*Panthera tigris*, below).
Pencil, pen-and-ink and sepia wash; 118 x 110; LT

37. Still life with book, bowl and sheep's skull, *c.*1885. Several interiors in the same vigorously linear, severe cross-hatched style date from this period (see 38). Pencil and pen-and-ink; 130 x 150; LT

38. An unidentified library, *c.*1885.
A pen drawing similar in style to one of her skull studies and several other interiors.
Pencil and pen-and-ink; 120 x 87; V&A

Opposite:
39. 'A Scottish garden in June from Nature', ?1882.
View of a garden on the Tay below Dunkeld: Beatrix Potter's largest extant drawing in this style of a landscape subject.
Watercolour and bodycolour heightened with white; 226 x 145; FLP

40. Interior of a watermill, 1884.
One of a number of architectural studies in chalks, made during a holiday at Bush Hall in 1884.
Black chalk; 246 x 182; V&A

Opposite:
41. Bush Hall, Hertfordshire, 1884.
'These chalk drawings, in singularly good perspective, must have been done when I was 18.'
Black chalk; 293 x 221; V&A

43. Dead stag, copied in chalks from a lithograph after Landseer. Beatrix also copied a portrait after Holbein in pen and wash, and a Constable sketch of Sty Head Tarn in watercolour.
Black, red and white chalks on grey paper; 337 x 444; V&A

Opposite:
42. Coniston Old Hall 'from nature', 1890. Most of her other chalk work was done at Bush Hall in 1884.
Pencil and black chalk; 291 x 227; FLP

Opposite:
44. Orange-winged Amazon parrot (*Amazona amazonica*), 1890.
The parrot, in profile and 'in full dress', belonged to the Moore family, recipients of Beatrix's picture letters. Like Brueghel, she inscribed her studies 'drawn from life'.
Watercolour and bodycolour; 250 x 175; FLP

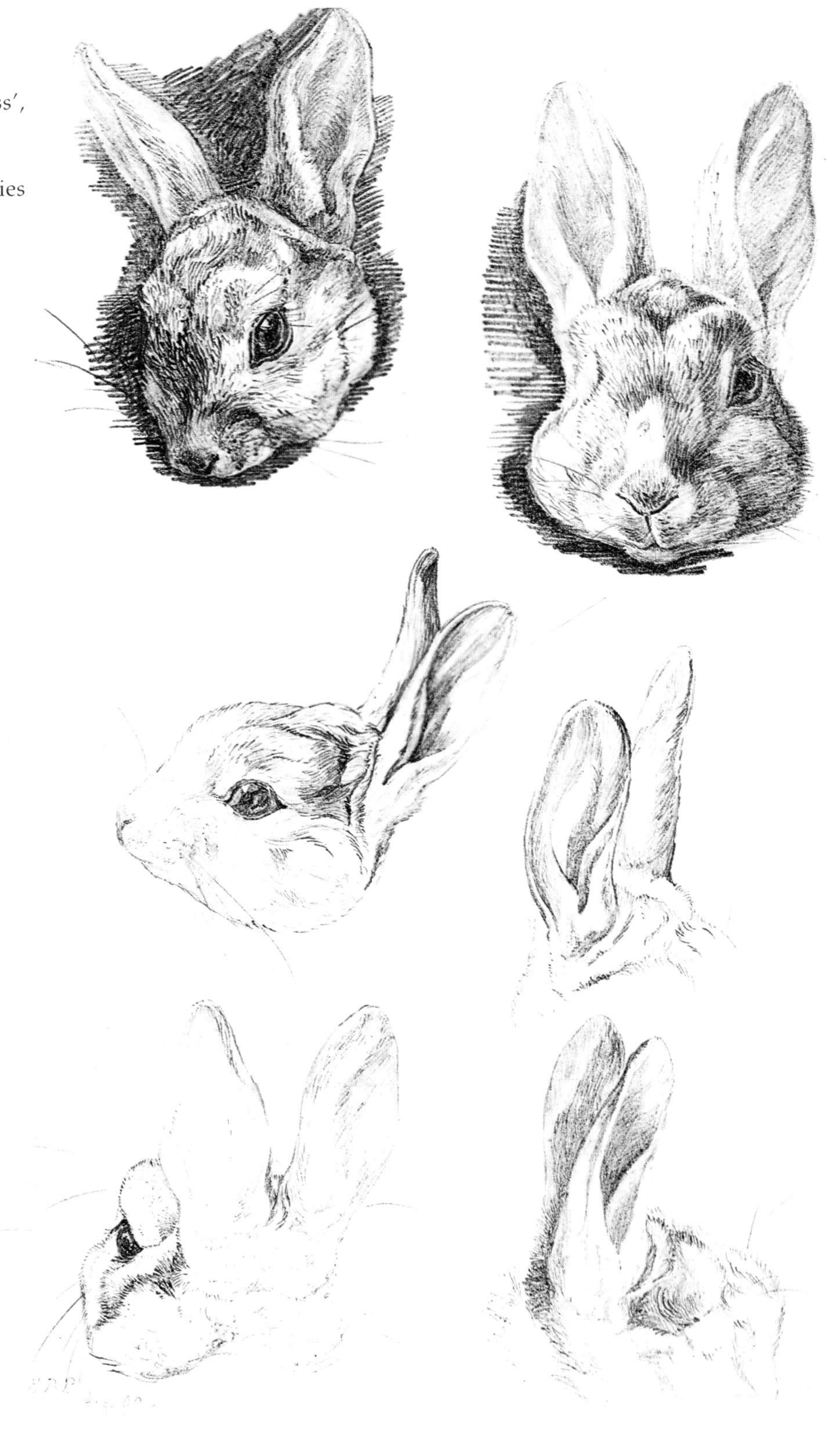

45. Rabbit's head, 1890.
Six studies of Benjamin Bunny's fine head, showing a sensitive portrayal of his ears. Endless practice and years of study perfected her natural history drawing.
Pencil; 255 x 162; V&A

46. The main staircase at Bedwell Lodge,
Hertfordshire, October 1891.
A fine study in perspective.
Watercolour; 254 x 162; LT

Opposite:
47. 'Sunlight & shadow' at Bedwell Lodge, 1891.
A bold grisaille technique coexists with the miniaturist style of her fantasy paintings.
Pencil, pen-and-ink and watercolour including grisaille heightened with white; 253 x 175; V&A

48. Mice in their store-room, 1891.
The backstairs at Bedwell Lodge embellished with a panelled passage-way. As a study in lighting it shows off Beatrix's management of space and command of perspective.
Pencil, pen-and-ink and watercolour including grisaille heightened with white;
188 x 148; V&A

49. Rabbits' potting shed, 1891.
Drawn at Bedwell Lodge in 1891 and later reborn as Mr. McGregor's potting shed in *The Tale of Peter Rabbit*.
Pencil, pen-and-ink and watercolour including grisaille; 189 x 146; V&A

SCENE 1

50. 'Appley Dapply', an 1891 rhyme sequence.
These three scenes have not been published together till now. Scenes 1 and 3 were reworked for *Appley Dapply's Nursery Rhymes* (1917); a new drawing was made for scene 2, the original having been mislaid.
Watercolour; 90 x 115 (each);
LT (1 and 3), private collection (2)

SCENE 2

SCENE 3

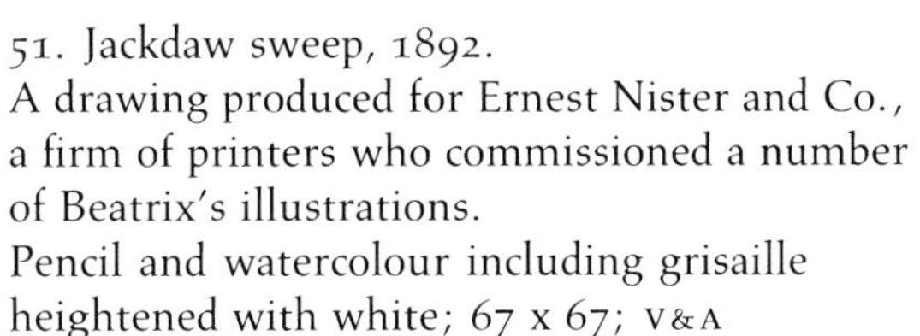
51. Jackdaw sweep, 1892.
A drawing produced for Ernest Nister and Co., a firm of printers who commissioned a number of Beatrix's illustrations.
Pencil and watercolour including grisaille heightened with white; 67 x 67; V&A

Opposite:
52. Two scenes from 'Three Little Mice', *c.*1892.
This project was originally planned as a booklet but never published; one picture was later redrawn for *The Tailor of Gloucester*. The bentwood chairs came from Camfield Place. The cat face behind the bars seems to echo an illustration by J. B. Zwecker in *National Nursery Rhymes* (1870).
Pen-and-ink and watercolour; 87 x 127 (each); V&A

53. Illustrations for 'The White Cat', 1894.
Sporting prints may have inspired these kittens with guns and game-bag. A third scene, showing a solitary kitten, was published in a Nister booklet.
Pencil, pen-and-ink and watercolour; 121 x 75, 100 x 79; V&A

54. Two scenes from 'The Rabbits' Christmas Party', *c.*1892.
A set of six paintings of which four were given to Beatrix's aunt Lucy, wife of Sir Henry Roscoe, and two to Henry P. Coolidge in 1927.
The first is uncannily reminiscent of Renoir's *Les Parapluies*, which Beatrix is unlikely to have seen.
Pen-and-ink and watercolour; 150 x 150 (each); V&A

55. 'The Squirrel's Gift', *c.*1895.
This drawing, on the borderline between observation and imagination, is almost a 'problem picture', since the spectator has to guess the story.
Pencil, pen-and-ink and watercolour including grisaille heightened with white; 187 x 138; V&A

Opposite above:
56. Squirrels and mistletoe, *c.*1891.
An early vignetted design, probably for a Christmas card. Around the picture are instructions to the printer.
Watercolour; 145 x 185 (sheet size); WA

Opposite below:
57. Squirrels on a log, *c.*1895.
The front and back views combine to make a greetings card design. It was never published as such, but in 1926 the pictures were considered by Beatrix's publishers, Warne, as possible covers for a calendar. Beatrix suggested they might illustrate 'October'.
Watercolour; 130 x 110 (each); WA

56. Squirrels and mistletoe (detail)

57. Squirrels on a log

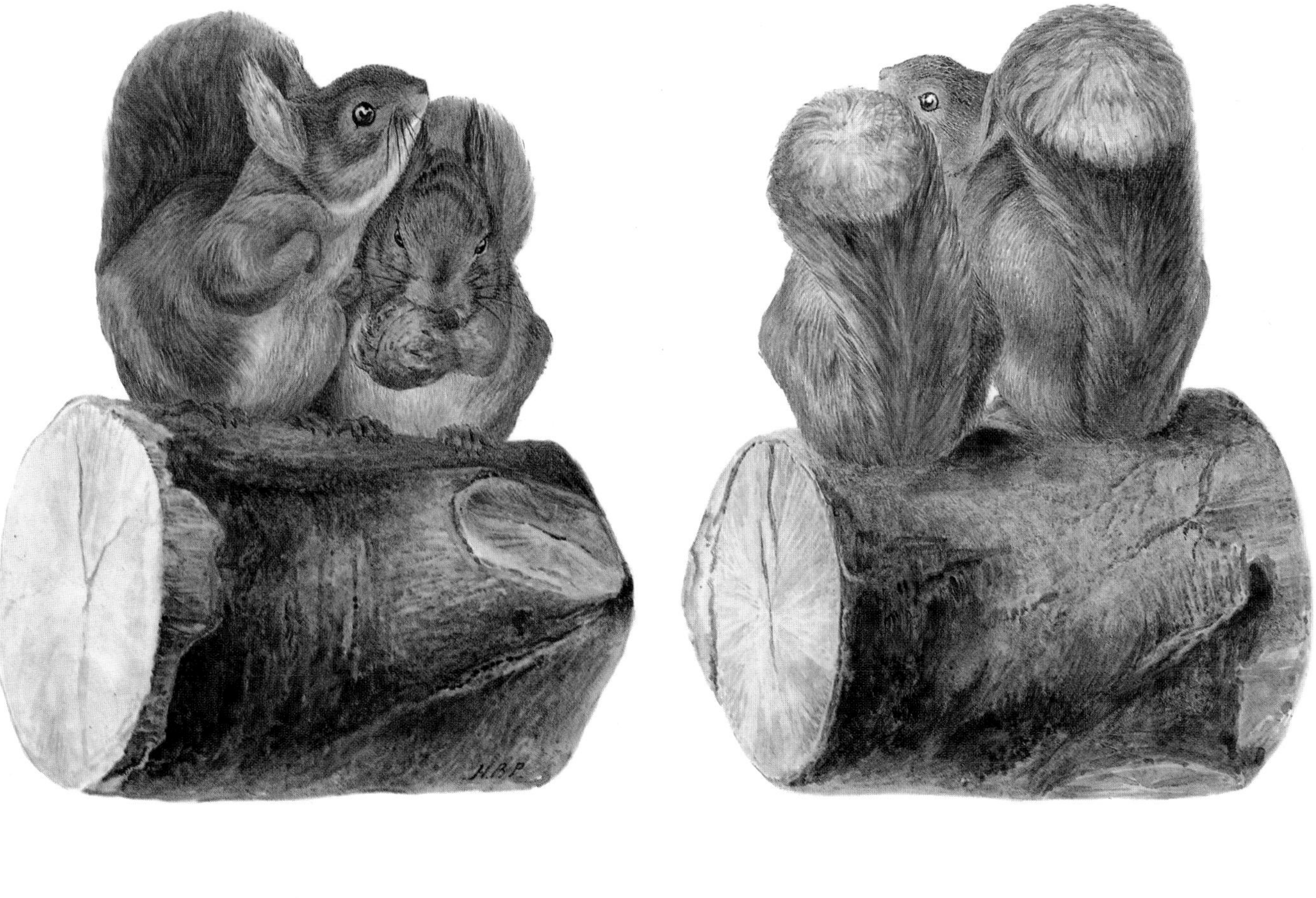

58. Seed pods of Stinking Iris (*Iris foetidissima*), *c.*1895.
'Lovelier in its orange seed than it is in flower' (Geoffrey Grigson, *Wild Flowers in Britain*, 1944).
Pencil and watercolour heightened with white; 167 x 78; V&A

Opposite above:
59. Insects, *c.*1890.
Bumble-bees (top row); bot-fly, hover fly, mud-wasp, soldier fly, deer-fly (second row); social wasp, ichneumon-fly, green lacewing (bottom row), exquisitely arranged on the page. An example of the Victorian love of examining, cataloguing and explaining the natural world, advocated by Ruskin.
Pencil and watercolour; 100 x 159; LT

Opposite below:
60. Boar fish and sea anemone, Weymouth 1895.
'In the morning I picked up a strange little red fish which I painted,' Beatrix records in her journal at Weymouth in 1895. According to the views of William Hunt, fish, with their variety of lustre and colour, were ideal subjects for the artist.
Pencil and watercolour heightened with white; 119 x 163; V&A

61. Scottish Blackface ram 'drawn from a stuffed specimen', ?1895.
This may have been copied at the Natural History Museum.
'I never saw anything so fearful as the stuffed animals.'
Watercolour grisaille heightened with white; 218 x 288; LT

62. Six heads of Herdwick rams.
Drawn some years later than the Scottish Blackface (61).
Pencil; 163 x 114; LT

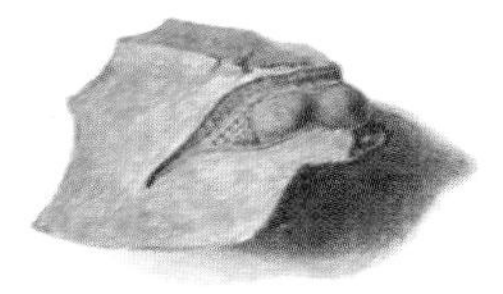

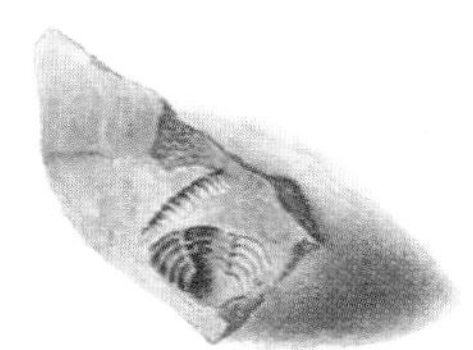
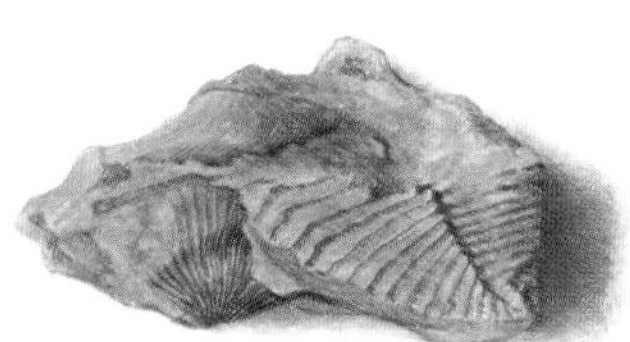

63. Six fossils from the Applethwaite Beds, found at Sour Howes, Troutbeck, 1895. Beatrix both photographed fossils and painted them in an illusionistic, photographic technique. The complicated textures of rocks and fossils fascinated nineteenth-century artists. Watercolour; 165 x 155; AT

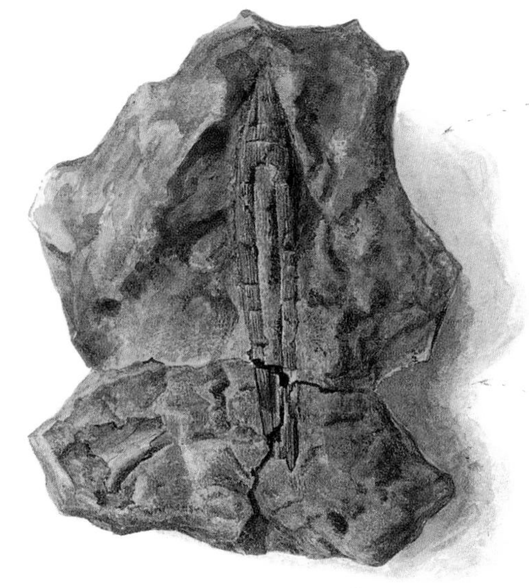

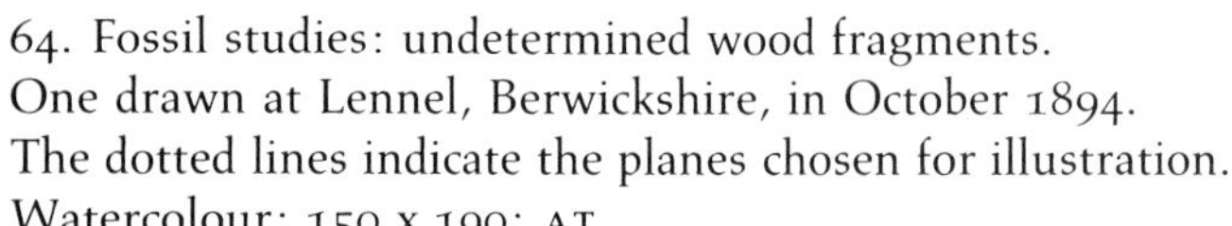

64. Fossil studies: undetermined wood fragments. One drawn at Lennel, Berwickshire, in October 1894. The dotted lines indicate the planes chosen for illustration. Watercolour; 150 x 190; AT

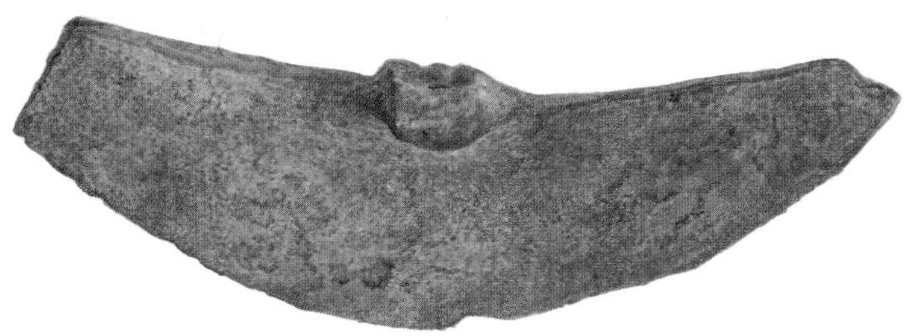

65–72:
Objects from the Bucklersbury excavations of 1872–3 were lent to Beatrix in 1894–5. Her drawings reflect the contemporary conventional approach to archaeological artefacts, but they are much more than aids to identification.

Above:
65. Two views of a turf cutter, July 1895. The rusty surface almost seems to grate on the skin, so compellingly is it observed. Watercolour and bodycolour; 120 x 145; AT

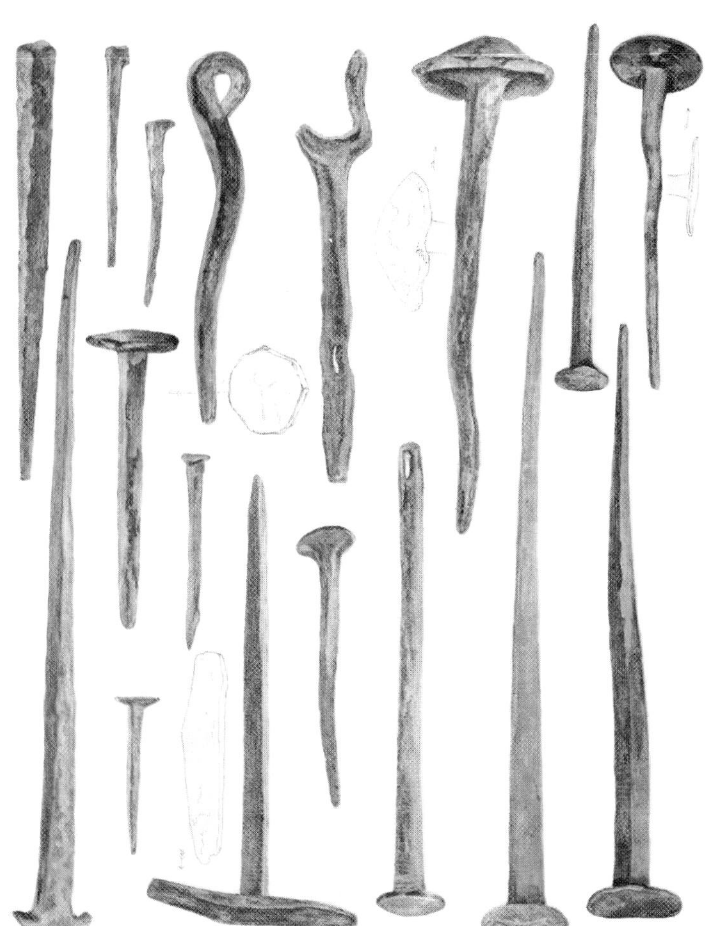

66. A comparative study of nails, 1895. Pen-and-ink and watercolour; 200 x 255; AT

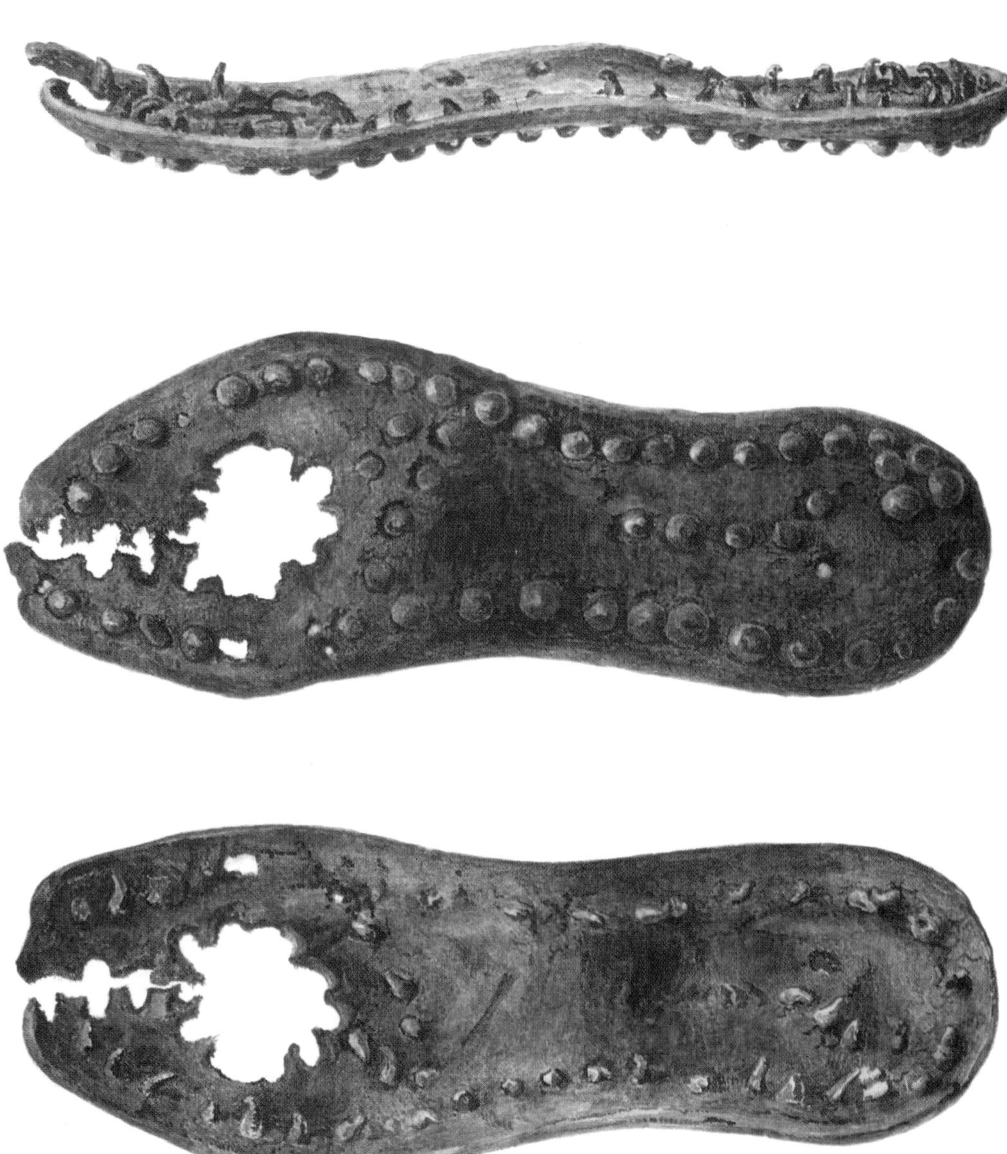

67. Three views of a Roman shoe leather, ?1895.
Found in Pickle Herring Street, City of London.
Watercolour and bodycolour; 235 x 205; AT

68. Fragments of potsherd, 1895.
Beatrix knew how to isolate an object and analyse its intrinsic qualities.
Watercolour and bodycolour; 85 x 270; AT

69. Roman shoe leather, painted in 1895.
This probably came from the Walbrook stream, in which many small articles were lost during the first century of Roman occupation.
Watercolour and bodycolour; 80 x 240; AT

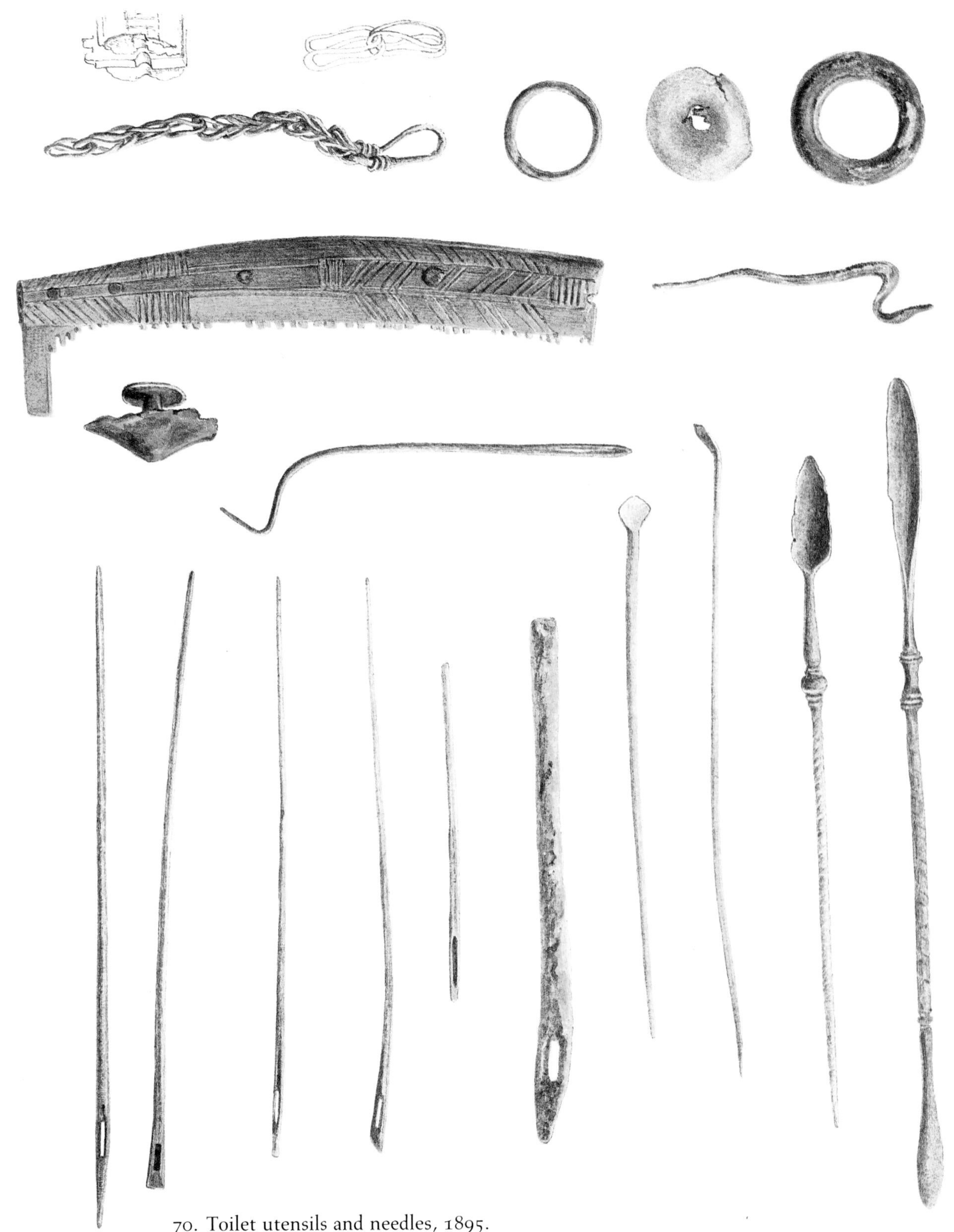

70. Toilet utensils and needles, 1895.
A more substantial fragment of comb provides the focal point.
Watercolour; 200 x 250; AT

71, 72. Fragments of Samian potsherd, 1895.
Watercolour and bodycolour heightened with white;
150 x 140, 100 x 185; AT

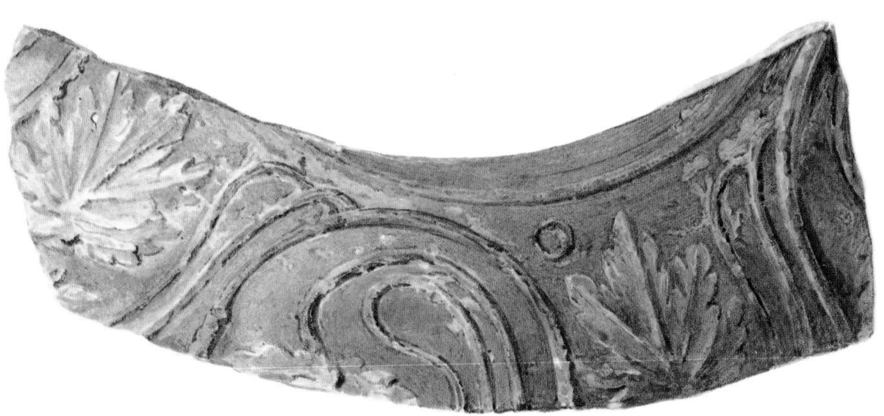

Opposite:
73. Fly Agaric (*Amanita muscaria*), with Polypody fern, beech leaves, mosses and lichen *Peltigera canina*, *c.*1890. A deliberately composed study, since its constituents come from different habitats. It appears to have been painted over an opaque ground, in the manner of William Henry Hunt. Watercolour and bodycolour; 201 x 170; NT

74. *Gomphidius glutinosus* from Hatchednize Wood, Coldstream, 1894. 'I found . . . joy of joys, the spiky *Gomphidius glutinosus*, a round, slimy, purple head among the moss' (*Journal*, August 1894). Watercolour; 170 x 200; AT

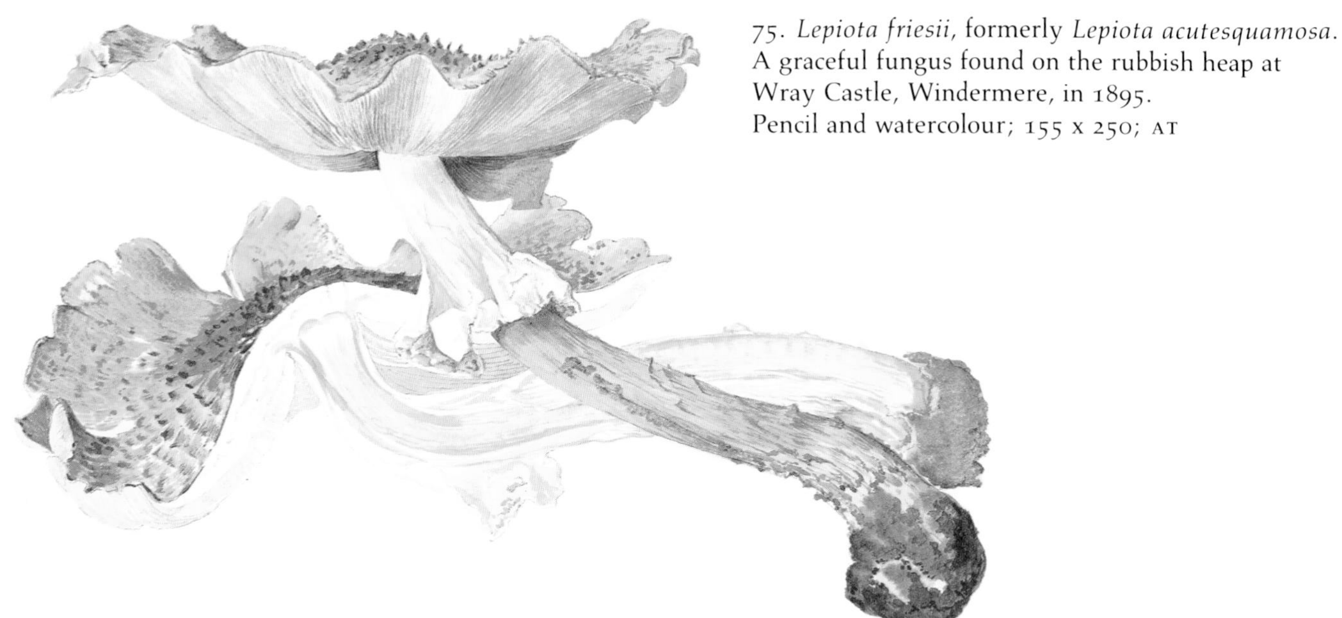

75. *Lepiota friesii*, formerly *Lepiota acutesquamosa*. A graceful fungus found on the rubbish heap at Wray Castle, Windermere, in 1895.
Pencil and watercolour; 155 x 250; AT

76. Larch Canker fungus (*Lachnellula wilkommii*, formerly *Dasyscypha calycina var. Trevelyani*) on fallen larch at Esthwaite, 1896.
Microscopic details including spores are shown, as well as the fungus on the larch canker.
Pencil and watercolour; 175 x 250; AT

77. Wax Cap (*Hygrophorus puniceus* or *Hygrocybe coccinea*), from Smailholm Tower, 1894.
'Lovely in colour and showing a kind of divination as well as imitative skill.' Ruskin's comment on the fungus drawings of William Hunt and Fred Walker could equally well refer to this painting.
Watercolour and bodycolour heightened with white; 175 x 230; AT

78. Brown Birch Bolete (*Leccinum scabrum*, formerly *Boletus scaber var. fulvus*), ?1895.
'Of all hopeless things to draw . . . the very worst is a fine fat fungus,' Beatrix wrote in 1892. Yet she succeeds in capturing each variety, matt or shiny, moist or slimy.
Watercolour; 235 x 210; AT

79. Jew's Ear fungus (*Auricularia* or *Hirneola auricula-judae*) on elder branch, Sidbury Camp, Devon, April 1898.
Pencil and watercolour; 130 x 275; AT

80. *Panaeolus semiovatus*, formerly *campanulatus*, from Smailholm Tower, September 1894.
The painting shows cap, gills and longitudinal section, according to the instructions on botanical drawing she received from Charlie McIntosh, the 'Perthshire naturalist'.
Watercolour; 170 x 160; AT

81. Old Man of the Woods (*Strobilomyces floccopus*, formerly *strobilaceus*).
Beatrix discovered this rare fungus, similar in appearance to a pine-cone, at Eastwood, Dunkeld in 1893. It was during this Scottish holiday, on the day after she painted the fungus, that Beatrix drew her first version of the Peter Rabbit story to send as a picture letter to a young friend.
Watercolour; 120 x 190; AT

82. *Pulcherricium caeruleum*, formerly *Corticium caeruleum*.
Inscribed 'Woodcote on Elder'.
Pencil and watercolour; 150 x 80; AT

83. Pine-cone, 1895.
Drawn in the technique of her best fungus and fossil studies.
Watercolour; 90 x 145; AT

84. Spectacular double portrait of Yellow Grisette (*Amanita crocea*) and Fly Agaric (*Amanita muscaria*), found near Derwentwater in 1897. She drew her fungi without modern aids such as a camera lucida. Pencil, pen-and-ink and watercolour; 241 x 365; V&A

85. Red Riding Hood meets the wolf, 1894.
Slate slabs and high walls give a feeling of claustrophobia among the meticulously drawn ferns, forest trees and fungus.
Pencil, pen-and-ink and watercolour grisaille heightened with white; 186 x 135; FLP

86. 'Subject drawing' for 'Mr. Wolf Makes a Failure', 1893.
One of nine pencil drawings for *Uncle Remus*, dating from 1893–6, set in pen-and-ink borders of expertly-drawn rabbits.
Pencil and pen-and-ink; 242 x 224; LT

87. 'Brother Rabbit rescues Brother Tarrypin', 1895.
A decidedly uncosy interior scene from *Nights with Uncle Remus*.
Pencil and pen-and-ink; 175 x 268; LT

88. A rabbit in his box.
A timed drawing inscribed '20 minutes'.
Pencil; 52 x 139; FLP

89. 'The Rabbit's Dream', *c.*1895.
Peter Rabbit dreaming of himself in No. 4 bedroom,
Camfield Place, framed by sketches of his sleeping positions.
An interweaving of fact, fantasy and wit.
Pencil and pen-and-ink; 207 x 182; V&A

90. Two designs for *Alice in Wonderland*, ?1895.
'The White Rabbit, splendidly dressed' and 'The Rabbit . . . scurried away into the darkness as hard as he could go.' Beatrix's pet rabbit Peter modelled for both Brer Rabbit and the White Rabbit.
Pencil, pen-and-ink and watercolour; 84 x 70 (each); LT

91. Peter Rabbit on his old quilt in the schoolroom, 1899.
The brushstroke has become freer, the emotion more obvious.
Watercolour; 93 x 182; LT

92. A rabbit's eye view from inside the burrow, *c.*1895.
Pencil and watercolour; 122 x 165; V&A

93. Crouching rabbit.
The original Peter Rabbit was probably the model for this grisaille painting. The same pose was captured in pencil.
Pencil, pen-and-ink and watercolour grisaille heightened with white;
64 x 143; V&A

94. 'Cinderella's carriage going to fetch her from the ball, intended for *moon*light', *c.*1895.
In grey wash on cream-tinted card, this is a remarkable study in atmosphere in which format is suited to subject.
Pencil, pen-and-ink and watercolour; 139 x 278; V&A

Opposite above:
95. Sketch for Cinderella's carriage, *c.*1895.
Pencil and pen-and-ink; 117 x 206; V&A

Opposite below:
96. Cinderella's carriage, *c.*1895.
The finished drawing: the carriage waits at the palace door in a blaze of light.
Sepia ink, pen-and-ink and sepia wash; 180 x 240; WA

97, 98:
Two of four designs for 'The Sleeping Beauty', made between 1898 and 1902, partly based on wood engravings by Ludwig Richter. The theme of the 'Briar Rose' borders complements their central subject. This style, asymmetric in the Art Nouveau or Japanese manner, was fashionable in the 1890s. 'I cannot design pattern borders, but I like drawing flowers,' Beatrix wrote to her publishers.

97. 'All round the castle there grew up a hedge of thorn . . .', 1902.
Pen-and-ink and watercolour; 303 x 240; FLP

Another of these decorative borders from the same series can be seen on the part title on page 25.
Pencil, pen-and-ink and watercolour; 196 x 169; V&A

98. 'The Prince coming into the courtyard of the palace', 1898.
Pen-and-ink and watercolour; 304 x 240; FLP

99. 'Ninny Nanny Netticoat', ?1897. One of several designs for this rhyming riddle in which the action pivots on the candle. Most of her best fantasy work dates from the 1890s. This illustration was redrawn for *Cecily Parsley's Nursery Rhymes*, 1922.
Pen-and-ink and watercolour; 128 x 148; NT

Below:
100. 'Golden Corn', October 1899, with a partial border of oats. A scene familiar at that period, with human gleaners instead of mice.
Pencil, pen-and-ink and watercolour; 216 x 280; V&A

101. 'A Dream of Toasted Cheese', 1899.
Devised in honour of her uncle's book, *First Step in Chemistry*. Fact and fantasy combine to make sly reference to NH3 (ammonia gas) and the Bunsen burner. The learned mouse appears elsewhere in Beatrix's pictures, reading a newspaper and on the *Tailor of Gloucester* cover.
Pen-and-ink and watercolour; 230 x 148; private collection

102. Harvest scene overlooking Esthwaite Water, *c.*1895.
A painting circulated within the Drawing Society to which Beatrix belonged at this time and generally praised, with however the comment that its hurried foreground spoilt the effect.
Pencil and watercolour; 255 x 355; V&A

103. Male Fern (*Dryopteris filix-mas*), 1901.
Beatrix Potter was interested in lichens, mosses and ferns as well as fungi.
Pencil and watercolour; 268 x 161; V&A

104. Sidmouth, March 1899.
The Potter family often took their spring holiday in the West Country.
Sidmouth became Stymouth in *The Tale of Little Pig Robinson.*
Watercolour; 115 x 202; LT

Opposite:
105. 'Rain': August in the Lake District, at Lingholm on Derwentwater in 1898.
The house is seen from an unconventional viewpoint.
Dampened paper is used to create the effect of a damp atmosphere.
Pencil and watercolour; 291 x 228; V&A

Kirkcudbright bay -
Sept. 27th 99 -

106. Mutchill, Kirkcudbright Bay, September 1899.
Several seascapes, and a study of sea lavender (108), date from this second visit to Galloway.
Watercolour; 173 x 251; LT

107. Nodding or Musk Thistle (*Carduus nutans*).
Inscribed 'A weed'.
Pencil and watercolour; 252 x 158; V&A

108. Sea Lavender (*Statice* or *Limonium*),
Kirkcudbright Bay, September 1899.
Pen-and-ink and watercolour; 260 x 179; LT

109. Snowdrops.
A life-size close-up, seen at eye level.
Beatrix Potter drew plants in context,
in profile, or, as here, as near-abstracts.
Pencil and watercolour; 90 x 85; LT

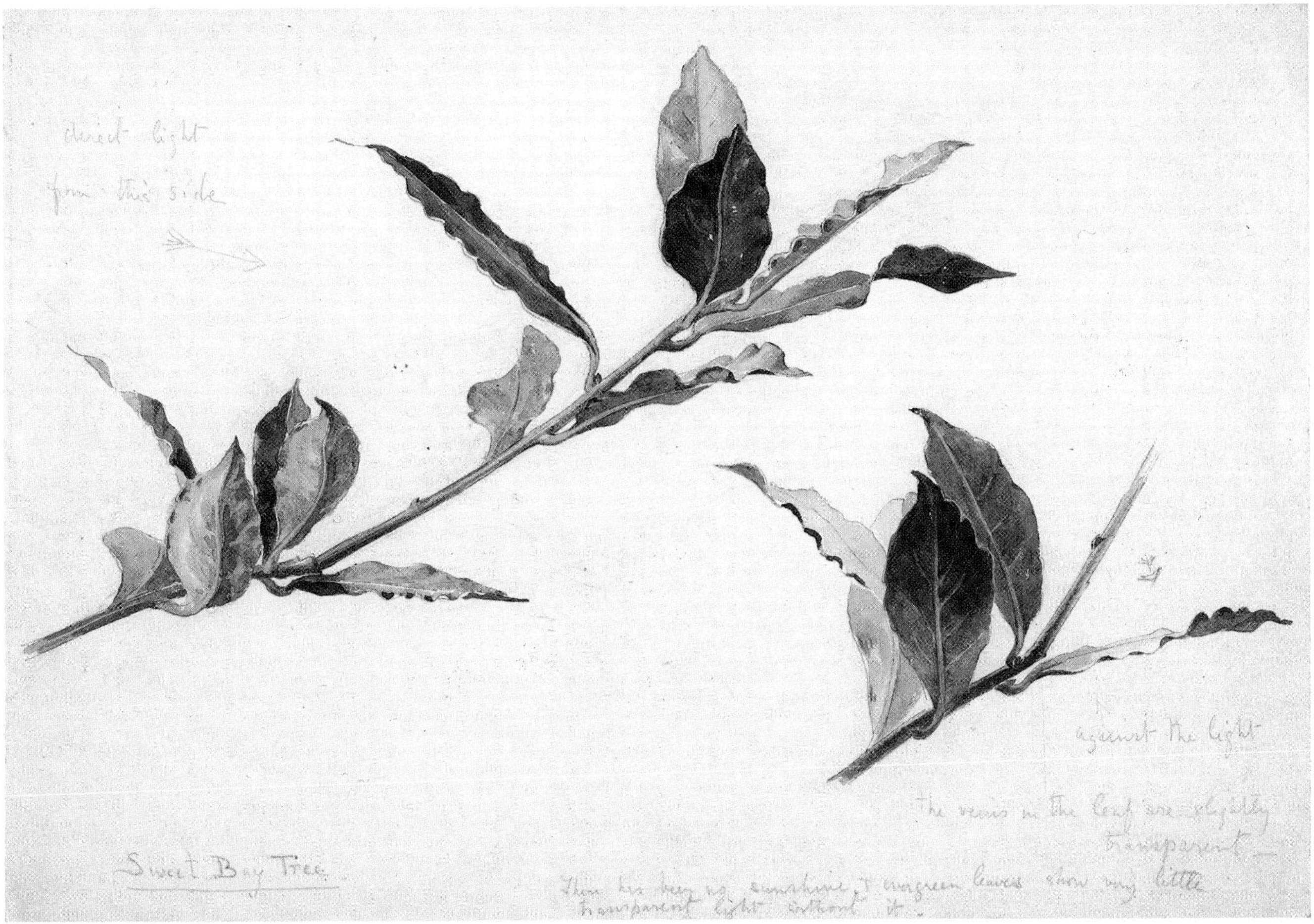

110. Sprays of Sweet Bay (*Magnolia virginiana*), 1900.
Included are Beatrix's notes on the direction of the light:
'Against the light. The veins in the leaf are slightly transparent.
There has been no sunshine & evergreen leaves show very
little transparent light without it.'
Pencil, pen-and-ink and watercolour;
178 x 254 (sheet size); V&A

111. *Cladonia floerkeana* with *Cladonia polydactyla* (centre).
Two red-tipped lichens.
Watercolour; 65 x 70; AT

112. Posy of wild flowers.
Light and colour are more important than line in this subject.
Watercolour; 278 x 228; LT

Opposite:
113. 'Fruit', *c.*1900.
A painting of raspberries and blackcurrants submitted to the Drawing Society. Damned with faint praise by the members, it is none the less an attractive and well-executed design.
Pencil, pen-and-ink and watercolour; 240 x 213; LT

114. 'Old Mister Prickly Pin', *c.*1902. Painted for the 1905 Book of Rhymes. She considered it 'about the best drawing I ever made' (writing in 1920).
Pencil, pen-and-ink and watercolour; 131 x 163; V&A

115. 'Old Mr. Pricklepin', *Appley Dapply's Nursery Rhymes*, 1917.
His predecessor was altogether cosier and less farouche.
Sepia ink and watercolour; 149 x 190; NT

116. Daffodils in a jug.
The Drawing Society thought it 'very pretty and well painted', approving of the indistinct background, which echoes the colours in the glaze. A similar jug sustains Mr. Pricklepin (*opposite*).
Pencil and watercolour heightened with white oil paint; 194 x 170; V&A

117. Garden at Tenby with fish-pond and attendant cat, *c.*1900. This picture was circulated by the Drawing Society. Members described it as 'too elaborate – but otherwise beautifully drawn'. The colours are reminiscent of oils. The fish-pond was later the model for the lily-pond in *The Tale of Peter Rabbit*.
Pencil, pen-and-ink and watercolour heightened with white; 227 x 291; V&A

118. From *The Tale of Peter Rabbit*, 1902. 'A white cat was staring at some gold-fish.' Its 'innocent whiteness becomes a dreadful *absence* of color' (Maurice Sendak, 'Beatrix Potter', 1965).
Pen-and-ink and watercolour; 98 x 83; WA

119. Unfinished drawing of foxgloves. It may have been a study for *The Tale of Jemima Puddle-Duck*, 1908. Pencil and watercolour; 273 x 207; V&A

120. 'An English Garden', Lakefield, Sawrey, 1900. Vivid in hue but according to a Drawing Society member 'wanting in colour, and life'. Pen-and-ink and watercolour; 228 x 292; V&A

121. 'At evening's close': Lakefield, Sawrey, *c.*1902.
Painted about two years later than the previous picture, from a different viewpoint and in a different style.
Sepia ink and watercolour; 293 x 228; LT

122. 'Spring', ?1903.
The Nuttery at Harescombe Grange, Gloucestershire, house of the Hutton family. 'The Nuttery' is still the same, but the large tree has gone.
Pencil, pen-and-ink and watercolour; 292 x 226; LT

123. From *The Tale of Johnny Town-Mouse*, 1918. Beatrix respected and admired dogs, sheep and horses, but found them difficult to draw. This illustration pleased her, however, and she wrote 'Old Dimond our farm horse is my favourite of the pictures.'
Pen-and-ink, sepia ink and watercolour;
101 x 75; NT

124. The old Court House at Hawkshead, *c*.1900. Rupert Potter photographed Beatrix outside this building in 1896.
Watercolour; 253 x 354; LT

125. 'Hen Blackbird drawn from nature'.
Some of Beatrix Potter's earliest extant drawings are studies of dead birds. She much admired Thorburn's paintings of birds in landscapes.
Watercolour heightened with white; 128 x 222; FLP

126. Studies of a thrush, 1902.
The bird was 'picked up dead in the snow' at Woodcote, Surrey, home of her uncle, Sir Henry Roscoe. It is recorded with a naturalist's eye and a clear, transparent palette.
Pencil, pen-and-ink and watercolour; 214 x 267; V&A

127. Microscopic study of *Electra pilosa* (formerly *Flustra pilosa*), Eastbourne, 1886.
Part of a colony of zooids (tiny marine animals), growing on what is probably a strand of seaweed.
Visible are the protective surface spines.
Watercolour heightened with white;
268 x 205 (sheet size); FLP

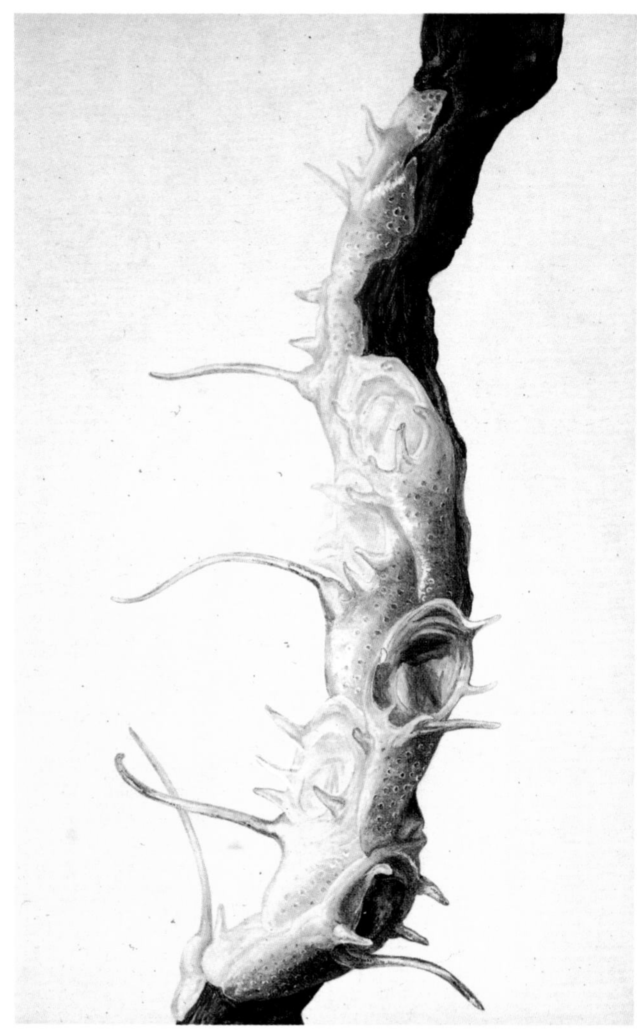

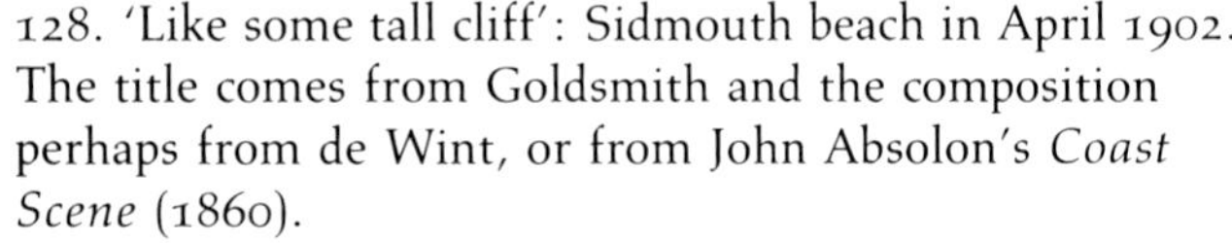

128. 'Like some tall cliff': Sidmouth beach in April 1902.
The title comes from Goldsmith and the composition perhaps from de Wint, or from John Absolon's *Coast Scene* (1860).
Pencil and watercolour; 202 x 273; V&A

129. 'A winter evening' at Derwent Cottage, Winchelsea, January 1900.
An interior view with open door, rag rug and gleaming furniture. During a winter holiday here Beatrix made at least fifteen drawings and sent several picture letters.
Watercolour heightened with white; 226 x 274; LT

130. Dressing-room at Derwent Cottage, Winchelsea, 26 January 1900.
Pencil; 205 x 255; LT

131. 'A Welsh dresser – date 1696'.
Drawn at Gwaynynog, North Wales in 1903.
Pencil and sepia ink; 240 x 210; LT

132. 'Gentlemen came every day', a nursery rhyme illustration. This version, drawn for her young friend Noel Moore in 1902, was later redrawn for the frontispiece of *Cecily Parsley's Nursery Rhymes* (1922), where one pipe becomes a newspaper. Pen-and-ink and watercolour heightened with white; 157 x 183; V&A

133. Archway in Gloucester, from *The Tailor of Gloucester*, 1903. Originally sketched 'on very warm spring days', sitting on a doorstep, during Beatrix Potter's first visit to Gloucester in 1897. Pen-and-ink and watercolour; 111 x 92; TG

134. Unused painting for *The Tailor of Gloucester*, 1903.
The book version firms up the composition but loses both unconventionality and clock; Beatrix thought this one equally good.
Pen-and-ink and watercolour; 112 x 94; WA

135. 'No more twist', from *The Tailor of Gloucester*, 1903.
The waistcoat and other late eighteenth-century costumes were copied from originals at the Victoria and Albert Museum.
Pen-and-ink and watercolour; 111 x 92; TG

136. From *The Tale of Squirrel Nutkin*, 1903.
A fine appreciation of colour and texture in this practical approach to ninepins.
Pen-and-ink and watercolour; 100 x 90; NT

Opposite above:
138. Derwent Bay, in a sketchbook dating from 1901.
This picture was reworked soon afterwards for *The Tale of Squirrel Nutkin*. The diagonals provide compositional interest.
Pencil and watercolour; 140 x 227; NT

Opposite below:
139. Squirrel sketch, ?1903.
The page was detached from a sketchbook containing squirrel drawings for *The Tale of Squirrel Nutkin*, 1903.
Pencil and watercolour; 111 x 115; V&A

137. From *The Tale of Squirrel Nutkin*, 1903.
Nutkin with 'robin's pin-cushion'.
Pen-and-ink and watercolour; 80 x 88; NT

138. Derwent Bay

139. Squirrel sketch

140. Squirrels on Derwentwater, alternative version of a picture in *The Tale of Squirrel Nutkin*, 1903. This view, without the figures, appears in Beatrix's 1903 sketchbook, known as the 'Derwentwater sketch-book' (*above*). The figures enhance the sense of distance. Pencil and watercolour; 90 x 130; NT (above); pen-and-ink and watercolour; 125 x 90; WA (left)

141. Squirrel in a wood near Derwentwater, 1903.
A background study for *The Tale of Squirrel Nutkin*.
Pencil, sepia ink and watercolour; 178 x 137; V&A

142. 'Flower-pots, and frames and tubs', 1903.
Background sketch at Fawe Park, Keswick, for *The Tale of Benjamin Bunny* (1904).
Pencil, pen-and-ink and watercolour; 226 x 190; LT

Opposite:
143. The garden at Fawe Park, with visiting cat, 1903.
An unused background for *The Tale of Benjamin Bunny*.
Pencil, pen-and-ink, sepia ink and watercolour;
292 x 226; private collection

Beatrix Potter
Fawe Park

144. Broad bean in flower.
Another background study for *The Tale of Benjamin Bunny*, painted at Fawe Park in 1903. Sepia ink and watercolour; 243 x 193; LT

145. Onions at Fawe Park, 1903. The fluent sepia line, made glossy by added gum arabic, is enhanced with transparent wash. A study for *The Tale of Benjamin Bunny*. Pencil, sepia ink and watercolour; 95 x 289; V&A

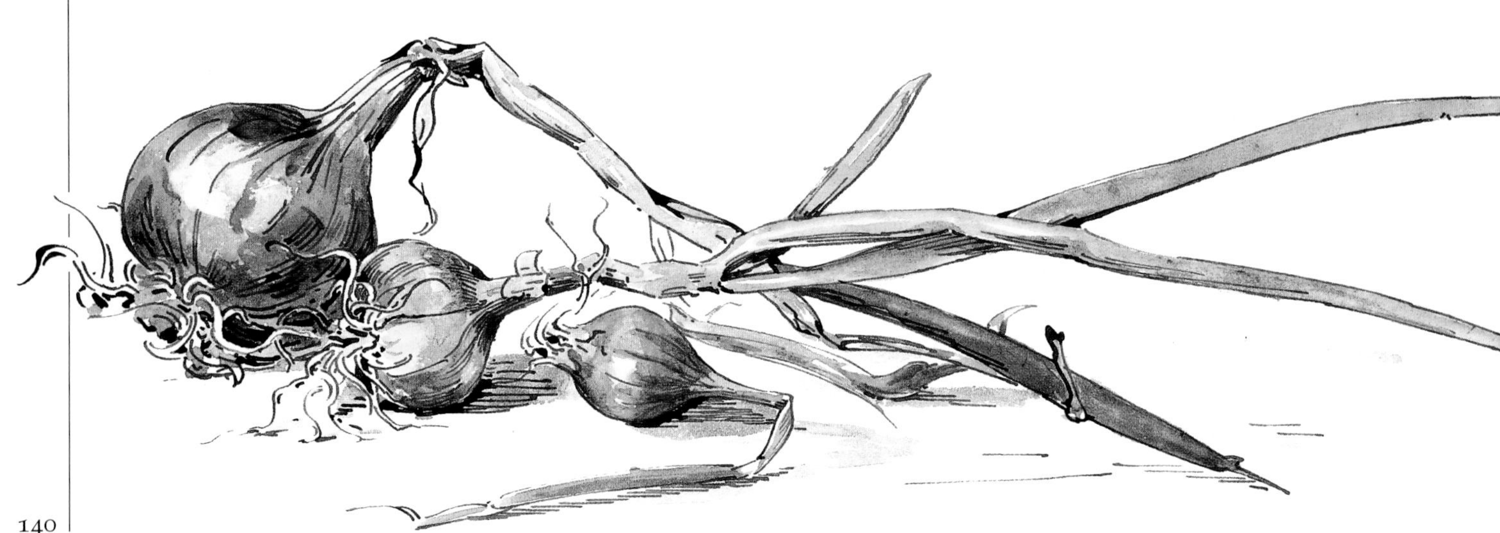

146. The garden wall at Fawe Park, 1903.
Pencil, pen-and-ink and watercolour; 226 x 187; LT

A background for *The Tale of Benjamin Bunny*, drawn at the same time as the vegetables and in a similar technique.

Opposite:
147. The garden steps at Fawe Park, 1903.
Another background for *The Tale of Benjamin Bunny.*
Pen-and-ink and watercolour; 227 x 190; FLP

148. Carnation, ?1903.
Study for a proposed frontispiece to *The Tale of Benjamin Bunny.*
Pencil, pen-and-ink and watercolour; 205 x 163; V&A

Opposite:
151. Buttressed wall at Melford Hall, Suffolk. Beatrix also photographed this view, in 1903. Photographs were useful aids for artists. Pencil and watercolour; 227 x 189; LT

149. The Newlands Valley, 1903, from the 'Derwentwater sketchbook'. The same view was re-used, slightly modified, in *The Tale of Mrs. Tiggy-Winkle.* Pencil and watercolour; 130 x 90; NT

150. Pheasant's Eye Narcissus (*Narcissus poeticus*) in delicate pen-and-wash. Here spring flowers are skilfully interpreted in a transparent medium. Pencil, pen-and-ink and watercolour; 279 x 150; V&A

Opposite:
152. Interior at Melford Hall, Christmas 1903. The shadowy figure by the exuberantly scrolled fireplace is Beatrix's young cousin, Stephanie Hyde Parker.
Pencil and watercolour; 227 x 189; LT

153. Studies of 'Chippendale' and Queen Anne chairs at Fawe Park, 1903.
Pencil and sepia ink;
269 x 210 (sheet size); V&A

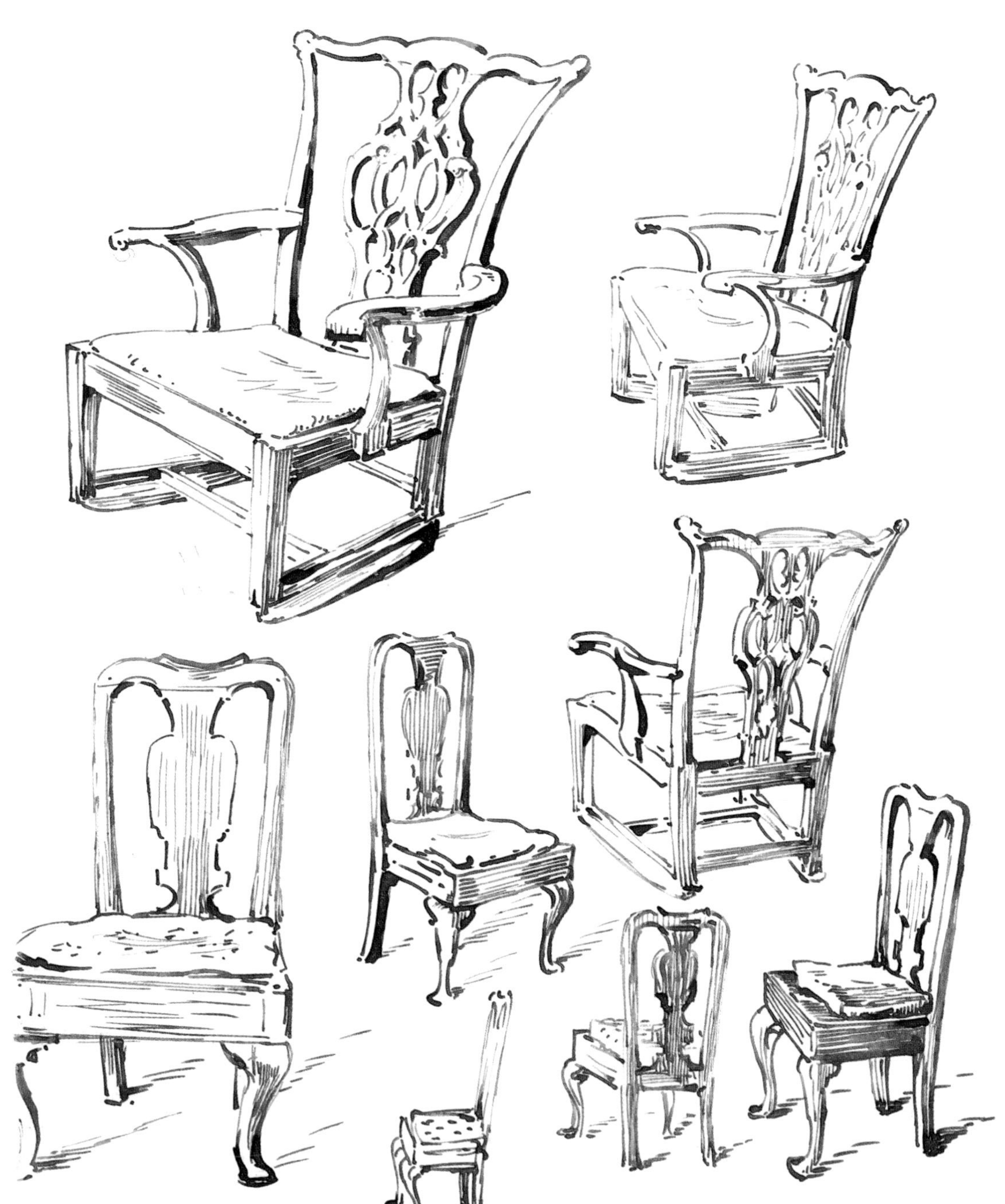

Opposite:
154. 'A November day', *c.*1905.
Bolton Gardens, Kensington, at dusk, seen from the schoolroom window through mist and a lattice-work of branches, with twinkling lights and a creeping sensation of damp.
Pencil and watercolour; 269 x 184; V&A

155. Bedford Square, November 1905.
Drawn from the viewpoint of No. 8, house of the Warne family, Beatrix's publishers.
Pencil and watercolour; 190 x 165; private collection

156. Lyme Regis, 1904.
This picture of the main street, descending steeply to the sea, was redrawn with figures for the American edition of *The Tale of Little Pig Robinson*, 1930.
Sepia ink; 230 x 205; LT

157. The Cobb at Lyme Regis, ?1904.
Golden Cap can be seen in the background.
Pencil and sepia ink; 269 x 199; FLP

158. Brookthorpe Farm, Gloucestershire, October 1904. A line block was made of this drawing and printed by Edmund Evans & Co., possibly for a greetings card. Pen-and-ink; 267 x 215; LT

Opposite:
159. 'An old mill on the Stour, Suffolk', *c.*1905. Several studies of buildings date from this period. Pencil and watercolour; 227 x 189; LT

160. 'The Town Mouse and the Country Mouse', *c.*1900.
A design that shows Art Nouveau influence; a later design, 'The Country Mouse and the Town Mouse', is less stylized.
Pen-and-ink and watercolour; 185 x 157; LT

161. 'The Country Mouse and the Town Mouse', *c.*1905.
As so often, Beatrix returns to a subject in a different style. The curve of a tail completes the harmony of the composition.
Pen-and-ink and watercolour; 196 x 167; LT

162. Tommy Tittlemouse, ?1905.
An unfinished design for the 1905 Book of Rhymes. Tommy is an obvious precursor of the bank vole, Timmy Willie, in *The Tale of Johnny Town-Mouse*. The foliage shows Art Nouveau influence (see also 171).
Pencil, sepia ink and watercolour; 202 x 152; LT

163. Cecily Parsley brewing cider, 1905.
In a later version for *Cecily Parsley's Nursery Rhymes* (1922) the apples were changed to cowslips at the insistence of her publishers, who felt that cowslip wine was more appropriate than cider for a children's book.
Pen-and-ink and watercolour; 157 x 182; LT

164. 'Butter and milk from the farm': frontispiece of *The Pie and The Patty-Pan*, 1905.
Hill Top, the farm that Beatrix Potter bought in 1905, can be seen behind, with Coniston Old Man in the distance. The squarely-planted house, cat and cows impart a sense of settled respectability.
Pen-and-ink and watercolour; 168 x 128; NT

165. Interior scene from *The Pie and The Patty-Pan*, 1905.
Authentic details include the North Country open range and long-case clock, the jug and rabbit skin rug.
Pen-and-ink and watercolour; 168 x 128; NT

166. From *The Pie and The Patty-Pan*, 1905.
Using artistic licence Beatrix combines the doorway of one Sawrey house and the garden of another. This cottage garden luxuriance was very much in vogue. The figure of Duchess has been pasted on to the background.
Pen-and-ink and watercolour; 168 x 128; NT

167. Turk's-cap Lily (*Lilium martagon*), *c.*1903.
The lucid wash enhances the bold penwork.
Pencil, sepia ink and watercolour; 275 x 155; V&A

168. Duchess on the sofa, from *The Pie and The Patty-Pan*, 1905. This book illustration parodies Briton Rivière's *Cupboard Love*, a portrait of Kate Potter, Beatrix's cousin. 'Should not have known Kate, but it is rather a pretty picture. The chief part of it, however, is taken up by the cupboard,' Beatrix wrote in her journal for 1882.
Pen-and-ink and watercolour; 168 x 228; NT

169. Magpie and horse from *The Pie and The Patty-Pan*, 1905. She sketched this magpie at the Zoological Gardens, making notes on the colour. Though happy to keep every kind of manageable animal at home, she also visited the Zoo for wild specimens and the Natural History Museum for stuffed ones. Pen-and-ink and watercolour; 168 x 128; NT

170. A characteristic page of frog studies.
Over the years Beatrix Potter consciously or unconsciously collected material for her book illustrations.
Pencil; 185 x 168; V&A

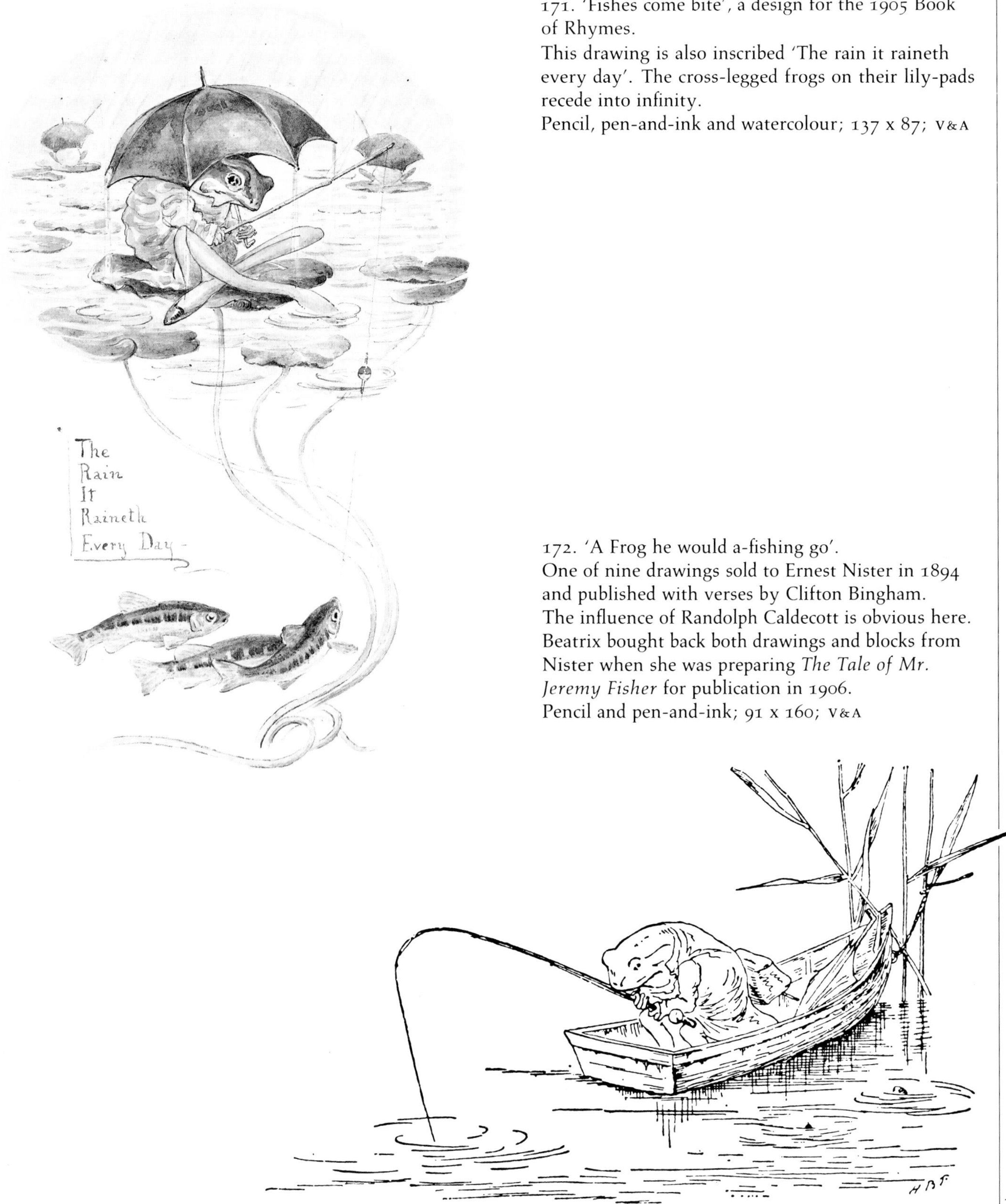

171. 'Fishes come bite', a design for the 1905 Book of Rhymes.
This drawing is also inscribed 'The rain it raineth every day'. The cross-legged frogs on their lily-pads recede into infinity.
Pencil, pen-and-ink and watercolour; 137 x 87; V&A

172. 'A Frog he would a-fishing go'.
One of nine drawings sold to Ernest Nister in 1894 and published with verses by Clifton Bingham.
The influence of Randolph Caldecott is obvious here.
Beatrix bought back both drawings and blocks from Nister when she was preparing *The Tale of Mr. Jeremy Fisher* for publication in 1906.
Pencil and pen-and-ink; 91 x 160; V&A

173. Waterlilies on Esthwaite Water, 1906.
Similar waterlilies appear in *The Tale of Mr. Jeremy Fisher,* who by 1906 was being drawn in a Lake District setting rather than in his former habitat on the River Tay. A variant design (see jacket) has even more definition and sense of pattern.
Pen-and-ink and watercolour; 228 x 293; V&A

174. From *The Tale of Mr. Jeremy Fisher,* 1906.
'Mr. Jeremy bounced up to the surface of the water, like a cork and the bubbles out of a soda water bottle.'
Pen-and-ink and watercolour; 105 x 93; NT

175. 'Toads' Tea Party', for the 1905 Book of Rhymes. Exquisite petal and leaf tints contrast with the squat shapes. Pencil, sepia ink and watercolour heightened with white; 123 x 120; V&A

176. Polite kitten drinking tea.
Probably drawn as a greetings card design for Nister and Co. in the 1890s but apparently never printed. It has the same spontaneity as her later unfinished cat drawings (see below).
Pencil, pen-and-ink and watercolour; 74 x 74; V&A

177. One of fourteen paintings for a panoramic tale, 'The Sly Old Cat', 1906.
These were never prepared for publication. The colour is unfinished, and so still subservient to the line. Closest to Caldecott of her works, 'The Sly Old Cat' epitomizes his marriage of picture and text. The flow of the story is accelerated by the format.
Pencil, sepia ink and watercolour; 100 x 79; V&A

178. The Puddle-Ducks of Sawrey, from *The Tale of Tom Kitten*, 1907. A harmonious composition in ruralist vein. Farmyard mud and manure are hardly in evidence: on the whole, artists of her time saw no point in showing the disagreeable side of country life.
Pen-and-ink, sepia ink and watercolour; 90 x 110; NT

179. From *The Tale of Jemima Puddle-Duck*, 1908.
Springtime woods above Sawrey frame the foolhardy heroine. This book contains some of Beatrix Potter's most idyllic landscapes.
Pen-and-ink and watercolour; 103 x 110; NT

180. Bird's-eye view from Hill Top Farm, in *The Tale of Samuel Whiskers*, 1908.
'The chimney stack stood up above the roof like a little stone tower.' Beatrix Potter liked this drawing, which she put in because 'there was such a string of sooty inside pictures'.
Sepia ink and watercolour; 160 x 125; NT

Opposite:
183. Interior at Gwaynynog, Denbighshire, 1904.
This was the house of Beatrix's Burton cousins where she learned to enjoy fine furniture and Staffordshire pottery. The cotton plant, emblem of the family success, was incorporated into the ornament of fenders and furniture.
Sepia ink and watercolour;
230 x 190; LT

Above:
181. From *The Tale of Samuel Whiskers*, 1908.
Samuel Whiskers at the head of Hill Top stairs: a cat's perspective.
Sepia ink and watercolour;
115 x 135; NT

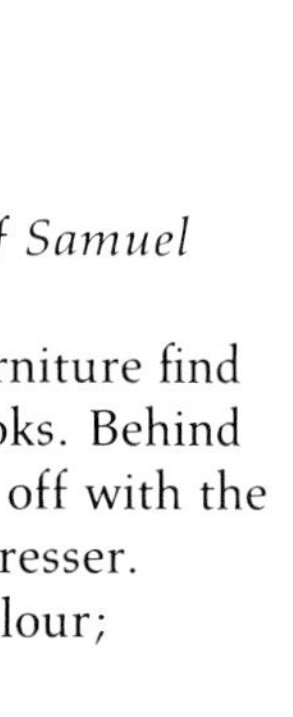

182. From *The Tale of Samuel Whiskers*, 1908.
Favourite pieces of furniture find their way into the books. Behind Anna Maria, running off with the dough, is a Hill Top dresser.
Sepia ink and watercolour;
133 x 154; NT

Opposite above:
184. The harbour at Teignmouth, ?1910.
In luminous wash over schematic underdrawing.
Pencil and watercolour; 140 x 228; FLP

Opposite below:
185. Beached boats at Teignmouth, ?1910.
A strong composition which focuses on essentials.
Pencil and watercolour; 140 x 229; V&A

Above:
186. A cottage at Teignmouth, ?1910.
An architectural peculiarity which caught her eye.
Pencil and watercolour; 227 x 140; LT

187. Hill Top by night, *c.*1910.
A welcoming light streams from the doorway.
Pencil and watercolour; 101 x 68; V&A

188. Scotch Fly, an 'extremely good sheep dog', ?1929.
Sometimes the roughest sketches have the greatest vitality.
Pencil; 200 x 160; WA

189. Airy landscape at Gwaynynog, Denbighshire, May 1912.
Beatrix uses the device of *contre-jour*, by which the shadowed station point draws attention to the sunlit distance.
Pencil and watercolour; 173 x 235; FLP

190. From *The Tale of The Flopsy Bunnies*, 1909.
The garden at Gwaynynog is the setting for this poignant scene, in which she has captured the soft greens of the English countryside.
Pen-and-ink and watercolour; 96 x 86; NT

191. Kitchen interior for *The Tale of Mr. Tod,* 1912.
Emphatically-framed line drawings in a bold woodcut style echo the archaizing style of contemporary private presses.
Sepia ink; 76 x 91; NT

192. Preliminary drawing for *The Tale of Mr. Tod,* 1912.
An uncharacteristic format, in which long horizontal lines give an impression of calm belied by the fox's watchful presence. The forty-two line drawings for *Mr. Tod,* originally drawn in brown ink, were printed in black for the book.
Pencil and sepia ink; 80 x 200; LT

193. A 'picturesque' composition from *The Tale of Mr. Tod*, 1912. The figures are framed in trees, and mountains close the distant view. Sepia ink and watercolour; 112 x 93; NT

Opposite:
194. Hillside under snow, with sheep and stone walls, 4 March 1909.
Pencil and watercolour; 255 x 180; V&A

195. Sawrey village under snow, March 1909.
In March 1909 Beatrix spent five out of six consecutive days sketching out of doors in and around Near Sawrey. Here her station point was the Tower Bank Arms.
Pencil and watercolour; 239 x 185; V&A

Jan 11, 13

197. Esthwaite Water, glassy with cold in December 1913. Atmospheric conditions make it appear wider than in reality; mist has almost drained the landscape of colour. The transparent quality of watercolour is particularly suited to interpreting a watery atmosphere.
Pencil and watercolour; 127 x 183; V&A

Opposite:
196. Hillside under snow with a stormy sky. Painted in January 1913 near 'Jemima's Wood'.
Pencil and watercolour; 254 x 178; V&A

Above and left:
198, 199. Landscapes.
From a group of late *plein air* sketches, *c.*1909–13, done in a fast impressionistic wash. These two autumn landscapes date from 1909. The crossroads (*opposite*) is a more finished example in the same bold manner.
Pencil and watercolour; 178 x 255 (above), 178 x 130 (left); FLP

Opposite:
200. The crossroads behind Hill Top, 1909.
Figures were added to this landscape for the frontispiece of *The Tale of Pigling Bland*. The eye is drawn to the sunlit background.
Pencil and watercolour; 255 x 179; LT

201. Kep, Beatrix's favourite collie, *c.*1907.
A proud and lifelike figure of Kep in clay was modelled in that year.
Pencil and watercolour; 240 x 179 (detail); FLP

Opposite:
202. Cart track in snow, and fields beyond Sawrey, probably January 1913.
In the style of the crossroads painting (200).
Pencil and watercolour; 254 x 178; V&A

203. Heads of an amiable pig, ?1910.
Drawn as preparatory studies for *The Tale of Pigling Bland*. 'The poor little cherub had such a sweet smile.'
Pencil and watercolour; 245 x 158; LT

204. Sheep's head, in a daringly experimental style and a vivid palette. Particles of pure colour shimmer with light.
Pencil and watercolour; 120 x 180; V&A

205. Two hens' heads, December 1912.
Red and white are set off by the black background; the brushstroke realistically conveys the fluffiness of feathers.
Pencil and watercolour; 253 x 176; FLP

206–209:
Illustrations for *The Fairy Caravan*, 1929.
The late pen-and-inks, for *The Fairy Caravan*, and also for the American edition of *The Tale of Little Pig Robinson* (1930), are as accomplished as any of her line work. Sophisticated little 'ends' could be put at the head or foot of the page, as she wanted.

206. Rocky hillside with foxes.
The background was taken from one of her brother Bertram Potter's landscape etchings. Beatrix understood the geological structure beneath her landscapes just as she understood the skeleton beneath the skin.
Pen-and-ink; 130 x 125; WA

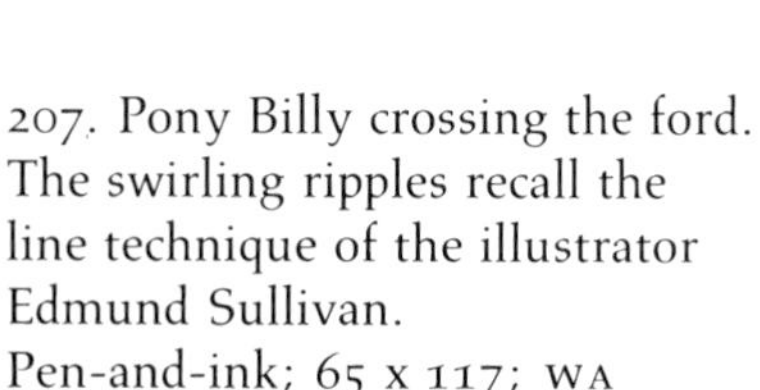

207. Pony Billy crossing the ford.
The swirling ripples recall the line technique of the illustrator Edmund Sullivan.
Pen-and-ink; 65 x 117; WA

208. A favourite drawing of the cat Tomasine.
Pen-and-ink; 164 x 123; WA

209. Cedar at Birds' Place, Camfield.
Headpiece for Chapter 7.
Pen-and-ink; 55 x 107; WA

Index

Figures in *italics* refer to plates

Unused vignette for *The Fairy Caravan*. Pen-and-ink; 27 x 129; WA